KU-201-055

VICTIMS OF CRIME

SECOND EDITION

EDITORS
ROBERT C. DAVIS
ARTHUR J. LURIGIO
WESLEY G. SKOGAN

SLS

UNIVERSITY OF WOLVERHAMPTON LEARNING RESOURCES	
Acc No. 2225828	CLASS 322
CONTROL 076190154X	362. 880
DATE 31. OCT 2000	SITE UN 973 VIC

SAGE Publications
International Educational and Professional Publisher
Thousand Oaks   London   New Delhi

Copyright © 1997 by Sage Publications, Inc.

All rights reserved. No part of this book may be reproduced or utilized in any form or by any means, electronic or mechanical, including photocopying, recording, or by any information storage and retrieval system, without permission in writing from the publisher.

For information address:

SAGE Publications, Inc.
2455 Teller Road
Thousand Oaks, California 91320
E-mail: order@sagepub.com

SAGE Publications Ltd.
6 Bonhill Street
London EC2A 4PU
United Kingdom

SAGE Publications India Pvt. Ltd.
M-32 Market
Greater Kailash I
New Delhi 110 048 India

Printed in the United States of America

Library of Congress Cataloging-in-Publication Data

Main entry under title:

Victims of crime / editors, Robert C. Davis, Arthur J. Lurigio, Wesley
    G. Skogan.—2nd ed.
        p.   cm.
    Includes bibliographical references (p.) and index.
    ISBN 0-7619-0154-X (acid-free paper). — ISBN 0-7619-0155-8
(pbk.: acid-free paper)
    1. Victims of crimes—United States.   I. Davis, Robert C. (Robert
Carl)   II. Lurigio, Arthur J.   III. Skogan, Wesley G.
HV6250.3.U5V54   1997
362.88'0973—dc21   96-45872

97 98 99 00 01 02 03 10 9 8 7 6 5 4 3 2

Acquiring Editor: C. Terry Hendrix
Editorial Assistant: Dale Grenfell
Production Editor: Diana E. Axelsen
Production Assistant: Karen Wiley
Typesetter/Designer: Yang-hee Syn Maresca/Andrea D. Swanson
Indexer: Virgil Diodato
Cover Designer: Candice Harman
Print Buyer: Anna Chin

Contents

Foreword

In less than 20 years, there has been a revolution in the criminal justice system. Each criminal case involves more than the government versus the defendant. There is another party with a burning interest and with legal rights: the clerk robbed at gunpoint, the sexually assaulted 13-year-old, or the elderly couple bilked out of their life savings. Today, we also vindicate their rights, provide services to ease their pain, and prevent their revictimization by the court system.

Twenty-four years ago, I walked into a courtroom to try my first case. As a prosecutor, I had no special training to work with victims, nor did the police officers. There was no such thing as a victim-witness specialist to make arrangements for the witnesses to come to court. There were no witness waiting rooms. There were no sexual assault counselors or domestic violence advocates. There was no support network for parents of murdered children. And there were no laws establishing and protecting the rights of victims and witnesses in our criminal justice system.

The process was intimidating and did not encourage citizens to come forward and get involved. Witnesses and victims experienced long, tedious waits in dim, dirty courthouse corridors, only to find that the case had been adjourned yet again. Victims faced anxiety and confusion about what had happened and what was going to happen in court, and frustration over their inability to have any say in the outcome.

Today, almost every state in the nation has adopted a bill of rights for victims of crime. Nationally, the Victim and Witness Protection Act of 1982 and thousands of state and federal laws have been enacted to establish and protect the rights of crime victims. The federal Crime Victims Fund and state funds provide millions of dollars annually to fund programs and personnel dedicated to serving and protecting crime victims and witnesses.

Although most of this is a relatively new phenomenon, these laws, programs, and services for crime victims are accepted as an everyday fact in the criminal justice system. Often established as a reaction to increasing levels of crime and victimization, they are also the product of a movement dedicated to expanding victim rights and protections further. Without a doubt, this movement will continue to grow and reshape the entire nature of our criminal justice system. As stated by Attorney General Janet Reno:

> Of paramount importance to crime victims and witnesses is their treatment by criminal justice personnel, who should care about their suffering, enforce their rights and protection, offer support to help them heal, and hold the criminal accountable for the harm caused. For too long, the rights and needs of crime victims and witnesses were overlooked by the criminal justice system. (Attorney General Guidelines for Victim and Witness Assistance, 1995)

A study of crime victims and the process of victimization, this book is essential because it explains the dramatic changes in our criminal justice system over the past two decades. In doing so, it will shape the course of changes yet to come.

Thomas P. Schneider
United States Attorney
Eastern District of Wisconsin

1 Another Look at Victim Problems, Policies, and Programs

ROBERT C. DAVIS

ARTHUR J. LURIGIO

WESLEY G. SKOGAN

The first edition of *Victims of Crime* was published 6 years ago (Lurigio, Skogan, & Davis, 1990). The current volume, like its predecessor, takes stock of recent advances and highlights the state of the art in crime victim research, policies, and programs. The chapters cover a wide range of topics, including the psychological impact of crime; the prevalence and nature of criminal victimization; victims' legislation, services, and interventions; and the future of victims' services. In addition, this edition offers broader and more intense coverage of special populations of victims: child victims, victims of domestic violence, and victims of hate crimes. Finally, we preserve the international flavor of the first edition by including a chapter on crime victims' rights and services in Europe.

In the introduction to the first edition of this book, we discussed a number of important topics in the field of victims' rights and services. We described how victims' programs and legislation arose out of federal funding and a unique blend of grassroots activism by victims, victims' families, and feminists (i.e., the so-called "victims' movement"). Today, the movement has achieved many of its original goals. Kelly and Erez (Chapter 13 of this volume) note that victims' rights and victim compensation programs have been adopted in 50 states, that victim service programs have spread to all major metropolitan areas, and that victims' rights are currently being extended. For example, many states have recently enacted or are considering constitutional amendments giving victims legal recourse when their

rights are abridged by local government officials. In short, essential reforms in the criminal justice system's treatment of crime victims
have certainly already been accomplished.

In the introduction to the first edition, we
also discussed the lack of knowledge regarding the psychological consequences of victimization and the needs of crime victims.
Today, the aftermath of sexual assault has
been extensively studied (Resick and Nishith,
Chapter 3 of this volume). Furthermore, we
now have much better information about the
consequences of other serious crimes, thanks,
in part, to the careful investigations of Norris,
Kaniasty, and Thompson (Chapter 8 of this
volume). Nonetheless, more work needs to be
done on this topic. For example, no study to
date has included baseline (i.e., pre-crime)
measures of victims' psychological functioning. Hence we cannot be sure that victims'
symptoms are due only to the crimes and not
to preexisting emotional states.

In the first edition's introduction, we
brought attention to the paucity of data on the
effectiveness of victim services programs.
With respect to this topic, few advances in
knowledge have been made since then. Several years ago, we studied four victim programs to examine whether their services made
a difference in victims' lives (reported in
Davis & Henley, 1990). Our results confirmed
the findings of earlier studies: The impacts of
victim services programs are difficult to assess. To isolate effects, investigators must carefully select appropriate target populations, develop more sensitive outcomes measures, and
design studies with longer follow-up times. In
a real sense, however, the issue of whether
victim services make a discernible difference
is moot: Victim services programs have become entrenched in state and federal government budgets and have developed strong political constituencies. The more relevant
question for future researchers may be "What
types of services or methods of delivery are
most effective?"

Emerging Themes

The current edition of *Victims of Crime* is
not simply an update of the original. Its chapters reflect the considerable changes that have
occurred within the crime victims' movement
in the past 6 years. At least four new themes
appear in this second edition of the book.

Nature of Criminal Victimization

Studies are becoming more concerned with
the nature of victimization. Laub (Chapter 2 of
this volume) presents data from the National
Crime Victim Survey (NCVS) that bear on this
theme. NCVS findings indicate that victimization is not randomly distributed across the
population; instead, it varies with people's
lifestyles and routine activities. The NCVS
data also show that many crimes—especially
violent victimizations—occur among acquaintances. Furthermore, the NCVS data suggest
that victimization can best be seen as a "situated transaction" between two or more parties
in which the behavior of victims, in the form
of precipitation or resistance, is likely to affect
the behavior of offenders and the outcomes of
encounters.

Davis, Taylor, and Titus (Chapter 9 of this
volume) tackle head on the nature of criminal
victimization. They contend that the view of
victims as simply persons who happen to be in
the wrong place at the wrong time is contrary
to empirical evidence. They suggest that some
individuals, by virtue of demographics and
behavior, are far more likely than others to
become victims. Moreover, persons who have
been crime victims once are at higher risk of
becoming crime victims again.

Fattah (Chapter 15 of this volume) sees
criminal victimization as a social construction.
He argues against the notion of an "active
aggressor" (i.e., offender) and a "passive sufferer" (i.e., victim). Instead, he emphasizes
that victims and offenders come from largely

overlapping populations. The roles of victim and offender are "neither fixed nor antagonistic but revolving and interchangeable." Abused children may grow up to become abusive parents, sexually molested children may become sex offenders, battered wives may kill their spouses, and persons preyed on by stalkers may retaliate. The proper response of society to crimes, therefore, should be not only to punish one party but also to restore the peace between the actors involved in an incident and to redress victim harm through mediation, reconciliation, restitution, and compensation.

Friedman and Tucker (Chapter 10 of this volume) argue that criminal victimization can dramatically alter the course of people's lives. Like Fattah, they contend that violence is transmitted from one person to another, with the roles of victim and offender sometimes becoming interchangeable. Dyads can become locked into a circle of repeated abuse. Violence can be transmitted vertically when abused children grow up to become abusive parents or spouses. Violence is transmitted horizontally when teens who are the targets of aggressive peers use weapons for self-defense.

New Roles for Victim Services

The new perspectives on victims introduced in the current book suggest new directions for victim services. Davis, Taylor, and Titus (Chapter 9 of this volume) discuss the implications of their view of victims as principal actors in criminal transactions for teaching victims to reduce their vulnerability to crime. If criminal incidents are, in part, the result of the characteristics and behaviors of potential victims, then it follows that potential victims can have some control in the prevention of crimes. Davis et al. emphasize the need for crime prevention training among persons who have been already victimized. Victim services programs can play a key role in training because program personnel have contact with victims shortly after the crimes, when they are

most open to information about how to reduce their vulnerability to future victimization.

Friedman and Tucker (Chapter 10 of this volume) contend that victim services are an important mechanism for freeing people from a "web of violence." Recognizing that victims are at increased risk of experiencing future violence (as either victims or offenders), they advocate the use of victim services to break the cycle of violence. Such services may be as simple as providing shelter for abused spouses or teaching teens techniques to resolve conflicts without resorting to violence. Services may also involve counseling to raise the self-esteem of battered women or long-term therapy to help violent offenders realize how their behaviors are conditioned by their own childhood histories of abuse and violence. Friedman and Tucker share with Davis et al. a forward-looking perspective on services for victims: "Those who work with victims need to recognize that our task is not merely to bind the wounds after the fact—it is also to reduce the risk of future injury."

Fattah's contention (Chapter 15 of this volume) that the roles of victims and offenders are often interchangeable leads him to address the need to heal victims through restorative justice rather than through protracted, adversarial court battles. Fattah sees prosecution as benefiting few victims. Instead, he believes that mediation, restitution, and compensation best serve the interests of victims and society. According to Fattah, constructive healing, not harsh punishment, should be the primary goal of both victim policy and victim services.

Smith and Hillenbrand (Chapter 14 of this volume) build on the theme of restorative justice for victims. They note the tremendous growth in state-run compensation programs for crime victims and in the use of restitution as a criminal sanction. They also discuss victim-offender reconciliation programs (VORPs), which bring the parties face to face to exchange information and to negotiate a disposition. They review research suggesting that victims and offenders who participate in VORPs tend to be quite satisfied with their experiences in the programs. However, they also note that VORPs have not taken hold on a large scale: Many victims are simply not interested in sitting across the table from offenders.

Young (Chapter 11 of this volume) looks at future trends in victim services. She argues that victim service programs will need to develop the capacity to reach out to America's growing minority populations, defined by ethnicity, age, and other factors, and serve them effectively. Advances in technology will make it necessary for victim services providers to become literate with computers and new communications methods. A growing emphasis on religion will require victim services providers to become better equipped to help victims deal with spiritual issues. A more dangerous world and more violence-prone youth will create a greater need for programs to promote conflict resolution skills at the individual and societal levels.

Institutionalization of Victim Services

The institutionalization of victim services and expanded roles for victims in criminal prosecutions are among the most important changes in the field. Kelly and Erez (Chapter 13 of this volume) discuss the widespread adoption of victim reforms in the justice process. Forty-five states have enacted victim bills of rights that contain provisions such as allowing victims to be present and heard in court and to be informed of key decisions in their cases. Nearly half of the states have adopted constitutional amendments giving victims greater influence and visibility in the criminal justice process. Kelly and Erez conclude that despite major changes in the laws, victims are still dependent on "sympathetic criminal justice personnel" to ensure that their rights are protected.

Maguire and Shapland (Chapter 12 of this volume) describe a sea change in attitudes toward crime victims in Europe. In Britain and

France, for example, victims' needs have become embedded in political agendas. Yet the institutionalization of victim services has not been extended to reforms that increase victim participation in the justice process. Maguire and Shapland note that attitudes toward victims' rights in the justice process are starting to change, most notably in Germany, where a comprehensive victims' rights bill has been enacted. However, as is true in the United States (see Kelly & Erez, Chapter 13 of this volume), legal changes have not always guaranteed the implementation of victims' rights.

The institutionalization of victim services has coincided with the professionalization of victim service providers. Maguire and Shapland describe the bureaucratization of victim services in England, where volunteer staff are being replaced by mental health professionals. Furthermore, volunteer staff are being asked to undergo more training to meet higher performance standards. Young (Chapter 11 of this volume) emphasizes the educational requirements and professional standards promoted by the federal Office for Victims of Crime (OVC). OVC has sponsored training programs in areas ranging from domestic violence to victim assistance in the military. She points out that the professionalization of victim services is reflected in the new National Code of Ethics for victim assistance professionals.

Sophistication of Research on Victims

Early investigations on the consequences of crime and the needs of victims led to valuable insights into victims' problems; these studies helped to develop victim services programs and to justify their continued funding. But they often used convenience samples of victims who sought services, poor research designs, and unstandardized outcomes measures.

As more empirical data on victims' problems were collected and theories of victimization were formulated, research became more sophisticated. Investigators drew more representative samples of the populations they were studying and used valid and reliable assessment tools. Norris, Kaniasty, and Thompson (Chapter 8 of this volume) have applied sound scientific methods to explore crime victims' reactions. They describe a series of extensive investigations on reactions to victimization that used a representative sample of Kentucky residents. They asked screening questions to divide the sample into victims of violent crimes, victims of property crimes, and nonvictims (the former two categories of respondents were oversampled to compensate for their relatively small numbers in the population). They assessed respondents three times over the course of a year, using measures of psychological symptoms, fear of crime, avoidance behavior, and worldviews. Their results provide the best evidence to date on the psychological impact of victimization.

Resick and Nishith (Chapter 3 of this volume) summarize research on sexual assault victims. They describe the various approaches that have been used to examine the effects of sexual assault, from longitudinal studies to population surveys. Resick and Nishith discuss theories of how victims are affected by sexual assault, ranging from crisis theory to conceptions of posttraumatic stress disorder. Finally, they report findings that demonstrate the usefulness of treating victims of sexual assault with cognitive therapy.

Special Victim Populations

As the victim movement has matured, more attention has been paid to special populations of victims. One of the earliest special populations to be acknowledged was victims of domestic violence. Garner and Fagan (Chapter 4 of this volume) provide a comprehensive overview of this burgeoning field. They describe the extent of domestic violence and discuss theories that purport to explain why it occurs. The bulk of their chapter is devoted to legal, social, and health responses to intimate violence. They conclude that "there is little conclusive evidence of either deterrent or protective effects of legal sanctions or treatment interventions for domestic violence." Finally, they stress the need for greater rigor in evaluation research and argue for treatment of domestic violence as a form of violent behavior rather than a unique phenomenon.

Child victims are another population with special needs. Finkelhor (Chapter 5 of this volume) documents the tremendous growth in the number of professionals concerned with children's welfare. Finkelhor's framework of "developmental victimization" encompasses the victimization of children from schoolyard assaults to child abuse, child molestation, and stranger abduction. He reviews findings on the incidence and effects of child victimizations. Furthermore, he addresses the question of why child victimizations are so common and how the circumstances that lead to them differ from those surrounding crimes against adults. Finkelhor calls for better data on the victimization of children under 12 years of age (who are not included in the NCVS).

Garofalo (Chapter 7 of this volume) discusses an even newer, special victim population: victims of hate crimes. He explores the prevalence and nature of hate crimes. Attempts to criminalize forms of hate expression have faced stiff constitutional challenges, but many states have passed hate crime reporting statutes and enhanced penalties for hate crimes. Garofalo indicates that municipalities are adopting multifaceted approaches to hate crimes that integrate law enforcement responses with victim services.

Wortman, Battle, and Lemkau (Chapter 6 of this volume) provide a compelling description of the experiences of persons who have suffered the sudden, traumatic death of a spouse or child from homicide, accident, or suicide. The authors detail the psychological ramifications of these types of losses and indicate how they differ from other types of deaths. They use social psychological theories to analyze why others often have a hard time responding in helpful ways to these victims. The authors argue that it is difficult for survivors of sudden deaths to find solace anywhere they search, from friends and family to church to therapy. They offer suggestions for ways those in the helping professions can better assist these victims and increase the chances for positive outcomes.

References

Davis, R. C., & Henley, M. (1990). Victim service programs. In A. Lurigio, W. G. Skogan, & R. C. Davis (Eds.), *Victims of crime: Problems, policies, and programs* (pp. 157-171). Newbury Park, CA: Sage.

Lurigio, A., Skogan, W. G., & Davis, R. C. (Eds.). (1990). *Victims of crime: Problems, policies, and programs.* Newbury Park, CA: Sage.

PART I

Victimization and Its Effects

2 Patterns of Criminal Victimization in the United States

JOHN H. LAUB

Crime is one of the most important problems facing the United States today. Yet despite a seemingly constant barrage of attention to crime in various media outlets, we still know relatively little about crime and its impact on society. Estimates as to the size and shape of the crime problem vary considerably even among so-called experts. In addition, until recently, information on the experiences of crime victims themselves was virtually nonexistent. And, perhaps most troubling, policy decisions regarding crime are often made in an ad hoc fashion, without the benefit of research. This situation cries out for good data and rational discussion: two things often lacking in current discourse on crime and crime control.

This chapter provides a comprehensive review of the current state of our knowledge about crime. Four important questions are ad-

dressed. The first concerns the *level* of victimization. How many victimizations occur each year? What is the rate of criminal victimization? Is the rate of criminal victimization increasing or decreasing over time? The next section examines the *correlates* of victimization. Who are the typical victims of crime? Do victim characteristics vary by crime type? How is victimization distributed across time and space? The following section addresses the *dynamics* of victimization. What is the nature of the relationship between victims and their offenders? Do victims in any way contribute to their victimizations? Conversely, do victims typically resist during victimization occurrences, and, if so, what are the results of that resistance? Finally, I examine the *consequences* of criminal victimization. How often do victims report their victimizations to the

AUTHOR'S NOTE: I thank James Alan Fox for providing me with the homicide data found in Figure 2.5 and with his technical assistance in producing the figures for this chapter. The research assistance of Roni Mayzer is also gratefully acknowledged. Finally, my chapter benefited enormously from Wes Skogan's skillful editing and helpful suggestions.

9

police? What is the extent of injury suffered by victims of crime? What is the extent of economic loss? Answers to these questions can provide a solid foundation on which to build theories of victimization, as well as to form effective policies relating to victims of crime. But before presenting the empirical findings, I turn to a brief discussion of the available sources of data.

Data Sources

Criminologists use several sources of data to learn about crime. These data are collected in different ways because they serve different purposes. Thus they tell us different things about crime. One source of data consists of records generated by criminal justice agencies (e.g., police, courts, and corrections). In contrast, other sources of data primarily include social surveys conducted independently of criminal justice agencies (e.g., victimization surveys and self-reported delinquency surveys). Unfortunately, efforts to obtain useful information on victims and victimizations from data sources such as the *Uniform Crime Reports* (UCR) face two interrelated problems. First, information regarding victim characteristics is not routinely collected by criminal justice agencies. On the contrary, criminal justice records tend to be *offender focused*. Second, and perhaps more important, information that is collected by criminal justice agencies relates only to those criminal events that have come to the attention of the criminal justice system. More precisely, crimes that are not reported (or recorded) to the police are not included in these measures.

If the reporting or nonreporting of crime to the police was a random process, there would be little concern about using crimes known to the police as an indicator of crime. Although we would not know about the precise *number* of crimes occurring, the data could be used with confidence to analyze the *correlates* and

characteristics of crime. In other words, the patterns might be the same independent of the overall number of offenses. However, the reporting of crimes to the police is not a random process. Factors such as weapon use and victim injury are systematically related to the likelihood that a crime will come to the attention of the police, that the police will record it, that an arrest will be made, and the case will be followed up on (see, e.g., Block & Block, 1980). This can lead to errors in describing the size and shape of the crime problem when relying on criminal justice system data.

To overcome these data problems, I will focus on the National Crime Victimization Survey (NCVS) data. This survey was designed to collect information on crime victims from a large sample of the U.S. population. Conducted by the Bureau of the Census and the Bureau of Justice Statistics (BJS), the NCVS is a household-based survey that is national in scope and has been ongoing since 1972. The NCVS is the only national data source that allows individual-level analyses of victims and their experiences across a variety of crime categories. It is also the only national indicator of the level of crime that attempts to record crimes that do not come to the attention of the police. These two characteristics make the NCVS a rich source of information on the nature and extent of criminal victimization and victims in the United States.

The offenses covered in the NCVS are rape (carnal knowledge through use of or threat of force), robbery (theft of property or cash by force or threat of force), aggravated assault (an attack with a weapon or an attack resulting in a serious injury), simple assault (an attack without a weapon that resulted in a minor injury), and personal larceny (theft with or without direct contact between the victim and the offender). In addition, such household crimes as burglary (unlawful or forcible entry of a residence or other structure such as a garage), household larceny (theft), and motor vehicle theft are included. Both attempted and completed crimes are included in the survey. Information is available regarding the basic demographic characteristics of the victim, what he or she knows about the alleged offender, the victimization event itself, and the consequences of the crime.

The NCVS excludes important types of crime and victims. For instance, no information on homicide is available. Because children under 12 are not interviewed, the NCVS data do not provide any information on child abuse or child pornography. Commercial robbery, burglary, and theft are not covered in the survey, nor is vandalism of public structures and facilities. Moreover, because respondents need to know about and understand them, it is extremely difficult to collect information on organizational crimes such as consumer fraud. So-called "victimless" crimes are also not studied in this survey. Respondent knowledge also limits the types of information that can be collected on the crimes contained in the survey. For instance, victims are asked only a few questions regarding offender characteristics.

How Much Crime Is There?

This section focuses on questions regarding the nature and extent of criminal victimization and the characteristics of victims. More detailed information is available in the BJS annual reports entitled *Criminal Victimization in the United States* and in special reports such as Bachman's *Violence Against Women* (1994).[1]

Rates of Victimization

In 1992, the NCVS counted 33.6 million victimizations (including both attempts and completed crimes) in the United States. In general, the more serious the crime, the less frequently it occurred. Thus property crimes were far more frequent than crimes of violence. In fact, the most frequently committed crime was a theft against a household or individual. Violent crimes accounted for 20% of all the victimizations reported to the NCVS in 1992, and the most common violent crime reported to survey interviewers was a simple assault. Of all household crimes reported, the most common was the theft of household property (BJS, 1994).

A better way of assessing victimization patterns is to calculate a *victimization rate* (the number of victimizations divided by the number of persons/households in a specific category of interest). Rates of victimization standardize the population for a given time and place and provide a measure of the *incidence* of victimization. In 1992, the victimization rate for violent crimes (rape, robbery, and assault) was 32 per 1,000 population age 12 and over. The overall victimization rate for personal crimes of theft (purse snatching and pocket picking, along with thefts away from home) was 59 per 1,000. The victimization rate for household crimes (burglary, larceny-theft, and motor vehicle theft) was 152 per 1,000 households. The victimization rate for burglary alone was 49 per 1,000 households (BJS, 1994).

Another way of assessing the extent of victimization is by constructing a *prevalence* rate of victimization. The prevalence rate is the number of persons/households who have been victimized one or more times in a given time period divided by the population of interest; it is the "percentage victimized" in a population. The BJS developed an indicator called "Households Touched by Crime" that measures the annual prevalence of victimization among households. In 1992, about 23% of the more than 97 million households in the United States were victimized by some type of NCVS crime. Again, the proportion of households touched by crime varies considerably by type of crime, with crimes of violence occurring less frequently (5%) than crimes of theft (16%; BJS, 1993).

To provide a context in which to understand victimization risk better, one can compare it to

Table 2.1   A Comparison of Crime Rates With the Rates of Other Life Events, 1990-1991 Data

Events	Rate per 1,000 per Year
Accidental injury, all circumstances	220.0
Accidental injury at home	66.0
Personal theft	**61.0**
Accidental injury at work	47.0
Violent victimization	**31.0**
Assault (aggravated and simple)	**25.0**
Injury in motor vehicle accident	22.0
Death, all causes	11.0
Victimization with injury	**11.0**
Serious (aggravated) assault	**8.0**
Robbery	**6.0**
Heart disease death	5.0
Cancer death	3.0
Rape (women only)	**1.0**
Accidental death, all circumstances	0.4
Pneumonia/influenza death	0.4
Motor vehicle accident death	0.2
Suicide	0.2
HIV infection death	0.1
Homicide/legal intervention death	**0.1**

SOURCE: Zawitz et al. (1993, p. 6).

risks for other untoward events (e.g., traffic accidents and serious illness). As revealed in Table 2.1, if all else is equal, the risk of criminal victimization is less than the risk of accidental injury. Although the risk of violent crime is higher than that of death by cancer, a person is more likely to die from a variety of causes other than criminal victimization. At the same time, the risk of personal theft is quite high relative to these other misfortunes (Zawitz et al., 1993).

Trends in Victimization

In 1992, the level of crime reported to the NCVS fell to its lowest level in the 20-year history of the survey (see Figure 2.1). This pattern of declining victimization rates generally held true for personal as well as household

crimes over the 1973-1992 period. What is particularly noteworthy is that the rates for robbery and burglary—crimes of high concern—declined 12% and 47%, respectively, between 1973 and 1992. At the same time, the rate of reporting crimes to the police by victims did not change dramatically. According to NCVS data, about half of all violent crimes, two fifths of all household crimes, and a little more than one fourth of all personal theft crimes are reported to the police each year (more details regarding victim reporting to the police are presented below). Not surprisingly, the number of households touched by crime also declined over the same period. In 1975, nearly one of three households was touched by crime compared with about one of four in 1992, the lowest percentage recorded since 1975, the first year the indicator was created (BJS, 1993).

A major concern among criminologists has been the comparison of NCVS and UCR trends over time (see, e.g., Gove, Hughes, & Geerken, 1985; McDowall & Loftin, 1992; O'Brien, 1985). UCR and NCVS trend data from 1973 to 1992 for the crimes of rape, robbery, aggravated assault, burglary, and motor vehicle theft reveal radically different portraits. Whereas the UCR shows percentage increases for four of these five crimes (the exception being burglary) over the 1973 to 1992 time frame, the NCVS data reveal a stable or declining trend for the same crime types. Whether the differences are artifacts of the different methodologies used to gather these data or whether they reflect the fact that the UCR and the NCVS measure different phenomena is unknown.

Who Are the Victims?

Several criminologists have argued that risk of criminal victimization is linked to lifestyle, routine activities, and opportunities (Cohen & Felson, 1979; Cohen, Kluegel, & Land, 1981;

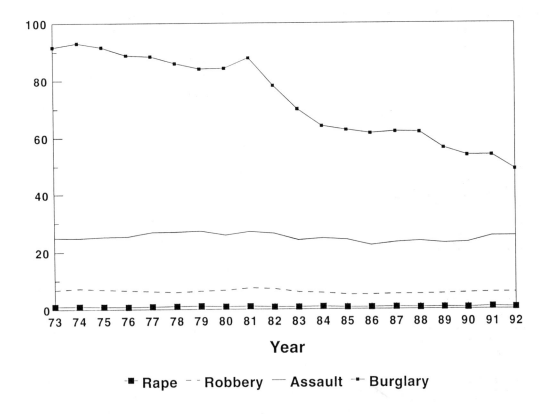

Figure 2.1. Victimization Rates (per 1,000 Persons/Households) for Selected Personal and Household Crimes, 1973-1992 National Crime Survey Data
SOURCE: Bureau of Justice Statistics (1994, p. 6).

Hindelang, Gottfredson, & Garofalo, 1978). What people do, where they go, and whom they associate with all affect their likelihood of victimization. Variations in lifestyle are important because they are associated with differences in exposure to "high risk times, places, and people" (Hindelang et al., 1978, p. 245). In large part, lifestyle and routine activities are adaptations to various role expectations and structural constraints (who people are, where they live, etc.). For example, teenagers typically go to school 5 days a week for 9 months of the year and associate primarily with other teenagers. This can be rather risky. On the other hand, elderly persons may spend considerable time at home, often do not work, and tend to associate with older friends or family members. This may be less risky. This section will explore how victimization is distributed across key demographic dimensions. There is considerable evidence that victimization follows the patterns suggested by the ideas of lifestyle and routine activity theorists.

Age

Age is one of the strongest correlates of victimization. The NCVS data show an inverse relationship between the age of the victim and the risk of both personal and house-

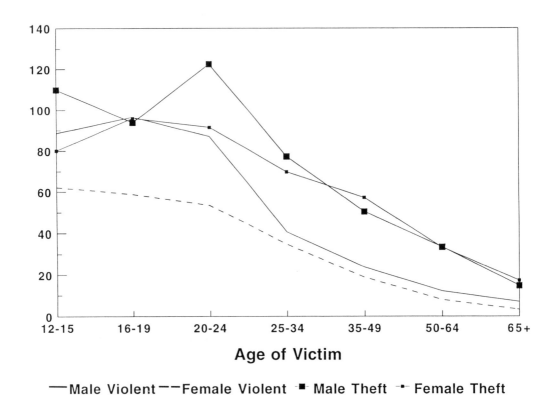

Age of Victim

—Male Violent ——Female Violent ■ Male Theft ⁻•⁻ Female Theft

Figure 2.2. Victimization Rates (per 1,000 Persons) by Type of Crime, Age, and Sex of Victim, 1992 National Crime Survey Data
SOURCE: Bureau of Justice Statistics (1994, pp. 24-25).

hold victimization. Persons age 65 and older are victimized at a rate far less than that of younger people. Rates of victimization seem to peak in the 16- to 24-year-old group, then decline as age increases. The relationship between age and victimization is especially strong with regard to the crimes of aggravated assault and robbery. The exception to this pattern is personal theft, which displays much more stability across age categories than any other crime type.

Sex

The NCVS data show that victimization by personal crimes is about 20% higher for males than females. The relationship between sex and victimization is especially strong for aggravated assault and robbery. The obvious exception to this pattern is rape. But also, the rate of victimization for males and females is virtually identical for personal thefts (see Figure 2.2), a category that includes purse snatching and pocket picking.

The relationship between sex and victimization is also influenced by the victim's age. As displayed in Figure 2.2, rates of violent victimization for those 35 and older differ far less by sex than do rates for younger age groups. Moreover, for crimes of personal theft, rates for females aged 25 and older surpass comparable rates for males of similar ages.

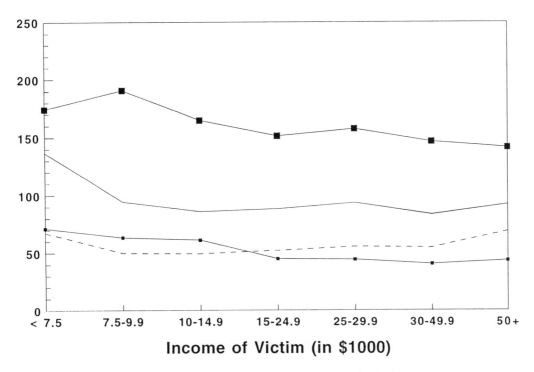

Figure 2.3. Victimization Rates (per 1,000 Persons/Households) by Type of Crime and Income of Victim, 1992 National Crime Survey Data
SOURCE: Bureau of Justice Statistics (1994, pp. 33, 46).

Race

Rates of victimization also vary by race. The NCVS data tell us that the rate of violent victimizations—especially aggravated assaults and robberies—is greater for blacks than for whites. However, for personal thefts, whites have a slightly higher rate than do blacks. The NCVS indicates that black males have the highest rate of violent victimization and white females the lowest. Blacks also have the highest rate of overall household victimization. This is particularly striking for the crime of burglary. The burglary rate is 68 per 1,000 black households, compared with 46 per 1,000 white households.

Family Income

Income is also related to risk of personal victimization: As income goes up, risk goes down. This is particularly true for robbery and aggravated assault. However, the pattern changes for personal theft. Whereas poor people are more often victimized by purse snatching and pocket picking, individuals with family incomes over $25,000 face higher risks for thefts of personal property (which involve no victim-offender contact; see Figure 2.3).

Although household victimization rates are highest for families in the $7,500 to $9,999 income category, the data reveal a decline in risk as income increases. For the crime of household burglary, Figure 2.3 reveals that rates are highest for lower-income households. It should also be noted that renters experience the greatest rates of household victimization, especially for burglary.

Urbanization

Those who live in urban areas are more afflicted by crime than are residents of suburban or rural areas. This pattern holds for all personal and household crimes and is particularly noteworthy for robbery. Robbery is a big-city phenomenon. Overall, even though there is considerable city-to-city variation, people who live in cities face higher crime rates independent of their personal characteristics. For example, the robbery rate for urban males in 1992 was 16.2 per 1,000, whereas for rural males it was 3.6 (BJS, 1994).

Of course, other correlates of victimization can be found in the NCVS data. For instance, marital status is related to victimization: Single and divorced or separated persons show higher rates of victimization than those who are married or widowed. Because most single people are also young, some of the risk may be accounted for by age. However, married people, regardless of age group, have the lowest rates of personal victimization. Furthermore, rates of victimization are related to a person's position in the labor force. The NCVS shows that employed persons, housewives, and retirees have lower rates of personal victimization than unemployed people do.

These relationships vary somewhat when one or more of the other demographic variables are taken into account and when specific subcategories of crime are examined. Nonetheless, the five correlates of victimization discussed above are quite general and persist when other variables are controlled for.[2]

Time and Place

In addition to examining the distribution of victimization across demographic groups,

lifestyle and routine activities theories hold that victimization patterns will vary across place and time. To the extent that lifestyle and routine activities increase an individual's chances of being in public places at night, for example, victimization risk is heightened.

Unfortunately, the NCVS gathers only crude indicators of the time and place that victimizations occur. For instance, the survey indicates that about half of all violent crimes take place at night, with the largest proportion occurring between 6:00 p.m. and midnight. Household crimes occur more frequently at night but overall are much more variable. In fact, 27% of household victims do not even know the time their victimization occurred. As for place, the most common site of personal victimizations was on the street. This was true for all personal crime categories. Overall, the NCVS data are in agreement with patterns found in police records regarding the time and place of crime (BJS, 1994).

Overall, the NCVS data on the correlates of victimization support the idea that individuals whose lifestyles and routine activities lead them away from home to public places, especially at night and in association with young people, are at greater risk of victimization. Although this general model of victimization fits fairly well with the existing data, much more theoretical work needs to be done to account for the distribution of victimization risk (for an overview, see Meier & Miethe, 1993). For example, direct behavioral and attitudinal measures of lifestyle and routine activities (including illegal and deviant activities) are essential to establish the viability of these theoretical accounts. Moreover, explanations of victimization need to be more sensitive to neighborhood factors as well as differences in crime type.

Offenders and Their Victims

This section examines the nature of the victim-offender relationship in criminal events.

One concern is whether the risk of victimization is greater from strangers or from loved ones. Another is whether the threat of victimization from strangers is greater for particular types of crime. Answers to these questions are crucial from both a theoretical and a public policy standpoint, in light of the widespread belief that at the core of fear of crime is a fear of victimization by a stranger (see Reidel, 1987).

In addition, this section analyzes interactions between the victim and the offender during the victimization event, specifically with regard to victim resistance and victim precipitation. From this perspective, criminal victimization can be seen as a "situated transaction" between two or more parties (Luckenbill, 1977, 1981; see also Felson & Steadman, 1983). A major policy concern is what concrete advice can be offered to potential victims of crime so that they may protect their property as well as themselves during a threatening encounter. Although it is relatively understudied, understanding the dynamics of victimization is critically important to develop reasonable victim-oriented policies.

Victim-Offender Relationships

Research on victimization has focused on three categories of victim-offender relationships: crimes committed by relatives, including spouses, ex-spouses, parents, and children; crimes committed by acquaintances, including casual acquaintances as well as close friends; and crimes committed by strangers, including those known by "sight only." Unfortunately, it is difficult to assess adequately the extent of crime committed by strangers for a variety of reasons. Most important is that victim-offender relationships can be determined only in crimes that typically involve some face-to-face contact, such as robbery and assault. In contrast, victims of burglary, auto theft, and household larceny do not typically see who their assailants were. However, even in crimes involving a confrontation, the victim-offender relationship may not be known or may be reported inaccurately. Indeed, the nature of the victim-offender relationship is unknown in 39% of the homicides reported to the police in 1993 (Federal Bureau of Investigation [FBI], 1994), due to a problem—the unavailability of the victim—that does not affect other types of crime. Second, research has consistently shown that a large number of crimes committed by relatives, friends, and lovers are not reported to the police *or* to NCVS interviewers (see Skogan, 1981). Therefore both data sources limit what is known about victim-offender relationships.

According to 1982-1984 NCVS data for the violent crimes of rape, robbery, and assault, 57% of the victimizations were committed by strangers, 31% were committed by acquaintances and friends, and 8% were committed by relatives (Timrots & Rand, 1987). This pattern has remained generally stable since 1973, when the NCVS was launched. The nature of the victim-offender relationship varies by type of crime. Generally, personal crimes involving theft are more likely to be committed by strangers than are crimes of violence. For instance, 81% of the robberies reported to survey interviewers were attributed to strangers, compared with 48% of the rape victimizations and 56% of assault victimizations (BJS, 1994, p. 52). National data on homicide for 1993 reveal that 14% of homicide victims were murdered by strangers (FBI, 1994, p. 17), and there is some evidence that over the last 20 years, stranger homicides have been on the rise (see FBI, 1994, pp. 283-287; Reidel, 1987, p. 240).

Crimes committed by strangers differ from crimes committed by nonstrangers in that stranger-to-stranger crimes are more likely to occur on the street, to involve two or more offenders, and to involve the presence of a weapon. However, those victimized by people that they know or recognize are more likely to be injured than those involved in stranger-to-stranger incidents (Timrots & Rand, 1987). Males, younger people, and single or divorced individuals also are more likely than their counterparts to be victimized by strangers. Persons living in areas characterized by high levels of family disruption and residential mobility and a large proportion of single individuals experience above-average risks of stranger violence independently of their personal characteristics (Sampson, 1987).

Victim Resistance and Precipitation

A small amount of research has been done on victim resistance and precipitation. *Victim precipitation* is defined here as actions by the victim that encourage a behavioral response or arouse emotions in the offender that increase the chance of victimization (Sparks, 1982, pp. 26-27). Unfortunately, this research suffers from a number of problems, ranging from inadequate or unavailable data to faulty conceptualization and measurement. The two topics are fraught with conceptual ambiguities, including a lack of a clear distinction between victim precipitation and victim resistance. There is also a tendency to interpret victim behavior during the victimization event solely in the context of the outcome of the event (Fattah, 1984). Although early victimology focused quite heavily on the role of the victim in crime causation, this perspective was not informed by sound research. Moreover, this focus can lead to what is known as "victim blaming" (Bard & Sangrey, 1979, p. 65). At the same time, issues surrounding victim resistance were virtually ignored until very recently.

In his seminal work on criminal homicide, Wolfgang (1958) defined victim-precipitated homicides as those in which

> the victim is a direct, positive precipitator in the crime. The role of the victim is characterized by his having been the first in the homicide drama to use physical force directed against his subsequent slayer. The victim precipitated cases are those in which the victim was the first to show and use a deadly weapon, to strike a blow in an altercation—in short, the first to commence the interplay of resort to physical force. (p. 252)

Using this definition, Wolfgang found 26% of the 588 homicides in Philadelphia during the period from 1948 to 1952 were victim precipitated. Similar results are to be found in more recent studies of homicide, although the growing proportion of unsolved murders makes such findings very tentative (see also Sparks, 1982, pp. 22-25, for a review).

Victim precipitation can be involved in assault, rape, and robbery. For instance, Mulvihill and Tumin (1969) found in their study in 17 large cities that 14% of aggravated assaults, 4% of rapes, and 8% of robberies can be classified as victim precipitated. Again, it is important to stress the definitional problems of victim precipitation plus the heavy reliance on police data in these studies. In fact, one researcher has suggested that "with the exception of homicide there is no adequate operational definition of victim precipitation; . . . the measures used in the past have been highly unreliable from a methodological point of view because they are highly dependent on a researcher's interpretation rather than on fixed criteria" (Silverman, 1974, p. 104).

Sparks (1982) attempted to distinguish a range of behaviors among victims that in some way may contribute to their victimization. His list includes precipitation, facilitation, vulnerability, opportunity, attractiveness, and impunity. The extent to which these concepts are useful in explaining variation in victimization risk and understanding the dynamics of victimization awaits further research. Unlike some criminologists, Sparks did not want to abandon the topic of victim precipitation, despite its serious conceptual and ideological difficulties.

Unlike research on victim precipitation, research on victim resistance has been more recent and often uses victimization data as well as police records. As Block and Skogan (1986) observed, "Police reports generally distort the apparent effects of victim resistance because they greatly underrepresent instances of *successful* resistance" (p. 242). People who are not injured and do not suffer any financial consequences are much less likely to notify the police about a crime.

Victims can and do resist their assailants in a variety of ways. According to available NCVS data, almost three of four victims of violent crime took some form of self-protective measures, ranging from trying to reason with the offender to using a weapon. The most common form of self-protection among victims who reported using such measures was nonviolent resistance and evasion. Victims of rape and assault were more likely to use self-protective measures than were victims of robbery. Also, victims were more likely to employ such measures when the offender was known to them (BJS, 1994).

In a study of resistance in stranger-to-stranger crime using NCVS data from 1973 to 1979, Block and Skogan (1986) distinguished two types of resistance: *nonforceful* resistance, which includes talking with the offender, yelling for help, and trying to flee, and *forceful* resistance, which includes physically fighting with the offender, with or without a weapon. Using a multivariate analysis, they found that forceful victim resistance may have reduced the likelihood of robbery completion, though such resistance may have increased the risk of physical attack to the victim. Forceful resistance in rape victimizations was related to a higher risk of attack and injury to victims, with no apparent effect on the likelihood of rape completion. In contrast, victims using nonforceful methods of resistance in robbery reduced the risk of robbery completion *and* suffered less attack and injury. Nonforceful resistance in rape victimizations was linked to a lower rate of completed rapes but was not related to attack or other nonrape injuries (Block & Skogan, 1986; but cf. Kleck & De-Lone, 1993).

A major weakness of any study using the NCVS (or most data from the police) is the lack of detailed information on the precise

timing and sequencing of events *during* the offense. We generally do not know whether resistance on the part of the victim is in response to some offender action or vice versa (see Cook, 1986). Such information is crucial for criminologists seeking to give advice to victims regarding resisting potential offenders.

The Consequences of Victimization

This section examines what happens after a victimization occurs. For instance, what is the nature and extent of victim reporting to the police? This issue is important because reports by victims trigger action by the criminal justice system. Citizens act as "gatekeepers" to the formal system of social control (Gottfredson & Gottfredson, 1988). Therefore the extent of victim reporting, as well as the reasons for nonreporting, can reveal critical information relating to victims, the police, and the criminal justice system at large.

This section also reviews what is known regarding the consequences of victimization, including the extent of physical injury and property loss. For example, how often are victims physically injured as a result of their victimizations? What is the severity of their injuries? Similarly, how often do victims suffer economic loss from their victimizations, and what is the extent of economic loss? What are the costs of crime for society at large? Answers to such questions are crucial for the development of adequate compensation programs, among other policy considerations. Note that mental and emotional trauma is not measured in the NCVS. Fortunately, the psychological aftermath of victimization is examined in Chapters 3 and 6 of this book.

Victim Reporting to the Police

Until the development of victimization surveys, there were no empirical data on the nature and extent of victim reporting to the police. Speculation about the "dark figure" of

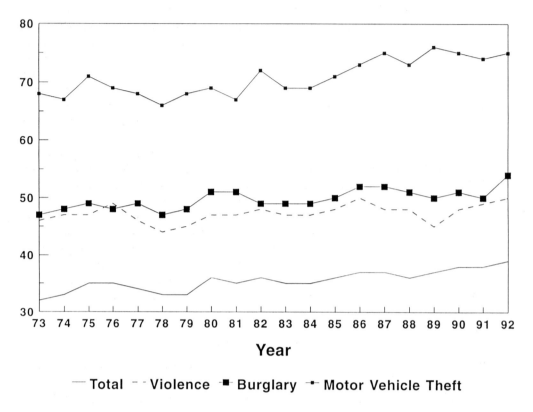

Figure 2.4. Percentage of Victims Reporting Victimizations to the Police for Selected Personal and Household Crimes, 1973-1992 National Crime Survey Data
SOURCE: Bureau of Justice Statistics (1994, p. 4).

unreported crime suggested that a considerable number of crimes did not come to the attention of the police. The NCVS confirmed this speculation. Indeed, according to the 1992 survey, a little more than a third of all crimes reported to interviewers were also reported to the police. Reporting rates vary by crime type. In 1992, violent crimes were more often reported to the police than were crimes of theft (50% vs. 30%), although the reporting rates for successful motor vehicle thefts (92%) are the highest (BJS, 1994). Importantly, rates of reporting to the police reveal no substantial variation over the period from 1973 to 1992. This is illustrated in Figure 2.4.

Research has consistently established that an important determinant of victim reporting to the police is the seriousness of the incident (Skogan, 1984). For example, completed thefts resulting in large losses and violent crimes involving injury or weapons are the most likely reported to the police. In contrast, reporting to the police seems to be largely independent of the victim's personal characteristics (Skogan, 1984). Small differences can be noted in reporting rates by sex and age: Older victims are more likely to report than younger ones, and female victims are more likely to report than males. No differences are related to race and income. Surprisingly, the

NCVS data reveal no differences in the extent of victim reporting to the police in crimes committed by strangers as compared with non-strangers. Given the weaknesses of survey measures of nonstranger victimizations, this finding is in all likelihood a methodological artifact and should be viewed cautiously.

In the NCVS, victims are also asked to state their reasons for reporting or not reporting their victimization experiences to the police. A large number are not reported because victims believe that the incidents were "not important enough" or that "nothing could be done/lack of proof," perhaps reflecting the nonserious nature of a number of crimes measured in the survey. However, a number of violent crimes were not reported to the police because victims felt they were "private matters." As to reasons for reporting, victims of violent crimes most often reported crimes out of a sense of duty or obligation or as a way of preventing recurrences of the victimization. On the other hand, victims of theft reported to recover their losses, primarily through insurance claims (BJS, 1994).

Physical Injury

Over 24,000 people are murdered in each year in the United States, and more than 2 million are injured in rapes, robberies, and assaults. About one of three victims of violent crime suffers some form of physical injury. However, serious injury—gunshot or knife wounds, broken bones, teeth knocked out, loss of consciousness—is less common. Of victims of violent crime who were injured, about half required some medical care, 19% were treated at a hospital, and 4% spent at least one night in the hospital (Zawitz et al., 1993, p. 15).

Not surprisingly, the likelihood of injury varies by crime and victim characteristics. The NCVS data from 1979 to 1986 show that victims of aggravated assault were more likely than other victims of violence (rape and robbery) to receive treatment in an emergency room or hospital and to have stayed in a hospital at least one night (Harlow, 1989, p. 4). With regard to victim characteristics, the rate of physical injuries is greater for males, blacks, persons aged 19 to 24, and those earning less than $10,000 per year. Also, blacks are more likely than whites to receive injuries that require hospitalization (BJS, 1994; Harlow, 1989).

It should be recognized that using hospitalization as a measure of injury severity has been criticized by some researchers (see Allen, 1986). Allen (p. 141) argued that hospitalization is dependent on a number of factors (e.g., delay in time between injury and medical intervention) in addition to the severity of injury itself. Therefore data on physical injury derived from the NCVS must be viewed with these considerations in mind.

Economic Loss

Victims may suffer a wide range of economic penalties. These include direct cash and property losses, property damage, medical expenses, work time loss, and security costs, as well as more intangible costs, such as fear of crime, a potentially trying involvement with the criminal justice system, and a general deterioration of the quality of their life.

The NCVS contains some information on the direct economic cost of crime to individual victims. For instance, 1991 NCVS data reveal that the direct cash and property losses for victims of personal robbery, personal and household larceny, household burglary, and motor vehicle theft totaled $19 billion. The bulk of these losses were from burglary, larceny, and motor vehicle theft. Among the violent crimes, robbery accounts for a disproportionate share of the total economic loss (Zawitz et al., 1993, p. 16). It is believed that these estimates are low and that they exclude important categories such as mental health costs (Cohen, 1988; Cohen, Miller, & Rossman, 1994).

The 1992 NCVS data show that 35% of all personal crimes and 24% of all household crimes involved losses of less than $50. In contrast, only 12% of personal crimes and 24% of household crimes resulted in losses greater than $500 (BJS, 1994, p. 94). Examining medical expenses among those injured victims who had acquired medical costs, the 1992 NCVS revealed that 8% incurred costs of less than $50, 15% incurred costs between $50 and $249, and 42% incurred costs greater than $250. Note, however, that 35% of the victims did not know the amount of their medical costs at the time of interview (BJS, 1994, p. 90).

In addition to the costs for individual victims, there are costs of crime to society at large. The BJS (1988, p. 114) has estimated that the cost of the criminal justice system at the local, state, and federal level is $45.6 billion a year. Moreover, private security costs have been estimated to be more than $20 billion (BJS, 1988, p. 114). Finally, Skogan (1986) has described the indirect effects of crime and fear of crime on neighborhood disinvestment, deindustrialization, and declining commercial vitality. Assessing the monetary cost of community decay is nearly impossible.

Homicide

Although the NCVS does not collect data on homicide, most criminologists believe that police reports can be used to assess the patterns and correlates of homicide victimization (but see Maxfield, 1989). There are numerous questions about homicide. First and foremost, is the rate of homicide in the United States increasing? Are the correlates of homicide victimization different from those of other violent crimes? Can homicide victimizations be explained by lifestyle and routine activities? What do we know about the circumstances of homicide?

In 1993, 24,526 murder or non-negligent manslaughter offenses—defined as intentionally causing the death of another person without extreme provocation or legal justification—were reported to the UCR; the rate per 100,000 inhabitants was 9.5. The murder rate is higher in urban areas than in suburban and rural areas, although there is a great deal of variation from city to city. There have been fairly large increases in the homicide rate since 1965, when the rate of homicide was 5.1 per 100,000 persons. Interestingly, whereas the homicide rate was 9.5 in 1993, the historical high occurred in 1980—a rate of 10.2 per 100,000 persons (FBI, 1994, pp. 283-287). Since 1985, homicide rates among young adults (18 to 24 years old) have increased by 77%. The rate increase for those aged 14 to 17 is even more dramatic: 152% (Fox, 1995, Table 1b). As displayed in Figure 2.5, handgun homicide victimization rates among those aged 14 to 17 have increased from 1976 to 1993, especially for black victims.

In 1993, 77% of homicide victims were males, 48% were between the ages of 20 and 34, and 51% were black. An examination of single-offender and single-victim incidents reveals that homicide is disproportionately an intraracial event, with blacks killing blacks and whites killing whites. In a similar vein, males were most often killed by other males; however, women were far more likely to be slain by men than by other women (FBI, 1994).

In 1993, firearms were the weapon of choice in 7 of every 10 homicides, with handguns accounting for 57% of all murders. Moreover, almost half of the murders in 1993 involved relatives or persons acquainted with the victim. Virtually 3 out of every 10 murders were the result of arguments, 19% were felony murders, and in 28% of the incidents the motives of the participants were not known (FBI, 1994).

Maxfield (1989) sorted out the various types of incidents that fall under the general rubric of homicide (see also Block & Block, 1992, for an interesting discussion of homicide syndromes). Specifically, he distin-

Rate per 100,000

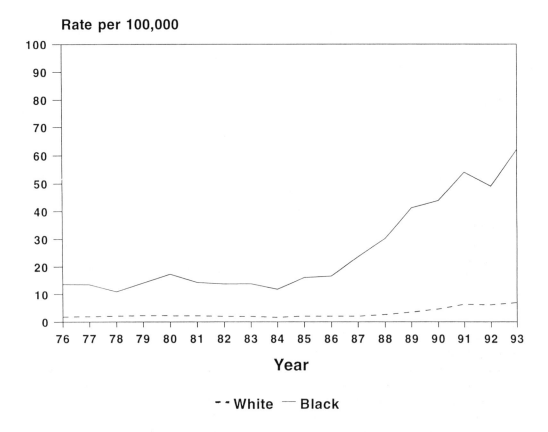

Figure 2.5. Handgun Homicide Victimization Rates for Males 14 to 17 Years of Age, by Race, 1976-1993
SOURCE: Federal Bureau of Investigation, Supplemental Homicide Reports (unpublished, supplied by James Alan Fox, Northeastern University).

guished between *conflict* homicides (generally resulting from arguments), *instrumental felony* homicides (resulting from other felonies, such as robbery or sexual assault), *property felony* homicides (resulting from burglaries and other such crimes), *drug* homicides, and *gang* homicides. These types of homicide clearly display differential risk-related patterns that reflect differences in lifestyle and routine activities (Block & Block, 1992; Maxfield, 1989). Thus successful prevention strategies must take into account different types of homicide.

Conclusion

Our knowledge regarding the nature and extent of victimization and the characteristics of victims in crimes other than homicide is almost wholly dependent on the NCVS. Of course, the NCVS is not without its problems, and a variety of questions have been raised regarding the validity and reliability of the NCVS design and data collection procedures. The importance of these methodological concerns depends in large part on the substantive question being asked: namely, whether one is interested in addressing the *level* of victimization (or changes in that level) or the *correlates* of victimization (Gottfredson, 1986). More important, perhaps, are the general problems inherent in victimization surveys. Victimization surveys attempt to capture in a uniform and systematic manner very complex interactions between people under stressful circumstances. Research has indicated that memory problems are significant in victim surveys (Skogan, 1981, pp. 15-22). In addition, affective factors such as shame and embarrassment make the reporting of certain events to survey interviewers more difficult. Finally, the nature of the interview—face to face in the home versus by telephone—may also alter the reporting of certain crimes such as domestic violence to survey interviewers. These problems can influence both estimates of the level of victimization in the United States and descriptions of the correlates of victimization.

Some evidence of systematic response bias has been discovered within the NCVS. For example, it is generally recognized that victimizations committed by offenders known to the victim, especially relatives, are less likely to be reported to survey interviewers, even though the incident was reported to the police (see Skogan, 1981). This is particularly problematic for the crimes of rape and assault, especially date rape, spouse abuse, and elder abuse.

In sharp contrast to the NCVS data, official data on crimes from the police and other agencies reveal that a much higher proportion of incidents of assaultive violence involve friends and family members (Skogan, 1981, pp. 30-31). Skogan argued that this makes the NCVS even more suspect "because we also believe that violence between friends and relatives is less likely than stranger violence to be reported to the police. That police files contain approximately $3\frac{1}{2}$ times more acquaintance violence than revealed in interviews does not add to our confidence in the validity of the survey findings" (p. 30). In addition, Cook

(1985) found that compared with police data, the NCVS undercounts (by a factor of about three) serious assaults that involve gunshot woundings.

Nevertheless, we can draw some broad conclusions using the available data:

1. The data clearly show that the more serious the victimization is, the less frequently it occurs, and that the risk of personal theft is greater than the risk of violent victimization. Serious crimes, especially violent offenses, are relatively rare events. The comparative risk of various life events reveals that accidental injuries at home and work are more likely than a victimization by a violent crime.

2. The NCVS shows an overall decline in crime over the period from 1973 to 1992. For the same time period, the survey indicates stability in the rates of victim reporting to the police. In contrast, the UCR reveals large percentage increases in many crime categories for the same time period. This suggests that the NCVS and UCR are measuring different phenomena and that one should exercise caution in making trend comparisons.

3. The risk of victimization is unevenly distributed across population groups, time, and space. Far from being a random event, victimization is largely consistent with the exposure to risks linked to lifestyle and routine activities. Although there are exceptions, young persons, males, blacks, and low-income groups are at greater risk of both personal and household victimization, perhaps due to their typical day-to-day behavior.

4. Homicide rates have increased since the mid-1980s. Homicide victims appear to getting younger, the result of increased firearm use among juveniles. Homicide is now the leading cause of death for young black males.

5. The dynamics of victimization events (e.g., the victim-offender relationship) and the consequences of victimization experiences (e.g., physical injury and economic loss) vary considerably by type of crime and, to a lesser extent, by characteristics of the victim.

6. Although the direct economic costs of crime for individual victims are not generally large, the indirect costs for the criminal justice system and communities as a whole are enormous. Although difficult to quantify, the indirect costs of fear of crime are believed to be quite large. At the same time, it should be recognized that although fear of crime is largely a fear of victimization by strangers, a large proportion of crimes, especially violent crimes, are committed by friends, lovers, and relatives.

Overall, these findings reveal the striking importance of the effect of crime on the quality of life in families and neighborhoods across the United States.

Notes

1. In July 1993, the NCVS implemented a redesigned interview schedule to elicit the reporting of more kinds of victimizations to survey interviewers to improve estimates of the difficult-to-measure crimes, such as rape, sexual assault, and domestic violence (Bastian, 1995). Because the comprehensive 1993 data are not available at this time, NCVS data from the 1973-1992 time period are presented in this chapter. However, the patterns in the available 1993 data regarding crime type distribution and the characteristics of victims appear to be the same as those found in 1992 using the previous survey instrument. The major changes from 1992 to 1993 appear in the estimates of the number of victimizations and victim reporting to the police. It appears that improved cues for certain questions induced respondents to report more crimes of a less serious nature that are less likely to be reported to the police (Bastian, 1995).

2. One puzzling finding has been the relationship between educational attainment and victimization. Sparks (1981, pp. 32-36) has found that variables linked to social class, such as educational attainment, positively affect the reporting of victimizations to survey interviewers. This suggests that highly educated members of the sample are more productive respondents rather than at greater risk of victimization. Skogan (1981) and Gottfredson (1984) have shown that once the educational effect is controlled, major patterns in the data (e.g., age, income, major activity) generally hold. In addition, the correlates of victimization found in the NCVS generally parallel those found in foreign victimization surveys such as the British Crime Survey (see Gottfredson, 1984, and more generally Block, 1984, for a review).

References

Allen, R. B. (1986). Measuring the severity of physical injury among assault and homicide victims. *Journal of Quantitative Criminology,, 2,* 139-156.

Bachman, R. (1994). *Violence against women.* Washington, DC: U.S. Department of Justice.

Bard, M., & Sangrey, D. (1979). *The crime victim's book.* New York: Basic Books.

Bastian, L. (1995). *Criminal victimization 1993.* Washington, DC: U.S. Department of Justice.

Block, R. (Ed.). (1984). *Victimization and fear of crime: World perspectives.* Washington, DC: Government Printing Office.

Block, R., & Block, C. (1980). Decisions and data: The transformation of robbery incidents into official robbery statistics. *Journal of Criminal Law and Criminology, 71,* 622-636.

Block, R., & Block, C. (1992). Homicide syndromes and vulnerability. *Studies of Crime Prevention, 1,* 61-87.

Block, R., & Skogan, W. G. (1986). Resistance and nonfatal outcomes in stranger-to-stranger predatory crime. *Violence and Victims, 1,* 241-253.

Bureau of Justice Statistics. (1994). *Criminal victimization in the United States, 1992.* Washington, DC: U.S. Department of Justice.

Bureau of Justice Statistics. (1993). *Crime and the nation's households, 1992.* Washington, DC: U.S. Dept. of Justice.

Bureau of Justice Statistics. (1988). *Report to the nation on crime and justice* (2nd ed.). Washington, DC: U.S. Dept. of Justice.

Cohen, L., & Felson, M. (1979). Social change and crime rate trends: A routine activity approach. *American Sociological Review, 44,* 588-608.

Cohen, L. E., Kluegel, J. R., & Land, K. (1981). Social inequality and predatory criminal victimization: An exposition and test of a formal theory. *American Sociological Review, 46,* 505-524.

Cohen, M. A. (1988). Some new evidence on the seriousness of crime. *Criminology, 26,* 343-353.

Cohen M. A., Miller, T. R., & Rossman, S. B. (1994). The costs and consequences of violent behavior in the United States. In A. J. Reiss & J. A. Roth (Eds.), *Understanding and preventing violence* (Vol. 4, pp. 67-166). Washington, DC: National Academy Press.

Cook, P. J. (1985). The case of the missing victims: Gunshot woundings in the national crime survey. *Journal of Quantitative Criminology, 1,* 91-102.

Cook, P. J. (1986). The relationship between victim resistance and injury in noncommercial robbery. *Journal of Legal Studies, 15,* 405-416.

Fattah, E. A. (1984). Victims' response to confrontational victimization: A neglected aspect of victim research. *Crime and Delinquency, 30,* 75-90.

Federal Bureau of Investigation. (1994). *Crime in the United States, 1993.* Washington, DC: Government Printing Office.

Felson, R., & Steadman, H. J. (1983). Situational factors in disputes leading to criminal violence. *Criminology, 21,* 59-74.

Fox, J. A. (1995, February). *Homicide offending patterns: A grim look ahead.* Paper presented at the annual meeting of the American Academy for the Advancement of Science, Atlanta.

Gottfredson, M. R. (1984). *Victims of crime: The dimensions of risk.* London: H.M. Stationery Office.

Gottfredson, M. R. (1986). Substantive contributions of victimization surveys. *Crime and Justice: An Annual Review of Research, 8,* 251-287.

Gottfredson, M. R., & Gottfredson, D. M. (1988). *Decision making in criminal justice.* New York: Plenum.

Gove, W. R., Hughes, M., & Geerken, M. (1985). Are uniform crime reports a valid indicator of the index crimes? An affirmative answer with minor qualifications. *Criminology, 23,* 451-503.

Harlow, C. W. (1989). *Injuries from crime.* Washington, DC: U.S. Dept. of Justice.

Hindelang, M. J., Gottfredson, M. R., & Garofalo, J. (1978). *Victims of personal crime.* Cambridge, MA: Ballinger.

Kleck, G., & DeLone, M. A. (1993). Victim resistance and offender weapon effects in robbery. *Journal of Quantitative Criminology, 9,* 55-81.

Luckenbill, D. F. (1977). Criminal homicide as a situated transaction. *Social Problems, 25,* 176-186.

Luckenbill, D. F. (1981). Generating compliance: The case of robbery. *Urban Life, 10,* 25-46.

Maxfield, M. G. (1989). Circumstances in supplementary homicide reports: Variety and validity. *Criminology, 27,* 671-695.

McDowall, D., & Loftin, C. (1992). Comparing the UCR and NCS over time. *Criminology, 30,* 125-132.

Meier, R. F., & Miethe, T. D. (1993). Understanding theories of criminal victimization. *Crime and Justice: An Annual Review of Research, 17,* 459-499.

Mulvihill, D., & Tumin, M. (1969). *Crimes of violence. A staff report submitted to the U.S. Commission on the Causes and Prevention of Violence* (Vol. 11). Washington, DC: Government Printing Office.

O'Brien, R. M. (1985). *Crime and victimization data.* Beverly Hills, CA: Sage.

Reidel, M. (1987). Stranger violence: Perspectives, issues, and problems. *Journal of Criminal Law and Criminology, 78,* 223-258.

Sampson, R. J. (1987). Personal violence by strangers: An extension and test of predatory victimization. *Journal of Criminal Law and Criminology, 78,* 327-356.

Silverman, R. (1974). Victim precipitation: An examination of the concept. In I. Drapkin & E. Viano (Eds.), *Victimology: A new focus* (pp. 99-109). Lexington, MA: Lexington.

Skogan, W. G. (1981). *Issues in the measurement of victimization.* Washington, DC: Bureau of Justice Statistics.

Skogan, W. G. (1984). Reporting crimes to the police: The status of world research. *Journal of Research in Crime and Delinquency, 21,* 113-138.

Skogan, W. G. (1986). Fear of crime and neighborhood change. In A. J. Reiss & M. Tonry (Eds.), *Communities and crime* (pp. 203-229). Chicago: University of Chicago Press.

Sparks, R. F. (1981). Surveys of victimization: An optimistic assessment. *Crime and Justice: An Annual Review of Research, 3,* 1-60.

Sparks, R. F. (1982). *Research on victims of crime.* Washington, DC: Government Printing Office.

Timrots, A. D., & Rand, M. R. (1987). *Violent crime by strangers and nonstrangers.* Washington, DC: U.S. Dept. of Justice.

Wolfgang, M. E. (1958). *Patterns in criminal homicide.* Philadelphia: University of Pennsylvania Press.

Zawitz, M. W., Klaus, P. A., Bachman, R., Bastian, L. D., DeBerry, M. M., Jr., Rand, M. R., & Taylor, B. M. (1993). *Highlights from 20 years of surveying crime victims.* Washington, DC: U.S. Dept. of Justice.

3 Sexual Assault

PATRICIA A. RESICK
PALLAVI NISHITH

Sexual assault is a problem of great personal and social significance. In random surveys of the population, the lifetime prevalence of sexual assault has been estimated between 13.5% and 44% of women (Kilpatrick, Best, et al., 1985; Koss, Gidycz, & Wisniewski, 1987; Russell, 1982). More recently, *Rape in America: A Report to the Nation* was released by the National Victim Center and the Crime Victims' Research and Treatment Center (Kilpatrick, Edmunds, & Seymour, 1992). Its researchers conducted a longitudinal survey of 4,008 adult American women and found that 507 (13%) reported having been raped at least once. Sexual assault is a problem that affects both the physical and psychological functioning of victims as measured by the prolonged use of medical and mental health services (Golding, Stein, Siegel, & Burnam, 1988; Koss, Dinero, Seibel, & Cox, 1988). Furthermore, nearly 20% of rape victims attempt suicide, and 44% contemplate suicide in its aftermath (Kilpatrick et al., 1987; Resick, Jordan, Girelli, Hutter, & Marhoefer-Dvorak, 1988). Sexual assault affects our nonvictimized population through fear of crime and restriction of lifestyles (Riger & Gordon, 1981).

Rape is probably the most thoroughly studied single-incident crime with regard to victim reactions. It has always been considered to be the most traumatic adult crime, short of murder, and has therefore been the subject of great scrutiny and the focus of considerable intervention. Whether rape does, in fact, produce greater trauma is, of course, an empirical question. Also in question is whether the rape reaction is different qualitatively or different only in degree from reactions to other traumatic events. If the latter is the case, then research that has been compiled on reactions to rape and treatment of rape victims should be directly applicable to other types of crime victims. The purpose of this chapter is to examine research on reactions to rape, to look at variables that moderate recovery, to describe current theories explaining these reactions, and to discuss the implications of these findings and theories for intervention with adult victims of rape.

The Psychological Aftermath of Rape

Research on Victim Reactions

Generally, three types of studies have examined the psychological reactions of rape victims. Each type has advantages and disadvantages in methodology. Together, they provide a very good picture of the reactions and recovery of rape victims. The first type of research is the longitudinal study (Atkeson, Calhoun, Resick, & Ellis, 1982; Kilpatrick, Resick, & Veronen, 1981; Resick, 1988; Rothbaum, Foa, Riggs, Murdock, & Walsh, 1992). In longitudinal studies, rape victims are compared to either nonvictims or other crime victims over a specified period of time to determine the pattern of reactions and recovery unique to rape victims. The advantage of these studies is that they are prospective: That is, they examine victims shortly after the crime and are sensitive to changes in victims' responses over time. This research clearly demonstrates that rape victims are indeed suffering from distinct symptoms beyond those found in the general population. This research also brings into question the validity of the crisis theory model of victim reactions. The disadvantage of longitudinal research is that findings are limited to those women who report the crime to some agency fairly soon after it occurs. It is known that many women do not report rape in the immediate aftermath and that some women do not define themselves as victims of rape even though they suffer from its effects. This is particularly true of acquaintance rape victims, who may have defined rape only as an attack by a stranger. Therefore, by definition, longitudinal research carries some potential bias.

Another possible source of bias is that researchers cannot control completely for attrition in longitudinal studies. Attrition has been examined by comparison of victims who completed versus victims who withdrew from longitudinal studies. Although no differences have emerged, it is possible that these groups differ on some variable(s) that have not been examined (Kilpatrick, 1984; Resick, Calhoun, Atkeson, & Ellis, 1981).

The second type of research is the random population survey (Burnam et al., 1988; Kilpatrick, Best, et al., 1985; Kilpatrick et al., 1992; Resnick, Kilpatrick, Dansky, Saunders, & Best, 1993). Because of the problem of nonreporting, this type of research was conducted to assess reactions of rape victims in the general population as well as to determine more accurately the prevalence of sexual assault. Random population surveys have been conducted by telephone survey, written questionnaire, and house-to-house survey. The purpose of random population surveys is to provide information regarding the long-term reactions of victims who may not have reported their crimes or perhaps even identified themselves as rape victims using everyday definitions. The greatest disadvantage of this type of research is that it is retrospective and is therefore subject to memory bias. Many of the women surveyed in these studies were victimized many years earlier and may not accurately remember events or their reactions to them. These studies also cannot control for intervening events that could account for reported symptoms. However, they do provide interesting information regarding current functioning in women who were sexually assaulted at some previous point in their lives.

The third type of research is designed to identify factors that may influence the reaction and recovery of rape victims. A range of studies have examined pre-crime, within-crime, and postcrime events and variables that may exacerbate or ameliorate the traumatic impact of rape. Although they provide important supplementary information regarding the effects of sexual assault, these studies are at times difficult to evaluate because they use idiosyncratic rather than standard questionnaires and interviews. It is difficult to generalize from one study to the next when every study uses a different methodology and different means of assessing the variables of interest. Although the results from the first two types of study (longitudinal and random population survey) have been rather consistent, the third type of research has produced a variety of findings that are frequently contradictory. Furthermore, these studies have rarely included comparison groups of other types of crime victims. Nevertheless, they have identified potentially important intervening variables for reactions and recovery.

Symptoms and Patterns of Recovery

Although most recent studies have focused on specific diagnoses of disorders, most of the research begun in the 1970s on reactions to rape did not use diagnostic categories or labels or examine the range and occurrence of individual symptoms (Atkeson et al., 1982; Kilpatrick et al., 1981; Kilpatrick, Veronen, & Resick, 1979a). Some of the early resistance to diagnosis stemmed from a reluctance to label victims as pathological when so little was known about what constituted a "normal" reaction to such an event. There was also concern with the classification models that existed prior to 1980, which were theory laden, subjective, and unreliable. Furthermore, no clear diagnostic category captured the essential features of rape reactions. With the advent of the third edition of the *Diagnostic and Statistical Manual* (*DSM-III*) in 1980 (American Psychiatric Association, 1980), diagnosis became much more empirically based than it had been previously. The new classification, posttraumatic stress disorder (PTSD), did appear to apply to the trauma reactions that had been observed in rape victims. By this time also,

enough evidence had been compiled to specify typical reactions to sexual assault.

Rather than determining whether and how many rape victims met the criteria for major depression or PTSD, most of the early studies merely compared whether rape victims suffered from more fear and anxiety or greater depressive symptoms than nonvictims or victims of other crimes. Generally, the longitudinal studies found that victims suffered from a wide range of symptoms for several months after the crime. Although much of the distress diminished by 3 months postcrime, there were often enduring problems with fear, anxiety, depression, social adjustment, sexual functioning, and self-esteem for a substantial minority of victims (Atkeson et al., 1982; Calhoun, Atkeson, & Resick, 1982; Kilpatrick et al., 1981; Kilpatrick & Veronen, 1983; Resick, 1988).

In a study of acute reactions to sexual assault, Veronen, Kilpatrick, and Resick (1979) reported that 96% of the victims said that immediately after the assault they were scared and worried and were shaking or trembling and that 92% reported being terrified and confused. These reactions were accompanied by depression (84%), exhaustion (96%), and restlessness (88%) in the 2 to 3 hours following the assault. These findings replicated those of Burgess and Holmstrom (1974, 1979a), who, in their study of rape conducted in an emergency room of a hospital, reported similar reactions immediately after the assault.

In a longitudinal study, Calhoun and her colleagues (Atkeson et al., 1982; Calhoun et al., 1982; Ellis, Calhoun, & Atkeson, 1980; Resick et al., 1981) compared the reactions of 93 rape victims and 87 nonvictims at six postcrime intervals: 2 weeks and 1, 2, 4, 8, and 12 months. They found that within 2 weeks postassault, the majority of the rape victims experienced clinically significant fear, depression, and other mood states. In addition, they reported problems with social adjustment, sexual functioning, and self-esteem. Rape victims scored higher than nonvictims on fear measures. Rape victims exhibited improvement between the second-week and second-month sessions but continued to report more fear and anxiety than nonraped women through the 12-month assessment. In addition, rape victims scored significantly higher than nonvictims on depression measures at 2 weeks, 1 month, and 2 months postcrime but not at later sessions. At the 2-week session, 75% of rape victims reported at least mild depressive symptoms.

Social adjustment was also disrupted until the 4-month assessment session. Of particular types of social adjustment, rape victims differed from controls in the area of family and work adjustment; work adjustment was affected the longest, for 8 months after the crime. With regard to sexual functioning, these researchers found that sexual activity was curtailed for the first month after the assault in 43% of the sample but that by 12 months postcrime, activity levels had returned to normal for those women who had had frequent or somewhat frequent sexual activity prior to the crime. Those women who had had infrequent sexual activity prior to the crime did not return to pre-crime levels by 12 months. They continued to avoid sexual contact. These findings replicate those of Burgess and Holmstrom (1979b), who reported that of the women who had been sexually active at the time of the crime, 38% gave up sex for at least 6 months, and 33% decreased the frequency of their sexual activity. At the 4- to 6-month follow-up, 30% still considered themselves not recovered. Sexual satisfaction for rape victims was lower than that for nonvictims (Feldman-Summers et al., 1979; Orlando & Koss, 1983; Resick, 1986), and the rape victims reported a greater number of sexual dysfunctions compared to nonvictims (Becker, Cunningham Rathner, & Kaplan, 1986; Becker, Skinner, Abel, & Treacy, 1982; Resick, 1986).

Kilpatrick and his colleagues also conducted a longitudinal study comparing rape victims with a sample of nonraped women (Kilpatrick, 1984; Kilpatrick et al., 1981; Kilpatrick & Veronen, 1983; Kilpatrick, Veronen, & Resick, 1979a, 1979b). For the most part, their findings are similar to those of Calhoun et al. (1982). Kilpatrick's project compared the two groups at the following postcrime intervals: 6 to 21 days, 1 month, 3 months, 6 months, 1 year, 2 years, and 3 years. In an early report with a smaller sample size of 35 rape victims, they reported that raped women scored significantly higher than nonraped women on 25 of 28 measures of distress at 1 month postcrime but scored higher on only 7 of the 28 measures at 3 and 6 months postcrime. All 7 measures were indicators of fear and anxiety. Greater fear reactions continued through the 3-year assessment. Depressive symptoms had disappeared by 3 months postcrime. However, in their final report for the project, analyses were conducted with a much larger sample of 149 rape victims (Kilpatrick, 1984). Within this larger sample, raped women continued to report significantly greater distress than nonraped women on 26 of 28 measures at 3, 6, and 12 months postcrime, including measures of depression. Throughout the 3-year assessment, differences were reported on fear and anxiety scales. Self-esteem was examined separately in a follow-up study by Murphy et al. (1988). An examination of nine self-esteem subscales indicated that rape victims experienced significantly poorer self-esteem than nonvictims across the 2 years examined. Particularly affected were self-esteem and relationships with parents and others.

In another longitudinal study, Resick (1988) compared the reactions of rape and robbery victims. She assessed these two groups at 1, 3, 6, 12, and 18 months postcrime to determine whether the reactions observed are unique to the crime of rape or similar to other life-threatening crimes. She found that both rape and robbery victims experienced considerable distress following their victimization. For example, at 1 month postcrime, on a measure of global distress, 48% of rape victims scored one standard deviation above the normative mean for the scale, and another 35% scored at least two standard deviations above the mean. In the sample of robbery victims, 37% scored one standard deviation above the mean, and another 31% were elevated at least two standard deviations. At 18 months postcrime, 55% of the rape victims and 36% of the robbery victims reported scores that were still elevated at least one full standard deviation. An examination of self-esteem indicated that rape-robbery victims had lower esteem regarding physical self, social self, and identity than either rape victims or robbery victims. Rape victims seeking therapy were also found to score lower than the population norms on the Tennessee Self-Concept Scale (TSCS; Fitts, 1965); in addition, attributions of self-blame were found to predict higher self-criticism scores on the TSCS (Resick et al., 1988; Resick & Schnicke, 1990).

In summary, most rape victims, immediately after the assault, experience acute reactions that last several months. By 3 months postassault, there is some stabilization in the initial symptoms. However, some victims continue to experience chronic problems for an indefinite time in the areas of fear/anxiety, depression, social adjustment, sexual functioning, and self-esteem. Furthermore, studies have also reported sleep disturbances (Burgess & Holmstrom, 1979a; Ellis, Atkeson, & Calhoun, 1981; Nadelson, Notman, Zackson, & Gornick, 1982; Norris & Feldman-Summers, 1981) and disturbances in memory and concentration (Horowitz, Wilner, Kaltrieder, & Alvarez, 1980; Nadelson et al., 1982) in rape victims.

Aside from psychological reactions following sexual assault, physical symptoms and problems may result either directly from the crime (e.g., injuries, sexually transmitted diseases, pregnancy) or as a result of stress. These physical reactions interact with psychological symptoms and may complicate recovery from the trauma. In approximately 5% of cases, pregnancy is a result of the rape (Beebe, 1991; Koss, Woodruff, & Koss, 1991). Sexually

transmitted diseases resulting from rape have been estimated to range from 4% to 30% of cases (Beebe, 1991; Jenny et al., 1990; Lacey, 1990; Murphy, 1990). Beyond the immediate effects of the violence, the prolonged stress reaction of victims may take a toll on their health. Women who have been the victims of rape and other crimes report more symptoms of illness and view their health as worse than nonvictims. They also visit their physicians more frequently—in fact, twice as often as nonvictimized women (Fellitti, 1991; Koss, Koss, & Woodruff, 1991).

Diagnosis of Psychological Disorders in Rape Victims

The two major psychological disorders that have been examined most frequently in rape victims are PTSD and major depression. Other disorders that have also been associated with rape are phobias (including simple phobias and social phobia), obsessive-compulsive disorder, and chemical dependency. Several studies have determined the frequency of these disorders (Steketee & Foa, 1987).

PTSD

In their retrospective study, Kilpatrick et al. (1992) reported that 31% of all the rape victims surveyed developed PTSD sometime in their life and that 11% still had PTSD at the time of the survey. They estimated that 3.8 million adult American women have had rape-related PTSD and that 1.3 million currently have it.

In a prospective study, Rothbaum et al. (1992), using structured diagnostic interviews, found that 94% of their rape victim sample met symptom criteria for PTSD (minus the time criterion of 1 month needed for diagnosis) at 1 week postrape. By 3 months postcrime, 47% still met criteria for PTSD. The women who eventually recovered continued to show gradual improvement through the 3 months of assessment, whereas the women who developed chronic PTSD reported more severe distress initially and showed little further improvement after the first month on any of the symptom scales. Similarly, Mechanic, Resick, and Griffin (1994), in a study of the natural course of recovery in recent rape victims, reported that at 2 weeks postrape, 72% of their sample ($N = 59$) met full symptom criteria for PTSD. At 3 months, 44% still met full criteria for PTSD.

Major Depression

Frank, Turner, and Duffy (1979), in an assessment of depression in 34 rape victims, found that 44% were moderately to severely depressed within the 1-month period of their assaults. Using semistructured interviews, Frank and Stewart (1984), in a sample of 90 recent rape victims, found that 43% met criteria for major depression. They reported that the depression diminished by 3 months postcrime. Atkeson et al. (1982) replicated this finding by reporting that rape victims were significantly more depressed compared to nonvictims at 2 weeks, 1 month, and 2 months postassault but not at later assessment periods. Another set of longitudinal studies have reported similar initial differences in levels of depression between rape victims and nonvictims (Kilpatrick & Veronen, 1984; Resick, 1988; Rothbaum et al., 1992); however, these differences apparently continue to persist from 1 year postcrime (Kilpatrick & Veronen, 1984; Resick, 1988) to 16 years postcrime (Ellis et al., 1981).

Kilpatrick et al. (1992) found that of the 507 rape victims surveyed, 30% had experienced at least one major depression, and 21% were meeting criteria for a current major depression at the time of the survey. In comparison, only 10% of the women who had never been raped had ever experienced major depression and only 6% were currently depressed. In another random survey of crime victims, Burnam et al. (1988) reported that a greater percentage of victims (17.9%) than nonvictims (4.7%) were

likely to experience a major depressive disorder. In a study of the natural course of recovery in recent rape victims, Mechanic, Resick, and Griffin (1993) reported a 35% prevalence at 2 weeks postrape and a 13% prevalence at 3 months postrape of current major depression. In another random survey of crime victims, Burnam et al. (1988) reported that a greater percentage of victims (17.93%) than nonvictims (4.68%) had experienced a major depressive disorder.

Finally, the high comorbidity between PTSD and major depression has focused research attention on suicidal ideation and suicide attempts in this population. Although the rates of suicidal behavior are not very high in the first month after victimization (2.9% in Frank et al., 1979; 2.7% in Frank & Stewart, 1984), Ellis et al. (1981) found that 50% of their long-term sample had considered suicide. Resick et al. (1988) reported that 43% of their treatment-seeking sample had considered suicide and that 17% had actually made a suicide attempt. In a random survey, Kilpatrick, Best, et al. (1985) reported that 44% of the rape victims had suicidal ideation and 19% had made an actual attempt. The national survey by Kilpatrick et al. (1992) found that 33% of rape victims had considered suicide compared to 8% of nonvictims. They also reported that 13% of the rape victims had made a suicide attempt compared to 1% of nonvictims.

Other Psychological Disorders

Kilpatrick et al. (1987) found that 3% of the nonvictims reported social phobia, whereas 12% of one-incident and 10% of two-incident rape victims reported meeting the diagnostic criteria for social phobia. Only 2% of the nonvictims reported obsessive-compulsive disorder, whereas 12% of the rape victims were currently experiencing the disorder. These findings were replicated by Resick (1988), who found that rape victims reported more obsessive-compulsive symptoms than robbery victims at 3, 6, and 12 months postcrime. A variety of phobic behaviors in rape victims have been documented by other researchers as well (Burgess & Holmstrom, 1979a; Masters & Johnson, 1976; Notman & Nadelson, 1976; Santiago, McCall-Perez, Gorcey, & Beigel, 1985; Turner & Frank, 1981).

As part of a larger epidemiology study, Burnam et al. (1988) found that 10% of the rape victims developed phobias compared to 3% of the nonvictims. Three percent of the victims developed panic disorder compared to 1% of the nonvictims, and 4% of the victims developed obsessive-compulsive disorder compared to 1% of the nonvictims. The victims of sexual assault were also more likely than the nonvictims to develop alcohol abuse or dependence (16%) or drug abuse or dependence (18%) than the nonvictims (7% each). These findings were replicated by Falsetti and Resnick (1994). Women who were assaulted first in childhood were more likely than those who were assaulted first in adulthood to develop an alcohol problem. Sexually assaulted men were more likely to develop alcohol abuse or dependence than women, but there were no other gender differences in reactions (Burnam et al., 1988).

Kilpatrick et al. (1992) reported that compared to nonvictims, rape victims were 3.4 times more likely to have used marijuana (52% vs. 16%), 6 times more likely to have used cocaine (15.5% vs. 2.5%), 10 times more likely to have used other hard drugs (12% vs. 1%), and 5 times more likely to have used prescription drugs nonmedically (15% vs. 3%). Compared to rape victims without PTSD, rape victims with PTSD were 5 times more likely to have two or more major alcohol-related problems and 4 times more likely to have two or more serious drug-related problems. Mechanic, Resick, and Griffin (1993), in a prospective study, found that 34% of the raped sample reported a lifetime history of substance abuse/dependence. The researchers concluded that the rates of currently reported substance abuse disorders may be underestimates of their true prevalence.

Overall, the preceding studies indicate that sexual assault causes significant disruption in the psychological functioning of rape victims. The findings are consistent for fear- and anxiety-related reactions, with about 50% of the victims developing chronic PTSD and associated sexual dysfunctions over their lifetime. The findings on depression are somewhat inconsistent, with some studies reporting an amelioration in symptoms within the 3 months postassault and others reporting persistent symptomatology accompanied by high rates of suicidal ideation for years after the crime. This discrepancy may be an artifact of sampling biases in these studies, but the collective results deserve attention by clinicians in their treatment planning for this population.

Variables Moderating Recovery

Despite the relative consistency of findings in the literature regarding the impact of sexual assault, the recovery profiles of victims are quite varied. Some women have mild- or short-term reactions, whereas others are devastated by the rape and go on to develop chronic PTSD. Research has focused on variables that may influence recovery. This process not only allows for theory development but also helps with refinement of existing treatment approaches.

Demographic Variables

The research on the relationship between demographic variables (age, race, socioeconomic status, and marital status) and postrape psychopathology is somewhat equivocal. Atkeson et al. (1982), McCahill, Meyer, and Fischman (1979), and Ruch and Chandler (1980) reported that victimization at a younger age posed fewer difficulties than victimization at an older age. However, Becker et al. (1982), Ruch and Leon (1983), Kilpatrick, Best, et al. (1985), Kilpatrick and Veronen (1984), and Kilpatrick, Veronen, and Best (1985) did not find any relationship between age and post-rape pathology. In a study of the effects of race on psychopathology, Ruch and Chandler (1980) found that Asian victims suffered from greater trauma than Caucasian victims; however, other studies failed to replicate this relationship (Burnam et al., 1988; Kilpatrick, Best, et al., 1985; Kilpatrick, Veronen, & Best, 1985; Ruch & Leon, 1983). Atkeson et al. (1982) found that lower socioeconomic status predicted depression at 12 months postcrime. Burgess and Holmstrom (1978), in their 4- to 6-year follow-up, also found that less economically advantaged rape survivors had more symptoms. However, Kilpatrick and colleagues (Kilpatrick et al., 1992; Kilpatrick, Saunders, Amick-McMullan, & Best, 1989) found no relationship between socioeconomic status and psychopathology in rape victims. In a study of the effects of marital status on post-rape pathology, Kilpatrick et al. (1989, 1992) and Ruch and Leon (1983) found no relationship between the two variables. However, McCahill et al. (1979) and Ruch and Chandler (1980) reported that married victims exhibited more post-rape difficulties than unmarried victims. Steketee and Foa (1987) suggested that the effect of marital status on post-rape difficulties is probably dependent on whether the spouse is a source of support or a source of stress. In general, demographic variables do not seem to predict post-trauma pathology but may affect it by influencing the victim's readiness to deal with the trauma.

Preassault Variables

Prior Psychological Functioning

The role of prior psychological functioning in recovery has been researched in various retrospective studies. Ruch and Leon (1983) found preexisting mental health variables to be one of the most influential variables affecting level of trauma at intake. The presence of a previous psychiatric history was found to relate to poorer post-rape adjustment (Burgess

& Holmstrom, 1978; Frank, Turner, Stewart, Jacob, & West, 1981; Frank & Anderson, 1987; Riggs, Foa, et al., 1992). Frank and Anderson (1987) found that on the basis of clinical interviews, victims with a prior diagnosis were significantly more likely to meet criteria for a psychiatric disorder in the first month after rape than those with no diagnosable disorder in their histories. Similarly, Frank et al. (1981) found that victims with a history of psychotropic medication, alcohol abuse, or suicidal ideation or attempts were more distressed in the first month after rape than victims without such histories. Other investigators have also found a history of substance use to predict post-rape pathology (Burgess & Holmstrom, 1978; Miller, Williams, & Berstein, 1982; Ruch & Leon, 1983). Looking at longer-term recovery, Atkeson et al. (1982) found that depression, a history of suicide, and poor sexual adjustment prior to the rape significantly predicted depression at 4 months postassault. Prior anxiety attacks and obsessive compulsive behaviors predicted depression at 8 months postcrime. At 12 months post-rape, prior anxiety attacks, obsessive-compulsive behaviors, and psychiatric treatment history predicted depression.

Previous Victimization History

Research on the effect of prior victimization on recovery has been somewhat inconsistent. Ruch and Leon (1983), in an evaluation of rape victims 48 hours and 2 weeks postcrime, found that women with no history of previous victimization showed a decrease in their trauma levels, whereas those with prior victimization exhibited an increase in trauma scores across the 2 weeks. They concluded that women who were multiple-incident victims were at risk for delayed responses. Other studies have also shown a relationship between a history of prior victimization and post-rape pathology (Kramer & Green, 1991; Riggs, Foa, et al., 1992; Roth, Wayland, & Woolsey, 1990).

In contrast, Frank et al. (1981) and Frank and Anderson (1987) found that victims of more than one sexual assault did not differ from single-incident victims on standardized measures of depression, anxiety, or fear from 1 to 4 months postrape. However, the multiple-incident victims did report poorer global social adjustment and greater disruption in social functioning in their immediate household. Looking at longer-term functioning, McCahill et al. (1979) found that multiple-incident rape victims were not different from single-incident rape victims at 1 year postrape; multiple-incident victims, however, reported more intense nightmares and a greater fear of being home alone. Extending the history of prior victimization beyond just prior rapes, Burgess and Holmstrom (1979a), in their 4- to 6-year follow-up, reported differences in recovery depending on type of victimization. They found that 86% of victims without a history of victimization were recovered in contrast to 53% of the victims with such a history at the 4- to 6-year follow-up.

In a different sample of treatment-seeking rape victims, Marhoefer-Dvorak, Resick, Hutter, and Girelli (1988) found that single- and multiple-incident rape victims did not differ on any of the standardized measures but that victims with a history of multiple-incident victimization differed on assertiveness and somatization. Women who had been victims of a crime that involved the threat of bodily harm were more assertive but had greater somatization symptoms. Resick (1988) categorized history of prior victimization in a more differentiated way than simple presence/absence. She found that at 1 month postcrime, history of previous criminal victimization predicted global distress, history of extensive domestic violence predicted global distress and fear, child sexual abuse predicted fear, and observation of violence in childhood predicted lowered self-esteem. At 12 months postcrime, physical child abuse, emotional abuse, and prior criminal victimization predicted greater global distress and fear. However, at 18 months postcrime, none of the variables predicted responses. Resick (1988) concluded that despite a relationship between previous victimization factors and recovery, no consistent patterns were apparent.

Ruch, Amedeo, Leon, and Gartrell (1991) followed 184 rape victims across a 2-year period from initial to follow-up services. Controlling for initial trauma level and time between assessments, they found that prior assault victims were more traumatized than first-assault victims at follow-up.

Life Stress

Research has shown that exposure to chronic stress prior to a sexual assault causes more postassault pathology than exposure to transient stress (Burgess & Holmstrom, 1978). In an extension of these findings, Ruch, Chandler, and Harter (1980) and Ruch and Leon (1983) reported that women who were exposed to major life stressors or no life stressors were more likely to be traumatized than women who were exposed to mild life stressors. They concluded that experience with some life stress may have an inoculating effect, whereas extreme stress probably interferes with the ability to develop coping methods to deal with an event as traumatic as rape. Similarly, other studies have shown that exposure to life-threatening stressors (loss of spouse, death of friend, major illness) predicts greater post-rape distress and fear (Kilpatrick & Veronen, 1984; Wirtz & Harrell, 1987).

Cognitive Appraisals

Research on the effects of preassault cognitive appraisals on postassault functioning suggests that victims who had a perception of unique invulnerability may have exacerbated reactions to a traumatic event (Bulman, 1979; Perloff, 1983). Support for this comes from studies that have found that rape victims who appraised the situation as "safe" prior to the assault had greater fear and depressive reactions than women who perceived themselves to be in danger (Frank & Stewart, 1984; Scheppele & Bart, 1983). At the same time, research on the relationship between prior victimization and post-rape pathology seems to suggest that victims with a multiple-incident history probably view themselves as vulnerable and are more likely to appraise situations as unsafe. In these victims, it is probably the confirmation of their existing cognitive appraisals that causes the post-trauma pathology. The role of preassault cognitive variables and attributions warrants further study.

In conclusion, prior psychological problems and major life stressors seem to impinge on recovery from rape. Further research is needed to examine other relevant variables possibly affecting reaction and recovery that have not been studied or have been understudied.

Assault Variables

Acquaintanceship Status

Research on the relationship between perpetrator-victim acquaintanceship status and post-rape pathology is equivocal. McCahill et al. (1979) found that victims raped by casual acquaintances or relative strangers were more severely maladjusted compared to victims raped by friends, family members, or total strangers. Similarly, Ellis et al. (1981) and Thornhill and Thornhill (1990) found that women assaulted by strangers had more problems with fear and depression than women assaulted by acquaintances. However, other researchers have not found this to be the case. Hassell (1981) found that victims who were attacked by acquaintances were more likely to have problems with their self-esteem initially but that these differences disappeared by 3 months postrape. Other researchers have also not found any differences between the symptoms of victims assaulted by strangers and those assaulted by acquaintances (Frank et al., 1981; Girelli, Resick, Marhoefer-Dvorak, & Kotsis Hutter, 1986; Kilpatrick et al., 1987;

Koss et al., 1988; Mechanic et al., 1994; Resick, 1988; Riggs, Foa, et al., 1992; Sales, Baum, & Shore, 1984). However, Koss et al. (1988) found that acquaintance rape victims were less likely to tell anyone about the incident. This result was supported by Stewart et al. (1987), who found that acquaintance rape victims were more likely to delay seeking treatment. The findings suggest that this group probably experiences more self-blame and that this is what interferes with recovery rather than acquaintanceship status per se.

Level of Violence

Research has shown that overall brutality of the assault is associated with more severe post-rape pathology (Cluss, Boughton, Frank, Stewart, & West, 1983; Ellis et al., 1981; McCahill et al., 1979; Norris & Feldman-Summers, 1981; Resick, 1988). On the other hand, Atkeson et al. (1982) and Sales et al. (1984) did not find a strong relationship between the degree of rape trauma and victim reactions. An examination of individual variables showed that presence of a weapon was related to negative victim adjustment in one study (McCahill et al., 1979) but not in five other studies (Frank et al., 1981; Girelli et al., 1986; Ruch & Chandler, 1983; Kilpatrick et al., 1987; Sales et al., 1984). Kilpatrick et al. (1989) and Sales et al. (1984) found that death threats contributed to poorer adjustment, but three other studies failed to find this effect (Frank et al., 1981; Girelli et al., 1986; Ruch & Chandler, 1983). Victims who were severely beaten showed poorer adjustment in three studies (McCahill et al., 1979; Ruch & Chandler, 1983; Kilpatrick et al., 1987; Sales et al., 1984) but not in three other studies (Frank et al., 1981; Girelli et al., 1986; Santiago et al., 1985). Sales et al. (1984) found the number of assailants to be related to victim adjustment, but this was not found in studies by Girelli et al. (1986) and Ruch and Chandler (1983). Similarly, Girelli et al. (1986) found that victim adjustment was unrelated to the number of sex acts inflicted, the use of restraint, and the length of detainment. However, Resick (1988) found restraint to be positively associated with PTSD severity. Perception of life threat (Cascardi, Riggs, & Foa, 1993; Cascardi, Riggs, Hearst-Ikeda, & Foa, 1996; Kilpatrick et al., 1989; Sales et al., 1984), and duration of assault (Riggs, Foa, et al., 1992) were also found to be positively associated with PTSD severity. Using path analysis, Riggs, Foa, et al. (1992) found that effects of assault brutality were mediated by cognitive factors such as perception of life threat.

Within-Crime Victim Reactions

Perception of Life Threat. Sales et al. (1984) suggested that "it is possible that the *actual* violence of an attack is less crucial to victim reaction than the *felt threat*" (p. 125). Girelli et al. (1986) found that subjective distress was predictive of later fear reactions, and Kilpatrick et al. (1987) and Falsetti, Resnick, and Resick (1992) also found cognitive appraisal of life threat to predict later PTSD. Resick (1988) also reported greater anger or anxiety during the assault as predictive of greater distress. Sales et al. (1984) found perception of life threat to be one of the strongest predictors of PTSD. In a more recent study, Riggs, Foa, et al. (1992) reported that the perception of life threat mediated the effects of the actual assault severity on postrape PTSD severity.

Dissociation. Dissociation is a disruption in the normal flow of consciousness that results in a lack of integration between thoughts, feelings, and physical sensations and our ongoing flow of awareness of the world around us. Dissociation during and following a trauma can occur in three areas: cognitions (thoughts), emotions (feelings), and the physical sensations of stimuli. In PTSD, dissociation of feelings is evidenced by emotional numbing (Litz, 1992), dissociation of cogni-

tions is evidenced by amnesia for some aspect of the traumatic event, and dissociation of physical sensations may be evidenced by higher pain thresholds. Dissociation has been studied as a factor moderating recovery from trauma. Dissociation used as a coping style within the trauma seems to interfere with the processing of the trauma, thereby increasing psychopathology (Davidson & Foa, 1991; Marmar et al., 1994; Spiegel, Hunt, & Dondershine, 1988). Support for this hypothesis comes from a study on within-assault emotions and cognitive states of rape victims. Resick, Churchill, and Falsetti (1990) reported that confusion/disorientation during the crime was the best predictor of subsequent, chronic PTSD symptoms: It accounted for more than 40% of the variance in their PTSD symptom scores.

Biological studies have reported alterations in the neurotransmitter and neurohormonal systems of the brain as a result of the trauma. Bremner, Davis, Southwick, Krystal, and Charney (1994), in a review of the literature, reported that these alterations in turn cause interference in information processing and memory encoding of the traumatic information, resulting in fragmentation of the traumatic memory, a phenomenon described as dissociation. Several authors have suggested that processing of the traumatic information is required for posttrauma recovery (Foa, Steketee, & Rothbaum, 1989; Horowitz, 1986). Thus victims who cope with the traumatic experience through dissociation will be more likely to develop chronic psychopathology. Indirect support for this comes from research showing that assault victims with a history of victimization dissociated more immediately and to a greater extent after the trauma than those without such a history (Chu & Dill, 1990; Dancu, Riggs, Shoyer, & Foa, 1991; Riggs, Dancu, Gershuny, Greenberg, & Foa, 1992) and that assault victims with PTSD dissociated more than assault victims without PTSD (Dancu et al., 1991; Dancu, Riggs, Hearst-Ikeda, Shoyer, & Foa, 1996).

Postassault Variables

Postassault variables are the least studied variables that affect recovery. Although variables such as initial reactions, social support, and post-trauma attributions have received some attention, other variables, such as the effects of participating in the criminal justice system, have been less thoroughly studied.

Initial Reactions

Kilpatrick, Veronen, and Best (1985) examined how initial reactions affect victims' functioning at 3 months postrape. They found that the level of distress that victims experienced within the first few weeks of the rape was highly predictive of subsequent distress. Riggs, Dancu, et al. (1992) found that initial anger, guilt, depression, anxiety, and rape-related fear were also higher in victims with persistent PTSD. Rothbaum et al. (1992) found that the severity and frequency of symptoms at 2 weeks postcrime could correctly classify the rape victims who would go on to develop chronic PTSD. Because most of the longitudinal studies have found that victim reactions stabilize at 3 months and then continue at that level, Kilpatrick, Veronen, and Best (1985) concluded that delayed reactions are not a significant problem for most rape victims and that an assessment of initial reactions will predict which victims are most likely to have difficulty recovering from the rape.

Cognitive Attributions and Appraisals

Disruption in Beliefs. McCann, Sakheim, and Abrahamson (1988) proposed that in response to a traumatic event, either one's prior positive beliefs about oneself and the world are disrupted or one's prior negative beliefs about oneself and the world are confirmed. In either case, the disruption or confirmation of prior beliefs affects the five areas of safety, trust, power/competence, esteem, and intimacy. Resick, Schnicke, and Markway (1991), in an attempt to explore the relationship between these beliefs and PTSD symptoms, administered their Personal Beliefs and Reactions Scale to 20 rape victims. They found that avoidance symptoms were predicted by negative trust beliefs, arousal symptoms were predicted by negative safety beliefs, and intrusive symptoms were associated with more negative beliefs about the rape and more attempts to "undo" or not accept the rape.

Scheppele and Bart (1983) found that women who believed the rape situation was safe prior to the crime were more likely to have severe reactions than those who had suspected they might be in danger. After reviewing a wide range of studies, Perloff (1983) proposed that nonvictims may perceive themselves as uniquely invulnerable to victimization. People who hold this view and are subsequently victimized appear to have more severe reactions than those who do not believe they are uniquely invulnerable. After being victimized, people's illusions of invulnerability are shattered, and they must reappraise their situation. Perloff proposed that victims who now feel uniquely vulnerable (more vulnerable than others) will have more problems than those who adopt a perception of universal invulnerability (being as vulnerable as others).

Guilt and Self-Blame. Postrape cognitive appraisals and attributions can be viewed as reactions to the assault and as attempts to cope with the event and reactions. Several researchers have observed feelings of guilt and self-blame in rape victims (Burgess & Holmstrom, 1979a; Fox & Scherl, 1972; Libow & Doty, 1979; Nadelson et al., 1982; Notman & Nadelson, 1976). A growing body of literature indicates that people have a strong need to search for the meaning of negative events (Silver & Wortman, 1980). Criminal victimization destroys the illusion that we live in a predictable, controllable, meaningful world. Foa, Zinbarg, and Rothbaum (1992) pointed out that animals subjected to unpredictable and uncontrollable events show disturbances that resemble PTSD. Some researchers who have focused on self-blame (Bulman & Wortman, 1977; Katz & Burt, 1988; Wortman, 1976) have proposed that victims are likely to accept responsibility for events to maintain a sense of control over their lives and to maintain the belief that the world is just and orderly. Riggs, Dancu, et al. (1992) found that guilt mediated the relationship between the brutality of the assault and severity of PTSD symptoms. Similarly, Wyatt, Notgrass, and Newcomb (1990) reported that rape victims who attributed their assault to internal factors (self-blame) experienced more negative reactions following the rape than rape victims who made external attributions (other-blame).

Bulman (1979) hypothesized that self-blame serves an adaptive function but that behavioral self-blame should be associated with more effective postrape adjustment than characterological self-blame. This hypothesis was not supported by Meyer and Taylor (1986) and Frazier (1990), who found both behavioral and characterological self-blame to be associated with poorer adjustment postrape. Schnicke and Resick (1990) also found self-blame to be associated with greater symptomatology, in particular depression, obsessive-compulsive symptoms, and self-criticism. More recently, Mechanic, Resick, Schnicke, and Griffin (1993) reported that 2-week measures of guilt frequency and guilt intensity were associated with PTSD status at the 3-month assessment. They also reported an association of guilt frequency and intensity with less positive views of oneself, the world, other people, and control over events.

Social Support

Research on the role of postrape social support is confounded by the quality and quantity of prerape relationships. Also, studies have varied in their assessment of specific aspects versus global indices of support, and the instruments used for assessing social support have varied from one study to the next. Evidence for the positive effect of social support on post-trauma recovery comes from several studies (Burgess & Holmstrom, 1978; Ellis et al., 1981; Moss, Frank, & Anderson, 1990; Norris & Feldman-Summers, 1981; Sales et al., 1984). Atkeson et al. (1982) found that social support predicted the level of depression the victims were experiencing at 4 and 8 months postrape. Norris and Feldman-Summers (1981) found that the presence of supportive men and women in the victim's life was related to less reclusiveness. Ruch and Chandler (1980) found that victims with supportive families experienced lower levels of trauma fairly soon after the assault. Similarly, Sales et al. (1984) found that victims reporting greater closeness to family members had fewer symptoms. The level of support may be mediated by the brutality of assault: That is, the more "stereotypic" rapes may have elicited more sustained social support (Resick, 1993b). Sales et al. (1984) did find a correlation between the violence of an assault and postassault family closeness.

Recently, Davis and his colleagues conducted an intensive examination of social support and its effects on recovery from sexual assault (Davis & Brickman, 1996; Davis, Brickman, & Baker, 1991; Davis, Taylor, & Bench, 1995). Their work conceptualized social support as composed of two independent dimensions, others' supportive behavior and others' unsupportive behavior. Sexual assault victims receive the same amount of supportive behavior as victims of nonsexual assault, but sexual assault victims also experience a greater amount of unsupportive behavior (Davis & Brickman, 1996). Consistent with recent literature in the social support field, this research has shown that adjustment to sexual assault is inversely related to unsupportive behavior but seems to be unrelated to supportive behavior (Davis et al., 1991).

Literature suggests that the absence of social support may exacerbate PTSD symptoms, but it is also likely that difficulties in relationships are caused by post-trauma pathology (Becker & Skinner, 1983; Resick et al., 1981). Foa and Riggs (1994) predicted that PTSD symptoms such as detachment from others and emotional numbing would interfere with victims' social interactions. Support for this came from a study by Riggs, Dancu, et al. (1992), who found that immediate symptoms of PTSD were related to poor social adjustment, which, in turn, was related to the severity of PTSD later on.

Participation in the Criminal Justice System

Few studies have thus far examined the effect of participation in the criminal justice system on victim recovery, perhaps because few cases actually reach the trial stage (Resick, 1993b). Cluss et al. (1983) found that at 12 months postrape there were no differences in the level of depression and social adjustment between victims who wished to prosecute the crime and victims who did not. However, women who wished to prosecute the crime did report greater self-esteem. Resick (1988) also reported that criminal justice participants reported greater self-esteem at 6 months postcrime. Sales et al. (1984) found that victims who began the process by reporting the case, and whose charges held, showed fewer symptoms at the initial interview and the 6-month follow-up. However, further progress toward the trial left victims with more symptoms, suggesting that extended court proceedings may inflict additional demands on these women and keep them in a victim role.

In conclusion, it appears that preassault, assault, and postassault variables may all play a role in victim reactions and influence the pattern of recovery. Victims' psychological functioning prior to the crime, their appraisal of danger during the crime, use of dissociation as a coping style, self-blame, and availability of social support after the crime are some of the variables that play an important role in moderating recovery.

Theories of Psychological Reactions to Sexual Assault

Crisis Theory

The first theory of victim reactions was crisis theory (Burgess & Holmstrom, 1974, 1979b; Sales et al., 1984). Crisis theory proposes that after an event that is beyond a person's normal resources and abilities to cope, he or she experiences psychological distress. If new attempts to cope are ineffective, the agitation and symptomatology will increase. However, it has always been proposed that such distress is time limited—that within 4 to 6 weeks, the person will resolve the crisis either adaptively or maladaptively (through inappropriate coping strategies such as denial or alcohol use). Either way, overt distress should be alleviated within approximately 6 weeks. The purpose of crisis therapy is to help the person resolve the crisis as quickly as possible and to avoid developing maladaptive coping strategies.

There are several major problems with crisis theory with regard to rape victims. Although no one would argue that many rape victims experience a "crisis" after the assault, crisis theory does nothing to explain why certain symptoms develop, to predict who is likely to have more problems with recovery, or to suggest which variables may affect reactions and recovery. Furthermore, longitudinal studies have all disconfirmed the time schedule proposed by crisis theorists. All of the studies have found that the bulk of improvement occurs within the first 3 months after the crime but that many rape victims continue reporting problems with fear, anxiety, depression, social adjustment, sexual dysfunctions, and self-esteem for years after the event. Rape victims report experiencing distress in these studies, so clearly they have not become symptom-free in 6 weeks.

Learning Theory

Two-factor learning theory was next proposed as the best explanation for the reactions of rape victims (Becker, Skinner, Abel, Axelrod, & Cichon, 1984; Holmes & St. Lawrence, 1983; Kilpatrick, Veronen, & Resick, 1982). Learning theory hypothesizes that at the time of the assault, victims' fear reactions are great enough to classically condition fear reactions to previously neutral cues that happen to be present during the crime. These cues, or stimuli, are then capable of triggering flashbacks and fear reactions in other nondangerous situations. Victims then develop escape and avoidance behavior to cope with what they subsequently perceive as dangerous situations (dangerous because they feel terror just as they did during the crime) or merely to avoid the unpleasant experience of fear even if they recognize that they are not really in danger in some other cue situation. Avoidance learning is the most powerful form of learning and is quite resistant to extinction or unlearning. Two-factor theory explains sexual dysfunctions and avoidance as well as other fear reactions and anxiety.

Depressive reactions also are explained by learning theory as being secondary to the anxiety reactions. Because of the helplessness experienced during the crime, victims may perceive that they are helpless in other situations in which they could have some control (Peterson & Seligman, 1983). This and the loss of the usual reinforcers in victims' lives that occur as a result of avoidance (refusing to go out in the evening, date, etc.) can lead to a state of depression. The treatments that have been developed on the basis of learning theory all emphasize anxiety management and/or exposure to nondangerous but fear-inducing cues that were conditioned during the assault and avoided in the aftermath of the rape.

Although two-factor theory explains many of the symptoms that develop and why they may persist indefinitely, it does not completely explain the intrusion symptoms of PTSD: that is, why the recurrent recollections, flashbacks, and nightmares occur. It could be argued that some possibly unrecognized cues in the environment trigger these memories, but it is more likely that there is some important cognitive function for the intrusive memories. Some of the experimental psychologists in the 1960s and 1970s recognized that a cognitive component should be added to two-factor theory and learned-helplessness theory. For the most part, the variables that were studied concerned attributions regarding events or expectancies regarding future events.

Cognitive Theories

A conceptual framework for cognitive assessment was provided by Kendall and Ingram (1987), who included four domains in their model. First, *cognitive structure* refers to the organization of information or how the person represents the information internally. Second, *cognitive propositions* refers to the content that is stored in these cognitive structures. The combination of structure and content forms a construct called a *schema*. The third domain, *cognitive operations,* refers to the processes by which information is encoded, stored, and retrieved. Based on an information-processing paradigm, research on cognitive processes or operations has included studies on selective attention, perceptual distortion, and selective encoding and retrieval. The final category, *cognitive products,* refers to the "by-products" of cognitive schemas and operations: the thoughts, self-evaluations, ideas, and feelings that a person experiences and is able to recollect consciously and report. In general, cognitive products are the easiest cognitive data to collect and evaluate and seem most useful for treatment planning (Merluzzi & Boltwood, 1989). They have been used most frequently in the cognitive treatment of anxiety and depressive disorders (Beck & Emery, 1985; Beck, Rush, Shaw, & Emery, 1979).

Given that PTSD is a response to an experience that is "out of the ordinary," it follows that rape victims with PTSD will be more likely to process trauma-related information differently from rape victims without PTSD. Support for this comes from a study by Zeitlin and McNally (1991); they found that combat veterans with PTSD showed an enhanced recall of combat-related words compared to those without PTSD.

The Stroop task has been used to study information processing as a cognitive operation in rape victims. The task entails the measurement of reaction time to naming the colors in which rape-related and non-rape-related words are painted. In a study of rape victims, Foa, Feske, Murdock, Kozak, and McCarthy (1991) found that rape victims with PTSD showed longer reaction times to trauma-related words but not to other words when compared to rape victims without PTSD. The results were interpreted as evidence for an attentional bias in PTSD victims toward trauma-related information. Similarly, Cassiday, McNally, and Zeitlin (1992), using a Stroop task, found that rape victims with PTSD were slower to color-name high-threat words than moderate-threat, positive, and neutral words. Rape victims without PTSD nevertheless exhibited greater Stroop interference for high-threat words than did nontraumatized subjects. Interference with high-threat words was correlated with intrusion symptoms on the Impact of Event Scale (IES; Horowitz, Wilner, & Alvarez, 1979). Therefore interference for trauma cues may provide a nonintrospective index of intrusive cognitive activity.

Emotional processing theory is one of the more recent cognitive theories based on information-processing research in rape victims. This theory is currently being applied to the study of rape victim reactions (Foa & Kozak, 1986; Foa et al., 1989). The emotional pro-cessing model draws from Lang's (1977) imagery-based information theory of fear and not only treats attributions and expectations as specific content but also focuses much of its attention on the structure and process by which information and events are encoded, integrated and retrieved in memory. Foa and colleagues proposed that when rape victims' concepts of safety are shattered, they develop an internal fear structure for escape and avoidance behavior that elicits the symptoms of PTSD. The fear structure consists of trauma memories that are fragmented, disorganized, and disintegrated from the existing schemas. Foa and Riggs (1994) proposed that repeated reliving of the rape memories during prolonged exposure (PE) treatment (Dancu & Foa, 1992; Rothbaum & Foa, 1992) decreases the anxiety associated with these memories through habituation and enables reevaluation of the meaning representations in the memory. This repeated reliving generates a more organized memory record that can be more readily integrated with existing schemas.

More recently, drawing from the work of McCann et al. (1988), Resick and Schnicke (1990, 1992b) proposed that reactions to a traumatic event represent more than a fear network. Victims report a wide range of affective reactions to traumatic events, not just fear. They proposed that PTSD results from an inability to integrate the event with prior beliefs and experiences. When new, incompatible events occur, the person either alters the new information to fit prior beliefs (assimilation) or alters the prior beliefs to accept the event (accommodation). Overaccommodation to the event is also possible, with victims making statements such as "No one can be trusted" or "I am never safe." Theorists have conceptualized the PTSD symptoms of intrusion and avoidance as representing unsuccessful attempts to assimilate or accommodate the event, which they term "stuck points." They have developed cognitive processing therapy (CPT), which tries to help clients process trauma-related affect and identify their stuck points (Calhoun & Resick, 1993; Ellis, Black, & Resick, 1992; Mechanic & Resick, 1994; Resick, 1992, 1994; Resick & Gerth Markaway, 1991). These stuck points are then systematically addressed and challenged in therapy, using education, exposure, and cognitive components, to help clients integrate the trauma into their preexisting schemas.

Treatment of Rape-Related PTSD

Treatment approaches to PTSD have derived from the theories that have been generated to explain the symptoms of intrusion, arousal, and avoidance that make up the disorder. Although there has not been extensive research thus far, several types of therapeutic techniques have been developed and appear promising to treat the symptoms that rape victims experience. Systematic desensitization (Becker & Abel, 1981; Frank, Anderson, Stewart, & Dancu, 1988; Frank & Stewart, 1983, 1984; Wolff, 1977), cognitive therapy (Forman, 1980; Frank & Stewart, 1984; Frank et al., 1988), flooding (Foa, Rothbaum, Riggs, & Murdock, 1991; Rothbaum & Foa, 1988), sexual dysfunction therapy (Becker & Skinner, 1983; Becker et al., 1984), and stress inoculation training (Foa, Rothbaum, et al., 1991; Kilpatrick et al., 1982; Pearson, Poquette, & Wasden, 1983; Resick et al., 1988; Rothbaum & Foa, 1988; Veronen & Kilpatrick, 1983) have all been used successfully with rape victims. Most of these therapy procedures reduce anxiety and change avoidance patterns to treat sexual dysfunctions or the symptoms of depression. Single case reports and the few treatment outcome studies that have been conducted indicate that cognitive and behavioral therapies are effective, with no one technique being better than any others.

Resick et al. (1988) compared stress inoculation training (SIT), assertion training, and supportive psychotherapy to a waiting-list control group. Rape victims in all three treatment groups showed reduction in postrape symptoms between pretreatment and posttreatment, and these gains were maintained at 6-month follow-up.

Foa, Rothbaum, et al. (1991) conducted a controlled study of short-term treatments for rape-related PTSD. They randomly assigned rape victims with PTSD to one of the four treatment groups: stress inoculation training (SIT), prolonged exposure (PE), supportive counseling, or a wait-list control group. At post-treatment, the groups differed with regard to the percentage of victims who continued to meet criteria for PTSD. Of the SIT group, 50% no longer met criteria for PTSD; 40% of those treated with PE also no longer met criteria for PTSD. In contrast, 90% of the supportive counseling group and all the victims on the waiting list still had PTSD. At a 3-month follow-up, although patients in all three groups remained improved, the mean scores of the PE group were the lowest. Foa, Rothbaum, et al. (1991) concluded that the reversal in the pattern of mean scores for SIT and PE from post-treatment to follow-up may imply that 3 months after treatment, patients who received SIT ceased to use the skills they acquired. On the other hand, patients who repeatedly relived trauma memories during PE may have remained somewhat distressed at the end of treatment, but exposure produced the expected organization of the rape memory, resulting in continued improvement.

Foa et al. (1994) examined the differential effects of SIT and PE on trauma symptoms by conducting a study on sexual assault victims that compared the efficacy of PE alone, SIT alone, and a treatment program that combined SIT and PE. Results showed that at post-treatment, PE alone was more effective than SIT alone and SIT/PE on a composite measure of psychological functioning. The superiority of PE was also demonstrated in analysis that crossed SIT and PE treatments. PE was associated with lower post-treatment reexperiencing, avoidance, arousal, and depression severity. SIT was only associated with lower avoidance severity.

In a single case study of PTSD and comorbid major depression, Nishith, Hearst, Mueser, and Foa (1995) treated a rape victim with the SIT/PE treatment package and found significant reductions in the victim's intrusion, arousal, and avoidance symptoms from post-treatment to the 3-month follow-up. Similar reductions were also seen in the victim's score on dissociative and trait anxiety symptoms. Although the depressive symptoms did not show a statistically significant change from pretreatment to post-treatment, there was a significant reduction in the depression scores from post-treatment to the 3-month follow-up. Nishith et al. concluded that an amelioration of the depressive symptoms was secondary to changes in PTSD symptoms.

In a treatment outcome study of CPT, Resick and Schnicke (1992a) compared 19 sexual assault survivors who received CPT in a group format with a 20-subject comparison sample who waited 12 weeks for the same therapy. The two groups were compared at pretreatment, post-treatment, and 3- and 6-month follow-ups. Results showed that CPT subjects improved significantly from pre- to post-treatment on both PTSD and depression measures and maintained their improvement at the 6-month follow-up. The comparison sample did not change from the pre- to post-treatment assessment sessions.

In a later study with a larger sample, Resick and Schnicke (1992b) reported that of the 52 women who had met full criteria for PTSD at pretreatment and had completed CPT, 88.2% no longer met criteria for PTSD at post-treatment. Of these, 44 had been assessed at the 3- and 6-month follow-ups. At 3 months, 86.4% no longer met criteria for PTSD, and at 6 months, 88.6% no longer met criteria for PTSD. At pretreatment, 53.7% met criteria for major depression. At post-treatment, only 13.2% were still depressed. At 3 months

postassault, 6.5% were depressed, and at the 6-month follow-up, 8.8% were still meeting criteria for a major depressive disorder.

In summary, both PE and CPT seem to be equally efficacious in treating PTSD and comorbid major depression. However, studies report a lower attrition rate with CPT (10%; Resick & Schnicke, 1992b) compared to PE (18%-29%; Foa, Rothbaum, et al., 1991). CPT also has another advantage over PE because it can be administered in a group format with equally efficacious results (Resick, 1993a). This not only renders it more cost-effective but also creates a setting that allows for the normalization of trauma reactions, provides more social support, facilitates cognitive restructuring, and increases homework compliance.

Conclusions and Implications for Practitioners

Practitioners in the criminal justice system are in an advantageous position to help in the recovery of rape victims with very little effort on their parts. They are also in a position to assess which victims may have more difficulty with recovery and to refer them for treatment. While obtaining statements about the crime, investigating officers are likely to hear from victims about whether they were terrified or fairly calm during the crime. In addition, they may hear from victims whether they believed the assailant was going to kill them. And, of course, they will learn about the extent of threats, restraint, violence, and the length of the criminal episode. Although the police who investigate cases may disagree with victims' appraisal of the imminent danger of the situation based on their experience, they should not disregard victims' perceptions, which will, in all likelihood, determine whether they suffer from a severe trauma reaction and whether they will recover from the crime. Investigators and other criminal justice system personnel should make a special effort to refer to counseling victims who describe the crime as an imminent death situation or who describe being terrified during the crime.

Over the months that follow the crime, the extent of avoidance can be assessed simply. Victim assistance counselors and attorneys are usually in a good position to do so. Rape victims sometimes profess to be recovered: That is, they are not depressed and are no longer having intrusive memories or anxiety reactions. However, they may be avoiding any reminders of the incident, or they may have inordinately restructured their lives. Specifically, they may deny having problems but on further questioning may admit that they are asymptomatic only because they refuse to go out after dark, date, be home alone, and so forth. Were they to attempt these activities, they would experience great distress.

It may still be painful for them to discuss the crime, and they may make great efforts not to think about it or encounter any reminders about the incident. A few simple questions about whether they are doing everything they did before the crime (going out, being home alone, etc.) should give a fairly accurate indication of whether they have recovered or are avoiding. If any of the facts regarding the case are known to the practitioner, specific questions can be asked about situations that are likely to be causing the victim problems. For example, if the victim was raped while home alone, the practitioner could ask if the victim is able to stay at home alone comfortably. If she was raped while out on a date, has she resumed dating or at least going out in the evening with friends? Resick (1988) found that among lifestyle questions, the best single predictor of the continuing problems with recovery was whether the victim avoided being alone. That question accounted for 73% of the variance in a measure of PTSD at 18 months postcrime in rape victims. Again, those who are exhibiting difficulties in recovery should be referred for therapy.

How victims are treated by criminal justice practitioners may affect how they psychologically process the event. Investigations can and should be conducted without implying that the victim brought on the crime (should be blamed for the incident, did not resist sufficiently, etc.), even when the investigator feels that the victim put herself at risk by her own behavior. Most people occasionally have less than optimal judgment as they move through the world, particularly if they believe that their corner of the world is safer than it actually is (e.g., locks are not always locked, they open their doors when someone knocks). Usually a lapse in judgment does not have catastrophic consequences. Teenagers are particularly naive and cannot always discriminate safe from potentially unsafe situations. Poor judgment is not an offense punishable by rape. Furthermore, it is impossible to know, after the fact, which and/or whether prevention or resistance techniques might have been effective with that particular assailant in that particular situation.

Police, counselors, and attorneys need to be careful in their phrasing of questions. For example, "What happened next?" or "What did you do then?" are neutral questions, whereas "Why did you . . . ?" implies blame and puts the victim on the defensive. Victims must understand that regardless of what they did, the offender had no right to rape them and that no one can second-guess how they should have behaved during the crime. They resisted and coped during the crime as best they could given that particular set of circumstances.

A few judicious statements by criminal justice practitioners may help greatly in the recovery of victims. Statements about the normal course of recovery (months, not days or weeks) and about symptoms such as flashbacks, nightmares, intrusive memories, the desire to avoid reminders, problems sleeping, and roller-coaster emotions may help victims understand that their reactions are common, and that they are not going crazy. Rape victims should be advised to take things one step at a time but to return to their routine activities as soon as they are able: in other words, not to avoid nondangerous "danger" cues that were conditioned during the crime. They should be encouraged to mobilize their social support network and tell loved ones what they need. Most often, families and friends want to be supportive but do not know what to do or say.

Finally, because the goal for victims is to accept what happened and recover rather than to develop amnesia, they should be warned that they may be given bad advice from well-meaning but uninformed people. Our society appears to subscribe to the "stiff-upper-lip school of psychology," in which people are supposed to disregard their emotions, forget the fact that someone almost killed them, put the event behind them, and get on with their lives in a few days or weeks. This advice, if followed, will give the appearance that victims have recovered. The advice serves to remove uncomfortable emotions and reactions from view of family, friends, and acquaintances. However, as everyone who works with crime victims knows, such behavior is just another form of avoidance that postpones recovery. In a recent treatment study, Resick and Schnicke (1993) reported that the average length of time until rape victims sought therapy was 8 years.

It is fairly common for mothers to have trauma reactions about their own unresolved rape when one of their children is assaulted years later. It is also common for victims to have their rape trauma suddenly reemerge years later, after some other trauma, such as the death of a loved one or another crime, or after an attempt to develop intimacy with someone. The intense reactions of the second event probably reactivate memories and emotions that were encoded years earlier. Postponing recovery from the rape trauma complicates recovery from later traumas because it appears that if the first event is not resolved and processed to the point at which the emotions dissipate, it is left encoded, with all of the intense emotions intact. Furthermore, it is probably more difficult to enlist social support years after an event than immediately after it occurs. Family and friends

are likely to be confused about why the victim is so upset years after an event has occurred.

Sexual assault is a shockingly common crime. It would be easy to conclude that because rape is a common occurrence in our society and is infrequently accompanied by other serious physical injuries, it is not very serious. This is not the case. Although the incidence of murder during rape is actually rather infrequent, rape is a life-shattering event because the victim perceives that she is about to die (due to threats, the presence of weapons, being choked, and so forth; Resick, 1988). The majority of victims experience severe psychological reactions in its wake that in many cases last for years. A substantial minority of victims are so distressed that they contemplate or attempt suicide. We have no statistics on how many successful suicides were precipitated by rape. Because of prevailing attitudes of victim blaming, victims frequently do not receive the support they need to recover successfully.

However, we do know that many victims do recover successfully. When they receive non-judgmental support from their loved ones and the professionals they encounter, they are many steps closer to recovery. Effective therapies for the treatment of rape victims are now available. Victims may need help in finding therapists who can supply appropriate treatment. Practitioners in the criminal justice system and victim assistance agencies are often in a crucial position to make appropriate referrals. Most of all, they are in the best position to lead the way in changing attitudes toward rape victims by their humane treatment of victims, by the example they set, and by the dissemination of accurate information and training to other professionals and the general public.

References

American Psychiatric Association. (1980). *Diagnostic and statistical manual of mental disorders* (3rd ed.). Washington, DC: Author.

Atkeson, B. M., Calhoun, K. S., Resick, P. A., & Ellis, E. M. (1982). Victims of rape: Repeated assessment of depressive symptoms. *Journal of Consulting and Clinical Psychology, 50,* 96-102.

Beck, A. T., & Emery, G. (1985). *Anxiety disorders and phobias: A cognitive perspective.* New York: Basic Books.

Beck, A. T., Rush, A. J., Shaw, B. F., & Emery, G. (1979). *Cognitive therapy of depression.* New York: Guilford.

Becker, J. V., & Abel, G. G. (1981). Behavioral treatment of victims of sexual assault. In S. M. Turner, K. S. Calhoun, & H. E. Adams (Eds.), *Handbook of clinical behavior therapy* (pp. 347-379). New York: John Wiley.

Becker, J. V., Cunningham Rathner, J., & Kaplan, M. S. (1986). Adolescent sexual offenders: Demographics, criminal and sexual histories, and recommendations for reducing future offenses. *Journal of Interpersonal Violence, 1,* 431-445.

Becker, J. V., & Skinner, L. J. (1983). Assessment and treatment of rape-related sexual dysfunctions. *Clinical Psychologist, 36,* 102-105.

Becker, J. V., Skinner, L. J., Abel, G. G., Axelrod, R., & Cichon, J. (1984). Sexual problems of sexual assault survivors. *Women and Health, 9,* 5-20.

Becker, J. V., Skinner, L. J., Abel, G. G., & Treacy, E. C. (1982). Incidence and types of sexual dysfunctions in rape and incest victims. *Journal of Sex and Marital Therapy, 8,* 65-74.

Beebe, D. K. (1991). Emergency management of the adult female rape victim. *American Family Physician, 43,* 2041-2046.

Bremner, J. D., Davis, M., Southwick, S. M., Krystal, J. H., & Charney, D. S. (1994). *Neurobiology of posttraumatic stress disorder.* In R. S. Pynoos (Ed.), *Posttraumatic stress disorder: A clinical review* (pp. 43-64). Lutherville, MD: Sidran.

Bulman, J. R. (1979). Characterological versus behavioral self blame: Inquiries into depression and rape. *Journal of Personality and Social Psychology, 37,* 1798-1809.

Bulman, J. R., & Wortman, C. B. (1977). Attributions of blame and coping in the real world: Severe accident victims react to their lot. *Journal of Personality and Social Psychology, 35,* 351-363.

Burgess, A. W., & Holmstrom, L. L. (1974). Crisis and counseling requests of rape victims. *Nursing Research, 23,* 196-202.

Burgess, A. W., & Holmstrom, L. L. (1978). Recovery from rape and prior life stress. *Research in Nursing and Health, 1,* 165-174.

Burgess, A. W., & Holmstrom, L. L. (1979a). *Rape: Crisis and recovery.* Bowie, MD: Robert J. Brady.

Burgess, A. W., & Holmstrom, L. L. (1979b). Rape: Sexual disruption and recovery. *American Journal of Orthopsychiatry, 49,* 648-657.

Burnam, M. A., Stein, J. A., Golding, J. M., Siegel, J. M., Sorenson, S. B., Forsythe, A. B., & Telles, C. A. (1988).

Sexual assault and mental disorders in a community population. *Journal of Consulting and Clinical Psychology, 56,* 843-850.

Calhoun, K. S., Atkeson, B. M., & Resick, P. A. (1982). A longitudinal examination of fear reactions in victims of rape. *Journal of Counseling Psychology, 29,* 655-661.

Calhoun, K. S., & Resick, P. A. (1993). Post-traumatic stress disorder. In D. H. Barlow (Ed.), *Clinical handbook of psychological disorders* (pp. 48-98). New York: Guilford.

Cascardi, M., Riggs, D. S., & Foa, E. B. (1993, October). *Assault characteristics as predictors of crime related PTSD: The role of severity, location, and identity of perpetrator.* Poster presented at the 9th annual meeting of the International Society for Traumatic Stress Studies, San Antonio, TX.

Cascardi, M., Riggs, D. S., Hearst-Ikeda, D., & Foa, E. B. (1996). Objective rating of assault safety as predictors of PTSD. *Journal of Interpersonal Violence, 11,* 65-78.

Cassiday, K. L., McNally, R. J., & Zeitlin, S. B. (1992). Cognitive processing of trauma cues in rape victims with post-traumatic stress disorder. *Cognitive Therapy and Research, 16,* 283-295.

Chu, J. A., & Dill, D. L. (1990). Dissociative symptoms in relation to childhood physical and sexual abuse. *American Journal of Psychiatry, 147,* 887-892.

Cluss, P. A., Boughton, J., Frank, L. E., Stewart, B. D., & West, D. G. (1983). The rape victim: Psychological correlates of participation in the legal process. *Criminal Justice and Behavior, 10,* 342-357.

Dancu, C. V., & Foa, E. B. (1992). Posttraumatic stress disorder. In A. Freeman & F. M. Dattilio (Eds.), *Comprehensive casebook of cognitive therapy* (pp. 79-88). New York: Plenum.

Dancu, C. V., Riggs, D. S., Hearst-Ikeda, D., Shoyer, B. G., & Foa, E. B. (1996). Dissociative experiences and post-traumatic disorder among females of criminal assault and rape. *Journal of Traumatic Stress, 9,* 253-267.

Dancu, C. V., Riggs, D. S., Shoyer, B. G., & Foa, E. B. (1991, November). *Dissociative symptoms among female crime victims.* Paper presented at the 7th annual meeting of the International Society for Traumatic Stress Studies, Washington, DC.

Davidson, J. R., & Foa, E. B. (1991). Diagnostic issues in posttraumatic stress disorder: Considerations for the DSM-IV. *Journal of Abnormal Psychology, 100,* 346-355.

Davis, R., & Brickman, E. (1996). Supportive and unsupportive aspects of the behavior of others toward victims of sexual and non-sexual assault. *Journal of Interpersonal Violence, 11,* 250-262.

Davis, R., Brickman, E., & Baker, T. (1991). Supportive and unsupportive aspects of the responses of others to rape victims: Effects on concurrent adjustment. *American Journal of Community Psychology, 19,* 443-451.

Davis, R., Taylor, B., & Bench, S. (1995). Impact of sexual and nonsexual assault on secondary victims. *Violence and Victims, 10,* 73-84.

Ellis, E. M., Atkeson, B. M., & Calhoun, K. S. (1981). An assessment of long-term reaction to rape. *Journal of Abnormal Psychology, 90,* 263-266.

Ellis, E. M., Calhoun, K. S., & Atkeson, B. M. (1980). Sexual dysfunction in victims of rape: Victims may experience a loss of sexual arousal and frightening flashbacks even one year after the assault. *Women and Health, 5,* 39-47.

Ellis, L. F., Black, L. D., & Resick, P. A. (1992). Cognitive-behavioral treatment approaches for victims of crime. *Innovations in Clinical Practice: A Source Book, 11,* 23-38.

Falsetti, S. A., & Resnick, H. (1994, November). *Frequency and severity of panic symptoms associated with trauma and PTSD.* Paper presented at the 10th annual meeting of the International Society for Traumatic Stress Studies, Chicago.

Falsetti, S. A., Resnick, H., & Resick, P. A. (1992, November). *Post-traumatic stress disorder, perceived life threat, and death anxiety.* Paper presented at the 8th annual meeting of the International Society for Traumatic Stress Studies, Los Angeles.

Feldman-Summers, S., Gordon, P. E., & Meagher, J. R. (1979). The impact of rape on sexual satisfaction. *Journal of Abnormal Psychology, 88,* 101-105.

Fellitti, V. J. (1991). Long-term medical consequences of incest, rape, and molestation. *Southern Medical Journal, 84,* 328-331.

Fitts, W. H. (1965). *Manual: Tennessee Self Concept Scale.* Los Angeles: Western Psychological Services.

Foa, E. B., Feske, U., Murdock, T. B., Kozak, M. J., & McCarthy, P. R. (1991). Processing of threat related information in rape victims. *Journal of Abnormal Psychology, 100,* 156-162.

Foa, E. B., Freund, B. F., Hembree, E., Dancu, C. V., Franklin, M. E., Perry, K. J., Riggs, D. S., & Moinar, C. (1994, November). *Efficacy of short term behavioral treatments of PTSD in sexual and nonsexual assault victims.* Paper presented at the 28th annual meeting of the Association for Advancement of Behavior Therapy, San Diego.

Foa, E. B., & Kozak, M. J. (1986). Emotional processing of fear: Exposure to corrective information. *Psychological Bulletin, 99,* 20-35.

Foa, E. B., & Riggs, D. S. (1994). Posttraumatic stress disorder and rape. In R. S. Pynoos (Ed.), *Posttraumatic stress disorder: A clinical review* (pp. 133-158). Lutherville, MD: Sidran.

Foa, E. B., Rothbaum, B. O., Riggs, D. S., & Murdock, T. B. (1991). Treatment of posttraumatic stress disorder in rape victims: A comparison between cognitive-behavioral procedures and counseling. *Journal of Consulting and Clinical Psychology, 59,* 715-723.

Foa, E. B., Steketee, G., & Rothbaum, B. O. (1989). Behavioral/cognitive conceptualizations of post-traumatic stress disorder. *Behavior Therapy, 20,* 155-176.

Foa, E. B., Zinbarg, R., & Rothbaum, B. O. (1992). Uncontrollability and unpredictability in post-traumatic stress disorder: An animal model. *Psychological Bulletin, 112,* 218-238.

Forman, B. D. (1980). Psychotherapy with rape victims. *Psychotherapy Theory, Research and Practice, 17,* 304-311.

Fox, S. S., & Scherl, D. J. (1972). Crisis intervention with victims of rape. *Social Work, 17,* 37-42.

Frank, E., & Anderson, B. P. (1987). Psychiatric disorders in rape victims: Past history and current symptomatology. *Comprehensive Psychiatry, 28,* 77-82.

Frank, E., Anderson, B., Stewart, B. D., & Dancu, C. (1988). Efficacy of cognitive behavior therapy and systematic desensitization in the treatment of rape trauma. *Behavior Therapy, 19,* 403-420.

Frank, E., & Stewart, B. D. (1983). Treating depression in victims of rape. *Clinical Psychologist, 36,* 95-98.

Frank, E., & Stewart, B. D. (1984). Depressive symptoms in rape victims. *Journal of Affective Disorders, 1,* 269-277.

Frank, E., Turner, S. M., & Duffy, B. (1979). Depressive symptoms in rape victims. *Journal of Affective Disorders, 1,* 269-277.

Frank, E., Turner, S. M., Stewart, B. D., Jacob, J., & West, D. (1981). Past psychiatric symptoms and the response to sexual assault. *Comprehensive Psychiatry, 22,* 479-487.

Frazier, P. A. (1990). Victim attributions and post-rape trauma. *Journal of Personality and Social Psychology, 59,* 298-304.

Girelli, S. A., Resick, P. A., Marhoefer-Dvorak, S., & Kotsis Hutter, C. (1986). Subjective distress and violence during rape: Their effects on long-term fear. *Victims and Violence, 1,* 35-46.

Golding, J. M., Stein, J. A., Siegel, J. M., & Burnam, M. A. (1988). Sexual assault history and use of health and mental health services. *American Journal of Community Psychology, 16,* 625-644.

Hassell, R. A. (1981). *The impact of stranger vs. non-stranger rape: A longitudinal study.* Paper presented at the 8th annual meeting of the Association for Women in Psychology, Boston.

Holmes, M. R., & St. Lawrence, J. S. (1983). Treatment of rape-induced trauma: Proposed behavioral conceptualization and review of the literature. *Clinical Psychology Review, 3,* 417-433.

Horowitz, M. J. (1986). Stress-response syndromes: A review of posttraumatic and adjustment disorders. *Hospital and Community Psychiatry, 37,* 241-249.

Horowitz, M. D., Wilner, N., & Alvarez, W. (1979). Impact of Event Scale: A measure of subjective stress. *Psychosomatic Medicine, 41,* 209-218.

Horowitz, M. J., Wilner, N., Kaltrieder, N., & Alvarez, W. (1980). Signs and symptoms of posttraumatic stress disorder. *Archives of General Psychiatry, 37,* 85-92.

Jenny, C., Hooton, T. M., Bowers, A., Copass, M. K., Krieger, J. N., Hiller, S. L., Kiviat, N., & Corey, L. (1990). Sexually transmitted diseases in victims of rape. *New England Journal of Medicine, 322,* 713-716.

Katz, B. L., & Burt, M. R. (1988). Self-blame in recovery from rape: Help or hindrance? In A. Burgess (Ed.), *Rape and sexual assault* (Vol. 2). New York: Garland.

Kendall, P. C., & Ingram, R. (1987). The future for cognitive assessment of anxiety: Let's get specific. In L. Michelson & L. Ascher (Eds.), *Anxiety and stress disorders.*

Kilpatrick, D. G. (1984, February). *Treatment of fear and anxiety in victims of rape* (Final Rep., NIMH Grant No. MH 29602). Washington, DC: National Institute of Justice.

Kilpatrick, D. G., Best, C. L., Veronen, L. J., Amick, A. E., Villeponteaux, L. A., & Ruff, G. A. (1985). Mental health correlates of criminal victimization: A random community survey. *Journal of Consulting and Clinical Psychology, 53,* 866-873.

Kilpatrick, D. G., Edmunds, C. N., & Seymour, A. K. (1992). *Rape in America: A report to the nation.* Arlington, VA: National Victim Center.

Kilpatrick, D. G., Resick, P. A., & Veronen, L. J. (1981). Effects of a rape experience: A longitudinal study. *Journal of Social Issues, 37,* 105-122.

Kilpatrick, D. G., Saunders, B. E., Amick McMullan, A., & Best, C. L. (1989). Victim and crime factors associated with the development of crime-related post-traumatic stress disorder. *Behavior Therapy, 20,* 199-214.

Kilpatrick, D. G., & Veronen, L. J. (1983). Treatment for rape-related problems: Crisis intervention is not enough. In L. H. Cohen, W. L. Claiborn, & G. A. Specter (Eds.), *Crisis intervention* (pp. 165-185). New York: Human Sciences Press.

Kilpatrick, D. G., & Veronen, L. J. (1984). *The psychological impact of crime.* Washington, DC: National Institute of Justice.

Kilpatrick, D. G., Veronen, L. J., & Best, C. L. (1985). Factors predicting psychological distress among rape victims. In C. R. Figley (Ed.), *Trauma and its wake* (pp. 114-141). New York: Brunner/Mazel.

Kilpatrick, D. G., Veronen, L. J., & Resick, P. A. (1979a). The aftermath of rape: Recent empirical findings. *American Journal of Orthopsychiatry, 49,* 658-669.

Kilpatrick, D. G., Veronen, L. J., & Resick, P. A. (1979b). Assessment of the aftermath of rape: Changing patterns of fear. *Journal of Behavioral Assessment, 1,* 133-147.

Kilpatrick, D. G., Veronen, L. J., & Resick, P. A. (1982). Psychological sequelae to rape. In D. M. Doleys, M. Ciminero, & A. R. Ciminero (Eds.), *Behavioral medicine: Assessment and treatment strategies* (pp. 473-497). New York: Plenum.

Kilpatrick, D. G., Veronen, L. J., Saunders, B. E., Best, C. L., Amick-McMullan, A., & Paduhovich, J. (1987). *The psychological impact of crime: A study of randomly surveyed crime victims* (Final Rep., Grant No. 84-IJ-CX-0039). Washington, DC: National Institute of Justice.

Koss, M. P., Dinero, T. E., Seibel, C. A., & Cox, S. L. (1988). Stranger and acquaintance rape: Are there differences in the victim's experience? *Psychology of Women Quarterly, 12,* 1-24.

Koss, M. P., Gidycz, C. A., & Wisniewski, N. (1987). The scope of rape: Incidence and prevalence of sexual aggression and victimization in a national sample of higher education students. *Journal of Consulting and Clinical Psychology, 55,* 162-170.

Koss, M. P., Koss, P., & Woodruff, W. (1991). Deleterious effects of criminal victimization on women's health and medical utilization. *Archives of Internal Medicine, 151,* 342-357.

Koss, M. P., Woodruff, W., & Koss, P. (1991). Criminal victimization among primary care medical patients: Prevalence, incidence, and physician usage. *Behavioral Sciences and the Law, 9,* 85-96.

Kramer, T. L., & Green, B. L. (1991). Posttraumatic stress disorder as an early response to sexual assault. *Journal of Interpersonal Violence, 6,* 160-173.

Lacey, H. B. (1990). Sexually transmitted diseases and rape: The experience of a sexual assault centre. *International Journal of STD and AIDS, 1,* 405-409.

Lang, P. J. (1977). Imagery in therapy: An information processing analysis of fear. *Behavior Therapy, 8,* 862-886.

Libow, J. A., & Doty, D. W. (1979). An exploratory approach to self-blame and self-derogation by rape victims. *American Journal of Orthopsychiatry, 49,* 670-679.

Litz, B. T. (1992). Emotional numbing in combat-related post-traumatic stress disorder: A critical review and reformulation. *Clinical Psychology Review, 12,* 417-432.

Marhoefer-Dvorak, S., Resick, P. A., Hutter, C., & Girelli, S. A. (1988). Single-versus multiple-incident rape victims. *Journal of Interpersonal Violence, 3,* 145-160.

Marmar, C. R., Weiss, D. S., Schlenger, W. E., Fairbank, J. A., Jordan, B. K., Kulka, R. A., & Hough, R. L. (1994). Peritraumatic dissociation and posttraumatic stress in male Vietnam theater veterans. *American Journal of Psychiatry, 151,* 902-907.

Masters, W. H., & Johnson, V. E. (1976). Principles of the new sex therapy. *American Journal of Psychiatry, 133,* 479-487.

McCahill, T., Meyer, L., & Fischman, A. (1979). *The aftermath of rape.* Lexington, MA: Heath.

McCann, I. L., Sakheim, D. K., & Abrahamson, D. J. (1988). Trauma and victimization: A model of psychological adaptation. *Counseling Psychologist, 16,* 531-594.

Mechanic, M. B., & Resick, P. A. (1994, July). *An approach to treating posttraumatic stress disorder and depression.* Paper presented at the 20th annual meeting of the National Association for Rural Mental Health, Des Moines, IA.

Mechanic, M. B., Resick, P. A., & Griffin, M. G. (1993, November). *Rape-related PTSD: Comorbidity of DSM-III-R Axis I disorders and associated symptoms.* Paper presented at the 27th annual meeting of the Association for the Advancement of Behavior Therapy, Atlanta.

Mechanic, M. B., Resick, P. A., & Griffin, M. G. (1994, November). *Post-rape reactions: Does knowing the rapist make a difference?* Paper presented at the 28th annual meeting of the Association for Advancement for Behavior Therapy, San Diego.

Mechanic, M. B., Resick, P. A., Schnicke, M. K., & Griffin, M. G. (1993, November). *The impact of guilt and self-blame on recovery from PTSD in rape victims.* Paper presented at the 27th annual meeting of the Association for the Advancement of Behavior Therapy, Atlanta.

Merluzzi, T. V., & Boltwood, M. D. (1989). Cognitive assessment. In A. Freeman, K. M. Simon, L. E. Beutler, & H. Arkowitz (Eds.), *Comprehensive handbook of cognitive therapy* (pp. 249-266). New York: Plenum.

Meyer, C. B., & Taylor, S. E. (1986). Adjustment to rape. *Journal of Personality and Social Psychology, 50,* 1226-1234.

Miller, W. R., Williams, M., & Berstein, M. H. (1982). The effects of rape on marital and sexual adjustment. *American Journal of Family Therapy, 10,* 51-58.

Moss, M., Frank, E., & Anderson, B. (1990). The effects of marital status and partner support on rape trauma. *American Journal of Orthopsychiatry, 60,* 379-391.

Murphy, S. M. (1990). Rape, sexually transmitted diseases and human immunodeficiency virus infection. *International Journal of STD and AIDS, 1,* 79-82.

Murphy, S. M., Amick-McMullan, A. E., Kilpatrick, D. G., Haskett, M. E., Veronen, L. J., Best, C. L., & Saunders, B. E. (1988). Rape victims' self-esteem: A longitudinal analysis. *Journal of Interpersonal Violence, 3,* 355-370.

Nadelson, C. C., Notman, M. T., Zackson, H., & Gornick, J. (1982). A follow-up study of rape victims. *American Journal of Psychiatry, 139,* 1266-1270.

Nishith, P., Hearst, D. E., Mueser, K. T., & Foa, E. B. (1995). PTSD and major depression: Methodological and treatment considerations in a single case design. *Behavior Therapy, 26,* 319-335.

Norris, J., & Feldman-Summers, S. (1981). Factors related to the psychological impacts of rape on the victim. *Journal of Abnormal Psychology, 90,* 562-567.

Notman, M. T., & Nadelson, C. C. (1976). The rape victim: Psychodynamic considerations. *American Journal of Psychiatry, 133,* 408-413.

Orlando, J. A., & Koss, M. P. (1983). The effects of sexual victimization on sexual satisfaction: A study of the

negative-association hypothesis. *Journal of Abnormal Psychology, 92,* 104-106.

Pearson, M. A., Poquette, B. M., & Wasden, R. E. (1983). Stress-inoculation and the treatment of post-rape trauma: A case report. *Behavior Therapist, 6,* 58-59.

Perloff, L. S. (1983). Perceptions of vulnerability to victimization. *Journal of Social Issues, 39,* 41-61.

Peterson, C., & Seligman, M. E. (1983). Learned helplessness and victimization. *Journal of Social Issues, 39,* 103-116.

Resick, P. A. (1986). Assesment of fear reactions in sexual assault victims: A factor analytic study of the Veronen-Kilpatrick Modified Fear Survey. *Journal of Behavioral Assesment, 8,* 271-283.

Resick, P. A. (1988). *Reactions of female and male victims of rape or robbery* (Final Rep., NIJ Grant No. 85-IJ-CX-0042). Washington, DC: National Institute of Justice.

Resick, P. A. (1992). Cognitive treatment of a crime-related post-traumatic stress disorder. In R. D. Peters, R. J. McMahon, & V. L. Quincey (Eds.), *Aggression and violence throughout the life span* (pp. 171-191). Newbury Park, CA: Sage.

Resick, P. A. (1993a, July). *Group versus individual format of cognitive processing therapy for PTSD in sexual assault victims.* Paper presented at the Lake George Conference on PTSD, Lake George, NY.

Resick, P. A. (1993b). The psychological impact of rape. *Journal of Interpersonal Violence, 8,* 223-255.

Resick, P. A. (1994). Cognitive processing therapy (CPT) for rape-related PTSD and depression. *Clinical Quarterly, 4,* 1-5.

Resick, P. A., Calhoun, K. S., Atkeson, B. M., & Ellis, E. M. (1981). Social adjustment in victims of sexual assault. *Journal of Consulting and Clinical Psychology, 49,* 705-712.

Resick, P. A., Churchill, M., & Falsetti, S. (1990, November). *Assessments of cognitions in trauma victims: A pilot study.* Paper presented at the 6th annual meeting of the International Society for Traumatic Stress Studies, New Orleans.

Resick, P. A., & Gerth Markaway, B. E. (1991). Clinical treatment of adult female victims of sexual assault. In C. R. Hollin & K. Howells (Eds.), *Clinical approaches to sex offenders and their victims* (pp. 261-284). New York: John Wiley.

Resick, P. A., Jordan, C. G., Girelli, S. A., Hutter, C. K., & Marhoefer-Dvorak, S. (1988). A comparative outcome study of behavioral group therapy for sexual assault victims. *Behavior Therapy, 19,* 385-401.

Resick, P. A., & Schnicke, M. K. (1990). Treating symptoms in adult victims of sexual assault. *Journal of Interpersonal Violence, 5,* 488-506.

Resick, P. A., & Schnicke, M. K. (1992a). Cognitive processing therapy for sexual assault victims. *Journal of Consulting and Clinical Psychology, 60,* 748-756.

Resick, P. A., & Schnicke, M. K. (1992b, November). *Cognitive processing therapy for sexual assault victims.* Paper presented at the 8th annual meeting of the International Society for Traumatic Stress Studies, Los Angeles.

Resick, P. A., & Schnicke, M. K. (1993). *Cognitive processing therapy for rape victims: A treatment manual.* Newbury Park, CA: Sage.

Resick, P. A., Schnicke, M. K., & Markway, B. G. (1991, October). *The relationship between cognitive content and PTSD.* Paper presented at the 25th annual meeting of the Association for the Advancement of Behavior Therapy, New York, NY.

Resnick, H. S., Kilpatrick, D. G., Dansky, B. S., Saunders, B. E., & Best, L. L. (1993). Prevalence of civilian trauma and posttraumatic stress disorder in a representative national sample of women. *Journal of Consulting and Clinical Psychology, 6,* 984-991.

Riger, S., & Gordon, M. T. (1981). The fear of rape: A study of social control. *Journal of Social Issues, 37,* 71-92.

Riggs, D. S., Dancu, C. V., Gershuny, B. S., Greenberg, D., & Foa, E. B. (1992). Anger and post-traumatic stress disorder in female crime victims. *Journal of Traumatic Stress, 5,* 613-625.

Riggs, D. S., Foa, E. B., Rothbaum, B. O., & Murdock, T. (1992). *Post-traumatic stress disorder following rape and non-sexual assault: A predictive model.* Unpublished manuscript.

Roth, S., Wayland, K., & Woolsey, M. (1990). Victimization history and victim-assailant relationship as factors in recovery from sexual assault. *Journal of Traumatic Stress, 3,* 169-180.

Rothbaum, B. O., & Foa, E. (1988). *Treatment of posttraumatic stress disorder in rape victims.* Paper presented at the World Congress of Behavior Therapy Conference, Edinburgh, Scotland.

Rothbaum, B. O., & Foa, E. B. (1992). Exposure therapy for rape victims with post-traumatic stress disorder. *Behavior Therapist, 15,* 219-222.

Rothbaum, B. O., Foa, E. B., Riggs, D. S., Murdock, T., & Walsh, W. (1992). A prospective examination of post-traumatic stress disorder in rape victims. *Journal of Traumatic Stress, 5,* 455-475.

Ruch, L. O., Amedeo, S. R., Leon, J. J., & Gartrell, J. W. (1991). Repeated sexual victimization and trauma change during the acute phase of the sexual assault trauma syndrome. *Women and Health, 17,* 1-19.

Ruch, L. O., & Chandler, S. M. (1980). An evaluation of a center for sexual assault. *Women and Health, 5,* 45-63.

Ruch, L. O., & Chandler, S. M. (1983). Sexual assault trauma during the acute phase: An exploratory model and multivariate analysis. *Journal of Health and Social Behavior, 24,* 174-185.

Ruch, L. O., Chandler, S. M., & Harter, R. A. (1980). Life change and rape impact. *Journal of Health and Social Behavior, 21,* 248-260.

Ruch, L. O., & Leon, J. J. (1983). Sexual assault trauma and trauma change. *Women and Health, 8,* 5-21.

Russell, D. (1982). The causal dimension scale: A measure of how individuals perceive causes. *Journal of Personality and Social Psychology, 42,* 1137-1145.

Sales, E., Baum, M., & Shore, B. (1984). Victim readjustment following assault. *Journal of Social Issues, 40,* 117-136.

Santiago, J. M., McCall-Perez, F., Gorcey, M., & Beigel, A. (1985). Long term psychological effects of rape in 35 rape victims. *American Journal of Psychiatry, 142,* 548-554.

Scheppele, K. L., & Bart, P. B. (1983). Through women's eyes: Defining danger in the wake of sexual assault. *Journal of Social Issues, 39,* 63-80.

Schnicke, M. K., & Resick, P. A. (1990, November). *Self-blame in rape victims.* Paper presented at the 6th annual meeting of the International Society for Traumatic Stress Studies, New Orleans.

Silver, R. L., & Wortman, C. B. (1980). Coping with undesirable life events. In J. Garber & M. Seligman (Eds.), *Human helplessness* (pp. 279-340). New York: Academic Press.

Spiegel, D., Hunt, T., & Dondershine, H. E. (1988). Dissociation and hypnotizability in posttraumatic stress disorder. *American Journal of Psychiatry, 145,* 301-305.

Steketee, G., & Foa, E. B. (1987). Rape victims: posttraumatic stress responses and their treatment: A review of the literature. *Journal of Anxiety Disorders, 1,* 69-86.

Stewart, B. D., Hughes, C., Frank, E., Anderson, B., Kendall, K., & West, D. (1987). The aftermath of rape: Profiles of immediate and delayed treatment seekers. *Journal of Nervous and Mental Disease, 175,* 90-94.

Thornhill, N. W., & Thornhill, R. (1990). An evolutionary analysis of psychological pain following rape: II. The effects of stranger, friend, and family-member offenders. *Ethology and Sociobiology, 11,* 177-193.

Turner, S. M., & Frank, E. (1981). Behavior therapy in the treatment of rape victims. In L. Michelson, M. Hersen, & S. M. Turner (Eds.), *Future perspectives in behavior therapy* (pp. 269-291). New York: Plenum.

Veronen, L. J., & Kilpatrick, D. G. (1983). *Stress reduction and prevention.* New York: Plenum.

Veronen, L. G., Kilpatrick, D. G., & Resick, P. A. (1979). Treating fear and anxiety in rape victims: Implications for the criminal justice system. In W. H. Parsonage (Ed.), *Perspectives on victimology* (pp. 148-159). Beverly Hills, CA: Sage.

Wirtz, P. W., & Harrell, A. V. (1987). Assaultive versus nonassaultive victimization: A profile analysis of psychological response. *Journal of Interpersonal Violence, 2,* 264-277.

Wolff, R. (1977). Systematic desensitization and negative practice to alter the aftereffects of a rape attempt. *Journal of Behavior Therapy and Experimental Psychiatry, 8,* 423-425.

Wortman, C. B. (1976). Causal attributions and personal control. In J. H. Harvey, W. J. Ickes, & R. F. Kidd (Eds.), *New directions in attributions research* (pp. 23-52). Hillsdale, NJ: Lawrence Erlbaum.

Wyatt, G. E., Notgrass, C. M., & Newcomb, M. (1990). Internal and external mediators of women's rape experiences. *Psychology of Women Quarterly, 14,* 153-176.

Zeitlin, S. B., & McNally, R. J. (1991). Implicit and explicit memory bias for threat in post-traumatic stress disorder. *Behavior Research and Therapy, 29,* 451-457.

4   Victims of Domestic Violence

JOEL GARNER

JEFFREY FAGAN

In 1969, the National Commission on the Causes and Prevention of Violence concluded that America was the world's leader in rates of homicide, assault, rape, and robbery. For most people, violent crime became a major concern; this concern, however, focused on violence outside the home. Like the commission, most Americans believed that their greatest risk of injury came from outside their home or their loved ones. Few people considered the home anything other than "a compassionate, egalitarian, peaceful affair in which violence played no part" (Wardell, Gillespie, & Leffler, 1983).

In the past three decades, research and social action have increased the public's awareness of the extent and seriousness of violence between spouses, sexual intimates, and family members. Consider the following facts. Victim surveys record millions of violent crimes each year, and we now know that approximately 40% of these violent incidents are between people who are friends or acquain-

tances, family members, or spouses. Estimates of dating or courtship violence range from 10% to 67% of all dating relationships (Sugarman & Hotaling, 1989). About 2,000 children under the age of 18 are killed each year by parents or caretakers. Homicides in the home account for 28% of all homicides of women. Nearly 30% of women presenting at emergency rooms for physical trauma are injured by spouses or boyfriends (Stark & Flitcraft, 1991). Research with both victims and batterers has increased our understanding of the factors that contribute to domestic violence.

Interest in domestic violence is part of a larger, sometimes cyclical, historical process of social reform in which what once were considered "private" family matters became matters for energetic state intervention (Pleck, 1987) but then fade from public attention. Recent reforms in both civil and criminal law have increased the legal remedies available to victims of domestic violence, and there has been a parallel growth of social and community-based services. One modern innovation is that research has documented the adoption and implementation of some of these reforms, promoted some innovations in policies and practice, and even generated information that has constrained enthusiasm for otherwise popular initiatives. As a result, our knowledge has also grown about how legal and social institutions respond to domestic violence and, when they do respond, about what is effective and what is not effective in preventing future violence. Many aspects of domestic violence, however, have not been subject to rigorous examination.

Social and research activism has developed evidence over the past three decades that although many relationships are nonviolent, virtually every form of family or intimate relationship has potential for being violent. However, many issues remain unsettled or controversial in the study of domestic violence. For example, the boundary of what is and is not violence remains a major issue, fraught with measurement and definitional ambiguity. Evaluative evidence on the effects of legal and social interventions has been weak or selective, and there is no consensus on the promise and limitations of legal or social interventions (Fagan, 1995). In this chapter, we review the current state of knowledge on the extent of domestic violence, contemporary theories of its occurrence, and evidence on the effects of social and legal policies to control it.

Definitions of Domestic Violence

There continue to be contentious debates over the definition of "domestic" violence. There has been no consensus on this definition among researchers or lawmakers. Differences in definition have led widely varying estimates of the prevalence and correlates of domestic violence (Fagan & Browne, 1994), as well as our understanding of effectiveness of interventions. There are two critical dimen-

sions to this debate: the nature of the acts that constitute "violence" and the types of relationships that qualify as "domestic."

Defining *Violence*

There is no consensus among researchers, activists, or lawmakers about what constitutes violent or abusive acts. Many contend that understanding violence, especially domestic violence, requires attention not only to numbers of physical assaults but also to other harmful behaviors, such as psychological or emotional abuse, economic deprivation, stalking, and threats toward other family members and property (Dobash & Dobash, 1979). These types of behavior co-occur with physical assault and can be part of an ecology of aggression that characterizes some domestic violence. These "nonviolent" but harmful behaviors may constitute antecedents of physical assault, part of a maintenance pattern of domination, or the displacement of aggression when the violence desists.

Others assert that definitions of domestic violence should include only acts that involve physical assaults. For example, the definition used in the first national survey of domestic violence focused only on physical violence and defined *violence* as "any act carried out with the intention or perceived intention of causing pain or physical injury to another person." There also is controversy regarding whether marital rape should be included in a definition of domestic violence.

There is no debate that domestic violence is violence. Defining *violence* in "traditional" terms such as homicide, rape, aggravated assault, and simple assault provides a basis for comparing and contrasting domestic violence with other types of violence. However, understanding domestic violence requires attention to a variety of sometimes interwoven and chronic behaviors such as harassment, stalking, intimidation, and threats of violence, and it is this chronic and diverse character that gives a distinctive quality to domestic violence. Both researchers and policy makers have increasingly turned to this broader definition in pursuing explanations and remedies for domestic violence.

Defining *Domestic*

The simple distinction between stranger and nonstranger is not adequate to explain the nature and distribution of domestic violence. In fact, our understanding of domestic violence is greatly informed by more refined distinctions among types of relationships between offenders and victims. Thus informed discussions of domestic violence benefit from identifying whether the victim is male or female and whether the victim and the offender are not merely not strangers but spouses or sexual intimates, ex-spouses, other family members, or simply friends and acquaintances.

The definition of what constitutes an "intimate" relationship has varied in research, law, and policy. Contemporary law recognizes a broad range of relationships that are eligible for criminal sanctions or civil relief under "domestic violence" statutes (Zorza, 1992). Definitions in research have varied widely. Although some studies have been limited to married or cohabiting couples, others have included noncohabiting couples (e.g., boyfriend/girlfriend), formerly married (separated, divorced) couples, and ex-boyfriends or ex-girlfriends. Whether gay or lesbian relationships qualify as "domestic" also has been controversial in both research and policy.

One result has been a confusing array of terms used to define the problems of violence between adult intimates or former intimates. The terms *wife assault* and *spouse assault* exclude former spouses and nonmarried cohabitants and are too limiting. Other terms, such as *partner assault* or *intimate assault,* are difficult to operationalize and defy a consensus on when these thresholds are achieved.

Most studies distinguish between parental violence toward children and violence between adult intimates. In fact, the literature on child abuse and neglect has developed separately from the literature on violence toward adult partners. There are several reasons for this: (a) A small number of families in national surveys report both adult intimate violence and violence toward children (Fagan & Browne, 1994); (b) state laws proscribe distinct legal sanctions for child abuse and partner or spouse abuse, including separate judicial forums; (c) different interest groups have been active in advocating for battered women and abused children;[1] and (d) the compartmentalized interests of researchers have led to segregation of the separate forms of "family" violence in the academic literature. So narrow have the interests of researchers been on all forms of "family" violence that its study has remained separate from the study of violence toward strangers. Criminologists have made few attempts to integrate the emerging knowledge of violence in the home with other research or theory on violence (Reiss & Roth, 1993).

In this chapter, we shall limit our discussion to violence toward adult intimate partners and refer to it as *domestic violence*. This is a practical as well as conceptual decision. The separate literatures have grown extensively over the past three decades, making a unified discussion of theory, research, and law all but impossible in one book, let alone one chapter.

Measuring Domestic Violence

Knowledge about domestic violence reflects not only differences in definitions but also differences in how it is measured and the data sources that are used.

Data Sources

The three main sources of information about domestic violence are official records, social surveys, and clinical or program data. Although each source has its limitations, it also has unique strengths that depend on the purpose for which it is used.

Clinical and program data are gathered primarily from women and men who are participants in a variety of services for domestic violence. Men in treatment programs for battering, women in shelters, and families in family counseling are three examples of clinical or program study subjects. These data are especially valuable because they may be the only way of obtaining information from a substantial number of severely battered women. However, because not all battered women seek help from these programs, their samples are not representative and are of limited value in determining either the extent of domestic violence or the reasons for its occurrence.

Official records include police, court, or social agency data on participants in their services or proceedings. As in clinical records, data from official records are limited to individuals who come to the attention of the agencies through either self-selection or official intervention. Only a small fraction of domestic violence incidents are reported to the police: no more than 20% (Dutton, 1995) and probably fewer. Official records often are difficult to use for research on domestic violence. Although police *contact* data may recognize domestic violence, police *arrest* records often fail to distinguish domestic assaults from other types of assaults. The same is true throughout the criminal justice system and often in the mental health and social service systems as well. Variations in the definitions and recording practices of official agencies often lead to disparate estimates on domestic violence (Weis, 1989).

Social surveys are important in overcoming the self-selection and official-selection biases in clinical data and official records. Social surveys of victimization typically inquire if the respondent has been a victim of a crime, if she or he knows the offender, and if so, the nature of their relationship—acquaintance, family member, intimate, spouse, or ex-spouse. Most violent crime is between strangers but for some groups, especially females, most violent incidents are committed by someone they know or live with or to whom they are or were married.

The usefulness of social surveys in domestic violence depends on the purposes to which they are put. As estimates of the extent and severity of domestic violence, they may be helpful depending on definitional and sampling considerations. However, broad surveys with general populations often are limited in several ways: They report very low base rates for individual types of violence, and, for all types of violence combined, the rates are typically less than 15%. Thus these surveys are limited in their ability to test theoretical explanations of violence. Usually it is difficult to survey both members of a household, and there often is disagreement between the members of a couple on whether domestic violence occurred and how serious it was (Straus & Gelles, 1990). The most severely battered women typically are unavailable for social surveys, for reasons of their own safety and as a reflection of their dangerous circumstances. Social surveys are prone to problems of recall and other difficulties typically associated with survey research (Weis, 1989).

Measuring Domestic Violence

Measurement has been one of the most contentious areas in research on domestic violence. Measurement of domestic violence through official records is limited because of the definitions imposed by agencies on what constitutes domestic violence, the diverse willingness of victims to mobilize these agencies, and the discretion of individuals in the agencies in what they determine is domestic violence and how they respond to it. Medical records often include measures of trauma but in many instances fail to recognize cases in which domestic violence has not caused physical injury (Stark & Flitcraft, 1991).

The most commonly used measurement device is a self-report scale, the Conflict Tactics Scale (CTS; Straus, 1979); however, it has generated considerable criticism while gaining widespread use. In contrast to the legal codification of "simple" and "aggravated" assault, the CTS includes detailed measures of specific types of acts that range from the most minor physical assaults (push, shove) to the most serious (shoot, stab). It includes threats of violence. Criticisms of the CTS have emphasized the procedures for its administration rather than the content of the items themselves. For example, criticisms include the absence of contextual factors (e.g., provocation vs. self-defensive violence), the inattention to injury or consequence, the exclusion of marital rape and other forms of sexual assault or forced sex in marriage, the exclusion of stalking and other forms of intimidation, and the embedding of CTS items in questions related to "conflict" rather than assault. (Dobash, Dobash, Wilson, & Daly, 1992).

The Extent and Severity of Domestic Violence

Estimates of the extent and severity of victimization vary by data source, definition, and method. Whereas initial estimates of the extent of domestic violence were confined to physical violence within marital relationships (e.g., Martin, 1976), more recent estimates have used more expansive sampling and measurement criteria. Advances in the precision of estimates have occurred at the cost of more complicated and often conflicting estimates of the problem. In this section, we provide estimates of the prevalence of different forms of domestic violence.

Assaults

Domestic violence is evident even before young people enter intimate adult relationships. Dating and courtship violence rates vary from 10% to 67% of all couples (Sugarman & Hotaling, 1989), but severe violence during courtship is reported by about one in four (27%) couples (Makepeace, 1983; Miller & Simpson, 1991). Many of these estimates

are based on samples of college students and older adolescents and exclude younger couples, who exhibit high rates of domestic violence.

Rates of violence among adults also vary by method. The National Crime Victimization Survey (NCVS) surveys all adults and measures violent victimizations by "intimates": boyfriends/girlfriends, spouses, or ex-spouses. Between 1987 and 1991, NCVS data showed that women were 10 times more likely than men to be assaulted in the past year by an intimate (5 victimizations per 1,000 women compared to 0.5 assaults per 1,000 men). The rates were highest for younger women (20-24 years of age), women living in cities, African American women, women in families with lower incomes, and women in families in which one member was unemployed.

Self-report surveys focused on domestic violence typically report prevalence rates higher than the victim reports in the NCVS. The National Family Violence Surveys (NFVS) conducted in 1975 and 1985, surveyed intact couples and portray a different level of violence (Gelles & Straus, 1988; Straus, Gelles, & Steinmetz, 1980). In these surveys, violence between partners occurred in about 16% of all households surveyed, and approximately 10% of both women and men reported some victimization in the past year. Three women in 100 were victims of "serious" violence. Women also were more likely to be injured (Stets & Straus, 1990). The prevalence of violence was stable across the 1975 and 1985 surveys. As with the NCVS, the risks of victimization to women were higher for younger, nonwhite, and lower-income households. When women are victimized, the average number of victimizations is three per year (Gelles & Straus, 1988).

The 10% victimization rate for women reported in the NFVS is actually low compared to rates in the studies reviewed by Fagan and Browne (1994). Table 4.1 shows that annual prevalence rates vary from about 10% (Schulman, 1979) to over 30% (e.g., Frieze, Knoble,

Table 4.1 Past-Year Prevalence Rates of Violence Among Intimates (Per 1,000 Population)

Study	Sample	Any Violence By: Husband or Male Partner	Wife or Female Partner
1. National Probability Samples			
Straus & Gelles (1990)	$N = 6,002$	116	124
Straus et al. (1980)	$N = 2,143$ couples	121	116
Straus & Gelles (1986)	$N = 3,520$ couples	110	120
2. Local or Statewide Probability Samples			
Schulman (1979)	$N = 1,793$ Kentucky women	100	-
Russell (1982)	$N = 644,$ San Francisco women[a]	260	-
Kennedy & Dutton (1987)	$N = 708$ 112	-	
Nisonoff & Bitman (1979)	$N = 297$ household sample	160	110
Smith (1986)[b]	$N = 315$	206	-
Smith (1987)	$N = 604$ Toronto women	144	-
3. Nonprobability Local Samples			
Makepeace (1983)[c]	$N = 244,$ dating couples, college students	137	93
Brutz & Ingoldsby (1984)	$N = 288,$ Quakers	146	152
Makepeace (1981)[b]	$N = 2,338$ students, dating couples	206	120
Meredith et al. (1986)	$N = 304$	220	180
Szinovacz (1983)	$N = 103$	260	300
Clarke (1987)	$N = 318,$ women	274	102
Lockhart (1987)	$N = 307,$ blacks and whites	355	-
Barling et al. (1987)[c]	$N = 187$	740	730
Frieze et al. (1980)	$N = 137$ Pennsylvania women, ever-married and comparison group	340	270
Levinger (1966)	$N = 600,$ divorce filings	370	-
Mason & Blankenship (1987)	$N = 155,$ Michigan undergraduates	18	22

SOURCE: Straus and Gelles (1990); Frieze and Browne (1989); Ellis (1989); Fagan and Browne (1994).
NOTE: Rates are for acts occurring during the past 12 months.
a. Currently or ever married at time of interview.
b. Rates only for lifetime prevalence.
c. Study did not report whether rates are for the previous year or lifetime.

Zomnir, & Washburn, 1980; O'Leary & Arias, 1988). The wide range of prevalence rates may be explained by differences in samples and methods in these studies. Studies using the CTS and other itemized scales are more likely than studies that ask single, global items to detect acts of intimate violence (Weis, 1989). Rates in telephone samples are likely to be lower than rates computed from face-to-face interviews because respondents are more likely in interviews to be in safe and anonymous conditions that encourage disclosure. Samples limited to married or cohabiting cou-ples are likely to underestimate intimate violence because NCVS and other data show that separated and divorced women face elevated risks of violence from their former partners. In short, method- and criterion-dependent biases influence prevalence estimates of partner or intimate assaults (Widom, 1990).

Gender Differences in Assaults

Whether men are victims of domestic violence has been a continuing controversy in domestic violence research. Despite the framing of partner violence as "wife battering" or "violence against women," some studies suggest that women are as likely to assault an intimate partner as are men (Straus, 1993; Straus & Gelles, 1986). However, studies that equate rates of intimate violence among men and women may overlook some important contextual factors that qualitatively distinguish women's violence toward male partners from male violence (Dobash, Dobash, Wilson, & Daly, 1992; Wardell et al., 1983). Women are more likely to be injured than men in partner violence: Males inflicted injury-assaults at a rate of 3.5 per 1,000 males, compared to 0.6 per 1,000 for women (Stets & Straus, 1990). Women are more likely to act in self-defense (Browne, 1993) and more likely to be sexually victimized and emotionally abused than men (Saunders, 1988). Crime victimization surveys show that women are 10 times more likely than men to report victimization by male partners or ex-partners (Bachman, 1994) and that men are far more likely than women to be arrested for partner violence (U.S. Dept. of Justice, 1994).

Injuries in Domestic Violence

Few studies have estimated the prevalence or risks of injuries to women from partner violence (Reiss & Roth, 1993). This is surprising because partner violence may be the most frequent source of injury to women, as well as the single most common cause of injuries for which women seek emergency medical attention (Stark & Flitcraft, 1991).

The relative risks and severity of injuries sustained in marital violence vary according to data sources. Recent analyses of the 1987 to 1990 NCVS longitudinal series by Wiersema and Loftin (1994) show that 18.5% of "domestic" assault victims report an injury of some kind over a 3-year period. Using crime victimization self-reports in the NCVS, Lentzner and DeBerry (1980) reported that over 75% of the victims of violence (assault, rape, and robbery) involving "related intimates" suffered

injuries, compared to 54% of victims of non-stranger violence. Over 80% of all assaults against spouses and ex-spouses resulted in injuries, and spouses and ex-spouses had the highest rates of internal injuries or unconsciousness (7.0%) and broken bones (6.9%).

Studies that measured both the frequency and severity of injury show the strong association between behavior and injury and between the frequency of behavior and the frequency and severity of injury. Among women who sought help from family violence intervention programs, 56% reported being the victim of abuse at least once a month (Fagan & Browne, 1994). Bruises, lacerations, broken bones, or more serious injuries were reported by 66% of the victims, and 59% reported being injured "occasionally" or "frequently." About one in three women who had children were victims of marital violence during pregnancy, and 4% of the women overall reported miscarriages due to marital violence.

Estimates of the prevalence of injury from spouse assault also have been compiled from studies using data from hospital emergency departments. Audits of records in emergency departments (Goldberg & Tomlanovich, 1984; McLeer & Anwar, 1989; Stark et al., 1981) show that at least 30% of women presenting for physical injury have been battered by a spouse or intimate partner, 19% of the women presenting to the emergency department with injury have a history of abuse, and 75% to 80% of the battering cases seen by medical institutions are recurring. Official medical records, however, identify only 1% of these cases as spouse assault. Goldberg and Tomlanovich (1984) found a prevalence rate of spouse assault of 22%; however, only 5% were identified from the ED record, and the majority were identified through in-depth interviews with medical staff in the ED. Implementation of identification protocols in a metropolitan hospital increased the identification rate for battered women from 5.6% to 30% among women presenting with injuries (McLeer & Anwar, 1989).

The severity of injuries in intimate violence is more difficult to gauge than their prevalence. Similar to the NCVS and NFVS studies, research from emergency departments often does not specify the nature of injuries or the distribution of injury severity, and the term *trauma* encompasses several types of injury.

Rape by Intimate Partners

Partner rape often was excluded from the research on domestic violence in the 1970s. It was not included in the CTS items in the National Family Violence surveys but was asked separately later on in the protocol. Nevertheless, the 1985 National Family Violence Survey (Straus & Gelles, 1990) showed that among the 2,942 currently married or "partnered" women, 1.3% reported that their partner had attempted to force them to have sex in the past year. Less than 1% (0.8%) reported that their partner had completed the attempt. Nearly all (93%) the women who experienced repeated attempts to force sex in the past year also had endured multiple incidents of other forms of marital violence.[2]

However, several other studies with different sampling criteria show far higher rates of marital rape. Among women who had ever been married in Russell's (1982) study of women in San Francisco, 14% said they had been raped by a husband or ex-husband. Finkelhor and Yllö (1983) found that 10% of the women cohabiting with a spouse or intimate male in a representative sample of 323 women in Boston reported at least one sexual assault and 50% reported that they had been raped at least 20 times by their spouses. Fagan, Friedman, Wexler, and Lewis (1984) reported that 6.3% of women seeking services from domestic violence intervention programs said they had sought help because of a sexual assault and that 23% reported having been sexually assaulted at some point in the relationship.

Empirical research has shown consistently that marital rape is an integral part of patterns of marital "violence" (Bowker, 1983; Fagan et al. 1984; Frieze, 1983; Russell, 1982; Shields & Hanneke, 1983; Walker, 1984) and may be an antecedent to marital homicide (Browne, 1987). Estimates of the incidence of sexual assaults among physically assaulted female partners range from 23% (Bowker, 1983) to 51% (Walker, 1984). Fagan and Browne (1994) showed that when marital rape items were added to the CTS, sexual assault scaled as the most serious of the CTS items.[3] Browne (1987) and Shields and Hanneke (1983) also found that sexual assault occurred as part of the most violent physical attacks.

Domestic Homicides

Gender disparity is evident in domestic homicide data. Using data from the Supplemental Homicide Reports of the FBI's Uniform Crime Reports, Mercy and Saltzman (1989) reported that women were 1.3 times more likely to be killed by a spouse than were men. Nearly 700 males are killed by their female partners or ex-partners each year, compared to 1,400 female victims of male partners or ex-partners. Moreover, the number of men killing women in "domestic" homicides has steadily increased over the past decade, and males accounted for over 60% of the assailants in domestic homicides by 1994.

These descriptions of domestic homicide can be misleading. In Table 4.2, we show the number and percentage of male and female homicides in 1992 (FBI, 1993). Although the numbers of males and females in the United States are roughly equivalent, the 22,000 homicides reported in 1992 included some 17,000 male victims and only 5,000 female victims. When the victim and offender had an intimate relationship (spouse, girlfriend or boyfriend, or family member), the numbers of male and female victims were roughly equivalent: 1,605 male victims and 1,925 female victims. However, the number of females killed by their spouses or sexual partners (1,256) was double the number of males killed by such relations (635), and more males (970)

Table 4.2   1992 Homicides by Relationship of Offenders and Victims

Relationship of Offender and Victim	Male Victim		Female Victim		Total	
	N	%	N	%	N	%
Total homicides	17,635	100	5,001	100	22,636	100
Unknown relationship	7,284	41	1,547	31	8,831	39
Known relationship	10,351	59	3,454	69	13,805	61
Total intimate	1,605	15.5	1,608	47	3,213	23
Spouse	388	2.2	900	18	1,288	9
Boyfriend/girlfriend	247	1.4	356	10	603	4
Other relative	970	5.5	352	10	1,322	10
Acquaintance/friend	6,102	34.6	1,100	22	7,202	52
Stranger	2,645	15.0	430	9	3,075	22

than females (352) were killed by other family members. Thus the ratio of male to female victims varies substantially depending on how *domestic* and *family* are defined.

In addition to gender differences, the social epidemiology of marital homicide reveals distinct patterns of risk by ethnicity. From police incident reports, Saltzman et al. (1990) found that the risk of fatal assaults was three times greater for nonwhites than for whites in Atlanta. Block (1987) found substantially fewer marital homicides in Chicago among Latinos than African Americans and whites, but there were differences in the male-female ratio by race: The percentage of marital homicides committed by males varied from 33.6% for non-Latino African Americans to 53.2% for non-Latino whites.

Gender differences in motives and methods in partner homicides also are evident. Browne (1987) found that abused women who killed their abusive partners had often endured years of severe assault and threat. Most had unsuccessfully searched for alternative solutions, killing only when they felt hopelessly trapped in a desperate situation from which they could see no practical avenue of escape. Almost all had sought police intervention.[4] Many of the women had attempted to leave the relationship but in retaliation were even more seriously threatened or attacked. A few had been separated or divorced from their partners for up to 2 years yet were still experiencing life-threatening violence and harassment before the final incident. In some cases, women who had endured abuse for years killed only when the partner's violence and threat turned toward their children. Most of the women in the Browne study had no prior history of violent or even illegal behavior. Their attempts to survive with an increasingly assaultive and threatening mate and their inability to find resources that would effectively mitigate the danger eventually led to their own acts of violence.

Theories and Explanations of Domestic Violence

Since the 1970s, theories of domestic violence have developed parallel to but often independently of theories of interpersonal violence toward nonintimates (Fagan & Browne, 1994). Early theories of marital violence, particularly those describing violence by husbands toward wives, viewed domestic violence as an outgrowth of a culture that engendered and maintained the dominance of men over women in every aspect of social life (e.g., Dobash & Dobash, 1979; Martin, 1976; Walker, 1979). Other perspectives on violence emphasized the personal characteristics of the offenders and the victims, such as their youth, socioeconomic status, and personal lifestyles, as enhancing the risks for participating in violence against family members or sexual partners. Similar to theories of "stranger violence," explanations of intimate or partner violence range from cultural to individually based theories. In addition, batterers are a heterogeneous population (Holzworth-Munroe & Stuart, 1994), and distinct types of assaultive partners or couples experiencing intimate violence tend to reflect unique etiological factors (Dutton, 1995).

In this section, we review some of the more prominent explanatory constructs and offer suggestions for an integration of theories to encompass individual and environmental influences. Our brief review of theories moves from ecological and cultural explanations to individual-level explanations.

Patriarchy, Social Networks, and Social Embedding

Dobash and Dobash (1979) described patriarchal influence as culturally normative (Bograd & Yllö, 1988), and Straus (1976) referred to the marriage license as a "hitting license." These theorists contended that the beliefs that support marital violence simply express more general cultural norms and values that uphold a hierarchical, patriarchal social organization. Such norms have been linked with wife assault in empirical studies in the United Kingdom (Dobash & Dobash, 1979), Canada (Smith, 1990), and the United States (Yllö & Straus, 1984).

To explain the contributions of patriarchy to marital violence, economic inequalities and cultural portrayals of women are cited as manifestations of male orientation and hegemony (Dobash & Dobash, 1979; Pagelow, 1984). Straus (1976) identified nine specific manifestations of a male-dominant structure that support wife assault and concluded that the relative weakness of criminal penalties in wife assault cases (until the 1980s) reflects cultural norms that have resulted in the insti-

tution of marriage carrying with it an (implied or explicit) immunity to prosecution for abuse by the male partner. Economic inequalities place a lesser value on women's labor and social contributions and reinforce the dominant role played by men in most labor markets. These cultural and economic indicators reflect women's lower social status, which reinforces male attitudes of superiority and the legitimation of domination. Societal supports for the subordinate position of women, together with situational interactions at a social or subcultural level, contribute to male violence toward women. Bowker (1983) contended that "the myriad peer-relationships that support the patriarchal dominance of the family and the use of violence to enforce it may constitute a subculture of violence. The more fully a husband is immersed in this subculture, the more likely he is to batter his wife" (p. 135).

Power, Control, and Domination

Applications of power and control perspectives from the alcohol literature (McClelland, 1975) to domestic violence suggest that assault is used to assert or maintain power within the relationship, particularly the power to gain victories in confrontations. Straus (1978) and Browne (1987) argued that one episode of violence can permanently alter the balance of marital power toward a strongly husband-dominant pattern. Coleman and Straus (1986), using 1975 NFVS data, found that marital violence was lowest in "egalitarian" couples that shared domestic chores and decisions.[5] However, both male and female aggression was highest in couples in which females were dominant (that is, had the greatest influence in decision making and control over resources).

Power motives and adherence to patriarchal ideology converge in research on patriarchy and marital violence. The translation of patriarchal ideology into specific attitudes or perceptions of marital power is evident in empirical work by Straus (1976, n. 29), Yllö and Straus (1984), and Smith (1990).[6] If males are socialized to expect dominance or power within the relationship, aggression may be initiated from frustration over their inability to control their female partners.

Issues of intimacy and the threat of dependency also may trigger violence in partner relationships. According to Browning and Dutton (1986), males experience anger most readily in circumstances in which they perceive an impending loss of control over either intimacy or distance. Similarly, increased demands for intimacy may be fear producing and may trigger verbal or physical assaults as a mechanism to produce distance and restore the "balance of power" to the male's control.

Finally, gratification that men experience from marital hegemony and male domination also may reinforce aggressive behaviors. Gratification from marital violence may come from achieving or maintaining the instrumental motive of dominance, from the expressive release of anger and aggression in response to perceived power deficits, from the attainment of positive social status that domination affords, or even from the "hearts and flowers" aftermath of many battering incidents.

Other sociological explanations focus on the absence of guardians and controls within intimate relationships. Intimate partners have frequent contacts in situations in which external social controls are weak or absent, in which they are in competition for resources and control, and in which violence becomes a primary form of redressing disputes and perceived attacks (Fagan, 1993; Gelles, 1983). External social controls, such as shaming and job loss, are further weakened in neighborhoods with low resources and weak social cohesion.

Early Childhood Socialization: Witnessing and Observing Violence

Social learning theories view aggressive habits as developing from the learning experiences of individuals and focus on the original milieus in which such habits are acquired (e.g., by observation in the family of origin), the instigators or aversive stimuli in the current environment that trigger aggression, and the maintenance of aggressive habits through the immediate consequences that reward or punish the aggression (Dutton, 1988). Thus sex-role socialization may interact with observation of instrumental violence in the family of origin to shape perceptions of aversive circumstances (such as female independence) and acceptable or socially desirable responses. Further, the salience of social and legal controls in later years may determine whether circumstances reinforce or extinguish these socially learned responses.

Children growing up in violent homes learn much about the instrumental value of violence. Bandura (1973) showed that children in a laboratory setting remember and then imitate aggressive actions that are modeled for them. He also found that boys imitated these behaviors more spontaneously than girls, even when not directly encouraged to do so. Acts performed by an adult male were more likely to be imitated than those performed by women, especially among male children. The context of these lessons is the cultural perpetuation of a dominant role for males, which facilitates the adoption of force or threat as a model for interpersonal interactions (Herzberger, 1983). When faced with the loss of control in adult (marital) relationships or frustration in their efforts to remain dominant, men raised in a violent home are more likely to respond with violence.

Like women victims, men who grow up in violent homes experience feelings of helplessness, fear, and loss of control over their own safety, even when they themselves are not the victims. As children, they may come to hate the abuser, yet they still learn that the most violent person in the household also seems to be the most powerful and the least vulnerable to attack or humiliation by others (Browne, 1987). Thus, when these men perceive a threat of emotional pain or loss of control in an adult relationship, they may follow early models by resorting to violence themselves in an attempt to avoid the potential for further victimization and pain.

Neutralization of Violent Behavior

When deviant behaviors occur that violate either personal standards or social norms, a variety of mechanisms may be mobilized to rationalize or externalize blame for the behavior (Sykes & Matza, 1957). Such processes appear to be evident among male perpetrators of marital violence. Shields and Hanneke (1983) found that 68% of male spouse assailants externalized the cause of their behavior by attributing it to the wife's behavior or to alcohol. "Excuses" for their spouse assaults were offered by 21% of the ($N = 75$) men studied by Dutton (1985). Although the remainder accepted *responsibility* for their actions, their *justifications* typically blamed the victim for these actions or discounted the behaviors as due to uncontrollable arousal or subgroup norms. Moreover, those who attributed their behavior to their wives were more likely to minimize the *severity* of their actions. Similar reports from men in treatment for spouse assault (Ganley, 1981) describe both the minimization of spouse assault and victim blaming or, alternatively, accepting responsibility but redefining the behavior as consistent with cultural norms.

This notion of disavowal of deviance by assaultive males essentially relocates blame for behavior from the individual to an attribute or behavior of their adversary or an imperative in the immediate context. When all else fails, disavowal leads to claiming conformity with cultural norms. This not only serves to excuse misbehavior but also reassures others that the behaviors themselves do not challenge the legitimacy of the violated norms. Thus wife assaulters do not challenge the sanctity of marriage or societal laws against assault.

Individual-Level Explanations

Violence toward intimates, like violence toward strangers, may also be explained by psychological abnormalities such as impulsivity, borderline personality, antisocial personality disorder, or mental illness. High rates of psychopathology are evident among men who assault their wives (Hamberger & Hastings, 1989). Dutton (1995) found high rates of posttraumatic stress disorder among violent male partners, a link from early childhood traumatic exposure to violence to intimate adult violence. Factors such as testosterone levels (Archer, 1991), serotonin (Virkkunen & Linnoila, 1993), and head injury (Lewis, Pincus, Feldman, Jackson, & Bard, 1988) have been linked to violence generally and, increasingly, to partner violence (Warnken, Rosenbaum, Fletcher, Hoge, & Adelman, 1994). These dysfunctions affect personality factors such as impulsivity, cognition, and aggression generally but have been detected at elevated rates among men who are assaultive toward female partners.

An Integrated Explanation of Marital Violence

When integrated, these perspectives suggest that cognitive and emotional factors are interpreted through social psychological processes and cultural beliefs to explain the occurrence of marital violence. Social networks and their subcultural *milieus* determine the social construction of behavior patterns and shape the cognitive and emotional processes that transform arousal to marital aggression. Victimization also influences cognitive processes: Dodge, Bates, and Petit (1990) showed in longitudinal research that

> harmed children are likely to develop biased and deficient patterns of processing social information, including a failure to attend to relevant cues, a bias to attribute hostile intentions to others, and a lack of competent behavioral strategies to solve interpersonal problems. These patterns in turn were found to predict the development of aggressive behavior [and] . . . lead a child to conceptualize the world in . . . ways that perpetuate the cycle of violence. (p. 1682)

These cognitive processes in turn are further influenced by cultural and situational factors that determine the norms, beliefs, and sanctions regarding behaviors following arousal during marital conflict or stress. Three major independent variables increase the probability of violence during microsocial interactions: (a) psychological proclivity toward the exercise of physical violence toward spouses (e.g., personality factors), (b) beliefs that instrumental goals will be achieved through the use of physical force, and (c) arousal that provides the motivation for the (male's) assaultive behavior against the spouse or partner. Each of these factors in turn influences cognitive processes that interpret both the situation and the appropriate behavioral response.

Cultural Factors

Cultural beliefs are expressed through the individual who believes, as he perceives social norms, that violence within families is an acceptable or normative response to marital conflict. Culture therefore has both direct effects, through expectancy of appropriate behaviors when angry or aroused, and indirect effects, through its influence on mediating cognitive processes that define complex emotions as anger. Cultural factors, including beliefs about permitted behaviors in specific milieus, and the cultural meaning of marital violence (ceremonies, spiritual or religious uses, social interaction) shape the context in which behavioral norms are interpreted. These settings and social contexts also influence the choice of behaviors: They convey the rules and norms proscribing behaviors, the cognitive interpretation of the situation, and, accordingly, the probability of marital violence while in that situation.

Personality Factors

An example of an individual personality factor is the propensity to use violence to resolve interpersonal conflicts or the habit strength of violence that has been socially reinforced through past experiences in childhood and during later stages of social and personality development (see, e.g., Megargee, 1983). Violence may be considered the "appropriate" response to anger or the behavior that individuals have learned best achieves their goals. Accordingly, the reinforcement of experiences learned from childhood exposure (either in the home or nearby in other closely observed relationships) provides a set of behaviors invoked in response to conditions that raise fear, anger, vulnerability, or other strong emotions.

The Specific Motivation

Arousal is a transitional state marked by emotional instability. Many of the socioeconomic markers of marital violence also may signify frustration from failure to achieve socially defined expectations of (male) success. This can contribute to a chronic state of frustration and arousal that assailants may label as anger (Browne & Dutton, 1990). These markers also may signify stresses that trigger fear, anxiety, self-derogation, or other states of emotional discomfort. Arousal also may come from threats of loss of control in the relationship, feelings of rejection or abandonment, threats from intimacy or emotional dependence on one's spouse or partner, or threats to social status from outside the relationship. Browne (1987) argued that even emotional states engendered in positive intimate relationships, such as desire or longing, may be reinterpreted by assaultive males as frustration or displeasure, with this effect again mediated by whether intimate relationships in childhood were anxiety provoking or nurturing.

The response to arousal will determine the occurrence of spouse assault. A complex calculus will determine whether the male partner becomes violent under conditions of arousal: earlier lessons about "what works" to quell anxiety or release anger, what he perceives as potential consequences, what he has seen others do in similar situations, and his control over his rage or fear (Browne, 1987; Dutton, 1995). Other factors also may influence whether an attack occurs, especially whether past attacks have been gratifying (that is, have resulted in the reduction of arousal, anger, or anxiety or in the restoration of control) and whether the gains have outweighed any aversive consequences.

Integrating Theories of Marital and Stranger Violence

What may set apart stranger from marital violence, or explain its overlap for a subset of offenders, are the concepts of culturally sanctioned sexual inequalities and traditional sex-role socialization. By integrating these perspectives into a general learning model, it may be possible to understand and explain the various manifestations of violent behavior and patterns of victim selection. Therefore, where sex-role socialization during early childhood is most traditional concurrently with socialization to violence, one would expect to find both extrafamilial and familial violence. In the presence of one of these primary socialization influences but not the other, we would expect to find men who confine their violence to either familial or extrafamilial domains. Where violence is learned, sanctioned, and reinforced through cultural or behavioral norms in the immediate community, violence is more likely to be chronic and/or more serious.

Distinctions between "generally" violent males, those violent only toward family members, and those violent only toward nonfamily members suggest that there are processes specific to victim selection in the development of violent behaviors. Social learning processes describe how socialization occurs where the utility and behavioral norms that express male dominance, as well as the functional value of violence, are passed on. Social supports for violence toward women or children may contribute to male sex-role socialization during childhood (Dobash & Dobash, 1979; Russell, 1982) and help explain in part the selection of family members as victims. When childhood and adolescent socialization includes the threat and/or use of male violence toward family members, there may exist a propensity to commit violent acts against family members during later adult years. It seems that victim selection also may be socially learned, like both violent behavior and its functional value and significance with both strangers and family members.

Summary

Rather than being a linear process, marital violence is more likely to be a reciprocal process in which arousal, personality, situational, and cultural factors have multiple and recursive interactions leading to aggressive or nonaggressive behaviors. Individuals form perceptions of their environments and internalize the expected responses to social situations through the development of personality, which itself is a socially determined process. Both psychological and social experiences with intimates, shaped by the arousal produced by marital dynamics or experiences outside the marital relationship, socialize partners not only to the responses to anger but also to the expected social behaviors that accompany that state. The boundaries of those responses are determined by three factors: (a) perceptions of the expected environment, (b) personality variables such as relative ego autonomy, and (c) responses to the specific marital context. These three processes are influenced strongly by social learning processes that carry forward the lessons of childhood and adolescence. The delicate interplay of these factors responds to the social cues of the setting in which couples interact. From these cues, marital violence by male spouses may follow logically from the controls that are internally activated and the social controls present in the setting.

Legal Responses to Domestic Violence

Beginning in the 1970s, social policy toward women victims of domestic assaults focused on improving legal responses to protect women and punish offenders. For many years, societal responses to domestic violence excluded legal intervention. Advocates for battered women claimed that male batterers were rarely arrested, prosecuted, or sentenced as severely as other violent offenders. Research showed that these claims were accurate. Police often exercised discretion in avoiding arrest in responding to domestic violence incidents in which there was probable cause. In many departments, policies for domestic "disputes" actively discouraged arrest, focusing instead on alternative responses such as family crisis intervention or counseling for batterers with alcohol abuse problems (Bard & Zacker, 1971). Prosecutors failed to actively pursue cases in which victims and offenders had intimate relationships, fearing that women might drop charges (Parnas, 1967). Sentences often were less serious for males convicted of domestic violence. For example, Davis and Smith (1982) showed that the presence of a victim-offender relationship led to less serious case assessments in prosecutorial screening, even after controlling for victim injury and weapon use.

The convergence of interests of feminists, victim advocates, and other criminal justice actors led to a series of reforms beginning in the late 1970s to strengthen legal responses to domestic violence (Lerman, 1981; Zorza, 1992). This "criminalization" of domestic violence cases sought to increase the certainty and severity of legal responses, thereby addressing historical, legal, and moral disparities in the legal protections afforded to battered women (Zorza, 1992). Law and policy emphasized the application of legal sanctions through arrest and prosecution of assailants or the *threat* of legal sanctions through civil legal remedies that carried criminal penalties if violated.

By 1980, 47 states adopted substantially revised domestic violence legislation. These laws took several forms. Many states increased access to protection orders, others enabled warrantless arrest for misdemeanor assaults, and some recognized a history of abuse

and threat as part of a legal defense for battered women who killed their abusive husbands.[7] The most visible of these efforts was directed at the police. Initially, the legislative efforts were designed to give the police additional authority to make misdemeanor arrests. Prior to 1980, in most states, the police were not authorized to make arrests in misdemeanor assaults between intimates or strangers unless the assault occurred in the presence of the police. This legal restriction explains in part why arrest rates for domestic violence reported prior to 1980 appear to be low. In some jurisdictions, the revised domestic violence legislation extended to police the authority to make arrests for all misdemeanor assault; in other jurisdictions, the new authority extended only to domestic assaults against women.

Success on this agenda in many jurisdictions was followed by efforts at both state and local levels to make arrest a mandatory or preferred policy in all instances of domestic violence. Many police departments changed their procedures. Some police agencies supported these policies and their increased authority to make arrests and support for making arrests; some agencies opposed these changes. These changes occurred not only in response to legislative reforms but also pursuant to successful litigation by women against police departments for their failure to enforce criminal laws and protect them from violent partners.[8] Civil court rulings established legal precedents for holding not only jurisdictions but individual police officers personally liable for not making arrests after repeated calls to the same location (Sherman, 1992).

Reforms in protective and restraining-order legislation enabled emergency, ex parte relief that included not only "no-contact" provisions but also economic and other tangible reliefs for battered women (Grau, Fagan, & Wexler, 1984). Police departments adopted proarrest or mandatory arrest policies (Sherman & Cohn, 1989). These reliefs, and the application of criminal laws as well, were extended to women in unmarried cohabiting couples and to divorced or separated women.[9] Domestic violence units were formed in prosecutor's offices (Lerman, 1981). Treatment programs for abusive husbands were launched in probation departments and among community-based groups to provide court-mandated treatment and supervision of batterers (Edelson & Tolman, 1993). A small number of jurisdictions developed coordinated, systemic responses that brought to bear the full range of social controls and victim supports for battered women (Hart, 1995).

At the same time, reforms in civil legal protection also have expanded nationwide (Grau et al., 1984; Harrell, Smith, & Newmark, 1993). Until the legal reforms of the late 1970s, women often could not obtain a restraining order against a violent husband unless they were willing to file for divorce at the same time (U.S. Commission on Civil Rights, 1982). When protective or restraining orders were available, their enforcement was weak, the penalties for violations were minor, and they were not available on an emergency basis.

Many of these reforms have been studied, and the resulting evaluations have produced information to allow us to assess their effects and to identify the factors that have contributed to or worked against their success.

Criminal Legal Sanctions

Experiments in Arrest

Efforts to deter domestic violence have focused primarily, if not unfairly, on the police. At the same time, we know more about the effects of police responses, especially arrest, than about any other legal reform. The Minneapolis Domestic Violence Experiment (Sherman & Berk, 1984) was a critical event in changing public and scholarly perceptions of domestic violence from a "family problem" amenable to mediation and other informal, nonlegal interventions to a law violation requiring a formal criminal justice sanction. In that experiment, street-level police officers'

selections of the most appropriate response to misdemeanor domestic violence were determined by an experimental design of random assignment to one of three treatments: (a) arresting the suspect, (b) ordering one of the parties out of the residence, and (c) advising the couple. Using victim interviews and official records of subsequent police contact, Sherman and Berk (1984, p. 267) reported that the prevalence of subsequent offending—assault, attempted assault, and property damage—was reduced by nearly 50% when the suspect was arrested.

The Minneapolis study's findings were reported in over 300 newspapers in the United States, three major television networks broadcast the study's results in prime time news programs or documentaries, and numerous nationally syndicated columnists and editorials featured the study and its findings (Sherman & Cohn, 1989). The Attorney General's Task Force on Family Violence endorsed the study's findings and recommended that state and local agencies adopt a proarrest policy toward domestic violence (U.S. Attorney General, 1984). Following the attention given to this study's results, a dramatic change in formal policy consistent with the study's proarrest findings has been reported by police departments in both large and small U.S. cities (Sherman & Cohn, 1989).

The enthusiasm for the deterrent effects of legal sanctions reported in the Minneapolis experiment was tempered by known limitations of its design and implementation: only 330 cases (with 114 arrests) from one imperfect study in one not particularly representative jurisdiction. In addition, criticisms of the overreach of its conclusions and concerns about the widespread publicity prior to substantiation of these results through secondary analysis and replication in other jurisdictions (Lempert, 1989) suggested more caution than the media reports conveyed. In fact, replications of the Minneapolis experiment in five other jurisdictions—Charlotte, Colorado Springs, Dade County, Milwaukee, Omaha—produced inconsistent results. Some jurisdictions found some deterrent effects for some measures but the consistent and strong deterrent effects in Minneapolis were not found elsewhere (Garner, Fagan, & Maxwell, 1995).

Whether deterrence through arrest is effective was tested only weakly in the Minneapolis experiment and the replications. In all six sites, the actual implementation of legal sanctions was strong compared to not arresting but relatively weak compared to other legal sanctions. Most offenders were not prosecuted once arrested. Legal sanctions were limited to booking for most of those arrested. Some arrestees were not even handcuffed, most spent only a few hours in custody, and only a small number were jailed overnight (Sherman, 1992). Only misdemeanor cases were included in most of the experiments, leaving out the more serious violent assailants.

Sherman, Smith, Schmidt, and Rogan (1992) examined one hypothesis about why the available evidence from different sites is inconsistent. They reported that for four of the experimental sites, deterrent effects existed for those offenders with stakes in conformity. Stakes in conformity were defined as being married or employed at the time of the arrest. However, for those individuals who were not married or not employed, arrest did not deter subsequent violence but was actually associated with increased rates of violence. Sherman et al. suggested that the disparate findings from Minneapolis and the replication studies stem from the different mix of suspects included in the studies and are not due to differences in police practices. All the available evidence from the police experiments suggests (a) that the effectiveness of arrest at reducing repeat domestic violence is at best marginal, (b) that the effectiveness of arrest and legal interventions may depend on the social context in which they are implemented, and (c) that arrest alone is not a sufficient societal response to domestic violence.

The proarrest policies adopted in the mid-1980s continue to be implemented by police agencies in the 1990s, with much of the debate focusing on whether police department policies should mandate arrest or whether arrest should be the preferred policy. Some officers in some departments responded to mandatory arrest policies by arresting both parties to a dispute, arguing that both arrests were mandated by policies that gave them little discretion. Other departments adopted creative policies to handle situations in which the suspect is absent when the police arrive. One study reported that offenders were absent in as many as 40% of the misdemeanor assaults to which the police were called (Dunford & Elliott, 1990). Policies that call for mandatory or preferred arrest typically pertain only to situations in which the offender is present when the police arrive.

The increased attention to domestic violence and the mixed results of the arrest studies have led researchers, reformers, and policy makers to look beyond the police and arrest to additional policies and practices that can be brought to bear against domestic violence. The innovations in the 1990s brought the resources of other criminal justice agencies to bear in identifying, preventing, and controlling violence.

Prosecution Experiments

Like the police, prosecutors also were accused of lacking interest in domestic violence cases, failing to file cases presented by the police, or discouraging willing victims from pursuing criminal complaints. Whether discouraged by the evidentiary problems in these cases, anticipating the ambivalence and lack of cooperation from victims to press forward with prosecution, assuming that women would ultimately reconcile with their partners and drop charges, adhering to patriarchal notions about family privacy and male prerogatives, or responding to signals from a judiciary who were unwilling to respond to prosecution with meaningful sanctions, prosecutors had little incentive to follow through with vigorous

presentation of domestic violence cases (Elliott, 1989; Ford, 1991).

The creation of special prosecution units
created an atmosphere and structure in prosecutors' offices that gave domestic violence
cases high status. These units created incentives for aggressive prosecution without competing for resources with other high-visibility
cases (Forst & Hernon, 1985). In these units,
screening of cases could include a wider range
of factors than simply the evidence in the case
or the severity of the victim's injuries. Prosecutors could entertain criteria such as the likelihood of future (severe) abuse, the history of
violence in the relationship, or the past frequency of victim injuries. Nevertheless, even
with these reforms, the rate of prosecution
remains extremely low, less than 10% for misdemeanor cases in many communities (Ford,
1993; Schmidt & Hochstadler-Steury, 1989).

Victim choices also influence prosecutorial
decisions to file cases. Victims may have
wider interests in mind than legal sanctions
when filing for prosecution. For example,
Ford (1991) suggested that victims' goals are
instrumental: obtaining money or property,
coercing partners to obtain counseling, or obtaining protection for themselves or their children. Successful prosecution and legal punishment may be secondary in the minds of some
victims to these other goals in increasing their
safety and well-being. To avoid these complications, some prosecutors adopted no-drop
policies that avoided the last-minute withdrawal of charges that frustrated police and
judges. However, this policy may conflict
with some victims' goals or interests and actually dissuade them from seeking prosecution
(Ford, 1993).

Despite the development of special prosecution units, few studies have documented the
effects of prosecution on the control or recurrence of spouse or partner assault. Fagan
(1989) found subgroup differences similar to
those reported by Sherman et al. (1991) for
arrests. Men who had prior arrest records or
lengthy histories of severe violence toward
their partners were more likely to reoffend if
prosecuted than men who were not prosecuted. Again, evidence of iatrogenic or coun-
terdeterrent effects raises serious questions
not only about the deterrent effects of legal
sanctions but also about the interactions of
violent men with legal institutions that may
produce this effect.

The most comprehensive prosecution study
has been the Indianapolis Domestic Violence
Prosecution Experiment (Ford, 1991, 1993).
This study found no significant protective effect for women from prosecution in general;
however, there was a significant reduction in
"severe" violence from *victim-initiated* prosecutorial actions compared with the traditional
police summons-and-prosecution procedure
(Ford, 1993). The results suggest small declines in the rates of recidivism from the victim's use or threat of prosecution.[10]

These studies raise the question of victim
empowerment and the hypothesis that the
threat of prosecution, placed in the hands of
the victim to use in her efforts to end her
partner's violence, may have deterrent effects
equal to the effects of punishment. Several
jurisdictions have encouraged the use of warrants in cases in which in-custody arrests were
not made, creating a "Sword of Damocles"
that hangs over the would-be assailant and
threatens him with further punishment (Dunford, 1990; Ford, 1993). This mechanism
combines the threat of criminal punishment
with the empowerment of victims. Deterrence
stems from the threat of punishment, and this
threat of legal sanctions—the use of warrants—deserves attention as an important
arena for future research and policy.

Batterer Treatment

Treatment interventions for batterers vary
in several respects. Most are court-mandated
programs, some are self-help, and others operate under the aegis of social service or private
agencies. Their underlying assumptions about
domestic violence vary. Their operational

characteristics vary as well, including the duration and frequency of contacts and the objectives of treatment. Most address the need for anger control techniques and the importance of power and control motivations in domestic violence. Most do not allow for "relapse" in the way that substance abuse treatment does (Maxwell, 1994).

There are several types of batterer treatment programs. Edelson and Syers (1991) distinguished three: self-help programs that emphasize anger management strategies and personal responsibility, educational programs that teach through passive learning about the sources of violence and the techniques of anger control, and some combination of the two methods. Harrell et al. (1991) studied programs in Baltimore County based on three types of models of causal and cessation processes: feminist models of power relations, social casework models that emphasize reduction of external stressors and interpersonal dynamics, and cognitive-behavioral models that stress anger management. The latter models also vary in their attention to psychopathological variables versus cognitive deficits in anger control. What is not in evidence in these programs is recognition of different types of batterers or efforts to match batterer profiles to specific treatment types (Saunders & Azar, 1989) or to match different types of batterers to specific types of programs (Andrews et al., 1990). It is unlikely that one program model will be equally effective with all batterers.

There is little systematic evidence to evaluate the effectiveness of batterer interventions. For example, Hamberger and Hastings (1989) reviewed 19 studies published in the 1980s. Only one reported sizable differences in recidivism between treated and untreated batterers. Harrell et al. (1991), comparing outcomes across treatment programs, found recidivism rates of over 60% and no differences among treatment groups. Dobash et al. (1994), evaluating a treatment program in the United Kingdom, found significant reductions in recidi-

vism for treated versus nontreated males in a program that combines treatment and supervision. In this program, cognitive-behavioral therapies are employed that teach recognition and control of anger cues that derive from patriarchal beliefs about gender roles. Supervision of batterers was designed to reinforce treatment gains while increasing surveillance of subsequent violence. The combination of treatment with legal controls is an innovation worthy of further testing and replication.

However, the majority of published studies of batterer treatment are not adequate for assessing the effects of batterer treatment. They have no comparison group, and the few that do rely on comparisons of completers with noncompleters, a bias that compromises the research (Sechrest, White, & Brown, 1979). Experimental designs using control groups of men who are under other forms of legal supervision are not evident in the literature. But such designs are of obvious importance, both to assess treatment effects substantively and to assess the marginal effects of treatment compared to other social or legal interventions. Current research by Robert Davis and colleagues at the New York City Victim Services Agency involves a randomized trial of batterer treatment that addresses many of the limitations of the previous studies (Davis, 1994). Although recidivism rates in batterer treatment are similar to recidivism rates generally for criminal cases, the absence of systematic controls makes it difficult to conclude that there are marginal gains from treatment compared to either incarceration or untreated probation supervision.

Systemic Responses:
The Domestic Violence Court

Recent innovations have focused on the creation of specialized courts to process domestic violence cases and intensive systemic reforms designed to align the components of the civil and criminal legal systems to ensure consistent application of sanctions and reliefs in cases involving domestic violence. "Systemic" programs, such as the comprehensive systems of coordination among legal and community-based programs in Duluth and San Francisco, embed legal sanctions in a dense web of social control that reinforces the messages of treatment and the threats of criminal punishment. However, these programs are difficult to evaluate. Establishing comparison conditions internally or across communities is difficult, making it difficult to sort out the effects of prosecution or advocacy from the effects of treatment. This makes it hard to answer the question of whether or how legal sanctions create a deterrent effect, and again the question of the deterrent effects of legal sanctions is unanswered.

Even within these programs, recidivism rates among treated batterers are comparable to rates for protective order and arrest studies: Recidivism in Duluth ranged from 40% to over half and was invariant over short and long follow-up periods (Hamberger & Hastings, 1989).

The creation of specialized courts for family violence cases responds to the devaluation of these cases in mainstream courts. In many courts, domestic violence cases may be assigned a lower priority for prosecution and punishment when compared to violence cases involving strangers. Specialized domestic violence courts provide substantive dispositions, often batterer treatment programs coupled with probation supervision, that create incentives for prosecutors to complete prosecution.

The Dade County Domestic Violence Court (DCDVC) illustrates these ideas. The DCDVC is a criminal court with a civil component designed by a team of representatives from every segment of the criminal justice system to serve as a coordinated, systemic response to the treatment of domestic violence cases in the courts. The DCDVC, which commenced in November 1992, handles only misdemeanor cases. The members of the court, led by the judiciary, work as a team to reduce family violence. From arrest to completion of sentence, only judges trained in family violence handle the cases. The court recognizes the necessity of expanding traditional roles and limits in an effort to create court reform in a system that has been seen to be ineffective and unresponsive. The founders of the DCDVC believe that the combination of intensive victim services, treatment for batterers, and an active judicial role in the social contexts of the community can improve the control of misdemeanor domestic violence and avoid its escalation to more serious violence and injuries (Goldkamp, Weiland, White, Collins, & Akaydin, 1995).

Civil Legal Sanctions: Protective Orders and the Prosecution of Violators

Reforms in restraining orders for battered women preceded reforms in arrest and criminal law. Beginning with the passage of the Pennsylvania Protection from Abuse Act in 1976, every state now provides for protection orders in cases of domestic violence (Klein, n.d.). How effective are protective orders in stopping domestic violence? Harrell et al. (1993) found that 60% of 300 women interviewed twice in one year after receiving a protective order suffered abuse at least once. Over one in five reported threats to kill, 29% reported severe violence, 24% reported other acts of violence, and 43% reported property damage. Threats and violence did not subside over time: There were no significant differences in the percentage reporting subsequent violence in the first 3 months of the year compared to the final 9 months of the year.

Klein (n.d.) used official records (new arrests for domestic violence, new restraining orders against the same defendant issued by the same victim) to measure reabuse in 644 cases in which temporary restraining orders had been issued. Nearly half (48.8%) of the men reabused their victims within 2 years of the issuance of a restraining order. Moreover, over half (54.5%) were rearrested for other crimes as well. Neither of these studies reported results for comparison or control groups. Grau et al. (1984) found no significant differences in subsequent abuse between women receiving restraining orders and women receiving other interventions; moreover, they reported that subsequent violence was more likely among men with histories of severe domestic violence or prior records of stranger crime.

In some jurisdictions, such as Colorado Springs, police officers can issue an emergency protection order that requires the offender not to return for at least 72 hours. If this order is violated, the police can and do make arrests, even if no new violence occurs. Research on the use of protection orders in the New Jersey courts found that they could be implemented more swiftly by a judicial hearing officer than by a judge but that the orders did not reduce the number of repeat calls to the police, regardless of who issued them (Fagan, Maxwell, Macaluso, & Nahabedian, 1995).

Social and Health Care
Responses to Domestic Violence

The criminal justice system is not the only source of assistance to victims of domestic violence. The expansion of social service options in the 1970s paralleled legal reforms. Today there are over 1,800 programs for victims of domestic violence. Among the most visible of these services are the 1,200 shelters in the United States for battered women and their children. In addition, social service programs offer a variety of services, including hotlines, temporary shelter services, support groups, group and individual counseling, legal advocacy, social service referral and advocacy, services for children of domestic violence, transitional housing, child care, and job training. These programs interface with both victims and other agencies through outreach, community education, and advocacy. Many private individuals, from clergy to social workers and psychologists, also provide services to victims of domestic violence.

In addition to shelters, domestic violence victims frequently request medical services from local doctors, hospitals, and emergency rooms, and the health professions have increased their attentiveness to the violence that causes these injuries as well as medical treatment for the bruises, cuts, head injuries, broken bones, and other injuries that the victims of domestic violence suffer (American Medical Association, 1995).

Shelters

Designed as safe locations where female victims can stay while they remove themselves from abusive relationships, shelters typically provide a range of services or access to services that provide victims of domestic violence with economic, social, psychological, and legal tools to control their lives and prevent future violence. Few studies have characterized the types of victims, primarily women, who are served by shelters. They tend to be from lower socioeconomic groups, often lacking economic resources for hotels or transitional or emergency housing (Fagan et al., 1984; Sullivan, Campbell, Angelique, Eby, & Davidson, 1994). Because shelters serve local populations, their ethnic and racial populations are likely to reflect the areas they serve. Shelter clients may have suffered more serious and prolonged violence than women seeking legal or other social service interventions (Fagan et al., 1984).

Shelters provide both direct and indirect help. Emergency housing and other services offered within shelters are critical interventions. But the indirect help also is essential in reducing the risks of abuse. Women in shelters receive a wide range of services, including legal and social service advocacy; transportation; counseling; child-focused interventions, including schooling and counseling; and employment-related services.

There have been few evaluations of shelters, and there are several challenges to research designs to evaluate shelter interventions. Many shelter residents have multiple stays in a lengthy process of change leading to separation from violence (Fagan et al., 1984; Walker, 1984), with several simultaneous interventions, adding both longitudinal and factorial considerations to measurement of outcome and psychological change. Outcome studies of shelter stays often are descriptive, typically comparing rates of violence before and after shelter stays. Comparisons of outcomes to other forms of intervention have been nonsystematic, with a variety of selection biases limiting their validity. In addition to design problems, shelter evaluations are complicated by decisions regarding which outcomes to measure. In addition to measuring subsequent physical violence and psychological abuse, other outcomes such as victim empowerment present measurement problems. For example, there are no validated measures of empowerment, making comparisons of shelter outcomes across sampling and measurement conditions difficult.

Counseling

Counseling services for victims range in type, duration, underlying theories, and outcomes sought. Counselors may be peers, professionals, or "lay" people, depending on the philosophy and auspices of the program (Fagan et al., 1984). Counseling programs address different concerns. Some focus on concrete social and economic circumstances, others promote victim empowerment and the development of human agency to make decisions and take actions, and others may focus on specific psychological symptoms of battered women such as posttraumatic stress disorder (Gondolf, 1990; Koss, 1990; Resick, 1992). Few programs have been systematically evaluated, for many of the same reasons that have limited the types of evaluations conducted on shelter services.

Counseling services may focus on individuals or couples, and the latter has been a point of controversy in the literature on domestic violence. Some programs argue that couples counseling does not address the underlying dynamics of gender inequality and domination that promote domestic violence and that continued contact between victims and assailants may endanger women. Couples counseling and family systems treatment allocate responsibility equally between victims and offenders, failing to sanction adequately the violent behavior of batterers and risking further violence. In several cases in which family therapy directly precipitated an escalation of violence leading to homicide. Proponents of family or couples counseling suggest that these interventions may best appropriate for couples in discordant but nonviolent relationships or relationships in which violence is rare and less serious (e.g., O'Leary, Heyman, & Neidig, 1995).

Interventions for Child Witnesses of Domestic Violence

The serious developmental and long-term behavioral consequences of childhood exposure to domestic violence have become a focus of interventions for domestic violence. Children of victims of domestic violence have exhibited psychological symptoms indicative of emotional disturbance and in some cases posttraumatic stress disorder (PTSD; Groves et al., 1993; Jaffe, Wolfe, & Wilson, 1990; Wolfe, McPherson, Blount, & Wolfe, 1986).[11] Childhood exposure to domestic violence also is one of the most consistent risk markers for adult battering (Fagan & Browne, 1994; Hotaling & Sugarman, 1986).

Interventions for child witnesses of domestic violence are still relatively new and developing, and there are few evaluation data to describe or assess these programs. These services are provided by mental health providers, within shelters, and in some cases in family preservation programs offered by child welfare agencies. Programs vary in their definitions of "witnessing," and some provide services only to children who were abused themselves, whereas others treat children who express awareness of parental violence. There are legal complications also in the delivery of this service. Child witnessing of parental violence is a reportable form of child abuse in some states, and women who disclose that their children witnessed domestic violence may risk losing them. This provides disincentives for women to seek services for their children.

Health Care Interventions

The modern recognition of child abuse began in health care settings. Although elaborate procedures and laws have been enacted to promote identification and reporting of child abuse, efforts to identify and serve adult victims of domestic violence have lagged far behind (Stark & Flitcraft, 1991). The most common interventions involve protocols to be administered by nursing or medical staff to identify domestic violence victims and make appropriate referrals. Education and training efforts are aimed at implementing protocols so that health care staff have the necessary skills to help battered women confidently. The protocols focus on patterns of injuries and medical histories and the types of treatments and referrals to address medical and other needs. Evaluation data suggest that systematic implementation of domestic violence protocols can improve reporting and referral rates (McLeer & Anwar, 1989; Tilden & Shepard, 1987).

These efforts are focused primarily on the education of health care workers to recognize patterns of injuries and psychological symptoms and to act with appropriate referrals and direct interventions. Because there are no mandatory reporting laws for domestic violence with adult victims, the incentives for identification and reporting are primarily professional and cultural. Efforts to link health care and legal interventions have focused on the health care worker's role in gathering forensic evidence to support legal interventions and also to educate victims about their legal options. These efforts will become even more critical as managed health care becomes the dominant mode of health care financing and decision making.

Coordination of Services

Increasingly, police, health care providers, and social service agencies work together. The police may recommend or even transport victims to shelters or hospitals, hospitals report serious injuries to the police, and shelters protect victims and may assist in promoting victims' willingness to prosecute criminal charges.

Whereas the primary thrust of reform and research in the 1970s and 1980s was to mobilize the police to develop effective alternatives for victims of domestic violence, the primary thrust in the 1990s is for a coordination of a variety of legal, social service, and private resources at the community level. In part, this is derived from the realization that police action alone is unlikely to be sufficient to reduce the amount or severity of domestic violence; it is also in concert with the community policing movement that encourages patrol officers to work with other community resources in solving individual and community problems. Coordination of community resources takes many forms, from increased communication among existing criminal justice and public and private social service agencies to the development and implementation of strategic plans that directly guide the work of many agencies in a consistent program of violence reduction (Hart, 1995).

Programs that address the issue of domestic violence need not focus on individuals; they can be implemented at the community level. Some jurisdictions promote the dissemination of information to victims about the availability of services and to the general public that are designed to change attitudes toward and acceptance of domestic violence. This approach attempts to influence the social context directly and is in many ways comparable to the community approaches used by the public health service. The community-level approach to domestic violence, however, is still embryonic, and many questions remain as to the appropriate ways to coordinate public and private responses to domestic violence. In some communities, the police take an active role in developing and implementing a community-wide approach. This is due in part to the police role as a 24-hour-a-day service and the typically large size of police agencies compared to other social services. But, in other communities, the coordination of services is led by private organizations, and it is not clear, in theory or in practice, what the structure of community coordination should look like. Though showing much promise, the experience with community coordination as an approach to respond to domestic violence is too limited to determine how much coordination is needed and when additional coordination is unnecessary or even gets in the way of effective individual action and innovation.

Why Sanctions Have Not Worked

There is little conclusive evidence of either deterrent or protective effects of legal sanctions or mandatory treatment interventions for domestic violence. Several issues can be identified to explain why past research has failed to locate deterrent effects and whether and how law influences the control of domestic violence. The issues fall into three general domains: the complex social and individual contexts in which domestic violence exists, weak research designs and limitations on policy experiments, and the theoretical issues in male violence.

Social and Economic Contexts of Deterrence

The experiments on arrest on domestic violence raised important hypotheses concerning the interaction of criminal punishment with extralegal social bonds. The lesson of these studies is that formal (legal) sanctions tend to be effective when reinforced by informal social controls and weakened when those informal controls are absent (Tittle & Logan, 1973). In other words, the deterrent effects of arrest will be greater for batterers who perceive higher social costs associated with the act of violence and with arrest (see Bowker, 1983). These costs include loss of job, relationship and children, and social status in the neighborhood, in addition to whatever substantive punishment batterers receive. When batterers perceive that punishment is not a cost worth avoiding, legal sanctions alone are unlikely to induce compliance with the law.

In both Minneapolis and the other arrest replication sites, the cases disproportionately came from neighborhoods with concentrations of the risk factors for violence generally: high unemployment, poverty, and divorce rates. The lower potential in these neighborhoods for job or relationship loss or for social stigmatization from neighbors or relatives may attenuate the development of informal social controls and in turn undermine the effectiveness of legal controls. This suggests that opportunity structures at the neighborhood or community level have direct effects on the availability of informal (or extralegal) individual-level controls that are critical reinforcers of legal sanctions.

The Complexity of Domestic Violence

Domestic violence differs significantly from other forms of violence in several important ways. First, there are strong emotional ties between victims and assailants. The parties often love one another, or, at least, the victim may love the assailant. The bond may be traumatic (Dutton & Browning, 1988), complicating victim resolve to enter into a lengthy adversarial proceeding to invoke punishments and creating internal conflict regarding separation. The victim may be financially dependent on the assailant or face the prospects of a severely diminished standard of living if separated. Arguably, she faces an economic life at or below the official threshold of poverty on leaving the relationship (Sidel, 1986). Because of these ties to assailants, victims may be less concerned with deterrence than with using legal institutions to guarantee their own safety, survive economically, protect their children, or get counseling help for their assailants (Ford, 1991). Thus victim choices about invoking legal sanctions may be less concerned with punishment and deterrence and may ultimately seek to use the law for other goals.

Second, domestic violence often is a recurring event between individuals in daily contact, usually without the forms of guardianship and surveillance that are available in public spaces. Unlike robberies, in which victims and offenders often are unacquainted, or other assaults involving acquaintances, victims and assailants often occupy the same space, share and compete for resources, and have emotional ties. In this context, threats are readily conveyed and quite believable. On the other hand, it is extremely difficult to mount and maintain a deterrent threat within a context of ongoing and unsupervised contact between victim and assailant.

Third, the scale of domestic violence makes it difficult to control solely through legal sanctions and deterrent threats. The base rates remain quite high relative to other violent crimes. The high rates of domestic violence make it difficult for police departments to arrest every man who commits a misdemeanor or felony assault against his partner, much less to arrest him every time he does it, without paralyzing their own agencies and the courts. Police departments are challenged to maintain a credible deterrent threat in cases in which arrests do not occur, in the face of a high base rate of the crime.

Finally, the deterrence logic of criminalization assumes a rational offender-actor who weighs the costs of offending—costs associated both with the act itself and the legal actions that ensue—against whatever benefits may accrue from their behavior. This logic is strained in the context of domestic violence. Episodes of rage during more serious assaults often obviate rational calculations and perceptions of costs (Browne, 1987). Studies with batterers in treatment suggest conditions of impaired cognition, hostility, and antisocial personality disorder (Dutton, 1995). The logic of deterrence is compromised among batterers whose behavior is patterned over time and for whom rational calculations are not possible during the arousal or rage in a violent assault. Among violent men whose behaviors are increasingly spiraling out of control, the threat of punishment may be remote and inconsequential under conditions of arousal and cognitive distortion.

Weak Research and Evaluation Designs

With few exceptions, the empirical literature on the effectiveness of the use of legal sanctions in response to domestic violence is characterized by weak evaluation designs. Experiments are rare as are clinical trials for treatment interventions. Most studies have small samples and limited experimental power. Follow-up periods are short, making it impossible to see longer-term impacts that may accrue. Budgetary limitations for many grant programs historically have constrained the results of research and evaluation on domestic violence. If the development and testing of theory is a cumulative process from repeated experiments, the foundations of empirical knowledge to advance theory and practice are not available for domestic violence.[12]

A related concern is the narrow range of sanctions in most experiments on legal interventions. Since the 1970s, the range of legal sanctions for batterers has expanded at a glacially slow pace. Although arrests have increased, the substantive sanction in most cases remains simply the process of arrest. The range of sanctions in the arrest experiments expanded in small increments. A small percentage of the arrestees spent any time in jail. Prosecution rates remain low. Pretrial and postconviction treatment regimens vary widely in the intensity of the treatment and the burdens they place on assailants. There is limited evidence of the use of incarceration or more intensive forms of supervision unless injuries are serious. When the range of punishments or sanctions is narrow in this way, the validity of tests of deterrence is intrinsically weak and the likelihood of detecting a reduction in violence appears remote.

Finally, exogenous influences on sanction effects often are not addressed in research on domestic violence. For example, subcultural influences may overwhelm the effects of legal sanctions or treatments in motivating domestic violence. That is, high divorce rates may devalue marriage or coupling, weakening the informal controls on violence that work reciprocally with legal sanctions. Residential mobility, high rates of poverty, and weak social cohesion are dimensions of social disorganization that weaken informal social controls on violence generally and undermine motivations for compliance with the law.

Heterogeneity of Batterers

Most research on the effects of legal sanctions for domestic violence has treated batterers as a homogenous group. This obscures potentially important subgroup differences in the effects of legal sanctions. Yet it is likely that legal sanctions will have different effects for different types of batterers. Just as domestic violence is best understood from the characteristics of batterers (Hotaling & Sugarman, 1986), so too may differing effects of legal sanctions be best understood from differences in the battering careers of violent males.

Several studies have suggested typologies of batterers that distinguish them along several dimensions. Holzworth-Munroe and Stuart (1994) identified three dimensions that distinguish among subtypes of batterers: severity of

marital violence, generality of violence (toward strangers as well as intimates), and psychopathology or personality disorders. On the basis of these dimensions, three types of batterers are hypothesized: family-only, generally violent, and dysphoric or borderline personality batterers. Each of these types is hypothesized to be involved in different levels of severity of domestic violence. There is utility in typologies such as these to predict responses to legal sanctions. For example, impulsivity and low self-control characterize generally violent batterers—personality variables that may complicate the rationality logic of deterrence logic. The "family-only" batterer engages in the least severe forms of violence and also exhibits the lowest levels of impulsivity and may be most amenable to legal sanctions.

These dimensions are rarely considered in research on domestic violence, yet they should be an important component of sanction and treatment research. Treatment research with offenders generally has recognized the importance of "responsivity" of different types of individuals to various interventions (Andrews et al., 1990). Understanding the effects of legal sanctions for batterers must account for the different responses of different types of batterers to both types of sanctions and their "doses." These factors also may be important and useful in sorting cases for prosecution or in determining the extent to which sanctions may risk victim safety.

Theories of Interpersonal Violence Versus Theories of Domestic Violence

A corollary concern is the extent to which theories of violence generally inform research on domestic violence, including the effects of legal sanctions. The typology suggested by Holzworth-Munroe and Stuart (1994) is based on a range of personality and developmental variables that were derived not only from research on batterers but from the literature on violence generally. Yet theory and research on domestic violence has segregated theories of violence from theories of battering. The social and ideological constructions of battering have limited the types of variables considered in research on domestic violence. Assuming that patriarchy and power relations alone cause domestic violence leads us toward conclusions that do not consider a full array of explanatory variables from other disciplines (Fagan & Browne, 1994). However, assuming that domestic violence is caused by a more complex set of hierarchical influences—for example, weak social controls, situational arousal, or even psychopathology—may lead us in quite another direction. The importance of recognizing factors from theories of violence that may influence the effects of legal sanctions is evident from the types of variables that define the typologies of batterers. Their inclusion offers a significant advance over the current level of empirical knowledge.

Conflicts in Goals

Criminal legal institutions—police, prosecutors, judges, probation—tend to have objectives that may or may not coincide with improving the safety of victims of domestic violence. As we have seen, the evidence that arrests reduce domestic violence is mixed, and the evidence for the effectiveness of other criminal justice interventions virtually nonexistent. Legal reforms in the previous two decades have promoted more aggressive and in most cases more punitive responses to domestic violence. These goals conform to the traditional goals of many criminal justice professionals and the organizations for which they work: More arrests, more prosecutions, and more convictions are good and in themselves measures of success.

However, these goals may not promote and in some instances may be in conflict with the goal of increased safety for the victims of domestic violence. As we have seen, as a general strategy, arrest may not affect subsequent domestic violence; other types of criminal justice sanctions or mandated treatment programs may have similarly weak or nonexistent effects. By focusing on the goal of more punishment for batterers, we may overlook the ultimate goal of less violence. The punitive legal reforms of the 1980s have assumed that more arrests, more prosecutions, and more convictions will result in less violence—deterrence goals that have eluded social policy in other domains of illegal behavior. The difficulty lies in the traditional use of the criminal law to achieve legitimate social aims.

One result of the reforms in domestic violence is the coexistence of policy goals in legal institutions both to *punish offenders* and to *protect victims*. These goals may be reciprocal as policy but may be in conflict at the operational level. Creating expectations for police and prosecutors to invoke informal social controls, in which legal sanctions play an indirect role, may require tasks and roles for which agency personnel are not well trained or that may contradict the roles and expectations in their jobs with respect to other types of crimes. It may require legal actors to pursue goals in domestic violence cases that they do not pursue in other types of crimes. Also, for crimes of the scale of domestic violence, it may be unrealistic to expect legal institutions to control effectively crimes that affect significant portions of the population.

Domestic violence is best explained by the characteristics of men, and social control is most effective when legal controls interact reciprocally with extralegal social controls. This suggests that legal institutions may be most effective in stopping domestic violence when focusing on the detection, punishment, and control of batterers and less effective when focusing on the coordination of extralegal services to protect battered women.

The Future

In the future, victims of domestic violence may suffer from the same personal, cultural, and economic structures that generate the level of violence manifest in our society today, or these structures may change. Recent policy initiatives may prove inadequate or even counterproductive in reducing violence. More likely, as Pleck's (1987) historical account suggests, the current level of policy and research attention will not be sustained in the ebb and flow of public attention.

The future need not be like the past. There are many indications that the contemporary focus on the victims of domestic violence can have permanent effects on how our society responds to knowledge about role of violence in the family and the alternative ways in which a variety of legal and social institutions have (and have not) addressed this violence. First, the current attention has been relatively long lasting, spanning 25 years, and there are no signs that this concern shows any sign of abating. Second, the widespread reforms have attracted considerable research attention. The number of articles and books about domestic violence and about the relative effectiveness of alternative responses is voluminous, and the amount of knowledge has grown substantially. Third, what began as a plank in the program of a radical political movement has succeeded in building collaborative relationships with more established and traditionally conservative social institutions such as police agencies, court systems, and medical services. The broad political and ideological spectrum of support for addressing violence in the home suggests the possibility of breaking historical cycles of attention and lack of interest. Last, reform and research have worked together in a generally supportive collaboration. This has not always been the case and will not always be the case. The Minneapolis Domestic Violence Experiment promoted proarrest policies, but the replication experiments suggested caution about the existence and the size of arrest's deterrent effects. Research on domestic violence is substantial compared to other areas of violence or criminal justice operations, and the concomitant growth in knowledge has supported the policy discussion and contributed to the direction of reforms.

The greatest threat to the two decades of sustained attention to domestic violence may come more from its success than from indifference. Domestic violence has grown to be a separate reform movement and a separate academic discipline, and it is this separation that may result in domestic violence becoming lost in a rapidly changing society. There is little theoretical rationale for treating domestic violence as different from other forms of violence, and the contemporary focus is on violence generally, not specific types of victims. Like other forms of violence, domestic violence, especially repeat violence that escalates toward fatalities, is preventable when interventions are carefully and strategically allocated to those offenders and victims at risk (Petrie & Garner, 1990).

The growth of social services, police programs, prosecutorial units, legal protections, shelters, coordinated programs, batterer treatments, and other approaches to addressing domestic violence has preceded solid empirical evidence that these approaches are the most effective approaches. If any of these approaches were a drug, they would all require years of testing by the Food and Drug Administration to protect victims from ineffective or even violence-enhancing efforts. We do not recommend against innovation; on the contrary, we do not want contemporary innovations, most of which have little or no evidence that they do in fact reduce violence, to become a new orthodoxy that precludes the introduction of new and perhaps more effective methods to help victims of domestic violence. It is inevitable that some current practices and programs will have negative consequences for victims. Without adequate knowledge of why those practices and programs were not successful, we will not make steady progress toward less violence in our lives and our society.

Notes

1. Child welfare and advocacy groups were active in promoting recognition of child abuse, and feminist activists and victim-witness advocates were critical in the development of legislation and programs for victims of adult partner abuse (Gordon, 1988).

2. Researchers studying marital rape typically avoid the term *rape* and instead usually ask respondents if they were ever sexually assaulted by their spouse or partner (Fagan et al., 1984), or if they were "forced to have sex" with their partner (Walker, 1984). Some studies ask about "unwanted sexual experiences" (Russell, 1982) or having sex in response to force or the threat of force or violence (Finkelhor & Yllö, 1983). Pagelow (1984) asked women if they had submitted to sexual demands to prevent beatings or other reprisals. Such diversity in item construction obviously suggests caution in comparing studies or drawing conclusions.

3. The Guttman procedure yielded a coefficient of scalability of .639 and a coefficient of reproducibility of .890, both well above the common standard for accepting scale validity.

4. During the period in which these women were living with their partners—from the mid-1960s to the late 1970s—legal and extralegal resources targeted for abused wives were either not available or only just beginning to be put in place.

5. Gelles (1983) discussed resource theory as an example of violence by males that is compensatory for a lower social or economic position within the couple.

6. Others, such as Dobash and Dobash (1979), view patriarchy as a system of economic and cultural control that preserves the dominance and power of males over women.

7. The "battered woman's" defense was applied not only in cases in which the woman killed the man during an attack but also in cases in which the man was not actively threatening or abusing the woman at the time of the incident (Browne, 1987).

8. See, for example, *Thurman v. City of Torrington* (1984).

9. However, throughout this period in nearly every state, civil and criminal legal sanctions have remained separate though parallel remedies, with divergent underlying legal theories and behavioral assumptions. Although legislatures have acted to increase the use of both civil and criminal legal sanctions to control domestic violence, there is continuing discussion of how the court system can most effectively protect domestic violence victims.

10. These conditions reduce the statistical power of the experiment and limit its impact on theory and policy. Statistical power is an estimate of the probability of falsely rejecting a null hypothesis—that is, detecting a significant effect when in fact it may not be valid (Cohen, 1988). In this case, the small effect size and limited sample sizes suggest that these findings may well result from chance.

11. Symptoms of emotional disturbance include depression, anxiety, withdrawal, hostile attribution, poor social skills, and behavioral disturbances such as aggressive or hostile behavior. PTSD symptoms include sleep disturbances, concentration problems, flashbacks, and hypervigilance.

12. There have been advances in research designs used. Prior to the Minneapolis Domestic Violence Experiment, alternative police responses were judged on the basis of the safety of the responding officers, not the safety of the victim of domestic violence (Garner & Clemmer, 1986).

References

American Medical Association. (1995). *Report card: Violence in America.* Chicago, IL: American Medical Association.

Andrews, D. A., Zinger, I., Hoge, R. D., Bonta, J., Gendreau, P., & Cullen, F. T. (1990). Does correctional treatment work? A clinically relevant and psychologically informed meta-analysis. *Criminology, 28,* 369-397.

Archer, J. (1991). The influence of testosterone on human aggression. *British Journal of Psychology, 82,* 1-28.

Bandura, A. (1973). *Aggression: A social learning analysis.* Englewood Cliffs, NJ: Prentice Hall.

Bard, M., & Zacker, J. (1971). Assaultiveness and alcohol use in family disputes: Police perspectives. *Criminology, 12,* 281-292.

Barling, J., O'Leary, K. D., Jouriles, E. N., Vivian, D., & McEwen, K. E. (1987). Factor similarity of the Conflict Tactics Scales across samples, spouses, and sites: Issues and implications. *Journal of Family Violence, 2,* 37-55.

Binder, A., & Meeker, J. W. (1988). Experiments as reforms. *Journal of Criminal Justice, 16,* 347-358.

Block, C. R. (1987, November). *Lethal violence at home: Racial/ethnic differences in domestic homicide in Chicago, 1965 to 1981.* Paper presented at the annual meeting of the American Society of Criminology, Chicago.

Bograd, M., & Yllö, K. (1988). *Feminist perspectives on wife abuse.* Beverly Hills, CA: Sage.

Bowker, L. (1983). *Beating wife-beating.* Lexington, MA: D. C. Heath.

Browne, A. (1987). *When battered women kill.* New York: Macmillan.

Browne, A. (1993). Violence against women by male partners: Prevalence, incidence, and policy implications. *American Psychologist, 48,* 1077-1087.

Browne, A., & Dutton, D. G. (1990). Risks and alternatives for abused women: What do we currently know? In R. Roesch, D. G. Dutton, & V. F. Sacco (Eds.), *Family violence: Perspectives in research and practice.* Vancouver, BC: Simon Fraser University.

Browning, J. J., & Dutton, D. G. (1986). Assessment of wife assault with the Conflict Tactics Scale: Using couple data to quantify the differential reporting effects. *Journal of Marriage and the Family, 48,* 375-379.

Bruno v. Codd, 47 N.Y. 582, 393 N.E. 976, 419 N.Y.S. 901 (1979).

Brutz, J. L., & Ingoldsby, B. B. (1984). Conflict resolution in Quaker families. *Journal of Marriage and the Family, 46,* 21-26.

Clarke, C. (1987). *Domestic violence: A study of interpersonal homicide.* Unpublished manuscript. R&E Research Associates, San Francisco.

Cohen, J. (1988). *Statistical power analysis for the behavioral sciences.* Hillsdale, NJ: Lawrence Erlbaum.

Coleman, D. H., & Straus, M. A. (1986). Marital power, conflict, and violence in a nationally representative sample of American couples. *Violence and Victims, 1*(2):141-157.

Davis, R. C., & Smith, B. (1982). Crimes between acquaintances: The response of the criminal courts. *Victimology: An International Journal, 8,* 175-187.

Davis, R. C., & Taylor, B. G. (1994). Coordinated response to domestic violence: A field experiment. Proposal submitted to the National Institute of Justice.

Davis, R. C., & Taylor, B. G. (in press). A proactive response to family violence: The results of a randomized experiment. *Criminology.*

Dobash, R. E., & Dobash, R. P. (1979). *Violence against wives: A case against the patriarchy.* New York: Free Press.

Dobash, R. P., Dobash, R. E., Cavanagh, K. & Lewis, R. (1994). *Research evaluation of programmes for violent men.* Cardiff, Wales: University of Wales, Violence Research Unit.

Dobash, R. P., Dobash, R. E., Wilson, M., & Daly, M. (1992). The myth of sexual symmetry in marital violence. *Social Problems, 39,* 71-91.

Dodge, K. A., Bates, J. E., & Petit, G. S. (1990). Mechanisms in the cycle of violence. *Science, 250,* 1678-1683.

Dunford, F. W. (1990). Victim initiated warrants for suspects of misdemeanor domestic assault: A pilot study. *Justice Quarterly, 7,* 631-653.

Dunford, F. W., & Elliott, D. S. (1990). The role of arrest in domestic assault: The Omaha experiment. *Criminology, 28,* 183-206.

Dutton, D. G. (1985). An ecologically tested theory of male violence toward intimates. *International Journal of Women's Studies, 8*(4):404-413.

Dutton, D. G. (1988). *The domestic assault of women: Psychological and criminal justice perspectives.* Boston: Allyn & Bacon.

Dutton, D. G. (1995). *The domestic assault of women: Psychological and criminal justice perspectives* (2nd ed.). Boston: Allyn & Bacon.

Dutton, D. G., & Browning, J. J. (1988). Concern for power, fear of intimacy, and aversive stimuli for wife abuse. In G. T. Hotaling, D. Finkelhor, J. T. Kilpatrick, & M. Straus (Eds.), *Family abuse and its consequences: New directions for research* (pp. 163-175). Beverly Hills, CA: Sage.

Edelson, J. L., Syers, M., & Brygger, M. P. (1987). *Comparative effectiveness of group treatment for men who batter.* Paper presented at the third National Conference on Family Violence Research, Durham, NH.

Edelson, J. L., & Tolman, R. M. (1993). *Intervention for men who batter: An ecological approach.* Newbury Park, CA: Sage.

Elliott, D. S. (1989). Criminal justice procedures in family violence crimes. *Crime and Justice: An Annual Review of Research, 11,* 427-480.

Ellis, D. (1989). Male abuse of a married or cohabiting female partner: Applications of sociological theory to research findings. *Violence and Victims, 4*(4):235-256.

Fagan, J. (1989). Cessation from family violence: Deterrence and dissuasion. *Crime and Justice: An Annual Review of Research, 11* 357-426.

Fagan, J. (1993). Social structure and spouse assault. In B. Forst (Ed.), *The socio-economics of crime and justice* (pp. 209-254). Toronto: M. E. Sharpe.

Fagan, J. (1995). *The criminalization of domestic violence: Promises and limitations* (National Institute of Justice Research Monograph). Washington, DC: U.S. Dept. of Justice.

Fagan, J., & Browne, A. (1994). Violence against spouses and intimates. In A. J. Reiss, Jr., & J. A. Roth (Eds.), *Understanding and preventing violence* (Vol. 3, pp. 115-292). Washington, DC: National Academy Press.

Fagan, J., Friedman, E., Wexler, S., & Lewis, V. O. (1984). *Final report: National family violence evaluation* (Grant 80-JN-AX-0004, Office of Juvenile Justice and Delinquency Prevention). Washington, DC: U.S. Dept. of Justice.

Fagan, J., Maxwell, C., Macaluso, L., & Nahabedian, C. (1995). *Evaluation of the Domestic Violence Hearing Officer Pilot Program: Final report.* Trenton, NJ: Administrative Office of the Courts.

Federal Bureau of Investigation (FBI). (1993). *Crime in the United States.* Washington, DC: Government Printing Office.

Finkelhor, D., & Yllö, K. (1983). Rape in marriage: A sociological view. In D. Finkelhor, R. J. Gelles, G. T. Hotaling, & M. A. Straus (Eds.), *The dark side of families: Current family violence research.* Beverly Hills, CA: Sage.

Ford, D. (1993). *The Indianapolis Domestic Violence Prosecution Experiment* (Final Rep., Grant 86-IJ-CX-0012, to the National Institute of Justice). Indianapolis: Indiana University.

Ford, D. A. (1991). Prosecution as a power source: A note on empowering women in violent conjugal relationships. *Law and Society Review, 25,* 313-334.

Forst, B., & Hernon, J. C. (1985). *The criminal justice response to victim harm* (National Institute of Justice Research in Brief). Washington, DC: U.S. Dept. of Justice.

Frieze, I. H., & Browne, A. (1989). Violence in marriage. In L. Ohlin & M. Tonry (Eds.), *Family violence. Vol. 11: Crime and justice: An annual review of research.* Chicago: University of Chicago Press.

Frieze, I. H., Knoble, J., Zomnir, G., & Washburn, C. (1980, March). *Types of battered women.* Paper presented at the meeting of the Association of Women in Psychology, Santa Monica, CA.

Ganley, A. L. (1981). *Participants manual: Court-mandated therapy for men who batter. A three day workshop for professionals.* Washington, DC: Center for Women's Policy Studies.

Garner, J., & Clemmer, E. (1986). *Danger to police in domestic disturbances: A new look* (National Institute of Justice Research in Brief). Washington, DC: U.S. Dept. of Justice.

Garner, J., Fagan, J., & Maxwell, C. D. (1995). Published findings from the NIJ Spouse Assault Replication Program: A critical review. *Journal of Quantitative Criminology, 8,* 1-29.

Gelles, R. J. (1983). An exchange/social control theory. In D. Finkelhor, R. J. Gelles, G. T. Hotaling, & M. A. Straus (Eds.), *The dark side of families: Current family violence research.* Beverly Hills, CA: Sage.

Gelles, R. J., & Straus, M. A. (1979). Determinants of violence in the family: Toward a theoretical integration. In W. Burr, R. Hill, F. I. Nye, & I. L. Reiss (Eds.), *Contemporary theories about the family.* New York: Free Press.

Gelles, R. J., & Straus, M. A. (1988). *Intimate violence.* New York: Simon & Schuster.

Goldberg, W., & Tomlanovich, M. (1984). Domestic violence victims in the emergency department. *Journal of the American Medical Association, 251,* 3259-3264.

Goldkamp, J. S., Weiland, D., White, M., Collins, M., & Akaydin, S. (1995). Integrating batterer and substance abuse treatment in Dade County's Domestic Violence Court: Experimental assessment of treatment outcomes, Working Report II. Philadelphia: Crime and Justice Research Institute.

Gondolf, E. W. (1985). Fight for control: A clinical assessment of men who batter. *Social Casework: The Journal of Contemporary Social Work, 66,* 48-54.

Gondolf, E. W. (1990). *Psychiatric responses to family violence: Identifying and confronting neglected danger.* Lexington, MA: Lexington.

Gordon, L. (1988). *Heroes of their own lives: The politics and history of family violence.* New York: Viking.

Grau, J., Fagan, J., & Wexler, S. (1984). Restraining orders for battered women: Issues in access and efficacy. *Women and Politics, 4,* 13-28.

Groves, B., Zuckerman, B., Marans, S., & Cohen, D. (1993). Silent victims: Children who witness violence. *Journal of the American Medical Association, 269,* 262-264.

Groves, R. M., & Kahn, R. L. (1979). *Surveys by telephone: A national comparison with personal interviews.* New York: Academic Press.

Hamberger, K. L., & Hastings, J. E. (1989). Counseling male spouse abusers: Characteristics of treatment completers and dropouts. *Violence and Victims, 4,* 275-286.

Harrell, A. (1991). Evaluation of court-ordered treatment for domestic violence offenders: Final report. Washington, DC: Urban Institute.

Harrell, A., Smith, B., & Newmark, L. (1993). *Court processing and the effects of restraining orders for domestic violence victims: Final report to the State Justice Institute.* Washington, DC: Urban Institute.

Hart, B. J. (1995). *Coordinated community approaches to domestic violence.* Paper presented at the Strategic Planning Workshop on Violence Against Women, National Institute of Justice, Washington, DC.

Herzberger, S. (1983). Social cognition and the transmission of abuse. In D. Finkelhor, R. J. Gelles, G. T. Hotaling, & M. A. Straus (Eds.), *The dark side of families: Current family violence research.* Beverly Hills, CA: Sage.

Holzworth-Munroe, A., & Stuart, G. L. (1994). Typologies of male batterers: Three subtypes and differences among them. *Psychological Bulletin, 116,* 476-497.

Hotaling, G. T., & Sugarman, D. B. (1986). An analysis of risk markers in husband to wife violence: The current state of knowledge. *Violence and Victims, 1,* 101-124.

Jaffe, P., Wolfe, D., & Wilson, S. (1990). *Children of battered women.* Newbury Park, CA: Sage.

Jaffe, P., Wolfe, D. A., Telford, A., & Austin, G. (1986). The impact of police charges in incidents of wife abuse. *Journal of Family Violence, 1,* 37-49.

Kennedy, L. W., & Dutton, D. G. (1987). *Edmonton Area Series Report No. 53: The incidence of wife assault in Alberta.* Population Research Laboratory. University of Alberta, Edmonton.

Klein, A. R. (n.d.). *Re-abuse in a population of court-restrained male batterers.* Unpublished manuscript, Quincy Court Domestic Violence Program, Quincy, MA.

Koss, M. P. (1990). The women's mental health research agenda: Violence against women. *American Psychologist, 45,* 374-380.

Lempert, R. (1989). Humility is a virtue: On the publication of policy relevant research. *Law and Society Review, 23,* 145-161.

Lentzner, H. R., & DeBerry, M. M. (1980). *Intimate victims: A study of violence among friends and relatives.* Washington, DC: U.S. Dept. of Justice, Bureau of Justice Statistics.

Lerman, L. G. (1981). Criminal prosecution of wife beaters. *Response to Violence in the Family, 4*(3), 1-19.

Levinger, G. (1966). Sources of marital dissatisfaction among applicants for divorce. *American Journal of Orthopsychiatry, 36,* 804-806.

Lewis, D. O., Pincus, J. H., Feldman, M., Jackson, L., & Bard, B. (1988). Neuropsychiatric, psychoeducational, and family characteristics of 14 juveniles condemned to death in the United States. *American Journal of Psychiatry, 145,* 584-589.

Lockhart, L. L. (1987). A reexamination of the effects of race and social class on the incidence of marital violence: A search for reliable differences. *Journal of Marriage and the Family, 49,* 603-610.

Makepeace, J. M. (1981). Courtship violence among college students. *Family Relations, 30,* 97-102.

Makepeace, J. M. (1983). Life events stress and courtship violence. *Family Relations, 32,* 101-109.

Martin, D. (1976). *Battered wives.* New York: Kangaroo.

Mason, A., & Blankenship, V. (1987). Power and affiliation, motivation, stress and abuse in intimate relationships. *Journal of Personality and Social Psychology, 52,* 203-310.

Maxwell, S. R. (1994). *Formal and informal social control of drug treatment retention of offenders.* Unpublished doctoral dissertation, Rutgers University.

McClelland, D. C. (1975). *Power: The Inner Experience.* New York: Irvington.

McLeer, S., & Anwar, R. (1989). A Study of women presenting in an emergency department. *American Journal of Public Health, 79,* 65-67.

Megargee, E. I. (1983). Psychological determinants and correlates of criminal violence. In M. E. Wolfgang & N. A. Weiner (Eds.), *Criminal violence.* Beverly Hills, CA: Sage.

Mercy, J. A., & Saltzman, L. E. (1989). Fatal violence among spouses in the United States, 1976-85. *American Journal of Public Health, 79,* 595-599.

Meredith, W. H., Abbott, D. A., & Adams, S. L. (1986). Family violence: Its relation to marital and parental satisfactions and family strengths. *Journal of Family Violence, 1,* 299-305.

Miller, S., & Simpson, S. (1991). Courtship violence and social control: Does gender matter? *Law and Society Review, 25,* 335-367.

Nisonoff, L. & Bitman, l. (1979). Spouse abuse: Incidence and relationship to selected demographic variables. *Victimology, 4,* 131-139.

O'Leary, K. D., & Arias, I. (1988). Assessing agreement of reports of spouse abuse. In G. T. Hotaling, D. Finkelhor, J. T. Kirkpatrick, & M. A. Straus (Eds.), *Family abuse and its consequences: New directions for research* (pp.). Newbury Park, CA: Sage.

O'Leary, K. D., Heyman, R. E., & Neidig, P. H. (1995, July). *An empirical comparison of physical aggression couples treatment versus gender-specific treatment.* Paper presented at the 4th International Family Violence Research Conference, Durham, NH.

Pagelow, M. D. (1984). *Family Violence.* New York: Praeger.

Parnas, R. J. (1967). Police response to domestic violence. *Wisconsin Law Review, 31,* 914-960.

Petrie, C., & Garner, J. (1990). Is violence preventable? In D. Besharov (Ed.), *Family violence: Research and public policy issues* (pp. 164-184). Lanham, MD: AEI.

Pleck, E. (1987). *Domestic tyranny: The making of American social policy against family violence from colonial times to the present.* New York: Oxford University Press.

Reiss, A. J., Jr., & Roth, J. A. (1993). *Understanding and preventing violence.* Washington, DC: National Academy Press.

Resick, P. A. (1992). Cognitive treatment of crime-related PTSD. In R. Peters, R. McMahon, & V. Quinsey (Eds.),

Aggression and violence throughout the lifespan (pp. 171-191). Newbury Park, CA: Sage.

Russell, D. E. H. (1982). *Rape in marriage.* New York: Macmillan.

Saltzman, L. E., Mercy, J. A., Rosenberg, M. L., Elsea, W. R., Napper, G., Sikes, R. K., Waxweiler, R., & Collaborative Working Group for the Study of Family and Intimate Assaults in Atlanta. (1990). Magnitude and patterns of family and intimate assaults in Atlanta, Georgia, 1984. *Violence and Victims, 5,* 3-18.

Saunders, D. G. (1988). Other "truths" about domestic violence: A reply to McNeely and Robinson-Simpson. *Social Work,* 179-184.

Saunders, D. G., & Azar, S. T. (1989). Treatment programs for family violence. *Crime and Justice: An Annual Review of Research, 11.*

Schmidt, J., & Hochstadler-Steury, E. (1989). Prosecutorial discretion in filing charges in domestic violence cases. *Criminology, 27,* 487-510.

Schulman, M. (1979). *A survey of spousal violence against women in Kentucky* (Study No. 792701 for the Kentucky Commission on Women). Washington, DC: U.S. Dept. of Justice.

Sechrest, L., White, S. O., & Brown, E. D. (1979). *The rehabilitation of criminal offenders: Problems and prospects.* Washington, DC: National Academy Press.

Sherman, L. W. (1992). *Policing domestic violence.* New York: Free Press.

Sherman, L. W., & Berk, R. A. (1984). The specific deterrent effects of arrest for domestic assault. *American Sociological Review, 49,* 261-272.

Sherman, L. W., & Cohn, E. G. (1989). The impact of research on legal policy: The Minneapolis Domestic Violence Experiment. *Law and Society Review, 23*(1):27-55.

Sherman, L. W., Schmidt, J. D., Rogan, D. P., Gartin, P., Cohn, E. G., Collins, D. J., & Bacich, A. R. (1991). From initial deterrence to long-term escalation: Short custody arrest for poverty ghetto domestic violence. *Criminology, 29,* 821-850.

Sherman, L. W., Smith, D. A., Schmidt, J. D., & Rogan, D. P. (1992). Crime, punishment, and stake in conformity: Legal and informal control of domestic violence. *American Sociological Review, 57,* 680-690.

Shields, N., & Hanneke, C. R. (1983). Battered wives' reactions to marital rape. In D. Finkelhor, R. J. Gelles, G. T. Hotaling, & M. A. Straus (Eds.), *The dark side of families: Current family violence research* (pp. 132-147). Beverly Hills, CA: Sage.

Sidel, R. (1986). *Women and children first.* New York: Viking.

Smith, M. D. (1986). Effects of question format on the reporting of woman abuse. *Victimology, 11,* 430-438.

Smith, M. D. (1987). The incidence and prevalence of woman abuse in Toronto. *Violence and Victims, 2*(2):173-187.

Smith, M. D. (1990). Patriarchical ideology and wife beating: A test of a feminist hypothesis. *Violence and Victims, 5,* 257-274.

Sonkin, D. J., Martin, D., & Walker, L. E. (1985). *The male batterer: A treatment approach.* New York: Springer.

Stark, E., & Flitcraft, A. (1983). Social knowledge, social policy, and the abuse of women: The case against patriarchal benevolence. In D. Finkelhor, R. J. Gelles, G. T. Hotaling, & M. A. Straus (Eds.), *The dark side of families: Current family violence research* (pp. 330-348). Beverly Hills, CA: Sage.

Stark, E., & Flitcraft, A. (1991). Spouse abuse. In M. L. Rosenberg & M. A. Fenley (Eds.), *Violence in America: A public health approach.* New York: Oxford University Press.

Stark, E., Flitcraft, A., Zuckerman, D., Grey, A., Robinson, J., & Frazier, W. (1981). *Wife abuse in the medical setting: An introduction to health personnel* (National Clearinghouse on Domestic Violence, Monograph Series No. 7).

Stets, J. E., & Straus, M. A. (1990). Gender differences in reporting marital violence and its medical and psychological consequences. In M. A. Straus & R. J. Gelles (Eds.), *Physical violence in American families: Risk factors and adaptation to violence in 8,145 families.* New Brunswick, NJ: Transaction.

Straus, M. A. (1976). Sexual inequality, cultural norms, and wife beating. *Victimology, 1,* 54-76.

Straus, M. A. (1978). Wife beating: How common and why? *Victimology, 2,* 443-458.

Straus, M. A. (1979). Measuring family conflict and violence: The Conflict Tactics Scale. *Journal of Marriage and the Family, 41,* 75-88.

Straus, M. A., & Gelles, R. J. (1986). Societal change in family violence from 1975 to 1985 as revealed by two national surveys. *Journal of Marriage and the Family, 48,* 465-479.

Straus, M. A., & Gelles, R. J. (1990). *Physical violence in American families: Risk factors and adaptations to violence in 8,145 families.* New Brunswick, NJ: Transaction.

Straus, M. A., Gelles, R. J., & Steinmetz, S. K. (1980). *Behind closed doors: Violence in the American family.* Garden City, NY: Doubleday.

Sugarman, D. B., & Hotaling, G. T. (1989). Courtship violence. In M. A. Priog-Good & J. E. Stets (Eds.), *Violence in dating relationships.* New York: Praeger.

Sullivan, C. M., Campbell, R., Angelique, H., Eby, K. K., & Davidson, W. S., II. (1994). An advocacy intervention program for women with abusive partners: Six-month follow-up. *American Journal of Community Psychology, 22,* 101-122.

Sykes, G. M., & Matza, D. (1957). Techniques of neutralization: A theory of delinquency. *American Sociological Review, 22,* 667-670.

Szinovacz, M. E. (1983). Using couple data as a methodological tool: The case of marital violence. *Journal of Marriage and the Family, 45,* 633-644.

Thurman v. City of Torrington, 595 F. Supp. 1521 (1984).

Tilden, V. P., & Shepard, P. (1987). Increasing the rate of identification of battered women in an emergency department: Using a nursing protocol. *Research in Nursing Health, 10,* 209-215.

Tittle, C. R., & Logan, C. H. (1973). Sanctions and deviance: Evidence and remaining questions. *Law and Society Review, 7,* 371-392.

U.S. Attorney General's Task Force on Family Violence. (1984). *Final report.* Washington, DC: Government Printing Office.

U.S. Commission on Civil Rights. (1982). *Under the rule of thumb: Battered women and the administration of justice.* Washington, DC: Author.

Virkkunen, M., & Linnoila, M. (1993). Brain serotonin, type II alcoholism, and impulsive violence. *Journal of Studies on Alcohol, 11,* 163-169.

Walker, L. E. (1979). *The battered woman.* New York: Harper & Row.

Walker, L. E. (1984). *The battered woman syndrome.* New York: Springer.

Wardell, L., Gillespie, D. L., & Leffler, A. (1983). Science and violence against wives. In D. Finkelhor, R. J. Gelles, G. T. Hotaling, & M. A. Strauss (Eds.), *The dark side of families: Current family violence research.* Beverly Hills, CA: Sage.

Warnken, W. J., Rosenbaum, A., Fletcher, K. E., Hoge, S. L., & Adelman, S. A. (1994). Head-injured males: A population at risk for relationship aggression? *Violence and Victims, 9,* 153-166.

Weis, J. G. (1989). Family violence research methodology and design. *Crime and Justice: An Annual Review of Research, 11.*

Widom, C. S. (1990). Implications of biases in sampling techniques for child abuse research and policy. In D. Besharov (Ed.), *Family violence research and policy.* Lanham, MD: University Press of America.

Wiersema, B., & Loftin, C. (1994). Estimates of assault by intimates from the National Crime Victimization Survey, 1987 (Working Paper, University of Maryland, Institute of Criminal Justice and Criminology). College Park: University of Maryland.

Wolfe, D. (1994). The role of intervention and treatment services in the prevention of child abuse and neglect. In G. B. Melton & F. D. Barry (Eds.), *Protecting children from abuse and neglect: Foundations for a new national strategy* (pp. 224-303). New York: Guilford.

Wolfe, D. A., McPherson, T., Blount, R., & Wolfe, V. (1986). Evaluation of a brief intervention for educating school children in awareness of physical and sexual abuse. *Child Abuse and Neglect, 10,* 85-92.

Yllö, K. A., & Straus, M. A. (1984). Patriarchy and violence against wives: The impact of structural and normative factors. *Journal of International and Comparative Social Welfare, 1*(1): 16-29.

Zimring, Franklin E. (1989). Toward a jurisprudence of family violence. *Crime and Justice: An Annual Review of Research, 11,* 547-570.

Zorza, J. (1992). The criminal law of misdemeanor domestic violence, 1970-1990. *Journal of Criminal Law and Criminology, 83,* 240-279.

5 The Victimization of Children and Youth

Developmental Victimology

DAVID FINKELHOR

Concern about children's victimization is not new. In modern times, there have been recurring public alarms about child abduction, child molestation, and child abuse dating back to the turn of the century (Alix, 1978; Gordon, 1988; McCormack, 1938). What is new, however, is the sustained professional and scientific attention being directed at these problems.

This attention is the product of several social changes. There has been a tremendous growth in the number of professionals whose occupations are concerned with child welfare, in fields such as education, medicine, social work, mental health, law, and nursing. This has coincided with, and has been fueled to some extent by, the entry into the professions—and particularly those that are justice related—of

larger numbers of women (De Titta, Robinowitz, & More, 1991; Martin, Arnold, & Parker, 1988). These women have tended to have more interest in the problems of children, including child victimization (Kendall-Tackett & Watson, 1991). Women police, prosecutors, and judges have brought into their work new concern about children as victims.

At the same time, there has also been a disintegration of the traditional, culturally sanctioned veil of privacy surrounding the family. This has meant that it has been easier to study and gather testimony about the previously shrouded widespread violence and abuse that occurs among and against family members, including children (Carter, 1974).

Author's Note: I gratefully acknowledge the Boy Scouts of America for financial support and Kelly Foster for help in preparing the manuscript.

Table 5.1 Crime Victimization Rates: Adolescents Versus Adults, 1992

| Type of Crime | Rate per 1,000 | | Source |
	Age 12-17	Age 18+	
Simple assault	41.8	13.9	OJJDP92
Aggravated assault	20.1	7.7	OJJDP92
Robbery	10.9	5.4	OJJDP92
Rape	1.6	0.5	NCVS93
Homicide	0.09	0.1	UCR93

a. Source acronyms are as follows:
  • NCVS93—National Crime Survey, 1993 (Bureau of Justice Statistics, 1995)
  • OJJDP92—Office of Juvenile Justice and Delinquency Prevention (Moone, 1994)
  • UCR93—Uniform Crime Reports, 1993 (FBI, 1995)

Children Are More Victimized Than Adults

Unfortunately, with some exceptions (Best, 1990; Christoffel, 1990; McDermott, Stanley, & Zimmerman-McKinney, 1982; Morgan & Zedner, 1992), the interest in child victimization has been fragmented into specific topics such as child abuse, child molestation, or stranger abduction, and few researchers have considered the larger whole. The goal of this chapter is to assemble these individual problems into a larger framework, termed *developmental victimology,* that encompasses the study of the victimizations of children across the span of childhood. We review findings on the incidence, risk factors, and effects of child victimization and suggest some integrative concepts.

One reality not widely recognized about child victimization because of the fragmentation is that children are more prone to victimization than adults. This is clearly true for teenagers. According to the National Crime Survey (NCVS), the overall violent crime victimization rate for youth aged 12 to 17 in 1992 was 2.3 times higher than the average national rate (Moone, 1994). It was three times higher for rape, two times higher for robbery, more than two times higher for aggravated assault, and three times higher for simple assault (Table 5.1). Teenagers as a group are murdered somewhat less frequently than adults, but the rate for 16- to 17-year-olds is 50% higher than

the adult average, and the rate for all youth has been growing much faster than the overall average in the last decade.

With the exception of homicide, the picture for children under 12 is not so clear. Studies suggest that assaults and sexual assaults are very common below age 12 (Finkelhor, 1994; Kilpatrick, 1992). Kilpatrick found that 29% of forcible rapes occurred among girls under age 11, although this age group makes up only 17% of the population. Other studies show assault rates for youth ages 10 and 11 that are just as high as for older youth (Finkelhor & Dziuba-Leatherman, 1994a), and school observation studies show a great deal of assault throughout grade school (Olweus, 1991). However, for homicide, rates for children under 12 are quite low, running about a quarter of the adult rate. The only exception is for infants, whose intentional deaths are often masked as accidents and whose homicide rate, according to some estimates, may reach or exceed the level of the adult population (McClain, Sacks, Froehlke, & Ewigman, 1993).

It is unfortunate that few comparative statistics exist for younger children. But the victimization rates for 12- to 17-year-olds in the NCVS are so much higher than the rate for adults that the overall rate for all children aged 0 to 17 would still be higher than the overall rate for adults (Moone, 1994), even under the limiting assumption of no victimizations at all for children under 12.

Table 5.2 Family Violence Victimization Rate per
1,000: Children Versus Adults, 1985

Perpetrator-Victim Relationship	Any Violence	Severe Violence[a]
Spouse to spouse	158	58
Parent to child	620	107

SOURCE: National Family Violence Survey, 1985, Straus and
Gelles (1990).
a. Includes kicking, biting, hitting with a fist or object, beating up,
or using or threatening to use a knife or gun.

The disproportionate victimization of children would be even more evident if the NCVS
and other studies were not so deficient in their
counting of family violence (Garbarino,
1989). Children are enormously more vulnerable than adults to intrafamilial victimization.
For example, in the National Family Violence
Survey in 1985, adults reported that they inflicted twice as many severe acts of violence
(a category that includes beating up, kicking,
and hitting with a fist or object) against a child
in their household as against their adult partner
(Straus & Gelles, 1990; see Table 5.2). If we
include less severe acts of violence (e.g., slap-
ping), the differential is even greater. Moreover, because younger children experience
more family violence than older children, this
differential holds over the whole span of childhood.

One objection sometimes made to the portrait of youth as highly victimized is the idea
that on the whole, youth victimizations, even
if numerous, are of a minor nature and are *less
serious* (Garofalo, Siegel, & Laub, 1987).
Youth victimizations, as in the NCVS, have
been characterized as schoolyard fighting and
the like. However, NCVS data do not bear out
this benign stereotype. The same percentage
of youth and adult victims of robbery or assault—about a third—suffer an injury. Youth
are actually more likely to be assaulted by
multiple perpetrators, and they are just as
likely to be victimized with a firearm (Rand,
1994). Their only indicator of less serious

victimization is in the case of theft: Fewer of
their stolen objects are worth more than $50.
But overall, there is little support for the idea
that their victimizations are less serious than
those of adults.

Statistics on Child Victimization

Although there is no single source for statistics on child victimizations, national estimates have been made for a variety of specific
types. These types can be organized into four
roughly characterized categories.

Conventional violent crimes include the
crimes of homicide, assault, sexual assault,
theft, and robbery. The primary source for
these is the NCVS.

Child abuse and neglect includes physical
and sexual abuse as well as physical neglect
and emotional abuse. Not all these acts are
violent or criminal; they include victimizations that stem from the dependent status of
children and the social responsibility of parents to protect them and care for their needs.
In contrast to the crime data, most child abuse
statistics are based on agency reports. Their
categories also lack the standardized definitions that have been developed for crime, but
one of their main sources, the National Incidence Study (NIS; Sedlak & Broadhurst,
1996), does use uniform and detailed definitions in its data collection effort.

A category of *specialized crimes* includes
abduction of children by strangers and abduction of children by family members: two specific crimes that have attracted attention and
have been the subject of a national study
(Finkelhor, Hotaling, & Sedlak, 1990).

A final category is *noncriminalized violent
acts toward children.* One of the interesting
special features of child victimology is that
children suffer from certain types of violence
that have been largely excluded from traditional criminologic concern. The first is assaults against young children by other children, including violent attacks by siblings.

Prevailing ideology has tended to treat these as relatively inconsequential victimizations. But from the point of view of the child, it is not clear, for example, why being beaten up by a peer would be any less traumatic or violative than it would be for an adult (Greenbaum, 1989). Even if these acts do not warrant formal adjudication, they are deserving of attention from the point of view of victimology.

An even more problematic type of non-criminalized violence toward children is spanking and corporal punishment. Corporal punishment is not typically viewed as victimization and is even viewed as educational by many segments of society. However, there are signs that a normative transformation is in progress regarding corporal punishment (Greven, 1990). A majority of states have banned it in schools, several Scandinavian countries have outlawed its use even by parents, and the American Academy of Pediatrics has condemned it. Social scientists have begun to study it as a form of victimization with short and long-term negative consequences (Straus, 1994; Straus & Gelles, 1990). Several national surveys have been done about the use of corporal punishment as self-reported by parents (Daro & McCurdy, 1991; Straus & Gelles, 1990; Straus, Gelles, & Steinmetz, 1980).

This is far from an exhaustive inventory of all the victimizations children may suffer. There are many types even of criminal victimizations for which we could identify no reliable national statistics, such as involvement in child prostitution. Moreover, children could be plausibly described as victims when crimes are committed against the households in which they live or other members of their household (Morgan & Zedner, 1992).

A Guide to the Estimates

The national statistics about child victimization gleaned from more than a dozen sources are arrayed in Table 5.3 in rough order of magnitude. The categories by which they are listed are certainly not distinct or mutually exclusive. For example, rape estimates include some sexual abuse and vice versa; assault includes some physical abuse and nonfamily abduction.

Under some victimization categories, the estimates of several different studies have been listed, sometimes showing widely divergent numbers. These differences stem from two factors in particular: the source of the report and the definition of the activity. Of the three main sources of reports—children themselves, caretakers knowledgeable about children's experiences, and agencies such as the police and child protection services—children and caretakers are likely to provide many more accounts than are available from agencies alone. This in part explains, for example, why the estimate of physical abuse from the National Family Violence Survey (a caretaker study) is more than double that of the 50 State Survey (agency statistics). Estimates also diverge because some studies used more careful or restrictive definitions.

What follows are some specific notes and observations about the statistics in Table 5.3:

- Sibling assault appears to be the most common kind of victimization for children, affecting 80% of all children in some form and over half of all children in its more severe form (which includes hitting with an object, kicking, biting or punching, beating up, or threatening with a knife or gun).[1] These rates are confirmed in other smaller scale self-report studies of children (Goodwin & Roscoe, 1990; Roscoe, Goodwin, & Kennedy, 1987).

- Of the several estimates available for theft, assault, and robbery, the NCVS estimates tend to be substantially lower than other self-report estimates. This may be, in part, a result of the NCVS method, which interviews children in the company of the other family members, and whose context has, in the past, especially emphasized people's stereotypical ideas about crime (Wells & Rankin, 1995).

- Assault figures (as well as theft, robbery, vandalism, and rape) pertain only to older children (age 11 and older). However, it should not be

Table 5.3 Rates and Incidence of Various Childhood Victimizations

Age	Rate/1,000	No. Victimized[a]	Year	Source[b]	Report Type[c]
Sibling Assault					
3-17	800.0	50,400,000[d]	1975	NFVS-1	C
3-17	530.0	33,300,000[e]	1975	NFVS-1	C
Physical Punishment					
0-17	(498.6)	(31,401,329)	1985	NFVS-2	C
Theft					
11-17	(497.0)	—	1978	NYS	S
12-15	95.3	—	1993	NCVS93	S
Assault					
11-17	(310.6)	—	1978	NYS	S
Gr. 8	(172.0)	—	1988	NASHS	S
12-17	61.8	—	1992	OJJDP92	S
Vandalism					
11-17	(257.6)	—	1978	NYS	S
Robbery					
11-17	(245.8)	—	1978	NYS	S
Gr. 8	(160.9)	—	1988	NASHS	S
12-17	9.8	—	1992	OJJDP92	S
Rape					
Gr. 8	(118.0)	—	1988	NASHS	S
11-17	(78.0)	—[f]	1978	NYS78	S
12-15	1.8	—	1993	NCVS93	S
Physical Abuse					
0-17	(23.5)	(1,480,007)	1985	NFVS-2	C
0-17	9.1	614,100	1993	NIS	A
0-17	(3.5)	(252,900)	1993	NCCAN93	A
Neglect					
0-17	(19.9)	(1,335,100)[g]	1993	NIS	A
0-17	(7.3)	(510,980)	1993	NCCAN93	A
Sexual Abuse					
0-17	(2.2)	(151,611)	1993	NCCAN93	A
0-17	4.5	300,200	1993	NIS	A

assumed that they would necessarily be lower if younger children were included. For example, serious sibling assaults are actually *highest* for children aged 3 to 4 and decline with age (from 592 per 1,000 down to 309 per 1,000 for ages 15 to 17). It is possible that nonfamily peer assaults are also higher for primary-school-age children than for teens.

• The rape figures from the NCVS are extremely low and have been widely criticized—in this case, not just because they are elicited in interviews with other family members present but also because respondents prior to 1994 were only asked specifically about a rape if they volunteered a "yes" to a previous general question about assault (Russell, 1984). Many adult prevalence studies suggest that the higher figures in Table 5.3 are more accurate (Kilpatrick, 1992; Russell, 1984).

• The child abuse and neglect figures are relatively crude. All but one come from either the National Incidence Study (NIS) or the 50 State Survey, both of which counted only cases known to professionals. Much child abuse, however, is not identified by professionals (Garbarino, 1989).

Table 5.3 Continued

Age	Rate/1,000	No. Victimized[a]	Year	Source[b]	Report Type[c]
Family Abductions					
0-17	5.6	354,100[h]	1988	NISMART	C
Emotional Abuse					
0-17	7.9	532,200	1993	NIS	A
0-17	(0.8)	(53,000)[h]	1993	NCCAN93	A
Nonfamily Abductions					
0-17	0.05-0.07	3,200-4,600[h]	1988	NISMART	A
0-17	0.003-0.005	200-300[i]	1988	NISMART	A
Homicide					
0-17	(0.039)	2,697	1993	UCR93	A
Abduction Homicide					
0-17	0.001-0.002	43-147	1988	NISMART	A

NOTE: Numbers given in parentheses did not appear in original source, but were derived from data presented there.
a. Numbers were computed only for complete populations (i.e., ages 0-17).
b. Source acronyms are as follows:
- NASHS—National Adolescent Student Health Survey (American School Health Association, 1989)
- NCCAN93—National Center on Child Abuse and Neglect (1995)
- NCVS93—National Crime Survey, 1993 (Bureau of Justice Statistics, 1995)
- NFVS-1—National Family Violence Survey, 1975 (Straus & Gelles, 1990)
- NFVS-2—National Family Violence Resurvey, 1985 (Straus & Gelles, 1990)
- NIS—National Study of the Incidence and Severity of Child Abuse and Neglect, 1993 (Sedlak & Broadhurst, 1991)
- NISMART—National Incidence Study of Missing, Abducted, Runaway and Thrownaway Children, 1988 (Finkelhor, Hotaling, & Sedlak, 1990)
- NYS—National Youth Survey (Lauritsen, Sampson, & Laub, 1991)
- NYS78—National Youth Survey, 1978 (Ageton, 1983)
- OJJDP92—Office of Juvenile Justice and Delinquency Prevention (Moone, 1994)
- UCR91—Uniform Crime Reports, 1991 (FBI, 1992)
- UCR93—Uniform Crime Reports, 1993 (FBI, 1995)
c. Report types: A = agency reports, C = caretaker reports, S = self-reports.
d. Any violence.
e. Severe violence.
f. Girls only.
g. Physical neglect.
h. Legal definition.
i. Stereotypical kidnapping.

A Typology of Child Victimizations

Examining the figures in Table 5.3 and recognizing their methodological limitations, definitional imprecision, and variability, we nonetheless suggest that the types of child victimization reflected there should be broken into three broad categories according to seriousness and pervasiveness (Figure 5.1). First, there are the *pandemic* victimizations that occur to a majority of children at some time in the course of growing up. These include at a minimum assault by siblings, physical punishment by parents, and theft, and probably also peer assault, vandalism, and robbery. Second, there are what might be called *acute victimizations*. These are less frequent—occurring to a minority, although perhaps a sizable minority, of children—but may be on average of a greater severity. Among these we would include physical abuse, neglect, and family abduction. Finally, there are the *extraordinary* victimizations that occur to only a very small number of children but that attract a great deal

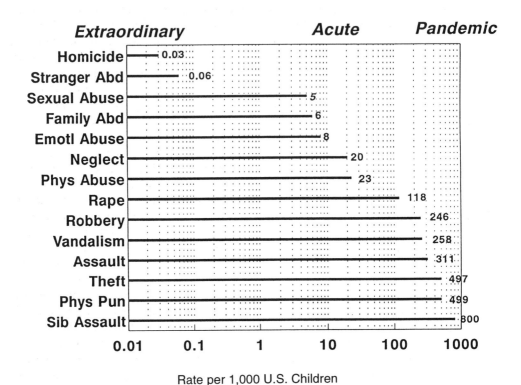

Figure 5.1. Rates of Child Victimization

of attention. These include homicide, including gang homicide, child abuse homicide, and nonfamily abduction.

Several observations follow from this typology. First, much more public and professional attention has been paid to extraordinary and acute victimizations than to pandemic ones. For example, sibling violence, the most frequent victimization, is conspicuous for how little it has been studied in proportion to how often it occurs. This neglect of pandemic victimizations needs to be rectified. For one thing, it fails to reflect the concerns of children themselves. In a recent survey of 2,000 children aged 10 to 16, three times as many were concerned about the likelihood of their being beaten up by peers as were concerned about

being sexually abused (Finkelhor & Dziuba-Leatherman, 1995). The pandemic victimizations deserve greater attention, if only for the alarming frequency with which they occur and the influence they have on children's everyday existence.

Second, this typology can be useful in developing theory and methodology concerning child victimization. For example, different types of victimization may require different conceptual frameworks. Because they are nearly normative occurrences, the impact of pandemic victimizations may be very different from the impact of extraordinary ones that children experience in relative isolation.

Finally, the typology helps illustrate the diversity and frequency of children's victimization. Although homicide and child abuse have been widely studied, they are notable for how inadequately they convey the variety and true extent of the other victimizations that children suffer. Almost all the figures in Table 5.3 have been promoted in isolation at one time or another. When we view them together, we note that they are just part of a total environment of various victimization dangers in which children live.

Why Is the Victimization of Children So Common?

When the victimization of children is considered as a whole and its scope and variety are more fully appreciated, a number of interesting and important theoretical questions arise. The first concerns why the victimization of children is so common. Obviously, this is a complex question; a complete answer will require the explanation of elevated risks for different categories of children for different kinds of victimization. However, some generalizations may apply. Certainly, the weakness and small physical stature of many children and their dependency status put them at greater risk. They can be victimized because they cannot retaliate or deter victimization as effectively as those with more strength and power. The social toleration of child victimization also plays a role. Society has an influential set of institutions, the police and criminal justice system, to enforce its relatively strong prohibitions against many kinds of crime, but much of the victimization of children is considered outside the purview of this system.

Another important generalization about why children are at high risk for victimization concerns the relationship between choice and vulnerability (Lynch, 1991). *Children have comparatively little choice over whom they associate with, less choice perhaps than any segment of the population besides prisoners.* This can put them into more involuntary contact with high-risk offenders and thus at

greater jeopardy for victimization. For example, when children live in families that mistreat them, they are not free or able to leave. When they live in dangerous neighborhoods, they cannot choose on their own to move. If they attend a school with many hostile and delinquent peers, they cannot simply change schools or quit. The absence of choice over people and environments affects children's vulnerability to both intimate victimization and street crime. Some adults—for example, battered women and the poor—suffer similar limitations, but still, many adults are able to seek divorces or change their residences in reaction to dangerous conditions. Adults also have more ready access to cars and sometimes have the option to live and work alone. Children are obliged to live with other people, to travel collectively, and to work in high-density, heterogenous environments (i.e., schools). To put it in more abstract language, children have difficulty gaining access to the structures and mechanisms in society that help segregate people from dangerous associates and environments. This makes them more vulnerable.

Differential Character of Child Victimization

A second interesting theoretical question concerns how the victimization of children differs from the victimization of adults. Children, of course, suffer from all the victimizations that adults do (including economic crimes such as extortion and fraud), but they also suffer from some that are particular to their status. The main status characteristic of childhood is its condition of dependency, which is partially a function of social and psychological immaturity. The violation of this dependency status results in forms of victimization (e.g., physical neglect) that are not suffered by most adults (with the exception of those such as the elderly and sick, who also become dependent).

The dependency of children creates a spectrum of vulnerability. Interestingly, the victimization categories that we identify in Table 5.3 can be arrayed on a continuum, according to the degree to which they involve violations of children's dependency status (Figure 5.2). At the one extreme is physical neglect, which has practically no meaning as a victimization except in the case of a person who is dependent and needs to be cared for by others. Similarly, family abduction is a dependency-specific victimization because it is the unlawful removal of a child from the person who is supposed to be caring for him or her. Emotional abuse happens to both adults and children, but the sensitive psychological vulnerability of children in their dependent relationship to their caretakers is what makes society consider emotional abuse of children a form of victimization that warrants an institutional response.

At the other end of the continuum are forms of victimization that are defined without reference to dependency and that exist in very similar forms for both children and adults. Stranger abduction is prototypical in this instance because both children and adults are taken against their will and imprisoned for ransom or sexual purposes. Homicide is similar; the dependency status of the victim does little to define the victimization. In some cases, to be sure, children's deaths result from extreme and willful cases of neglect, but there are parallel instances of adult deaths resulting from extreme and willful negligence.

Finally, some forms of child victimization should be located along the midsection of the dependency continuum. Sexual abuse falls here, for example, because it encompasses at least two different situations, one dependency related and one not. Some sexual abuse entails activities ordinarily acceptable between adults that are deemed victimizing in the case of children because of their immaturity and dependency. But other sexual abuse involves violence and coercion that would be victimizing even with a nondependent adult.

In the case of physical abuse, there is also some mixture. Although most of the violent acts in this category would be considered victimizing even between adults, some of them— for example, the shaken-baby syndrome— develop almost exclusively in a caretaking relationship in which there is an enormous differential in size and physical control.

The dependency continuum is a useful concept in thinking about some of the unique features of children's victimizations. It is also helpful in generating some hypotheses about the expected correlates of different types of victimization such as variations according to age.

Developmental Propositions

Childhood is such an extremely heterogenous category—4-year-olds and 17-year-olds having little in common—that it is inherently misleading to discuss child victimization in general without reference to age. We would expect the nature, quantity, and impact of victimization to vary across childhood with the different capabilities, activities, and environments characteristic of different stages of development. An apt term for the study of this phenomenon might be *developmental victimology*. Unfortunately, we do not have strong studies of the different types of victimization across all the ages of childhood with which to examine such changes.

Two plausible propositions about age and child victimization could be a starting place for developmental victimology. One is that victimizations stemming from the dependent status of children should be most common among the most dependent and hence the youngest children. A corollary is that as children get older, their victimization profile should come more and more to resemble that of adults.

We can examine such propositions in a crude way with the data that are available. In fact, we can see in Table 5.4 that the types of victimization that are most concentrated in the under-12 age group are the dependency-related ones (see the dependency continuum in Figure

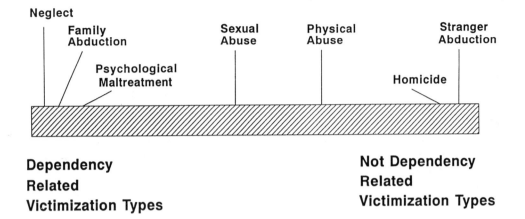

Figure 5.2. Dependency Continuum for Child Victimization Types

Table 5.4 Victimizations of Younger Children

Type of Victimization	% of Victims Under 12	Source[a]
Family abduction	81	NISMART
Physical neglect	70	NIS
Emotional abuse	58[b]	NIS
Physical abuse	56	NIS
Homicide	43[c]	UCR93
Sexual abuse	40	NIS
Stranger abduction	27	NISMART

a. Source acronyms are as follows:
- NIS—National Study of the Incidence and Severity of Child Abuse and Neglect, 1986 (Sedlak, 1991).
- NISMART—National Incidence Study of Missing, Abducted, Runaway and Thrownaway Children, 1988 (Finkelhor et al., 1990).
- UCR93—Uniform Crime Reports, 1993 (FBI, 1994).

b. Reflects the midpoint of two divergent estimates.
c. Age group for this category is under 10.

5.2), particularly family abduction and physical neglect. Victimizations such as homicide and stranger abduction, which we grouped at the nondependency end of the continuum, involve a greater percentage of teenagers. However, not everything falls neatly into place;

sexual abuse seems anomalously concentrated among teenagers too. We believe this to be an artifact of the NIS data on sexual abuse, which were based on reported cases only and thus undercounted sexual abuse of young children.[2] When we look at sexual abuse, using data from retrospective self-reports, we find that 64% of victimizations occur before age 12 (Finkelhor, et al., 1990), a pattern more consistent with the dependency hypothesis and the place of sexual abuse on the dependency continuum.

For additional insights about development and victimization, we can also look at child homicide, the type of victimization to which a developmental analysis has been most extensively applied (Christoffel, 1990; Christoffel, Anzinger, & Amari, 1983; Crittenden & Craig, 1990; Jason, 1983; Jason, Carpenter, & Tyler, 1983). Child homicide has a conspicuous bimodal frequency, with high rates for the very youngest and the oldest children (Figure 5.3). But the two peaks represent very different phenomena. The homicides of young children are primarily committed by parents using choking, smothering, and battering. In contrast, the homicides of older children are committed

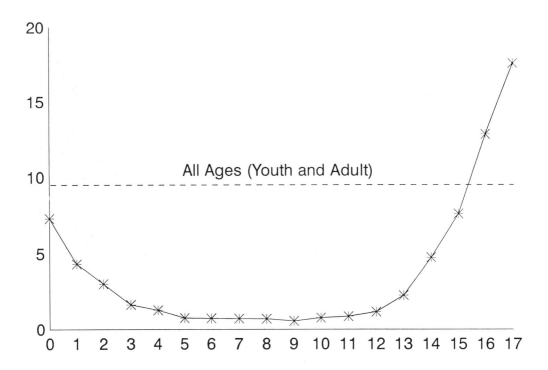

Figure 5.3. Homicide Rates (per 100,000 U.S. Youth) for Youth Aged 0 to 17, 1991-1992

mostly by peers and acquaintances, most often using firearms (Figures 5.4 and 5.5).

Although the analysts do not agree entirely on the number and age span of the specific developmental categories for child homicides, some propositions are clear. There is a distinct group of neonaticides—children killed in the first day or few weeks of life. The proportion of female and rural perpetrators is unusually high in this group (Jason et al., 1983). Homicide at this age is generally considered to include many isolated parents dealing with unwanted children.

After the neonatal period, there follows a period through about age 5 in which homicides are still committed primarily by caretakers using "personal weapons," but the motives and circumstances are thought to be somewhat different. These appear to be mostly cases of fatal child abuse that occur as a result of par-

ents' attempts to control child behavior or reactions to some of its aversive qualities (Christoffel, 1990; Crittenden & Craig, 1990). Because of their small size and physical vulnerability, many children at this age die from acts of violence and force by adults that would not be fatal to older children.

As children reach school age, the rate of child homicide declines and the nature of child homicide becomes somewhat different. Among school-age children, killings by parents and caretakers gradually decline and those by peers and acquaintances rise. There are more firearm deaths. Children are targeted by suicidal parents killing their whole families. Children are killed in sexual assaults and are innocent victims in robberies and arsons.

Then, at age 13, the homicide picture changes again and rapidly. The rate for boys diverges sharply from that for girls. Acquaintances be-

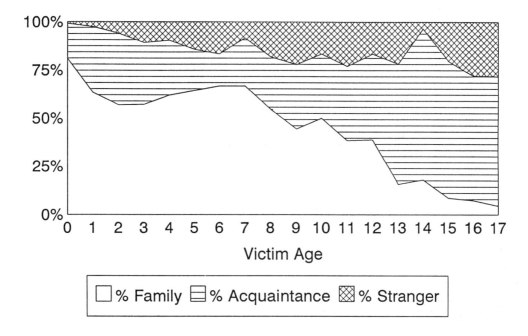

Figure 5.4. Relationship of Child Homicide Victims to Perpetrators, by Child's Age, 1991-1992

come the predominant killers. Gangs and drugs are heavily involved, and the rate for minority groups—African Americans, Hispanics, and Asians—soars.

These trends clearly suggest that the types of homicide suffered by children are related to the nature of their dependency and to the level of their integration into the adult world. They provide a good case for the importance and utility of a developmental perspective on child victimizations and a model of how such an approach could be applied to other types of victimization.

Intrafamily Victimization

Unlike many adults, children do not live alone; they mostly live in families, so another plausible principle of developmental victimol-

ogy is that more of the victimization of children occurs at the hands of relatives. We illustrated this in Table 5.2, and also Table 5.3, showing the sheer quantity of victimization by relatives apparent in the elevated figures on sibling assault, which outstrip those for any other kind of victimization.

The findings on homicide also suggest a developmental trend: Younger children have a greater proportion of their victimizations at the hands of intimates and correspondingly fewer at the hands of strangers. This is because they live more sheltered lives, spend more time in the home and around family, and have fewer of the characteristics that might make them suitable targets for strangers, such as money and valuable possessions.

An additional possible principle is that the identity of perpetrators may vary according to the type of victimization and its place on the

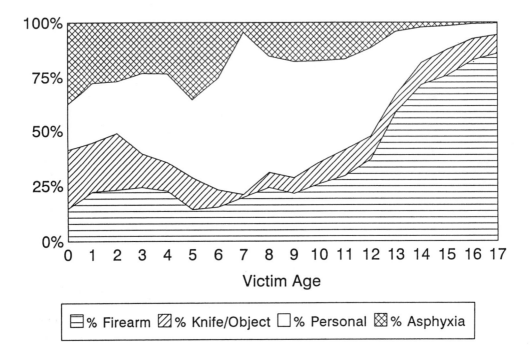

Figure 5.5. Homicide Weapon by Child Victim's Age, 1991-1992

dependency continuum (Figure 5.2). Victimizations that are more dependency related should involve more perpetrators who are parents and family members. As shown in Table 5.5, parents are 100% of the perpetrators of neglect (Sedlak, 1991), the most dependency-related victimization, but only 28% of the perpetrators of homicide (Federal Bureau of Investigation [FBI], 1992). This pattern occurs because the responsibilities created by children's dependency status fall primarily on parents and family members. They are the main individuals in a position to violate those responsibilities in a way that would create victimization. Thus, when a sick child fails to get available medical attention, it is the parents who are charged with neglecting the child, even if the neighbors also did nothing.

Gender and Victimization

Developmental victimology needs to take account of gender as well. On the basis of the conventional crime statistics available from the NCVS and Uniform Crime Report, boys would appear to suffer more homicide (2.3 to 1), more assault (1.7 to 1), and more robbery (2.0 to 1) than girls, whereas girls suffer vastly more rape (8.1 to 1; Bureau of Justice Statistics, 1992; FBI, 1992). But this primarily pertains to the experience of adolescents and does not consider age variations.

Because gender differentiation increases as children get older, a developmental hypothesis might predict that the pattern of victimization would be less gender specific for younger children. That is, because younger boys and girls are more similar in their activities and physical

Table 5.5 Childhood Victimizations Perpetrated by Parents

Type of Victimization	% Victimized by Parent	Source[a]
Physical neglect	100	NIS
Emotional abuse	100	NIS
Physical abuse	90	NIS
Abductions	80	NISMART
Sexual abuse	51	NIS
Homicide	28	UCR93

a. Source acronyms are as follows:
- NIS—National Study of the Incidence and Severity of Child Abuse and Neglect, 1986 (Sedlak, 1991).
- NISMART—National Incidence Study of Missing, Abducted, Runaway and Thrownaway Children, 1988 (Finkelhor et al., 1990).
- UCR93—Uniform Crime Reports, 1993 (FBI, 1994).

characteristics, there might be less difference between sexes in the rate of victimization.

This pattern does indeed appear to be the case at least for homicide, the type of victimization for which we have the best data. Rates of homicide are quite similar for younger boys and girls, even up to age 13, after which point the vulnerability of boys increases dramatically (Figure 5.6).

However, this increased differentiation with age is less apparent for other types of victimization. Physical abuse does appear to have such a trend in one data set, but not in another. Caretaker reports from the National Family Violence Survey show more abuse of boys after age 5, rising particularly high in later adolescence. But data from another source, the NIS, contradict this trend, showing girls to be the predominant victims of physical abuse during adolescence. It could be that the physical abuse of adolescent boys is particularly underdetected by professionals (on whose observations the NIS is based).

It is possible that a developmental pattern in gender differentiation may apply to some forms of victimization but not others. The mixed picture in regard to gender and age merits more study. Some victimization types may have unique gender patterns reflecting their particular dynamics.

Routine Activities Theory and Children

Routine activities theory (RAT), which has been a popular conceptual framework in the victimology field, has been applied to the analysis of youth victimization as it has to other issues. The application has tended to focus on how increased *exposure* and decreased *guardianship* heighten youth vulnerability. Young people are viewed as engaging in risky behaviors, such as staying out late, going to parties, and drinking, that compromise the guardianship provided by parents and adults and expose them to more possibilities for victimization (Jensen & Brownfield, 1986). Much of the RAT approach to youth victimization has particularly stressed its connection to *delinquent activities* (Lauritsen, Laub, & Sampson, 1992; Lauritsen, Sampson, & Laub, 1991). Delinquency is seen as a lifestyle that puts a person in close proximity to other offenders—aggressive or delinquent companions or rival gang members—and also greatly reduces guardianship because delinquents tend to avoid conventional social environments and through their activities also largely forfeit their claims on the protection of police and other authorities (Sparks, 1982). Empirical research has confirmed that delinquents are indeed more prone to victimization than other youth (Lauritsen et al., 1991, 1992).

However, this perspective on youth victimization has some obvious limitations. For one thing, many youth who get victimized have no involvement in delinquency. Delinquent activities are primarily the domain of adolescents, particularly adolescent boys. But even young children get assaulted, kidnapped, and sexually abused (Finkelhor & Dziuba-Leatherman, 1994b) without any connection to delinquent behavior. Moreover, the lifestyle and routine activities theories were designed

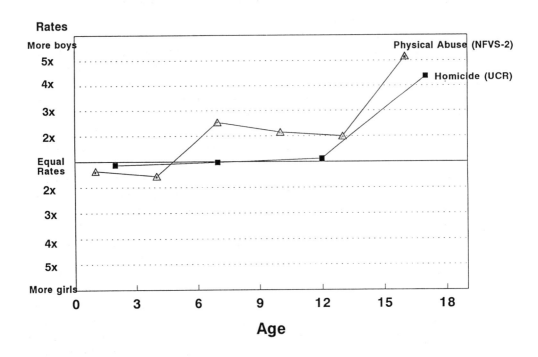

Figure 5.6. Gender Differences in Victimization Rates by Age, 1991-1992

for, and have always been best at explaining, variations in stereotypical street crime such as stranger assaults and robberies. But much of youth victimization occurs at the hands of acquaintances and family members. This is particularly true for younger children (Finkelhor & Dziuba-Leatherman, 1994b).

These acquaintance and intrafamily victimizations are not well suited to the RAT concepts. For example, routine activities studies often operationalize *guardianship* as the amount of time routinely spent within the family household. However, for a child at risk of parental violence, time spent in the family household does not increase guardianship. Nor does being out at night—another popular lifestyle variable—increase exposure. In fact, for intrafamily victimization, it is not entirely clear that time "exposed" outside or inside the family makes much difference at all.

Thus it is not surprising that theories developed to explain many specific forms of acquaintance and family victimization among youth have virtually ignored RAT and have relied on other concepts besides exposure and guardianship. For example, in trying to account for who becomes the target of bullying, observers have noted that these tend to be children who have "avoidant-insecure" attachment relationships with primary caregivers, lack trust, have low self-confidence, expect hostility from others, and are socially isolated (Smith, Bowers, Binney, & Cowie, 1993). Bullied boys tend to be physically weaker and may be more likely to have physical impairments (Olweus, 1993). Something about the behavior of these children—both their physical and psychological vulnerability and perhaps a relational style irritating to other children—seems to attract victimization. Interestingly, as opposed to lacking guardianship, this literature suggests that victims of bullies tend to be, if anything, overprotected by parents and bullied in part because of it (Smith et al., 1993).

The literature on parental assault on children also takes a very different tack from the lifestyles approach. This literature tends to equate victimization risk primarily with family and parental attributes, such as family stress, isolation, alcoholic and violence-prone caretakers, and parents who have victimization histories and unrealistic expectations of their children (National Research Council, 1993). To the extent that victim factors play a role, particularly in the case of adolescents, the parental assault literature notes that such youth may be more at risk if they are disobedient, uncooperative, or temperamental or if they have problems or impairments that are a burden or source of disappointment for caregivers (Berdie, Berdie, Wexler, & Fisher, 1983; Garbarino, 1989; Libby & Bybee, 1979; Schellenbach & Guerney, 1987).

A still different victimization literature, the one on child sexual assault, notes some other risk factors. For this form of victimization, girls are at substantially greater risk than boys (Finkelhor, 1994). Also at risk are children from step-parent families and children whose parents fight or are distant and punitive (Finkelhor, 1993). Finkelhor (1984) hypothesized that risk for sexual abuse is increased by factors that reduce parental supervision as well as those that create emotional deprivation. Emotional deprivation makes children and youth vulnerable to the offers of attention and affection that sexual predatory offenders sometimes use to draw children into sexual activities.

A challenge for the field of developmental victimology is to find ways to blend the theoretical approaches relevant to specific forms of child victimization together with the insights of RAT to the extent that they apply. Elsewhere, Finkelhor and Asdigian (1996) have proposed a framework for beginning this task.

Effects of Child Victimization

Inflicted injuries, neglect, and criminal acts are responsible for the deaths of more than 2,000 children per year, and homicide is currently one of the five leading causes of child mortality in the United States (Goetting, 1990; Martinez-Schnell & Waxweiler, 1989). Victimization also results in a substantial toll of nonfatal injuries that are more difficult to count accurately. The NIS estimated that, as a result of abuse or neglect over the course of one year, 565,000 children suffered serious injuries (i.e., life threatening conditions, long-term physical, mental, or emotional impairment) and 822,000 others suffered moderate injuries (i.e., observable injuries or impairments that lasted for at least 48 hours) (Sedlak & Broadhurst, 1996). From the NCVS, one can estimate that approximately half a million teenagers aged 12 to 17 sustained physical injury due to an assault in a single year and that about 100,000 received hospital care as a result of any kind of violent crime (BJS, 1995). Another national survey of 10- to 16-year-olds suggests that the annual number of injured youth is on the order of 2.8 million, with 250,000 needing medical attention (Finkelhor & Dziuba-Leatherman, 1994a). A Massachusetts study suggested that each year 1 in every 42 teenage boys receives hospital treatment for an assault-related injury (Guyer, Lescohier, Gallagher, Hausman, & Azzara, 1989).

Children's level of development undoubtedly influences the nature and severity of injuries resulting from victimization, although few analyses have taken such a developmental approach. An obvious example is the greater vulnerability of small children to death and serious harm as a result of blows inflicted by hands and other so-called "personal objects." Another obvious example is the higher likelihood of older children to contract sexual-abuse-related HIV infection because older children suffer more penetrative abuse (Kerns & Ritter, 1992).

In addition to physical injury, a growing literature documents that victimization has grave short and long-term effects on children's mental health. For example, sexually victimized children appear to be at substantially increased lifetime risk for virtually all categories of psychiatric disorder (Table 5.6), a finding supported by Saunders, Villeponteaux, Lipovsky, Kilpatrick, and Veronen (1992). Scott (1992) estimated that about 8% of all psychiatric cases within the population can be attributed to childhood sexual assault.

Although they do not involve such specific epidemiological assessments, other studies have also demonstrated increased rates of mental health morbidity for other types of childhood victimization, including physical abuse (Kolko, 1992), emotional abuse (Briere & Runtz, 1990), and physical punishment (Straus & Gelles, 1990). A national survey has demonstrated that victimized youth have higher levels of posttraumatic stress disorder (PTSD) and depression, that a wide variety of specific forms of victimization result in such effects, and that such effects are independent of prior levels of symptoms (Boney-McCoy & Finkelhor, 1995; in press). A number of other studies also show the traumatic impact of violence exposure and in particular its serious effects on those from minority communities and communities with higher violence rates (DuRant, Getts, Cadenhead, Emans, & Woods, 1995; Martinez & Richters, 1993; Singer, Anglin, Song, & Lunghofer, 1995).

In addition to general mental health impairments, a proposition that has been established across various types of victimization is that a history of such victimization increases the likelihood that someone will become a perpetrator of crime, violence, or abuse. Although this popular shibboleth has been criticized and qualified (Kaufman & Ziegler, 1987), evidence to support it comes from a wide variety

Table 5.6 Increased Risk for Psychiatric Disorders Among Victims of Child Sexual Abuse

Disorder	Risk Ratio
Any disorder	3.8
Any affective disorder	2.4
Any substance abuse or dependence	3.1
Drug abuse or dependence	5.2
Alcohol abuse or dependence	2.1
Phobia	3.4
Depression	3.4

NOTE: Only risks significantly different from risk for nonvictims are included.
SOURCE: Scott (1992).

of methodologies—longitudinal follow-ups (McCord, 1983; Widom, 1989a), studies of offender populations (Hanson & Slater, 1988; Lewis, Shanok, Pincus, & Glaser, 1979), and surveys of the general population (Straus et al., 1980)—and concerns a wide variety of perpetrations, including violent crime, property crime, child abuse, wife abuse, and sexual assaults (for review, see Widom, 1989b). An important qualification is that victims are not necessarily most prone to repeat their own form of victimization. But the proposition that childhood victims are more likely to grow up to victimize others is firmly established.

Theory about PTSD is being applied to, and may be a unifying concept for, understanding common psychological effects of a wide variety of child victimizations (Eth & Pynoos, 1985). Terr (1990) has made some effort to cast PTSD in a more developmental framework, but its application is mostly anecdotal.

Sexual abuse is the only area in which a developmental approach to the psychological impact of victimization has been advanced on the basis of empirical studies (Kendall-Tackett, Williams, & Finkelhor, 1993). For example, in reaction to sexual abuse, symptoms of sexualization seem to appear more frequently among preschool than among school-age girls, who seem more aware of appropriate and inappropriate sexual conduct (Friedrich et al., 1992). This is the direction that the whole area of child victimization needs to take.

One of the challenges for a field of developmental victimology is to document how victimization at different stages of development can have different kinds of effects (Trickett & Putnam, 1993). Such developmentally specific effects can be related to three different aspects of development, according to a formulation Shirk (1988) made in regard to physical abuse: (a) differences in the developmental tasks children are facing at the time of victimization, (b) differences in the cognitive abilities that affect children's appraisal of the victimization, and (c) differences in the forms of symptom expression available to the child at that stage of development. Each of these processes is worthy of further study (Finkelhor & Kendall-Tackett, in press).

A number of models in the developmental literature point to pivotal tasks that children need to accomplish at various ages (Egeland & Sroufe, 1981; Erikson, 1968) and the related idea that there are sensitive periods during which developmental tasks or processes are particularly vulnerable to disturbance (MacDonald, 1985). Several specific examples exist in the research literature of attempts to document how victimization can interfere with such stage-specific processes. For example, young children victimized at an early age by their primary caretakers seem to suffer a big developmental impact in the form of insecure attachments to caregivers (Carlson, Cicchetti, Barnett, & Braunwald, 1989; Crittenden, 1988; Egeland & Sroufe, 1981). Children victimized during preschool years, when children experiment with normal dissociative skills, may be those who become most likely to use dissociation as a defense mechanism and to develop a pattern of dissociation that becomes chronic (Kirby, Chu, & Dill, 1993). And sexual abuse and other trauma can hasten the

onset of puberty (Herman-Giddens, Sandler, & Friedman, 1988; Putnam & Trickett, 1993).

A second developmental component to the impact of victimization concerns how children's beliefs about what happened may mediate the experience of victimization (Rutter, 1989). For example, victims seem to be more affected by crime in which they believed they were going to die or be seriously injured or in which they felt helpless and out of control (Kilpatrick et al., 1989; Resnick, 1993). But this cognitive appraisal process works very differently among children, who know much less about the world or make assumptions different from those of adults (Dalenberg, Bierman, & Furman, 1984), and these cognitive appraisal skills, including those that apportion responsibility and blame for bad events, change over the course of development.

Finally, in addition to stage-specific vulnerabilities and cognitive appraisals, a third domain highlighted by Shirk (1988) is developmental differences in symptom expression. Whatever the stage at which a child may have been victimized or whatever appraisals a child may make, the subjective distress from that victimization will usually be expressed within a vocabulary of behaviors or symptoms specific to the current stage of development. Thus distress expressed by preschool-age children in the form of disruptive behavior in preschool may take the form of self-blame or depression at a later stage. Shirk labels this process "developmental symptom substitution." In understanding how children respond to victimization over the course of development, all these processes need to be better described, documented, and related to the child victimization literature.

Research Needs

The research needs in this field of child victimization are vast and urgent, given the size of the problem and the seriousness of its impact, and they range from studies of risk factors to studies of treatment efficacy. But in the limited space of this review, I will mention only three important points.

First, if we are to take it seriously, we need much better statistics to document and analyze the scope, nature, and trends of child victimization. The NCVS records only crime victimizations down to age 12. The Uniform Crime Reports in the past have made no age information available about crimes with the exception of homicide (something that may change under a proposed new National Incident Based Reporting System [NIBRS], but the implementation of this system is still a long way off). The national data collection system about child abuse fails to include all states and has severe methodological limitations such that the information cannot be aggregated nationally or compared across states (National Center on Child Abuse and Neglect, 1992).

We need comprehensive, yearly national and state figures on all officially reported crimes and forms of abuse committed against children. These need to be supplemented by regular, national studies to assess the vast quantity of unreported victimization, including family violence, child-to-child violence, and indirect victimization. Although there are methodological challenges in such efforts, studies such as those referenced in this chapter demonstrate that this is feasible.

Second, we need theory and research that cut across and integrate the various forms of child victimization. A good example is the work on PTSD in children, which has been applied to the effects of various victimizations: sexual abuse, stranger abduction, and the witnessing of homicide (Boney-McCoy & Finkelhor, 1995, in press; Eth & Pynoos, 1985; Terr, 1990). Similar cross-cutting research could be done on other subjects (e.g., what makes children vulnerable to victimization or how responses by family members buffer or exacerbate the impact of victimization). To be truly synthesizing, this research needs to study the pandemic victimizations, not just the acute

and extraordinary victimizations, which have been the main focus in the past.

Finally, the field needs a more developmental perspective on child victimization. This would start with an understanding of the mix of victimization threats that face children of different ages. It would include the kind of factors that place children at risk and the strategies for victimization avoidance that are appropriate at different stages of development. It would also differentiate how children at different stages react and cope with the challenges posed by victimization.

A Final Word

It is ironic that the problem of children as aggressors has until recently had more attention in social science than children as victims, reflecting perhaps the priorities of the adult world. It is encouraging that as the needs of children are more fully recognized, this balance is finally changing.

Notes

1. The 1975 Family Violence Survey actually gathered its information about sibling assault *perpetrations* rather than victimizations. This means the figures may be underestimates because for every sibling perpetrator there was at least one, but possibly several, sibling victims.

2. The undercount stems from two problems. First, most sexual abuse reports, unlike other forms of child maltreatment, start from children's own disclosures, which are more difficult for younger children to make. Second, much sexual abuse goes on for extended periods of time before being disclosed, and the age data in the NIS are based on age at the time of report, not age at onset.

References

Ageton, S. S. (1983). *Sexual assault among adolescents.* Lexington, MA: Lexington.

Alix, E. K. (1978). *Ransom kidnapping in America, 1874-1974.* Carbondale: Southern Illinois University Press.

American School Health Association. (1989). *The National Adolescent Student Health Survey: A report on the health of America's youth.* Kent, OH: Author.

Berdie, J., Berdie, M., Wexler, S., & Fisher, B. (1983). *An empirical study of families involved in adolescent maltreatment.* San Francisco: URSA Institute.

Best, J. (1990). *Threatened children: Rhetoric and concern about child-victims.* Chicago: University of Chicago Press.

Boney-McCoy, S., & Finkelhor, D. (1995). The psychosocial impact of violent victimization on a national youth sample. *Journal of Consulting and Clinical Psychology, 63,* 726-736.

Boney-McCoy, S., & Finkelhor, D. (in press). Is youth victimization related to PTSD and depression after controlling for prior symptoms and family relationships? A longitudinal study. *Journal of Consulting and Clinical Psychology.*

Briere, J., & Runtz, M. (1990). Differential adult symptomatology associated with three types of child abuse histories. *Child Abuse and Neglect, 14,* 357-364.

Bureau of Justice Statistics. (1992). *National crime survey.* Washington, DC: U.S. Dept. of Justice.

Bureau of Justice Statistics. (1995). *Criminal victimization in the United States, 1993: A national crime victimization survey report.* Washington, DC: U.S. Dept. of Justice.

Carlson, V., Cicchetti, D., Barnett, D., & Braunwald, K. (1989). Disorganized/disoriented attachment relationships in maltreated infants. *Developmental Psychopathology, 25,* 525-531.

Carter, J. (Ed.). (1974). *The maltreated child.* London: Priory.

Christoffel, K. K. (1990). Violent death and injury in US children and adolescents. *American Journal of Diseases of Children, 144,* 697-706.

Christoffel, K. K., Anzinger, N. K., & Amari, M. (1983). Homicide in childhood. *American Journal of Forensic Medicine and Pathology, 4,* 129-137.

Crittenden, P. A., & Craig, S. E. (1990). Developmental trends in the nature of child homicide. *Journal of Interpersonal Violence, 5,* 202-216.

Crittenden, P. M. (1988). Distorted patterns of relationship in maltreating families: The role of internal representational models. *Journal of Reproductive and Infant Psychology, 6,* 183-199.

Dalenberg, C., Bierman, K., & Furman, W. (1984). A re-examination of developmental changes in causal attributions. *Developmental Psychology, 20,* 575-583.

Daro, D., & McCurdy, K. (1991). *Current trends in child abuse reporting and fatalities: The results of the 1990 Annual Fifty State Survey.* Chicago: National Center on Child Abuse Prevention Research, National Committee for Prevention of Child Abuse.

De Titta, M., Robinowitz, C. B., & More, W. M. (1991). The future of psychiatry: Psychiatrists of the future. *American Journal of Psychiatry, 148,* 853-858.

DuRant, R. H., Getts, A., Cadenhead, C., Emans, S. J., & Woods, E. R. (1995). Exposure to violence and victimization and depression, hopelessness, and purpose in life among adolescents living in and around public housing. *Developmental and Behavioral Pediatrics, 16,* 233-237.

Egeland, B., & Sroufe, L. A. (1981). Developmental sequelae of maltreatment in infancy. *New Directions for Child Development, 11,* 77-92.

Erikson, E. (1968). *Identity, youth and crisis.* New York: Norton.

Eth, S., & Pynoos, R. S. (1985). *Post-traumatic stress disorder in children: Progress in psychiatry.* Washington, DC: American Psychiatric Press.

Federal Bureau of Investigation. (1992). *Crime in the United States, 1991: Uniform crime reports.* Washington, DC: U.S. Dept. of Justice.

Federal Bureau of Investigation. (1994). *Crime in the United States, 1993: Uniform crime reports.* Washington, DC: U.S. Dept. of Justice.

Finkelhor, D. (1984). *Child sexual abuse: New theory and research.* New York: Free Press.

Finkelhor, D. (1993). Epidemiological factors in the clinical identification of child sexual abuse. *Child Abuse and Neglect, 17,* 67-70.

Finkelhor, D. (1994). Current information on the scope and nature of child sexual abuse. *Future of Children, 4*(2), 31-53.

Finkelhor, D., & Asdigian, N. L. (1996). Risk factors for youth victimization: Beyond a lifestyles theoretical approach. *Violence and Victims, 11*(1), 3-20.

Finkelhor, D., & Dziuba-Leatherman, J. (1994a). Children as victims of violence: A national survey. *Pediatrics, 94,* 413-420.

Finkelhor, D., & Dziuba-Leatherman, J. (1994b). Victimization of children. *American Psychologist, 49,* 173-183.

Finkelhor, D., & Dziuba-Leatherman, J. (1995). Victimization prevention programs: A national survey of children's exposure and reactions. *Child Abuse and Neglect, 19,* 125-135.

Finkelhor, D., & Kendall-Tackett, H. K. (in press). A developmental perspective on the childhood impact of crime, abuse, and violent victimization. In D. Cichetti & S. Toth (Eds.), *The effects of trauma on the developmental process.* Rochester, NY: University of Rochester Press.

Finkelhor, D., Hotaling, G. T., & Sedlak, A. (1990). *Missing, abducted, runaway and thrownaway children in America: First report.* Washington, DC: Juvenile Justice Clearinghouse.

Friedrich, W. N., Grambasch, P., Damon, L., Hewitt, S. K., Koverola, C., Lang, R., & Wolfe, V. (1992). Child Sexual Behavior Inventory: Normative and clinical comparisons. *Psychological Assessment, 4,* 303-311.

Garbarino, J. (1989). Troubled youth, troubled families: The dynamics of adolescent maltreatment. In D. Cicchetti & V. Carlson (Eds.), *Child maltreatment: Theory and research of the causes and consequences of child abuse and neglect* (pp. 685-706). New York: Cambridge University Press.

Garofalo, J., Siegel, L., & Laub, J. (1987). School-related victimizations among adolescents: An analysis of National Crime Survey (NCVS) narratives. *Journal of Quantitative Criminology, 3,* 321-338.

Goetting, A. (1990). Child victims of homicide: A portrait of their killers and the circumstances of their deaths. *Violence and Victims, 5,* 287-296.

Goodwin, M. P., & Roscoe, B. (1990). Sibling violence and agonistic interactions among middle adolescence. *Adolescence, 98,* 451-467.

Gordon, L. (1988). *Heroes of their own lives: The politics and history of family violence.* New York: Viking.

Greenbaum, S. (1989). *School bullying and victimization NSSC resource paper.* Malibu, CA: National School Safety Center.

Greven, P. (1990). *Spare the child: The religious roots of punishment and the psychological impact of physical abuse.* New York: Knopf.

Guyer, B., Lescohier, I., Gallagher, S. S., Hausman, A., & Azzara, C. V. (1989). Intentional injuries among children and adolescent in Massachusetts. *New England Journal of Medicine, 321,* 1584-1589.

Hanson, R. L., & Slater, S. (1988). Sexual victimization in the history of sexual abusers: A review. *Annals of Sex Research, 4,* 485-499.

Herman-Giddens, M. E., Sandler, A. D., & Friedman, N. E. (1988). Sexual precocity in girls: An association with sexual abuse? *American Journal of Diseases of the Child, 142,* 431-433.

Jason, J. (1983). Child homicide spectrum. *American Journal of Diseases of Children, 137,* 578-581.

Jason, J., Carpenter, M. M., & Tyler, C. W. J. (1983). Under-recording of infant homicide in the United States. *American Journal of Public Health, 73,* 195-197.

Jensen, G. F., & Brownfield, D. (1986). Gender, lifestyles, and victimization: Beyond routine activity theory. *Violence and Victims, 1,* 85-99.

Kaufman, J., & Ziegler, E. (1987). Do abused children become abusive parents? *American Journal of Orthopsychiatry, 57,* 186-192.

Kendall-Tackett, K. A., & Watson, M. A. (1991). Factors that influence professionals' perceptions of behavioral indicators of child sexual abuse. *Journal of Interpersonal Violence, 6,* 385-395.

Kendall-Tackett, K. A., Williams, L. M., & Finkelhor, D. (1993). Impact of sexual abuse on children: A review and synthesis of recent empirical studies. *Psychological Bulletin, 113,* 164-180.

Kerns, D. L., & Ritter, M. L. (1992). Medical findings in child sexual abuse cases with perpetrator confessions. [Abstract]. *American Journal of Diseases of Children, 146,* 494.

Kilpatrick, D. (1992). *Rape in America: A report to the nation.* Charleston, SC: Crime Victims Research and Treatment Center.

Kilpatrick, D. G., Saunders, B. E., Amick-McMullan, A., Best, C. L., Veronen, L. J., & Resnick, H. S. (1989). Victim and crime factors associated with the development of crime-related post-traumatic stress disorder. *Behavior Therapy, 20,* 199-214.

Kirby, J. S., Chu, J., & Dill, D. L. (1993). Correlates of dissociative symptomatology in patients with physical and sexual abuse histories. *Comprehensive Psychiatry, 34,* 258-263.

Kolko, D. J. (1992). Characteristics of child victims of physical violence: Research findings and clinical implications. *Journal of Interpersonal Violence, 7,* 244-276.

Lauritsen, J. L., Laub, J. H., & Sampson, R. J. (1992). Conventional and delinquent activities: Implications for the prevention of violent victimization among adolescents. *Violence and Victims, 7,* 91-108.

Lauritsen, J. L., Sampson, R. J., & Laub, J. H. (1991). The link between offending and victimization among adolescents. *Criminology, 29,* 265-292.

Lewis, D. O., Shanok, S. S., Pincus, J. H., & Glaser, G. H. (1979). Violent juvenile delinquents: Psychiatric, neurological, psychological and abuse factors. *Journal of the American Academy of Child Psychiatry, 18,* 307-319.

Libby, P., & Bybee, R. (1979). The physical abuse of adolescents. *Journal of Social Issues, 35,* 101-126.

Lynch, J. P. (1991). Victim behavior and the risk of victimization: Implications of activity-specific victimization rates. In G. Kaiser, H. Kury, & H. J. Albrecht (Eds.), *Victims and criminal justice* (pp. 543-566). Freiburg, Germany: Max Planck Institute.

MacDonald, K. (1985). Early experience, relative plasticity, and social development. *Developmental Review, 5,* 99-121.

Martin, S. C., Arnold, R. M., & Parker, R. M. (1988). Gender and medical socialization. *Journal of Health and Social Behavior, 29,* 333-343.

Martinez, P., & Richters, J. E. (1993). The NIMH community violence project: II. Children's distress symptoms associated with violence exposure. In D. Reiss, J. E. Richters, M. Radke-Yarrow, & D. Scharff (Eds.), *Children and violence* (pp. 22-35). New York: Guilford.

Martinez-Schnell, B., & Waxweiler, R. J. (1989). Increases in premature mortality due to homicide: United States, 1968-1985. *Violence and Victims, 4,* 287-293.

McClain, P. W., Sacks, J. J., Froehlke, R. G., & Ewigman, B. G. (1993). Estimates of fatal child abuse and neglect, United States, 1979 through 1988. *Pediatrics, 91,* 338-343.

McCord, J. (1983). A forty year perspective of effects of child abuse and neglect. *Child Abuse and Neglect, 7,* 265-270.

McCormack, A. H. (1938). New York's present problem. *Mental Hygiene, 20,* 4-5.

McDermott, M. J., Stanley, J. E., & Zimmerman-McKinney, M. A. (1982). The victimization of children and youths. *Victimology, 7,* 162-177.

Moone, J. (1994). *Juvenile victimization: 1987-1992* (Fact Sheet No. 17). Washington, DC: U.S. Dept. of Justice, Office of Juvenile Justice and Delinquency Prevention.

Morgan, J., & Zedner, L. (1992). *Child victims: Crime, impact, and criminal justice.* Oxford, UK: Clarendon.

National Center on Child Abuse and Neglect. (1992). *National child abuse and neglect data system. Working Paper No. 1: 1990 summary data component* (DHHS Publication No. ACF 92-30361). Washington, DC: Dept. of Health and Human Services.

National Center on Child Abuse and Neglect. (1995). *Child maltreatment 1993: Reports from the states to the National Center on Child Abuse and Neglect.* Washington, DC: Government Printing Office.

National Research Council. (1993). *Understanding child abuse and neglect.* Washington, DC: National Academy Press.

Olweus, D. (1991). Bully/victim problems among schoolchildren: Basic facts and effects of a school based intervention program. In D. J. Pepler & K. H. Rubin (Eds.), *The development and treatment of childhood aggression* (pp. 411-448). Hillsdale, NJ: Lawrence Erlbaum.

Olweus, D. (1993). Bullies on the playground: The role of victimization. In C. H. Hart (Eds.), *Children of playgrounds: Research perspectives and applications* (pp. 85-128). Albany: State University of New York Press.

Putnam, F. W., & Trickett, P. K. (1993). Child sexual abuse: A model of chronic trauma. In D. Reiss, J. E. Richters, & M. Radke-Yarrow (Eds.), *Children and violence* (pp. 82-95). New York: Guilford.

Rand, M. R. (1994). *Handgun victimization, firearm self-defense, and firearm theft: Guns and crime* (Crime Data Brief NCJ-147003). Washington, DC: U.S. Dept. of Justice.

Resnick, P. A. (1993). The psychological impact of rape. *Journal of Interpersonal Violence, 8,* 223-255.

Roscoe, B., Goodwin, M., & Kennedy, D. (1987). Sibling violence and agonistic interactions experienced by early adolescents. *Journal of Family Violence, 2,* 121-137.

Russell, D. E. H. (1984). *Sexual exploitation: Rape, child sexual abuse, and workplace harassment.* Beverly Hills, CA: Sage.

Rutter, M. (1989). The role of cognition in child development and disorder. In S. Chess, A. Thomas, & M. E. Hertzig (Eds.), *Annual progress in child psychiatry and child development: 1988* (pp. 77-101). New York: Brunner/Mazel.

Saunders, B. E., Villeponteaux, L. A., Lipovsky, J. A., Kilpatrick, D. G., & Veronen, L. J. (1992). Child sexual assault as a risk factor for mental disorders among women: A community survey. *Journal of Interpersonal Violence, 7,* 189-204.

Schellenbach, C. J., & Guerney, L. F. (1987). Identification of adolescent abuse and future intervention prospects. *Journal of Adolescence, 10*(1), 1-12.

Scott, K. D. (1992). Childhood sexual abuse: Impact on a community's mental health status. *Child Abuse and Neglect, 16,* 285-295.

Sedlak, A. J. (1991). *National incidence and prevalence of child abuse and neglect: 1986—Revised report.* Rockville, MD: Westat.

Sedlak, A. J., & Rankin, J. H. (1995). *Third national incidence study of child abuse and neglect.* Washington, DC: U.S. Department of Health and Human Services.

Shirk, S. R. (1988). The interpersonal legacy of physical abuse of children. In M. B. Straus (Ed.), *Abuse and victimization across the life span* (pp. 57-81). Baltimore: Johns Hopkins University Press.

Singer, M. I., Anglin, T. M., Song, L. Y., & Lunghofer, L. (1995). Adolescents' exposure to violence and associated symptoms of psychological trauma. *Journal of the American Medical Association, 273,* 477-482.

Smith, P. K., Bowers, L., Binney, V., & Cowie, H. (1993). Relationships of children involved in bully/victim problems at school. In S. Duck (Ed.), *Learning about relationships* (pp. 184-205). Newbury Park, CA: Sage.

Sparks, R. F. (1982). *Research on victims of crime.* Washington, DC: Government Printing Office.

Straus, M. A. (1994). *Beating the devil out of them: Corporal punishment in American families.* New York: Lexington.

Straus, M. A., & Gelles, R. J. (1990). *Physical violence in American families: Risk factors and adaptations to violence in 8,145 families.* New Brunswick, NJ: Transaction.

Straus, M. A., Gelles, J., & Steinmetz, S. K. (1980). *Behind closed doors.* Newbury Park, CA: Sage.

Terr, L. (1990). *Too scared to cry.* New York: Harper/Collins.

Trickett, P. K., & Putnam, F. W. (1993). Impact of child sexual abuse on females: Toward a developmental psychobiological integration. *Psychological Science, 4,* 81-87.

Wells, E. L., & Rankin, J. H. (1995). Juvenile victimization: Convergent validation of alternative measurements. *Journal of Research in Crime and Delinquency, 32,* 287-307.

Widom, C. S. (1989a). The cycle of violence. *Science, 244,* 160-166.

Widom, C. S. (1989b). Does violence beget violence? A critical examination of the literature. *Psychological Bulletin, 106,* 3-28.

6 Coming to Terms With the Sudden, Traumatic Death of a Spouse or Child

CAMILLE B. WORTMAN

ESTHER S. BATTLE

JEANNE PARR LEMKAU

- John and Peg R. lost their only son, Tim, 7, in a drunk driving incident. Tim and another child were struck and fatally injured while on a 2-mile hike with Tim's Cub Scout troop. The drunk driver, who had lost his license several times previously, crashed into the hikers as they walked along a sidewalk near Tim's elementary school.

- Sarah and George M. were a successful, middle-aged couple who were at the peak of their careers. They depended on each other for support because they had no children and no nearby extended family. Sarah had a position as a human resources administrator for a large industry. One Friday afternoon, an enraged employee who had lost his job stormed into Sarah's office. He shot and killed her before turning the gun on himself.

- Annie T., a divorced mother, was asked by her 10-year-old son, Brett, if he could go next door and play with his friend, Michael. Shortly after Brett left, Annie thought she heard gunshots. Apparently Michael had decided to show Brett his father's revolver, which was kept loaded and unlocked in the bedroom. The gun misfired as the boys were handling it, and Brett was seriously injured. He was rushed to the hospital but was pronounced dead on arrival. Annie was not aware that Michael's family owned a gun.

- Jane and Bob S., who had been married for 42 years, were on their way to visit their newest grandchild when Bob pulled over to help at the scene of an accident. Jane stayed in their car while Bob approached the disabled vehicle up ahead. Just as he reached the vehicle, he heard a deafening crash. A semi-truck driver lost control and went onto the shoulder, destroying Jane's car on impact. Jane was killed instantly as Bob looked on in horror. The truck driver had been on the road for many hours and had fallen asleep at the wheel.

- Greg B. was an honor student and a varsity athlete. When he turned 17, he began working evenings and weekends at a pizza restaurant to save money for college. He would be the first person in his family to attend college. The repeated complaints of his manager that there was inadequate security at the restaurant were ignored by the owners. One evening at about 10:00 p.m., Greg and the store manager were murdered during a botched hold-up attempt. The assailants were never captured.

The survivors of each incident described above experienced the sudden, traumatic death of a spouse or child. In a single instant, their lives were fundamentally changed. In each case, the death occurred as a result of the carelessness, negligence, or willful misconduct of others. Death of a child under any circumstances and deaths caused by accidents, disasters, war, suicide, or homicide are all considered to be traumatic (Rando, 1993). Although the reader might assume that incidents such as those described above are "freak accidents" that rarely happen in real life, they are surprisingly prevalent. In fact, accidental deaths resulting from motor vehicle crashes, medical malpractice, occupational accidents, drowning, poisoning, and firearms are the leading causes of death among individuals from 1 to 44 years old (Statistical Abstract of the United States, 1994). Approximately 100,000 fatalities of this kind occur each year in the United States alone, and the number continues to increase each year (Rando, 1993). Deaths from homicide are also very prevalent, particularly in the 15 to 24 age range, in which they constitute the second leading cause of death after accidents (Statistical Abstract of the United States, 1994).

Our research and clinical work on bereavement has focused primarily on people who have endured a loss of this sort. We decided to devote a chapter to the impact of traumatic deaths because, despite their prevalence, such losses have attracted little attention from researchers or clinicians writing about bereavement. Although there are hundreds of studies and articles dealing with bereavement, only a handful have addressed the unique problems encountered by those who have endured the sudden, traumatic death of a loved one.

As these families attempt to pick up the shards of their lives and move forward, what lies ahead for them? Most people have conceptions about what it is like to grieve for a loved one. Usually, these expectations are based in part on cultural norms, and in part on past experience in dealing with loss—usually the loss of an elderly parent or grandparent. Drawing from experiences with these kinds of losses, most people expect survivors to experience tearfulness, sadness, and other symptoms of grief for several months after a death. After a year or so, however, survivors of sudden, traumatic losses are expected to pretty much be "over" the death and to be able to put the loss behind them and move on with their lives.

In contrast, research and our professional experience have shown us that the grief process following the sudden and traumatic death of a spouse or child is usually intense and prolonged. Powerful feelings of confusion, anger, and anxiety are usually unleashed, as well as the feelings of depression typically associated with grief. The survivor may experience painful and disruptive symptoms that many people do not associate with grief, such as intrusive thoughts and nightmares and a desire for vengeance against the perpetrator. The timetable is also different for these kinds of losses. Although distress usually declines over time, symptoms often last for many years. In fact, there is some debate over whether survivors of sudden and traumatic loss ever fully recover. Many become reconciled to what happened, but, as one bereaved mother expressed, "You don't get over it, you get used to it." Because outsiders are frequently not aware that people who experience sudden and traumatic losses have debilitating and long-lasting symptoms, they often convey to the bereaved that they should be feeling better than they are. Of course, the failure to live up to others' expectations only leaves the survivors feeling more isolated. Because survivors often share the cultural expectations that they should have recovered in about a year, they are often confused, frightened, and ashamed by the nature, intensity, and duration of their distress.

In this chapter, our goal is to provide a full understanding of what people go through when they experience the sudden, traumatic death of a spouse or child. First, we detail the psychological ramifications of this type of loss and indicate how they are different from those of other types of deaths. Second, we provide an analysis of the social responses that survivors of such losses typically receive from others. Although they have powerful needs for support, there is convincing evidence that survivors of a traumatic loss have special problems in eliciting support from others. Drawing from social psychological theories, we detail why contact with those who have experienced tragedies is often disturbing. Interaction with someone who has suffered a traumatic loss forces people to recognize that such a tragedy could happen to them. The discomfort evoked in such interactions often leads individuals to react in ways that enhance their own comfort (e.g., avoidance, derogation, blame) but that are perceived as insensitive and judgmental by survivors of trauma. Third, we describe why survivors' interactions with the church, the legal system, and people at the workplace are often unsatisfying and disappointing. We explain why such tragedies make it difficult to enjoy leisure activities, recreational pursuits, or holidays. We also describe how such deaths affect ties with close friends, members of the extended family, and even members of the immediate family. Finally, we discuss the unique

difficulties faced by survivors of a sudden, traumatic loss in obtaining effective psychological treatment and the problems faced by professionals working with these clients.

Psychological Ramifications of Sudden and Traumatic Loss

The death of a loved one is a stressor experienced by virtually everyone at some point. A child may lose a grandparent or some other elderly relative while in grade school. In the adult years, most people are faced with the loss of one or both parents. As they continue through life, many people experience the loss of their spouse—a loss that usually, but not always, is preceded by illness. In the grief literature, losses of this kind are usually referred to as "normal" or "on-time" losses. Although there are striking individual differences in how people respond to such losses (Wortman & Silver, 1987), these kinds of deaths are often accompanied by feelings of shock or numbness, with most respondents agreeing that "it's hard to believe." It is common to experience considerable anguish and to be preoccupied with the deceased. Other acute symptoms of grief may include wrenching of the gut, sighing, feeling empty inside, and frequent welling up of tears. Feelings of despair, fatigue, restlessness, irritability, anger, and guilt are also typical. Over time, the symptoms of acute grief usually become less intense and less frequent, and there is a gradual return to feelings of well-being. Although there is no consensus about how long grief will last, most investigators have suggested that it lasts from a few months to a year, depending on the importance of the relationship, the nature of the death, and the coping resources (e.g., social support) available to the survivor (see Shuchter & Zisook, 1993, for a more detailed discussion of the course of normal grief).

The psychological aftermath of a traumatic death differs in many ways from that which follows a loss reflecting a normal part of the life cycle, that is an "on-time" loss. Sudden traumatic losses include (a) deaths that occur suddenly or without warning; (b) deaths that are untimely, including the death of one's child at any age (loss of a child can be viewed as untimely no matter how young or old the child is because parents expect do not to outlive their children); (c) deaths involving violence, mutilation, or destruction; (d) situations involving multiple deaths; (e) deaths viewed as random; (f) deaths perceived as unnecessary or preventable; and (g) deaths that involve a direct threat to the personal safety of the survivor (see Green, 1990, or Rando, 1993, for a more detailed discussion of these factors). As Rando (1993) has noted, these characteristics of sudden, traumatic deaths have a cumulative impact; the more of them that occur together, the more intense and prolonged the grief reaction is likely to be. Most cases of traumatic loss involve two or more of these factors. This is true of the case illustrations that appeared at the beginning of the chapter. For example, John and Peg R. were faced with the sudden death of their son, Tim, a pedestrian who was struck by a drunk driver. The death was violent and mutilating. They also had to contend with the fact that the accident was preventable because if the drunk driver's license had been permanently revoked after his repeated offenses, the accident would not have happened.

We have contrasted losses that are sudden and traumatic with losses that might be considered normal, given how and when they occur during the life course. However, there is no clear dividing line that neatly separates losses into two groups. Some losses that might be considered normal given the point in the life course when they occur, such as the death of one's parents, can still have traumatic elements. Consider the case in which adult children are deprived of their elderly parents in a violent automobile crash resulting from someone else's negligence. The involvement of such traumatic elements (suddenness, violence,

mutilation, etc.) can complicate the grieving process, even for "on-time" losses.

Among those who have experienced a traumatic loss, what pattern of symptoms can be expected? In most cases, the individual experiences the symptoms of normal grief described earlier, which include feelings of shock, intense anguish, and depression. However, these symptoms are usually overlaid with posttraumatic stress symptoms as a result of how the loss occurred (Rando, 1993). If the loss was sudden, occurred without warning, and was perceived as random, feelings of shock may be profound. The survivor may feel completely helpless, confused, out of control, and unable to grasp the implications of what has happened. If the loss was untimely and/or viewed as preventable, feelings of anger may be predominant. Most mourners find it difficult to live with the fact that their loved one is gone and that it did not have to happen—that indeed it would not have happened except for the misconduct of someone else. Particularly if harm was intended or if the perpetrator was cruel or callous, the survivor must grapple with the realization that others can and will commit malevolent acts. Such losses typically evoke intense death anxiety and fears of annihilation, often accompanied by powerful feelings of generalized rage as well as rage specifically directed toward the perpetrator. Moreover, as a result of confronting a violent, mutilating death or viewing the body of the deceased, images of what has happened (or what the survivor imagines to have happened) are often seared into the mind of the bereaved. Such images often return later as intrusive thoughts or fragments of dreams or nightmares.

Because of the way the death occurred, survivors of traumatic deaths are typically flooded with intense and painful affect during the early stages of the trauma. Their defenses are often completely overwhelmed by what has happened. As one survivor expressed it, "It was as though someone cut my insides out" (Burgess, 1975, p. 392). This overwhelming assault to the system almost always leads to the development of posttraumatic stress disorder, or PTSD, symptomatology (see Freedy & Hobfoll, 1995, for a review). PTSD has been defined as "the most common and severe type of post-trauma mental health problem that can occur" (Freedy & Donkervolt, 1995, p. 9). The three hallmark symptoms of PTSD are *re-experiencing symptoms* (e.g., flashbacks or intrusive thoughts); *avoidance* or *numbing symptoms* (e.g., avoiding reminders of the trauma; feelings of detachment or estrangement); and *arousal symptoms* (e.g., difficulty falling or staying asleep; irritability).

Recent evidence suggests that exposure to trauma brings about permanent neurobiological changes that cause persistent hyperarousal, resulting in many of the PTSD symptoms that are experienced (Everly & Lating, 1995). Unfortunately, PTSD can develop into a chronic, debilitating condition with lasting symptoms of personality change such as increased hostility, suspiciousness or paranoia, feelings of emptiness or hopelessness, impulsivity, and constant feelings of danger or impending doom. Individuals' efforts to cope with this pattern of symptoms often create additional difficulties. Because the affect associated with the trauma is so painful, survivors often withdraw from others at the first sign of tension or conflict, limiting their capacity to become involved in encounters that could be soothing or healing (Rando, 1993). Increased use of alcohol among survivors of trauma may be viewed as an attempt to self-medicate or dampen the painful overarousal they are experiencing. However, excessive alcohol use often compounds the depression and sleep disturbances with which the bereaved person is struggling. Moreover, particularly among male survivors, alcohol use often becomes chronic and excessive. There is clear evidence indicating that survivors of traumatic deaths are at enhanced risk for the development of alcoholism and its associated problems.

In attempting to understand why a traumatic death can evoke so many debilitating symptoms, it is important to remember that the death typically provokes an existential crisis, shattering the survivor's most basic assumptions about the world. Because of the way the loss occurred, most mourners are forced to question assumptions that they previously took for granted (see Bowlby, 1969; Marris, 1975; Parkes, 1971). These include assumptions that the world is predictable and controllable, that the world is meaningful and operates according to principles of fairness and justice, that one is safe and secure, that the world is benevolent, and that, generally speaking, other people can be trusted (Janoff-Bulman, 1992).

The traumatic death of a loved one shakes these fundamental assumptions to their very core. Often, the bereaved simply cannot absorb what has happened; the loss does not make sense. The tragedy demonstrates that life is capricious and unpredictable. Depending on the type of death and the violence associated with it, the loss may force the mourner to confront the unfairness of life or even the evil and destructiveness of other people. The dismantling of these basic assumptions often invalidates much of the bereaved's past behavior. For example, two young parents did everything humanly possible to protect their 3-year-old son, such as putting locks on the cabinets and buying the best car seat. Nonetheless, they lost him in a drunk driving crash. In addition to the loss itself, it is painful for parents to recognize that everything they did to protect their child was in vain. The shattering of such assumptions will also have serious implications for them in the future, particularly if they have other children. The trauma makes it clear that there is danger lurking everywhere and that no matter what they do, they cannot keep themselves or their loved ones safe.

The profound impact of traumatic losses and the associated destruction of one's assumptions about the world often results in attempts to preserve or restore one's worldview. These responses are very common, although they often elicit judgmental reactions from others. One such reaction is expressed in a compulsive need for information about what happened to the deceased. Parents who have lost a child will often pore over autopsy reports and comb the site for clues about what happened. This reflects a deep need to understand how and why their child died. Information seeking can benefit the bereaved by providing a means of taking control of the situation and warding off feelings of helplessness. Another set of reactions that may puzzle outsiders has to do with the difficulties mourners have in accepting the reality of this sort of loss. In one study in which people were interviewed 4 to 7 years after the death of their spouse or child in a motor vehicle crash, nearly 40% reported that they sometimes felt the death was not real and held the fantasy that they would wake up and it would not be true (Lehman, Wortman, & Williams, 1987). Powerful wishes override the survivor's knowledge that their loved one is gone forever. Because of the profound difficulties in accepting the loss, the bereaved often have trouble getting rid of the loved one's things or dismantling his or her room. They may choose to keep pictures and other memorabilia in view longer than others might feel is appropriate.

A desire for retribution against the perpetrator is also common among survivors. Particularly if one's loved one has been murdered or killed in a motor vehicle crash by a perpetrator who received only a minimal sentence, the bereaved may harbor fantasies of vengeance. Although others are sometimes critical of the survivor's need for retribution, it is natural for survivors to believe that the person who caused their loved one's death should receive punishment commensurate with the heinous act that was committed. In these cases, the bereaved are especially disturbed if the perpetrator fails to show remorse for what has happened.

How long does it take people to recover from a traumatic death? Some investigators have pointed out that terms such as *recovery* or *resolution* are not applicable to losses of

this sort because they imply a type of once-and-for-all closure that typically does not occur (see, e.g., Rando, 1993). As a result of a traumatic death, the survivor often becomes a changed person who realizes that things will never be the same. The empirical evidence is clear that the effects of such losses are long-lasting and do not conform to the "3 months to a year" timetable expected by most outsiders. In one study focusing on the long-term effects of the sudden, unexpected loss of a spouse or child in a motor vehicle accident 4 to 7 years earlier, interviews were conducted with bereaved respondents and with a control group of nonbereaved individuals. Significant differences between bereaved and control respondents were found on depression and on other psychiatric symptoms, role functioning (e.g., at work, as a spouse, as a parent), and quality of life. Moreover, bereavement was associated with an increased mortality rate, a decline in financial status, and, in the case of bereaved parents, a higher divorce rate. A majority of the respondents—between 60% and 70%—indicated that they had not been able to find any meaning in their loved one's death, had thoughts that the death was unfair, and had had painful memories of their spouse or child during the previous month (Lehman et al., 1987). People continue to experience painful upsurges of grief for many, many years following a traumatic death. These periods of intense distress are often triggered by reminders of the deceased (Rando, 1993). Occasions such as birthdays, anniversaries, weddings, or retirement parties may evoke a strong desire for the loved one's presence (Rando, 1993). Taken together, these results are consistent with Herman's (1992) conclusion that "the impact of a traumatic event continues to reverberate throughout the survivor's life cycle" (p. 211).

Because the symptoms following a traumatic loss are so debilitating, it is common for caregivers, laypersons, and the bereaved themselves to assume that they are indicative of personal weakness, prior maladjustment, or character flaws on the part of the survivor. Such assumptions do the survivor a great disservice because there is considerable evidence that the nature of the traumatic event itself, not the personal characteristics of the survivor, determines the amount of psychological harm that occurs (see Herman, 1992, or Rando, 1993, for reviews). As Rando (1993) has indicated, "Psychological trauma can produce posttraumatic symptomology in almost anyone, regardless of premorbid characteristics" (p. 571). There is evidence to suggest that when confronted with a traumatic loss, those who have previously experienced trauma may exhibit a more intense grief reaction, with more PTSD symptoms, than those who have not previously experienced trauma. Nonetheless, it should not automatically be assumed that a survivor who shows an intense reaction to the loss experienced earlier trauma or was psychologically impaired prior to the death.

Two sets of factors have repeatedly been shown to influence the grieving process and the course of adjustment following the loss. The first of these is the presence of concomitant stressors. Because traumatic deaths tend to overwhelm the survivor, they place an enormous burden on coping resources. If the survivor's resources are already depleted due to the presence of other stressors, such as unemployment, divorce, or physical health problems, coping will be even more difficult.

A second factor that affects the grieving process is social support. People who are hurt or suffering have a special need for supportive relationships with others. Several studies have indicated that perceived support is associated with good emotional adjustment among the bereaved (Stylianos & Vachon, 1993). Although only a few studies have focused on the impact of social support following traumatic loss (see, e.g., Lehman, Ellard, & Wortman, 1986), the evidence suggests that in the aftermath of trauma, social support is particularly important. Because trauma shatters survivors' assumptions about the world and other people, support from others can play a critical role in the healing process (Herman, 1992). When the deceased has been a significant support person for the survivor, the impact of the death is amplified by the loss of a major source of support.

Unfortunately, survivors of traumatic loss often have difficulty in obtaining the support they need. In fact, it appears that survivors experience many of their interactions as unhelpful at best and as alienating and offensive at worst. This phenomenon, known as secondary wounding or the "second injury" (Ochberg, 1988; Symonds, 1980), is believed to result from the needs of others to defend themselves against the belief that something terrible could happen to them. These fears lead them to respond to survivors with self-protective responses such as avoidance, derogation, and blame. This is deeply wounding to survivors, who are hurt by the very people they are counting on for assistance.

Because the dynamics of seeking and obtaining support are complex and important in ameliorating suffering among survivors of traumatic loss, we describe them in more detail below.

Support

People who have suffered a major loss usually value opportunities to discuss the loss (Lehman et al., 1986; Pennebaker, 1993). This wish to discuss what has happened often occurs because the bereaved individual is preoccupied with thoughts of the deceased and wants to have the opportunity to share these thoughts. This provides the chance to clarify what is happening in one's own mind, as well as to be understood by others. Conversations with others can also provide reassurance that one's reactions to the loss are normal, appropriate, and understandable. Because their symptoms are so overwhelming, such reassurances can be particularly helpful to survivors of traumatic loss.

Mental health professionals and laypersons often encourage survivors to talk about what they have been through on the assumption that it is harmful to keep negative feelings "bottled up" inside. In handbooks for mental health professionals dealing with trauma, therapists are usually advised to encourage clients to talk about what happened in detail. Repeated discussions of this sort are regarded as necessary to the healing process (McCann & Pearlman, 1990; Rando, 1993). This is a recognized approach among professionals treating posttraumatic stress disorders. Unfortunately, however, evidence from our own and others' work suggests that any benefits from expressing one's feelings about the trauma in a social context may be outweighed by the costs.

To understand the problems inherent in seeking social support from others—most of whom do not understand the nature and course of traumatic loss—it is important to examine the attitudes and expectations that others hold when they enter into interactions with survivors. As far as understanding what survivors go through when they experience the traumatic death of a spouse or child, most people are "clueless." Having never experienced a loss of this sort, they are simply unable to comprehend the human suffering that is unleashed following a traumatic death. Any personal knowledge they may have about death usually comes from a "normal" or "on-time" loss such as the death of an elderly parent. Unfortunately, many people rigidly and inappropriately apply the understanding derived from such losses to traumatic deaths. As a result, they are often judgmental toward survivors who display symptoms for more than a few months. In fact, in a study of survivors who lost a loved one in a drunk driving crash, nearly 20% of the respondents reported being upset because after only a month following the crash, friends and relatives thought that the grief process should be over and that the sur-

vivor's life should be resumed as normal (Lord, 1987).

In part because of their expectations of a quick recovery, outsiders often believe that survivors of a traumatic death have more control over their symptoms than is in fact the case. As we noted earlier, outsiders often regard the survivor's continuing distress as a character weakness rather than as a legitimate response to the loss (Coyne, Wortman, & Lehman, 1988). It is commonly believed that if they really wanted to, survivors could control their displays of distress and resume normal functioning. Unfortunately, evidence of distress is frequently attributed to a lack of will power; the survivors are believed to be "wallowing in their grief."

Another factor that shapes others' reactions to survivors of a traumatic loss has to do with the kinds of feelings that are elicited by such losses. Interacting with a survivor of a traumatic loss evokes powerful feelings of helplessness and vulnerability in others (Wortman & Lehman, 1985). Feelings of helplessness are evoked because there is so little one can do or say to effect any real improvement in the survivor's situation following a traumatic death. The more distressed the survivor, the more helpless others are likely to feel. Regarding feelings of vulnerability, several theories in social psychology have relevance for understanding reactions to survivors of traumatic loss. These theories suggest that the evaluations that people make about others who are less fortunate are determined in large part by their own needs for security and self-esteem (e.g., Lerner's "just world" theory; see Wortman, Carnelley, Lehman, Davis, & Exline, 1995). Such feelings can lead others to avoid, derogate, and blame survivors of a traumatic death for their fate. In so doing, people can maintain the belief that the world is just and that because they do not deserve to suffer, nothing bad will happen to them.

These beliefs and feelings on the part of others often result in behaviors toward survivors of trauma that are unintentionally damaging. One set of behaviors involves avoidance and withdrawal. One woman whose child was murdered confided to us that people avoided her at the supermarket, presumably because they were uncomfortable in her presence and did not know what to say. This was so painful to her that she drove to the next town to do her grocery shopping. It is common for the survivors of a traumatic loss to point out that many of their supporters stopped calling or visiting after the first few weeks.

Survivors may also be distressed by others' inappropriate questions about the loss. Regarding the accident, they might be asked about such matters as whether the deceased was wearing a seatbelt, to what extent the body was crushed as a result of the impact, whether there was a lot of blood, or specifically how the loved one died. People also ask questions about such matters as money, insurance, and whether the survivor intends to file a lawsuit. In one study of families who lost a loved one in a drunk driving crash, 20% of respondents were exposed to insensitive questions of this sort on the day of the funeral (Lord, 1987). It is not clear whether such questions stem from morbid curiosity, from a desire to learn something about what has happened that will enable the person to feel protected from a similar fate, or from an attempt to fill socially awkward moments. Learning that the deceased driver of a motor vehicle crash was not wearing a seatbelt could reassure the questioner that as long as a seatbelt is worn, there will be protection from such a tragedy.

Other responses to the bereaved that are usually regarded as unhelpful include discouraging expression of feelings (e.g., "Tears won't bring him back"), minimizing the loss (e.g., "You had many good years together"), encouraging the survivor to recover more quickly (e.g., "You should get out more often"), portraying their own experiences as similar to those of the survivor (e.g., "I know how you feel. I lost my second cousin"), and

offering advice (e.g., "You should consider getting a dog; they're wonderful companions"). Such lines of conversation may be regarded as unhelpful because they close off communication with the bereaved person and/or inhibit displays of distress (Davidowitz & Myrick, 1984; Lehman et al., 1986). What survivors do find helpful is talking with others who are receptive and nonjudgmental and who allow them to express their feelings if and when they choose to do so (Lehman et al., 1986).

Finally, the most devastating responses that survivors endure at the hands of others are those involving derogation and blame. A child had climbed out of his car seat shortly before a drunk driver collided into their car and he was killed. His devastated mother reported that several people said, "If he had been secured in his seat, he probably would have lived." As she expressed it, "It may be true, but it broke my heart to hear them say it."

Intuitively, one might expect unhelpful remarks or behaviors to be more prevalent among strangers or casual acquaintances than among the survivors' relatives or close friends. However, this does not appear to be the case. In one study, slightly more than half of all unhelpful comments were made by relatives or friends. Because those closest to the survivor may have the greatest stake in his or her recovery, it is perhaps not surprising that they have little tolerance for displays of distress. Another reason that family members may have difficulty providing support to one another following a traumatic loss is that in most cases, bereavement is a crisis of the entire social network. As Stylianos and Vachon (1993) have suggested, "The joint experience of suffering may render network members unable to support the individual for whom the loss is most immediate and profound" (p. 397).

Repeated exposure to insensitive comments from others is experienced by most survivors as deeply wounding. Such reactions tend to exacerbate feelings of vulnerability, frustration, and injustice (Rando, 1993). As a result, many survivors withdraw from others and give up on the possibility of meaningful social exchanges (see Pennebaker, 1993, for a more detailed discussion). Interactions in which they are blamed, derogated, or discouraged from expressing their pain only serve to make them feel more isolated.

Withdrawal is likely to have a number of negative consequences. One problem is that social withdrawal reduces the likelihood of interactions that could ameliorate the loss. Some investigators have maintained that social connections are essential to the healing process and that those who cut themselves off from others have a bleak prognosis (Herman, 1992). There is also evidence to suggest that those who are unable to discuss their trauma may show an increase in ruminations about the loss and a greater number of health problems (Lepore, Silver, Wortman, & Wayment, 1996; Pennebaker, 1993). Moreover, if the bereaved fail to exhibit their distress and instead hide it from others, this will contribute to false social expectations that most people recover quickly and that displays of intense distress are atypical or indicative of maladjustment (Wortman et al., 1995).

Attempts to Find Solace

Following the traumatic loss of a spouse or child, most people attempt to find solace for their pain—typically in such places as the church or the legal system, through involvement in work or leisure activities, or through interactions with friends or family members. In part because the people encountered in these settings often lack an understanding of what survivors are going through, solace is frequently not found. Instead, the survivor often continues to accumulate experiences are painful and alienating. In this section, we provide a brief overview of the sorts of difficulties that survivors may encounter in those places where solace may be sought.

The Church

Even among people who are religious, the traumatic loss of a spouse or child can evoke a crisis of faith. Parents may become angry toward God for taking an innocent child who brought so much joy to others. Such losses make it difficult to maintain the view of God as a protector. As one woman explained it, "I said the Rosary, 'Protect me in the midst of danger,' so many times, but God did not protect my husband. It's hard for me to say the Rosary now." Feelings that God has betrayed them often occur among those who were actively involved in religion and who tried to uphold the teachings of the church prior to their loss.

For a variety of reasons, attending church may also be difficult following a traumatic loss. Sometimes church attendance can bring home the finality and reality of the loss. As one woman said, "Whenever I go to church, I see my son's casket." In the case of a woman whose parents were murdered, it was painful for her to see someone else playing the church organ, which her mother had played for many years before her death. A man who had attended church with his wife for many years found it jarring and unpleasant to attend without her. Survivors may also feel self-conscious or "on display" at church and may become uncomfortable with repeated questions about how they are holding up. They may also be the recipients of support attempts that they experience as unhelpful, such as "You'll see Richie in the next life" or "God needed him more than you did."

The Legal System

Those who lose a loved one as a result of another's negligence, as in medical malpractice, may decide to file a civil suit against the perpetrator.

If the loved one was murdered or if willful misconduct was involved, as in the case of homicide (vehicular or other), criminal proceedings may ensue. In both types of cases, survivors' concerns are the same. They want to see the perpetrator held accountable for what has happened and to receive some acknowledgment from the legal system that what happened to their loved one was wrong. They want the enormity of their loss and of their continuing pain to be registered publicly. They hope that as a result of their legal action, what happened to their loved one will be less likely to happen to somebody else.

Participation in the judicial system has the potential of having a positive impact on survivors' mental health. In one study of family survivors of homicide victims (Amick-McMullan, Kilpatrick, Veronen, & Smith, 1989), the most important determinant of the anxiety and depression that participants reported was their satisfaction with treatment by the criminal justice system. For a variety of reasons, however, what begins as a search for justice may end in profound disillusionment. In part, this is due to aspects of the judiciary process that are not well understood by laypersons. The outcome or sentence is often disappointing because it is perceived as not commensurate with what the perpetrator has done. Disillusion may also result from reactions of others who may be critical of the survivor's decision to become involved in the legal system.

One aspect of the judiciary process that upsets most survivors is that the attorney for the perpetrator may attempt to shift blame for the death to either the survivors or to the deceased. In one case, a 9-year-old girl was struck and killed by a drunk driver while riding her bicycle. Her parents brought charges of vehicular homicide against the driver. The girl was wearing a helmet and was apparently riding with care. Nonetheless, the parents were criticized during the trial for not providing an iridescent safety flag for their daughter's bicycle.

The judicial process may also expose survivors to painful reminders of the accident. In the above case, the daughter's mangled bicycle was brought into the courtroom as an exhibit by the defense. The parents received no forewarning that they would be confronted with the bicycle. During the trial, survivors may also be exposed to new information about the accident that is profoundly disturbing. A woman who lost her husband in a motor vehicle crash was horrified to learn that her husband's body was dragged along the pavement for 200 yards. Another problem confronting survivors is that during the trial they may be instructed to behave in ways that are foreign or upsetting to them. For example, they may be told to keep their emotions under control or to avoid looking at the defendant. They may also be upset by rulings made during the course of the trial. In one case, an 18-year-old had stopped along the highway to help a disabled vehicle when he was struck and killed by a drunk driver who had crossed the median and was speeding in the wrong direction. The family was horrified when evidence that the man was drunk was withheld from the jury on the grounds that it was prejudicial (i.e., would unfairly prejudice the jury against the defendant).

Most people are not prepared for the many delays that they encounter during the judicial proceedings. Postponements, continuances, and appeals often prolong a legal battle for several years. The repeated delays are painful for survivors, who repeatedly go through the process of psychologically preparing themselves for the courtroom. Most survivors have considerable anxiety about testifying in front of a judge and jury about their loss. It almost seems as if they are on trial and must prove how much they are suffering if justice is to be done. The process can be especially hard on people who are stoic or who do not feel comfortable expressing their distress in a public forum.

Another difficult aspect of judicial proceedings is that they bring survivors into direct contact with the perpetrator. As noted earlier, most survivors harbor intense feelings of rage toward the perpetrator. Face-to-face contact at trial may prove trying, particularly if the perpetrator expresses no remorse about what has happened. Burgess (1975) described the situation encountered by a man whose brother was murdered. He repeatedly expressed a desire to "get his hands on the guy." During the trial, his strong desire for revenge made face-to-face contact with the murderer almost unbearable: "I sat there and looked at his hands . . . remembering what he did. I wished so much that he would come near me. I wanted to choke him to death and I really wanted him to come near me so I would have the chance" (pp. 393-394).

Many survivors feel that they and their loved ones have been given a life sentence of pain and loss. Hence, if the perpetrator receives anything less than a lengthy prison term, this may seem inappropriately lenient. In many cases, the punishment meted out to the perpetrator may be minimal, such as receiving a traffic ticket or paying a fine. In such cases, the disparity between the harm caused by the perpetrator and his or her punishment is likely to be extremely upsetting for the survivor. If the perpetrator receives a minimal sentence from the judge or jury, this typically conveys to the survivor that his or her loved one's life had no meaning. As one father expressed it, "It was as if they said, 'Your daughter was killed. So what!'" Of course, even a lengthy prison sentence can be whittled away through appeals or parole. Once the sentence has been served, the survivor must contend with the perpetrator's release. In some cases, it upsets survivors to recognize that the person responsible for their loved one's death is now free to live a normal life. In other cases, survivors may fear retaliation once the perpetrator has been released.

One reason that court decisions are often not more favorable for survivors is that jurors and judges may typically harbor the same erroneous beliefs about traumatic loss that were discussed earlier. Hence they may be relatively unsympathetic toward survivors who express distress several years after the event. Because such incidents are threatening, jurors may be motivated to believe that the survivor or the deceased was at fault.

In addition to the indignities stemming from the legal system itself, survivors may have to cope with the reactions of family members and friends who are not sympathetic to litigation. Survivors are sometimes told that pursuing legal action is fruitless because it "will not bring their loved one back" or because "no matter what you do, there will always be drunk drivers." If respondents are involved in a civil case, others may not understand why they are seeking monetary damages. Many people are unaware that in most cases, the survivor's primary interest in pursuing such a claim is in seeing justice done, not in obtaining a monetary reward for its own sake. Others may also subject the survivors to a barrage of unpleasant questions and comments about the legal proceedings, such as telling them how lucky they are that they received a settlement and asking what they plan to do with the money.

Work

Following the traumatic loss of a spouse or child, most survivors take some time off from work. Surprisingly, many people return to work a few days or weeks after the funeral, although some do not return for several weeks or months. In some cases, people return to work before they feel ready to do so because of financial concerns. In other cases, returning to work is voluntary. Many survivors find it too painful to remain at home with their thoughts and memories. Although they may not feel ready to resume the demands of their job, they return to work hoping that "keeping busy" and burying themselves in work will help distract them from their grief and fill the awful emptiness they feel inside.

On returning to work, many people find it helpful to be reestablishing a more normal life routine and to have some means of structuring their time. Many are fortunate to have at least some coworkers who are genuinely supportive and caring. Unfortunately, survivors may also encounter a variety of experiences at work that are distressing. Many survivors feel very self-conscious around others, often making remarks such as "I felt everyone was staring at me" or "I felt that my presence was making everyone uncomfortable." Survivors frequently report experiences such as walking up to a group of people who are conversing and having the conversation stop cold. Especially during the first several weeks on the job, most survivors also have trouble keeping their emotions under control. They may become tearful on encountering any reminder of the loss, such as dealing with a customer who has the same name as their loved one. Survivors find that they often have to retreat to a private space such as the bathroom until they can regain their composure.

Most people have major problems with concentration and memory following a traumatic loss. This can significantly reduce the chances of successful performance at work. People who are in contact with the public find that they can no longer remember the names of their customers. Survivors who work with numbers or figures find that they have to keep checking and rechecking everything they do. Those who work with heavy machinery often worry that a lapse in concentration will result in an injury for themselves or someone else. This lack of concentration is often accompanied by significant problems in maintaining motivation for one's work. Following a traumatic loss, it is common to feel that nothing matters very much, including one's job. Many people report that they no longer find their job satisfying or interesting, that they have to force themselves to do tasks that they performed easily before the tragedy, and that previous plans for long-term career advancement have lost their meaning.

Survivors also report difficulty in dealing with the day-to-day office banter of their colleagues. A woman whose teenage son was struck and killed by a drunk driver found it upsetting to hear a colleague complain about the high insurance premiums he had to pay for his son's automobile insurance. A man whose wife was killed had trouble showing sympathy for a colleague who complained because his wife was away on a trip for a week. These indignities are sometimes suffered in silence, but at other times they become public, adding to the survivor's discomfort. For example, a man who lost his teenage daughter just before she was planning to leave for college was approached by a subordinate who wanted to take a few days off so that he and his daughter could visit colleges. When he heard this request, his eyes teared up even though it had been a few years since his daughter had died. This reminded the subordinate of what had happened. The incident was extremely awkward and uncomfortable for both of them.

Certain types of jobs have a high likelihood of exposing the survivor to difficult interactions. This is the case for people who work in consulting, sales, or other professions that bring them into periodic contact with their customers. Particularly at first, many of the people they are calling on may not know about the loss and may innocently inquire about their spouse or children. The survivor is then in the position of having to tell them about the loss and deal with their reaction to it. Telling a coworker or customer about the loss for the first time is a particularly emotional experience for bereaved family members; "It's as if it just happened," explained a woman whose husband had been killed in a robbery 18 months before. One woman who was often placed in a difficult situation by customers had worked for Welcome Wagon, an organization that greets newcomers to the community. This woman had had two young children and had lost one of them in a motor vehicle accident. She returned to work after a few weeks but had to quit the job because newcomers would invariably ask how many children she had. As she put it, "I couldn't say two because that was a lie, and I couldn't say one because that seemed to dishonor the child who had died—who will always be my child. I couldn't say,

'I had two, but one died' because this would make both the customer and me very sad, and I would start to cry."

Leisure and Recreation

For most people, leisure and recreational activities serve as a source of replenishment. Following a traumatic loss, however, it is often difficult for survivors to continue with hobbies or recreational activities that were enjoyed with the deceased. A father who used to go hunting and fishing with his teenage son may find it very difficult to derive relaxation from these activities after his son's death. Engaging in previously shared activities alone often evokes a vivid sense of who is missing and what has been lost. Many people are never able to resume activities that they enjoyed with the family member who died.

Vacations and other special outings also present challenges to survivors of traumatic loss. If the family returns to a regular vacation spot following the death, the trip is likely to trigger bittersweet memories of the past and an almost palpable sense that things are not right because the loved one is missing. If a new destination is chosen, the vacation may evoke a painful sense of what the deceased has missed and how much he or she would have enjoyed the experience. One couple who had lost a toddler in a motor vehicle crash took their surviving child to Disney World the following year. It was extremely painful to encounter Barney because Barney had always been their toddler's favorite character.

Even such mundane experiences as eating dinner or watching television may change markedly as a result of a traumatic death. A family of four may have difficulty coping with the empty kitchen chair where the deceased used to sit; as a result, they may elect not to have their dinners together or to sit on the couch and watch TV during dinner. It may be hard for survivors to relax while watching TV because they never know when they will be confronted with a vivid reminder of the de-

ceased or of the incident in which their loved one died. A couple who lost a blond toddler in a drunk driving crash may find it difficult to be confronted with the endless series of blond toddlers who appear in diaper and cereal commercials. A young man who lost his wife in a plane crash may become upset if footage of a plane crash is shown on TV or in a movie. Even reading the newspaper is likely to be a profoundly altered experience for most survivors. A man who lost his child may become incensed on seeing a feature about parents who abuse their children. A woman whose child was killed in a gun accident may find it painful to encounter an article about the easy availability of weapons.

The Nuclear Family

It is important to understand the structure and functioning of the family as a system, above and beyond the relationships between any two members of that family unit. To assess the impact of a traumatic loss on any particular family member, it is essential to develop a thorough understanding of the family system before the loss.

Each family has rules about the expression of emotion, the distribution of power within the family, the roles played by individual family members, and the boundaries between the family and outsiders. With a traumatic loss, the family structure and function are often disrupted, with serious consequences. When Jack was killed in a church outing because the defective brakes on the bus gave way, his wife and three children were cast adrift. Jack had been a strong disciplinarian. When he died suddenly, his three adolescent children began to disobey their mother and act out in the community with drinking and vandalism. Although the family had been emotionally contained and retiring, Jack's wife, Elaine, could not control herself and cried in church and at work when she encountered reminders of Jack and his death. Jack's daughter, Karen, had been particularly close to him. When he died, she dropped out of college (rejecting Jack's goal) and moved in with a boyfriend who was considerably older than herself. This formerly happy, church-going family became angry and avoidant of their parish, which in turn withdrew from them because of their collective sense of guilt about Jack's death while in the service of the church.

Because interactions with the outside world are often troubling, trauma survivors are in special need of support and understanding from members of the immediate family. However, even the closest of human ties—those between husband and wife and between parent and child—suffer profound changes following a traumatic loss. The atmosphere at home may become gloomy and tense. Family members may become more irritable and impatient following a traumatic loss. Moreover, as individual family members struggle with their anguish, there is sometimes a contagion effect as grief reverberates through the family. Each family member is troubled by his or her own pain with respect to the loss and also by his or her awareness of how much other family members are hurting and how much they have lost. A mother's heart may break when she sees her son's tears at the realization that his father will not be at his championship soccer game. Following the traumatic loss of a child, a father who has had a relatively good day at work may plummet to despair by returning home and finding his wife sobbing.

The home contains endless reminders of the person who has died, even if many of the loved one's personal belongings have been removed. A wife may become overwhelmed with grief when she goes out onto the deck that her husband had built just before he was killed; parents may be deeply saddened when they go into the den where their teenage son put up shelves in that room just prior to his death. Moreover, most family members have countless memories of their loved one doing things at home—a husband barbecuing steaks on the grill, a child swinging on the swing set—and

these memories are easily evoked by merely being at home. Bereaved family members with PTSD may use their home as a retreat in an effort to avoid unexpected situations that may stir up threat, anxiety, or out-of-control feelings with their loss. On the other hand, family members may find that the reality of their loved one's death hits hardest when they are at home. It is not uncommon for individual family members to avoid the home or to move, contributing to a growing sense of disconnectedness (Lehman et al., 1987).

Impact on the Marriage

Even the best marriages are greatly strained. Men and women often grieve differently. Men often feel compelled to "be strong" because they feel that this is in the best interests of the family. Furthermore, men are brought up to restrain the open expression of painful feelings. A man may find that he can succeed in maintaining control of his feelings only by distancing himself from his more openly distressed wife. It is typical for men to deal with their distress by keeping as busy as possible; this is often accomplished by spending increased time at work. Women often feel a powerful need to talk about the tragedy. If the husband gives off cues that he does not want to hear about the wife's feelings, she is likely to become resentful. A wife may interpret her husband's lack of expressiveness, as well as his desire to stay busy, as a sign that he really did not care about the child who died. Wives may worry that as a result of "keeping his feelings bottled up inside," their husbands will experience negative health consequences such as ulcers or high blood pressure. Loss of sexual interest is a common symptom of depression. Husbands and wives may have different preferences about sexual intimacy in the face of their bereavement. Women often have a complete lack of interest in sex following the loss of a child; men's interest may stay the same, decrease, or even increase as a defense against the feelings of loss. In any event, sex may become a source of contention between the couple, or their sexual relationship may be a casualty of the child's death.

Parenting

Following the loss of a family member, the surviving parent(s) typically struggle with a number of specific problems. Chief among them is that when one is in the throes of grieving, it is almost impossible to be emotionally available to surviving family members. Children who have lost one parent to death sometimes feel as if they have lost the other parent emotionally as a result of the tragedy. Another problem is that parents' preoccupation with the deceased, combined with the fatigue that is commonly experienced, makes it difficult for them to enforce consistent discipline. Following a traumatic loss, it is common for parents to expose their children to stretches of benign neglect punctuated by periods of irritability and harshness. It is also common for surviving parents to "spoil" children following a traumatic loss, usually by giving the child more material possessions. This may occur in part because, as a result of the death, parents believe that "life is short" and that it is not wise to delay gratification. In addition, parents are aware that the child has been through a rough time, and they may attempt to provide gifts as a way of comforting the child.

Because the tragedy has shattered feelings of safety and security, parents typically become overprotective following a traumatic loss. It is common for such parents to question children unmercifully about where they are going and what they are doing. Such increased scrutiny often contributes to the development of animosity in the household. As a result of a traumatic loss, activities previously enjoyed are now viewed as dangerous by the adults. Ten-year-old Becky was previously allowed to ride her bicycle to a friend's house a few blocks away. Since her younger brother was killed in a motor vehicle accident, her parents no longer let her ride unless she is supervised by an adult.

Because young children often express their grief differently from adults, they often manifest behaviors that make the task of parenting more challenging at a time when parental resources are at an all-time low. Aggression, anxiety, and regressive behaviors are common symptoms of trauma and depression in young children. Parents also may have to cope with children's sleep problems. The surviving child may insist on sleeping with or near the parent(s). Eleven-year-old Sam slept at the foot of his parents' bed for a year after his 14-year-old sister died. Bed-wetting is also common. Other symptoms of anxiety that are common among young children who have experienced traumatic loss are headaches, stomachaches, and difficulties tolerating separation from their parent(s). Parents also may find that their children ask difficult and painful questions, such as why a man shot their father or whether they can visit a sibling who died. Depending on their age, they may not understand the permanence of death. A 5-year-old insisted to her father, "I don't care what you say, I know Mommy is coming back." Children may also bring up the trauma at times when their parents would prefer not to deal with it, as in the case of a child who struck up a conversation with a customer in the checkout line of the supermarket and announced to her that "my brother died in a fire."

Teenagers may become more angry, rebellious, and uncooperative around the house following a traumatic loss, and it may be difficult to determine to what extent particular changes were caused by the loss and to what extent they reflect the child's reaching the teenage years. Because of their growing need for independence, teenagers often have substantial difficulty coping with parents who are overprotective. For all of these reasons, teenagers' comments are sometimes extremely hurtful, as in the case of one mother whose daughter yelled, "Why couldn't it have been *you* who died instead of Dad?" In other cases, the child may be thrown into a caregiver role with a bereaved parents who is unable to function, interfering with the child's healthy emotional development.

The Extended Family

Survivors generally expect that they will get emotional support from their parents, siblings, and other relatives following a traumatic death. Sometimes this is the case. It is typical for survivors to have one confidant—usually a mother or a same-sex sibling—to whom they can turn for comfort and understanding. To their surprise, however, most survivors encounter difficulties in dealing with their extended family, both individually and at family gatherings and celebrations.

One problem frequently discussed by survivors is the extended family members' refusal to acknowledge and talk about the deceased. Survivors often find it disturbing that family members who were formerly very close to their spouse or child now act as if the loved one never existed. This sort of behavior may occur because family members fear that they may upset the survivor by bringing up the deceased in conversation and also because they worry that they themselves will become distraught if they discuss the loved one.

It is also common for survivors to encounter family members who show the same kinds of unsupportive behaviors discussed above in the section on social support, such as minimizing the loss, providing unsolicited advice, or blaming the survivor for what happened. Parents who lose an adult son may feel compelled to give their daughter-in-law advice about how she should be raising the children and whether she should return to work ("Janet owes it to Gary to stay home and focus on the children"). Sometimes the circumstances surrounding the loss unfold so as to increase the likelihood that a specific person will be blamed by other family members, as when a father has purchased the motorcycle his son was riding when he was struck and killed in a motor vehicle accident, or when a mother asks her child to go to the store on an errand and the child is killed by a drunk driver as he is returning on his bicycle. In such cases, most survivors are already struggling with intense feelings of self-reproach and guilt. Accusatory comments by family members deepen their wounds.

Family occasions such as graduations, weddings, and baby showers are likely to be unbearably painful for people who have lost a spouse or child. Following the loss of a child, for example, attending such events heightens parents' awareness that their child will never graduate, go out on dates, marry, or have a family. If survivors do lose their composure at such an event, they may not receive much sympathy. One woman who lost her infant son in a motor vehicle crash became tearful at a baby shower thrown for her sister. She overheard her mother say that "it's too bad Peggy can't be happy for Susan instead of just focusing on herself and her own tragedy."

Even holiday gatherings can result in stunning displays of insensitivity by members of the extended family. One couple who lost their teenage son a few months previously was shocked when the husband's brother said a prayer at Christmas dinner that began, "Thank the Lord that the whole family is here together."

Treatment

Most people attempt to handle the impact of a traumatic loss on their own, perhaps with the help of a few family members or close friends. Of those who do seek formal assistance of some kind, it is usually limited to one or two visits with one's pastor or family physician. Unfortunately, physicians and pastors typically do not receive extensive training in grief dynamics or in the sequelae of traumatic loss. Only a small percentage of bereaved persons seek help from a mental health professional or a support group (in most studies, from 1% to 5%; see Jacobs, 1993, for a review), and the percentage is smaller still for those who have experienced traumatic loss.

The most likely reason for the avoidance of professional help is the wish to avoid situations that may stir up feelings and memories associated with the loss. The bereaved may also fail to seek treatment because of ignorance about what mental health professionals do and/or cultural beliefs that people should be able to handle their problems on their own. A stoic widower said, "I thought mental health professionals were only for people who are suicidal." Many see therapy as a crutch for weak-willed people who lack the inner strength to cope with the loss. Reluctance to seek professional help may also stem from survivors' concern about losing control over their feelings or not be able to stand the pain of discussing their feelings. As one client expressed it, "I'm afraid I might fall apart. . . . I might begin crying and never stop" (McCann & Pearlman, 1990, p. 214). Survivors may also worry that the therapist will not believe or understand what they are going through or will be repelled or disgusted by what they feel they need to talk about. One woman whose child was killed by a drunk driver was reluctant to discuss her elaborate fantasies of revenge against the perpetrator.

It is very difficult for survivors of traumatic loss to be healed on their own. In one horrific moment, their world has been permanently altered. Many of the symptoms they are experiencing—intense anxiety, sleep disturbances, flashbacks, concentration problems—are so disturbing that they cause survivors to question their sanity. These and other symptoms undermine survivors' coping resources at a time when the demands are monumental. And although the most difficult coping task may be learning to live without the spouse or child who played a central role in their lives, this is by no means the only loss that is encountered. Survivors may also need to grieve the loss of their hopes and dreams for the future, their belief in God as a benevolent protector, and their belief in a fair and just legal system. The incident is likely to shatter the normality of their home life and family rituals, including holidays and recreational pursuits. Their relationships with particular friends and family members, their motivation to excel at work, and (following child loss) the sexual intimacy they shared with their spouse may also be casualties of the trauma. Against the backdrop of these profound losses, survivors are also confronted with everyday-life problems that were brought on as a direct result of the trauma. These can include a sudden loss of income; hassling with tasks formerly handled by the loved one who died, as when a widow must struggle to get the taxes together or the furnace repaired; or having to deal with new problems that have emerged as a result of the tragedy, such as a young child's bed-wetting or sleep difficulties or an older child's uncooperativeness and rage.

In our experience, most survivors make a valiant effort to cope with the myriad problems that emerge in the wake of tragedy. As we described above, however, their attempts to find understanding, comfort, or justice through interactions with others or involvement in their work, the church, or the legal system are often unsuccessful. With each new instance of insensitivity, derogation, or blame, the survivor's spirit may be diminished a little more. Clinical depression, exacerbation of preexisting personal/family difficulties, or onset of stress-related physical problems may ensue.

Available evidence suggests that for all these reasons, time does not heal the wounds inflicted by a traumatic loss. What does happen as the days, months, and years go by? Most people alternately experience intrusive symptoms, such as flashbacks or nightmares, and numbing symptoms, such as feeling detached or dead inside (Herman, 1992; Horowitz, 1986). For the first few weeks and months following the trauma, symptoms of intrusive thoughts and feelings are likely to predominate as the survivor is flooded with intense, overwhelming emotions. Over time, these intrusive symptoms fade somewhat, but they are still triggered by a variety of cues, such as the loved one's birthday and anniversary, or hearing the loved one's favorite song. A major problem for survivors is that they encounter such cues when and where they least expect them and thus have little control over their emotions. One woman who lost her husband in an occupational accident was called by friends a few years after the accident. They offered to take her out to dinner the following weekend. They picked her up and drove to the restaurant they had selected. Unbeknownst to them, the survivor and her husband had gone to that same restaurant together to celebrate her birthday a few days before he was killed. The woman was unable to control her emotions on arriving at the restaurant. The friends suggested that they go to a different restaurant, but the woman felt too upset to go out for dinner at that point and asked to be taken home. What was anticipated as a pleasant evening became a distressing and awkward social encounter. Repeated experiences of this sort contribute to the survivor's feelings of helplessness and estrangement.

As time continues to pass, numbing or constrictive symptoms may come to predominate. Attempts to avoid the trauma may lead to a narrowing of the survivor's focus, a withdrawal from engagement with others, and ultimately, an impoverished life (Herman, 1992). To outside observers, it may appear as if the survivor is moving forward with life. But survivors often describe themselves as feeling "dead inside" or as "just going through the motions." Herman (1992) has noted that because these are negative symptoms, significant through what is missing, they are easy for outsiders to overlook. The effort of the bereaved to "put on a good front" in social situations coincides with the need of others for recovery to occur, but the underlying pain and distress are not alleviated.

In the field of bereavement, there is controversy about whether more effort should be made to encourage the bereaved to seek treatment. Some practitioners maintain that as long as the grief falls within normal limits, it can be handled with the assistance of family, friends, and community supports and that professional intervention is not necessary. We disagree strongly with this notion; in cases of sudden, traumatic loss, grief is never "normal," and mental health treatment is almost always warranted. As was detailed above, the survivor's grief is typically overlaid with PTSD symptoms. Because the symptoms are so debilitating and so unlikely to remit spontaneously, treatment is generally indicated. Without treatment, a person with this pattern of symptoms "is condemned to a diminished life, tormented by memory and bounded by helplessness and fear" (Herman, 1992, p. 49). With professional treatment, the bereaved may experience significant resolution of symptoms of posttraumatic stress and assistance in working through their grief.

Therefore one of the most important ways that people can assist bereaved individuals who have sustained a traumatic loss is by encouraging them to get professional help. Although a review of outcome studies is beyond the scope of this chapter (see Exline, Dorrity & Wortman, 1996, for a more detailed discussion), research provides clear support for the usefulness of individual therapy. Although the evidence regarding any one technique is not 100% consistent, controlled studies demonstrate the effectiveness of various techniques, ranging from exposure-based treatments such as flooding or systematic desensitization to psychodynamic therapy and family therapy. Regarding the efficacy of peer support interventions, the evidence is mixed. However, many of the available studies have methodological limitations that make them difficult to interpret. A few well-controlled studies provide convincing evidence that one-to-one peer counseling and peer support groups can facilitate the healing process (see Exline et al., 1996, for a more detailed discussion).

The role of medication (such as antidepressants and antianxiety drugs) in the treatment of traumatic loss is more controversial. There is growing interest in the use of medications consistent with the evidence of biological underpinnings for both PTSD and clinical depression. However, some clinicians believe that drugs can interfere with the process of remembering and reliving the trauma—a process they maintain is essential to healing. As scientific knowledge about PTSD symptomatology has continued to expand, it appears that this pessimism about the use of drugs may be unwarranted. In fact, evidence from several sources suggests that by stabilizing clients, medications can often free them to work through their painful feelings without becoming overwhelmed. Studies show that both trycyclic and selective serotonin reuptake inhibitors antidepressants (SSRIs) are helpful in mitigating PTSD symptoms associated with traumatic loss. There is also evidence to support the use of antianxiety medications such as the benzodiazepines, especially in the early stages of the trauma. They may help to reduce acute symptoms, such as heightened arousal, intrusive imagery, startle reactions, shaking, and disrupted sleep. Because of their rapid onset, many practitioners prefer these drugs to antidepressants for clients who are experiencing acute symptomatology. However, it should be kept in mind that antianxiety drugs can have addictive properties. Although it is unusual for survivors of traumatic loss to become dependent on antianxiety medications, the use of these drugs should be monitored carefully, especially if the client has a history of substance abuse.

In summary, evidence supports the judicious use of antidepressant and antianxiety drugs in the treatment of those who have experienced a traumatic loss. Yet because of the controversy surrounding their use, many people who could be helped substantially by medications are not receiving them. Clinicians must remain open-minded to the potential benefits of medications and must be willing to educate and counsel their patients about these options. There is general agreement that if medication is warranted, it should be prescribed in conjunction with psychological intervention (Davidson & van der Volk, 1996; Southwick & Yehuda, 1993).

Although people may benefit from attending support groups (see discussion below), in most cases, individual therapy or group therapy with a professional leader is a better choice for those who have suffered traumatic loss. In our judgment, the most important factor to consider when making a referral for treatment is whether the therapist has training and experience in treating grief, trauma, and PTSD, in addition to general professional competence.

In individual therapy, the major goals of treatment include empowering the survivor and freeing him or her from the grip of the trauma (see Rando, 1993, for a more detailed discussion). The intervention should focus not only on cardinal symptoms of PTSD, such as intrusion and avoidance, but also on the defenses that have been erected against those symptoms, such as withdrawal. The treatment should also focus on maladaptive behaviors such as alcohol use, which have been used to control the symptoms, and should foster the development of skills required to cope with problems created by the trauma (e.g., money management or job skills, or parenting skills to deal with uncooperative or "acting-out" behavior).

Symptoms of PTSD must be resolved before the treatment of the complicated grief can be pursued. During the course of treatment, therapists attempt to provide a safe haven where the emotions associated with the trauma can be identified, expressed, and worked through. Most therapists use some sort of exposure to the traumatic stimuli, to aid the client in developing the capacity to tolerate and modulate the painful feelings associated with the original trauma. Although some therapists have had success with implosive therapy, there is consensus that this technique risks retraumatizing the client, and that a gradual introduction of traumatic material, such as is accomplished through systematic desensitization, is less likely to overwhelm the client. As painful feelings emerge, it is important for the therapist to provide reassurance that the client's feelings and responses are normal under the circumstances. Normalizing the client's responses is particularly important following a traumatic loss because many symptoms (e.g., vivid flashbacks of the accident and fantasies of revenge against the perpetrator) are very frightening. Most threatening is the loss of a sense of personal control. As was noted above, clients are unlikely to receive validation for such symptoms from members of their social environment. Other techniques that may be used to alleviate the anxiety of PTSD include cognitive therapy, guided imagery, desensitization, and relaxation (see Rando, 1993, for a more detailed discussion). Having access to these techniques allows the bereaved to counteract feelings of helplessness associated with the trauma.

Once the PTSD symptoms have abated and the client is stabilized, grief becomes the appropriate focus of treatment. The therapist needs to support and guide the client in the process of accomplishing four interrelated tasks: (a) accepting the reality of the loss, (b) working through the pain of grief, (c) adjusting to an environment in which the deceased is missing, and (d) internally relocating the deceased so as to move on with life (Worden, 1991). During this process, the client begins to face the reality of the loss more directly and to express feelings generated by this realization.

The bereaved should also be encouraged to identify and grieve secondary losses resulting from the death. In losing a spouse, for example, direct losses may include losing a sexual partner, a source of social support, a repair person, and so forth. Secondary losses include such things as the loss of a home due to increased financial pressures or the loss of a planned-for vacation or retirement with the deceased. Recognizing and grieving these secondary losses is a necessary step toward adjusting to one's changed environment.

The survivor should also be assisted in resolving, as much as is possible, any "unfinished business" with the deceased. Clients need to be supported in expressing potentially unacceptable feelings toward the deceased, such as relief from problematic aspects of the relationship. They should also be assisted in expressing wishes or feelings that were not shared with the deceased while he or she was alive. For example, a man may regret that he never thanked his wife for certain sacrifices she made for his career.

Helping clients find ways to say goodbye to the deceased is as important as it is painful. Only when some degree of closure is accomplished and the finality of the loss accepted is the client able to move on and reinvest in the living. This reinvestment brings up a new set of issues that may need working through—for example, feelings of disloyalty toward a deceased spouse that might be generated by beginning to date.

Sometimes support groups can play a useful role in the treatment of traumatic loss. Such groups may be appropriate for clients who cannot afford psychotherapy but nonetheless desire some form of support. Some people are more comfortable in a group than in individual treatment. Support groups or one-on-one peer support programs can also serve as important adjuncts to individual psychotherapy. Listening to the stories of survivors who have experienced a similar loss can be uniquely empowering, reassuring the bereaved that their own feelings and behaviors are normal. Groups may also provide a forum for the exchange of information about grief, PTSD, and community resources. The group combats the tendency to withdraw and provides the opportunity for individuals to augment their support system by forming relationships with other group members. Finally, involvement in the group can combat feelings of helplessness by giving members opportunities to assist others or to work for social policy changes that could spare others the trauma they experienced (e.g., members of MADD working for drunk driving legislation).

Support groups and peer support programs are best conceptualized as adjuncts to, rather than replacements for, individual or family psychotherapy. Particularly during the first few months of treatment, it is important to monitor coping failures and risks of suicide and to ensure that the bereaved has the opportunity to receive appropriate medications when warranted. These treatment goals are best accomplished in individual psychotherapy. Moreover, many of the techniques effective in combating PTSD symptomatology are best employed by trained and experienced professionals in a one-on-one situation.

Support groups have their limitations. Many people feel uncomfortable discussing their difficulties with strangers, even if these strangers have experienced a similar fate. Because men are more reluctant to express their emotions in a public forum, most support groups are made up almost entirely of women. This can undermine the value of the experience for men who do attend, leading some experts to suggest that one-to-one peer interventions may be a better option for men than support groups. Unless such groups are specifically set up for those who have suffered traumatic loss, survivors may find that the majority of the people in the group have suffered "on-time" losses and have concerns that are different from theirs. Young widows may have difficulty finding an age-compatible group who are wrestling with similar issues, such as rearing their young children, dating, and/or wishing to remarry.

In groups composed primarily of those who have endured a traumatic loss, individuals may find it overwhelming to encounter so many people who have had their lives shattered as a result of the negligence or malevolence of others. One woman fled a group, stating, "I couldn't stand seeing all those people who, after 4 years, were just as upset as I was after 3 months." Interactions with the group can reinforce the view, triggered by the survivor's own experience, that the world is a place where horrible things can and do happen on a regular basis. Finally, there may be a greater threat of obtaining misinformation in a support group than in individual treatment. In one case, a woman who lost her only child was so distraught that she was put on a mild antianxiety drug by her physician. On attending a support group for the first time, she was chastised for taking the medicine and urged to flush it down the toilet while the group looked on and cheered. A few days later, the anxiety became so overpowering that she had to be hospitalized.

Challenges of Intervention With Survivors of Traumatic Loss

There are special challenges inherent in working with survivors of traumatic loss. Working with survivors of trauma is likely to have a profound psychological impact on the mental health professional (Figley, 1995). The work is accompanied by lasting changes in therapists' views about themselves, others, and the world. Moreover, the impact is typically pervasive, potentially affecting all domains of the therapist's life. As Pearlman and Saakvitne (1995a) have expressed it, it is impossible to do this kind of work and remain unchanged. The many changes in the therapist's identity, worldview, and inner experience that result from trauma work have been called "vicarious traumatization" (McCann & Pearlman, 1990).

Therapists who treat survivors of traumatic loss are routinely confronted with raw, intense emotions. Repeated exposure to such anguish can take its toll and can also bring therapists face to face with the limitations in their ability to alleviate suffering. Treatment of those who have endured sudden traumatic losses can also produce feelings of intense anxiety and vulnerability in the therapist, who is forced to recognize that tragedy can strike anyone at any time. Listening to vivid and graphic details of a client's description of an accident in which a loved one was killed or of encountering the loved one's body following an act of violence can result in intrusive imagery that can be profoundly disturbing. Repeated exposure to others' lives being shattered viciously and without warning can prompt an existential crisis in the therapist that may result in a diminished view of humanity. As therapists struggle to provide treatment in the face of such overwhelming needs and to integrate the disturbing material they are subjected to on a daily basis, they may develop many of the same symptoms of PTSD that plague their clients.

The frustration that therapists may experience as a result of doing this work can have a destructive impact on them and their clients. Feelings of vulnerability and helplessness evoked when treating these clients can lead therapists to engage in some of the same negative behaviors as nonprofessionals. They may derogate, blame, or punish their clients. The increasing cynicism that often develops can result in a variety of behaviors and practices that are disrespectful and inappropriate, including forgotten appointments, failure to return phone calls, and breaches in confidentiality (Pearlman & Saakvitne, 1995b). More serious types of professional mistreatment may also occur, such as abandonment of the client.

There is widespread agreement among clinicians that the feelings evoked in therapists who work with survivors of trauma must be acknowledged and processed. This requires ongoing support from and communication with other professionals who do this kind of work. With such support, therapists can examine their own feelings and reactions to their clients and develop strategies for coping more effectively with the stresses inherent in the work. Pearlman and Saakvitne (1995a) offered a number of specific strategies for minimizing vicarious traumatization, including self-talk (e.g., "The acute pain my client is expressing today will not last forever"), limit setting, and creating more balance in one's life. Failure to attend to the consequences of vicarious traumatization can lead to maladaptive attempts by the therapist to self-soothe, such as emotional disengagement or addictive behaviors.

As part of the process of working through the feelings evoked by trauma work, it is imperative that therapists examine and reexamine their own personal motives for involvement in this field. It is well known that people often enter this profession because they themselves have been traumatized at some point in the past (Pearlman & Saakvitne, 1995a). Therapists who are themselves trauma survivors often bring an energy and commitment to their work that is sustaining. However, they may also find themselves overidentifying with their clients and having difficulty setting boundaries. Specific treatment recommendations for clients may stem more from therapists' desire to heal themselves than from their desire to help the clients. Candid discussion of these matters with a colleague, supervisor, or personal therapist is encouraged, particularly at the early stages of one's career.

Those who work with survivors of traumatic loss are well aware that despite the stressors associated with it, the work is rich in rewards. It is extremely gratifying to witness the transformation that may take place in our clients as their symptoms abate and their lives become more satisfying. Moreover, these relationships with our clients have the capacity to contribute enormously to our growth as individuals. The intense connections we forge with our clients can impart wisdom and deepen our humanity (Pearlman & Saakvitne, 1995a). We have the satisfaction that through our work, we are helping to ameliorate the destructive impact of traumatic loss and promoting healing in a population that is often ignored or misunderstood.

Summary and Conclusions

Exposure to traumatic loss places survivors at enormous psychological risk. These people's lives are turned upside down as they attempt to cope with the tragedy and its aftermath. They experience powerful and disturbing symptoms that are not well understood by themselves or by others, and these symptoms continue much longer than people expect. The trauma typically provokes an existential crisis in which everything one has believed is suddenly thrown into question. The bereaved make valiant efforts to deal with the loss, but their efforts to seek solace are often unsuccessful. They accumulate reactions from others and from society that add to their growing disillusionment and alienation. Over time, they often choose to withdraw from others, further reducing the potential for meaningful social connections.

People who have experienced a traumatic loss rarely seek professional help. Instead, they attempt to handle the impact of the trauma on their own. Unfortunately, the intense grief reaction and accompanying PTSD symptoms are usually not amenable to a self-help approach. For this reason, professional help is almost always warranted following a traumatic loss. To enhance the likelihood of treatment effectiveness, the person providing the treatment should be trained in grief therapy and in specific techniques to treat PTSD.

Perhaps because of their own desires for self-protection, many people view deaths resulting from drunk driving accidents or homicides as highly unusual. In fact, such deaths represent the leading cause of death among individuals under the age of 44 and are important causes of deaths in most other age groups as well. Moreover, as a result of a variety of disturbing social trends, the frequency of traumatic deaths is increasing. These trends include the proliferation of media violence, the availability of guns, and the increasing pathology of those who commit violent crimes (see

Rando, 1993, for a cogent discussion of this topic). The rising frequency of such deaths, coupled with the failure to seek help, has created an enormous population of people who, through no fault of their own and despite their best coping efforts, are living diminished lives.

Although the individual helping professional can assist those who have suffered traumatic loss in some ways, it should be emphasized that the scope of this problem goes beyond the purview of the individual therapist. One enormous problem is the insufficient training received by most mental health professionals in the area of trauma. Rando (1993) has described this as a "shocking insufficiency of knowledge," and we wholeheartedly agree. An effort must be made to develop and expand training in trauma for mental health professionals who are currently in graduate school and for those who received their degrees before there were course offerings in the field of trauma. Such training is also of the utmost importance for family physicians and pastors because they may be the first and only professionals with whom the survivor has contact. A second problem is that there is no "quick fix" for the impact of a traumatic loss. Although long-term individual therapy is usually the best treatment choice, third-party payers often limit treatment to brief therapy or medication. As the demand on mental health services increases, these services will be increasingly subject to limitations, preapprovals, and third-party reviews by people without expertise in the long-term effects of trauma and bereavement.

It behooves all of us to ask what small contribution we might make to these entrenched and difficult problems. In this chapter, our goal has been to provide mental health professionals and laypersons with a more complete understanding of the impact of trauma and the difficulties in obtaining help. Only through awareness of these problems can we begin the challenge of finding ways to reach and heal those whose lives have been affected by a traumatic loss.

References

Amick-McMullan, A., Kilpatrick, D. G., Veronen, L. J., & Smith, S. (1989). Family survivors of homicide victims: Theoretical perspectives and an exploratory study. *Journal of Traumatic Stress, 2*(1), 21-33.

Bowlby, J. (1969). *Attachment and loss: Vol. 1. Attachment.* New York: Basic Books.

Burgess, A. W. (1975). Family reaction to homicide. *American Journal of Orthopsychiatry, 45,* 391-398.

Coyne, J. C., Wortman, C. B., & Lehman, D. R. (1988). The other side of support: Emotional overinvolvement and miscarried helping. In B. H. Gottlieb (Ed.), *Marshaling social support: Formats, processes and effects* (pp. 305-330). Newbury Park, CA: Sage.

Davidowitz, M., & Myrick, R. D. (1984). Responding to the bereaved: An analysis of "helping" statements. *Research Record, 1,* 35-42.

Davidson, J. R. T., & van der Volk, B. A. (1996). The psychopharmacological treatment of posttraumatic stress disorder. In B. A. van der Volk, A. C. McFarland, & L. Weisaeth, L., *Traumatic stress,* pp. 519-524. New York: Guilford.

Everly, G. S., & Lating, J. M. (1995). *Psychotraumatology.* New York: Plenum.

Exline, J. J., Dorrity, K., & Wortman, C. B. (1996). Coping with bereavement: A research review for clinicians. *In Session: Psychotherapy Practice, 2*(4), 3-19.

Figley, C. R. (1995). *Compassion fatigue.* New York: Brunner/Mazel.

Foa, E. B., Rothbaum, B. O., Riggs, D. S., & Murdock, T. B. (1991). Treatment of posttraumatic stress disorder in rape victims: A comparison between cognitive-behavioral procedures and counseling. *Journal of Consulting and Clinical Psychology, 59,* 715-723.

Freedy J. R., & Donkervolt, J. C. (1995). Traumatic stress: An overview of the field. In J. R. Freedy & S. E. Hobfoll (Eds.), *Traumatic stress: From theory to practice* (pp. 3-28). New York: Plenum.

Freedy, J. R., & Hobfoll, S. E. (1995). *Traumatic stress: From theory to practice.* New York: Plenum.

Green, B. L. (1990). Defining trauma: Terminology and generic stressor dimensions. *Journal of Applied Social Psychology, 20,* 1632-1642.

Herman, J. L. (1992). *Trauma and recovery.* New York: Basic Books.

Horowitz, M. J. (1986). *Stress response syndromes* (2nd ed.). Northvale, NJ: Jason Aronson.

Jacobs, S. (1993). *Pathological grief: Maladaption to loss.* Washington, DC: American Psychiatric Press.

Janoff-Bulman, R. (1992). *Shattered assumptions: Towards a new psychology of trauma.* New York: Free Press.

Lehman, D. R., Ellard, J. H., & Wortman, C. B. (1986). Social support for the bereaved: Recipients' and providers' perspectives on what is helpful. *Journal of Consulting and Clinical Psychology, 54,* 438-446.

Lehman, D. R., Wortman, C. B., & Williams, A. F. (1987). Long-term effects of losing a spouse or child in a motor vehicle crash. *Journal of Personality and Social Psychology, 52,* 218-231.

Lepore, S. J., Silver, R. C., Wortman, C. B., & Wayment, H. A. (1996). Social constraints, intrusive thoughts, and depressive symptoms among bereaved mothers. *Journal of Personality and Social Psychology, 70*(2), 271-282.

Lord, J. H. (1987). Survivor grief following a drunk-driving crash. *Death Studies, 11,* 413-435.

Lord, J. H. (1988). *Beyond sympathy: What to say and do for someone suffering an injury, illness or loss.* Ventura, CA: Pathfinder.

Marris, P. (1975). *Loss and change.* New York: Pantheon.

McCann, I. L., & Pearlman, L. A. (1990). *Psychological trauma and the adult survivor: Theory, therapy, and transformation.* New York: Brunner/Mazel.

Ochberg, F. (1988). *Post-traumatic therapy and victims of violence.* New York: Brunner/Mazel.

Parkes, C. M. (1971). Psychosocial transitions: A field for study. *Social Science and Medicine, 5,* 101-115.

Parkes, C. M. (1993). Psychiatric problems following bereavement by murder or manslaughter. *British Journal of Psychiatry, 162,* 49-54.

Pearlman, L. A., & Saakvitne, K. W. (1995a). *Trauma and the therapist: Countertransference and vicarious traumatization in psychotherapy with incest survivors.* New York: Norton.

Pearlman, L. A., & Saakvitne, K. W. (1995b). Treating therapists with vicarious traumatization and secondary traumatic stress disorder. In C. R. Figley (Ed.), *Compassion fatigue* (pp. 150-177). New York: Brunner/Mazel.

Pennebaker, J. W. (1993). Social mechanisms of constraint. In D. M. Wegner & J. W. Pennebaker (Eds.), *Handbook of mental control* (pp. 200-219). Englewood Cliffs, NJ: Prentice Hall.

Rando, T. A. (1993). *Treatment of complicated mourning.* Champaign, IL: Research Press.

Schuchter, S. R., & Zisook, S. (1993). The course of normal grief. In M. S. Stroebe, W. Stroebe, & R. O. Hanson (Eds.), *Handbook of bereavement* (pp. 23-43). New York: Cambridge University Press.

Southwick, S. M. & Yehuda, R. (1993). The interaction between pharmacotherapy and psychotherapy in the treatment of posttraumatic stress disorder. *American Journal of Psychotherapy, 47,* 403-408.

Statistical Abstract of the United States. (1994). *The national data book.* Washington, DC: Government Printing Office.

Stylianos, S. K., & Vachon, M. L. S. (1993). The role of social support in bereavement. In M. S. Stroebe, W. Stroebe, & R. O. Hansson (Eds.), *Handbook of bereavement,* pp. 397-410. New York: Cambridge University Press.

Symonds, M. (1980). The "second injury" to victims. *Evaluation and Change,* pp. 36-38.

Worden, J. W. (1991). *Grief counseling and grief therapy: A handbook for the mental health practitioner* (2nd ed). New York: Springer.

Wortman, C. B., Carnelley, K. B., Lehman, D. R., Davis, C. G., & Exline, J. J. (1995). Coping with the loss of a family member: Implications for community-level research and intervention. In S. E. Hobfoll & M. W. de Vries (Eds.), *Extreme stress and communities: Impact and intervention* (pp. 83-103). Dordrecht, the Netherlands: Kluwer.

Wortman, C. B., & Lehman, D. R. (1985). Reactions to victims of life crises: Support attempts that fail. In I. G. Sarason & B. R. Sarason (Eds.), *Social support: Theory, research and applications* (pp. 463-489). Dordrecht, the Netherlands: Martinus Nijoff.

Wortman, C. B., & Silver, R. C. (1989). The myths of coping with loss. *Journal of Consulting and Clinical Psychology, 57* 349-357.

7 Hate Crime Victimization in the United States

JAMES GAROFALO

Hatred is a relatively common motive for inflicting harm on others. Sometimes the hatred develops out of personal interaction. But hatred can also be directed toward groups of complete strangers, based only on some apparent characteristic of people in the group. This latter form of hate has been responsible for enormous amounts of victimization throughout history. In its most extreme form—genocide—concerted efforts are made to annihilate the group physically (Chalk & Jonassohn, 1990; Fein, 1993; Rummel, 1994). In its less extreme forms, hatred can be expressed in subtle forms of bias that inflict psychological harm, making victims feel angry, unwanted, inferior, and so forth.

At a very general level, hate victimization can be defined as harm inflicted on a victim by an offender whose motivation derives primarily from hatred directed at some apparent characteristic of the victim. The key is that any person perceived as having the characteristic is a potential victim of the hate-motivated offender. The offender acts because of what the victim is—an African American, a Mexican, a Jew—not because the victim has something that the offender wants and not because the offender bears some personal grudge against the individual.

This chapter focuses on hate crimes: those hate victimizations involving some form of behavior that is criminal, regardless of its motivation. This qualification excludes most verbal and written expressions of group hatred, at least in the United States,[1] as well as discriminatory behaviors that are covered by civil statutes. Furthermore, attention here is focused on the categories of victims whose characteristics are specified in most existing hate crime statutes and policies in the United States: race, ethnicity, religion, and sexual orientation. Obviously, hate victimizations can be motivated by other characteristics, such as gender, social class, or—as the 1995 bombing of a federal building in Oklahoma City suggests—even government employment. But current statutes in the United States do not routinely cover characteristics other than race, ethnicity, religion, and sexual orientation, and even sexual orientation is not covered universally.

This chapter presents an overview of hate crimes in the United States. It concludes with some discussion of actual and potential responses to this form of victimization.

Importance

If the focus is on acts that are crimes already, why is it important to give special attention to crimes that are motivated by hate? The answer is found in the notion that the element of hate adds to the harm suffered by victims of those crimes.

For individuals, hate crimes involve double victimization. In addition to the harm caused by the underlying crime—physical injury or property damage, for example—the hatred expressed in conjunction with the crime attacks what is often a central feature of the victim's identity. Victims of hate crimes cannot even draw on the limited comfort offered by the rationale that what happened to them could have happened to anyone, that they were simply unlucky to be in the wrong place at the wrong time. Hate crimes tell the victims that at least some people detest them and feel free to harm them because of who they are: African Americans, Jews, lesbians, and so forth (see Delgado, 1993, pp. 90-96; Weiss, 1993, pp. 182-183).

It is also reasonable to assume that hate crimes victimize communities in ways that go beyond the community harms associated with "common" crime. This is especially apparent in the aftermath of high-profile hate crimes, such as the Howard Beach and Bensonhurst killings in New York City during the 1980s. The demonstrations, counterdemonstrations, and angry exchanges in the media following

these events seemed to increase racial polarization or at least to give greater vent to underlying racial tensions (Kelly, Maghan, & Tennant, 1993, p. 29). Although these were widely publicized, serious crimes, there is no reason to think that an ongoing accumulation of less serious, less publicized hate crimes would not have similar effects on intergroup hostilities.

Sources of Information

During the past 10 years, new efforts have been mounted to document the prevalence and nature of hate crimes. However, it is not yet possible to describe hate crime victimizations with the same level of accuracy and detail as we can attain with descriptions of criminal victimization in general (see Chapter 2 of this volume).

The National Crime Victimization Survey does not differentiate between victimizations that are and are not hate motivated. The Uniform Crime Reporting (UCR) program has undertaken the task of collecting data about hate crimes that come to the attention of the police. However, the UCR effort is relatively new; it was developed under a provision of the 1990 Hate Crime Statistics Act (Pub. L. No. 101-275). To implement the collection of hate crime data, the Federal Bureau of Investigation (FBI) has had to elicit the cooperation of state and local law enforcement and crime statistics agencies and to provide training on new definitions and reporting procedures. A 1995 FBI hate crime publication indicated that 6,865 police agencies, representing jurisdictions with a combined population of 148 million people, participated in the hate crime reporting effort in 1993; 6,551 of these agencies provided all of the information necessary for FBI report tabulations (FBI, 1995, p. 5).

In addition to the federal reporting effort under the Hate Crime Statistics Act, 18 states have implemented mandatory hate crime re-

porting statutes in recent years (Anti-Defamation League [ADL], 1994, pp. 30-31). Data
have also been generated by private advocacy
organizations, state and local commissions,
and individual researchers. However, many of
these have been one-time data collection efforts covering one state or local jurisdiction;
some focus on a particular form of hate victimization; and some rely on data collection
techniques of questionable reliability.

Despite the shortcomings of the data
sources taken individually, some consisten-
cies emerge when the various sources are considered together. These regularities are discussed in the next two sections.

Extent of Hate Crime Victimization

The 6,551 law enforcement agencies providing full information to the FBI's Hate
Crime Statistics program reported 7,587 hate
crime incidents for 1993 (FBI, 1995, p. 9).
This figure was dominated by a few large
jurisdictions that had hate crime reporting programs in place before the FBI efforts began.
For example, New York City, Boston, and San
Francisco accounted for nearly 1,100 of the
reported incidents, and New Jersey, which has
an active statewide reporting system, contributed another 1,100. On the other hand, most
participating jurisdictions reported no incidents (FBI, 1995, Tables 13-19).

The FBI figure cannot be taken as a measure
of the "true" level of hate crime victimization
in the United States. The FBI program is in its
infancy, and many key jurisdictions are not
represented in the 1993 data (much of California, for example). Among many of the agencies that did contribute data, the practice of
identifying and recording hate victimization is
new, and these agencies will almost certainly
become more comprehensive in their reporting as they become more experienced with
identifying and documenting hate crimes. But
even when these problems are solved, the basic problem with all "crimes known to the

police" data—the extent to which victims do
not report crimes to the police—will remain.
Over the years, victimization survey data have
given us a basis for understanding the amount
of nonreporting and the factors associated
with nonreporting for crimes in general, but
we do not know if a hate victimization is more
or less likely than a nonhate victimization of
the same crime type (a simple assault, for
example) to be reported to the police.

There are indications that some hate victimizations—those directed against gays and
lesbians—are particularly unlikely to be reported to the police. As Berrill and Herek
(1992) pointed out, gay and lesbian victims
cannot always expect a positive response from
the criminal justice system, and reporting a
hate-motivated crime reveals the victim's sexual orientation, which could produce negative,
collateral responses from family, employers,
and landlords, for example. Berrill and Herek
(1992, pp. 293-294) mentioned a number of
studies suggesting that rates of reporting to the
police may be 20% or lower among gay and
lesbian victims.

If we cannot measure the level of hate victimization at one point in time with any confidence, can we make some reasonable estima-
tions about whether hate victimizations have
been increasing or decreasing over time? Unfortunately, the answer is no.

The FBI's hate crime reporting program is
new. As additional agencies begin to participate, as training workshops for agency personnel enhance detection and recording practices,
and as continuing special attention to hate
crimes increases sensitivity to them among
law enforcement agencies, the numbers recorded by the FBI will surely rise in coming
years. Similarly, private efforts to monitor
hate crimes, such as those by the ADL and the
Southern Poverty Law Center, can be expected
to improve and expand their monitoring procedures over time, thus recording greater numbers of victimizations. Because data collection
efforts need to mature, it will be some time
before we can make reasonable estimates of

increases or decreases in the level of hate victimization.

Even works that call attention to the problems of hate victimization and suggest that such victimizations may be increasing take note of the problems involved in drawing inferences from existing data (e.g., Berrill, 1992, pp. 35-37; Levin & McDevitt, 1993, pp. 200-201). Much more common are predictions that the problem of hate crime victimization in the United States is likely to worsen in the future because of various demographic, social, and economic trends (Levin & McDevitt, 1993, chap. 16; Tafoya, 1993).

The Nature of Hate Crime Victimization

This section attempts to provide a descriptive portrait of hate crime victimizations. Although it is not possible to document their true levels or trends, the incidents represented in existing data sets are a revealing "slice" of the universe of incidents. Our confidence in their representativeness is greater to the extent that the patterns they reveal are consistent across several sets of data.

Most of the findings cited in this section are derived from three sources. First is the 1993 national compilation provided by the FBI (1995). Despite its shortcomings, this is the most broad-based data source available. Second is a compilation of hate crimes reported by police agencies to the Minnesota Bureau of Criminal Apprehension in 1989. The report based on these data (Lane, 1990) covers some of the issues dealt with in this section. Third is a study of bias-motivated crimes handled by the New York City Police Department in 1987 and 1988 and by the Baltimore County (Maryland) Police Department from 1982 to 1988. This study, which I directed, included matched samples of nonbias crimes in both jurisdictions so that observations could be made about how hate crimes differ from "regular" crimes (Garofalo & Martin, 1993, p. 8).[2] These three are designated simply as the

FBI data, the Minnesota data, and the NYC data in the following discussion.

All three of these data sets pertain to hate crimes recorded by the police. Thus they are dependent on victims' willingness to report crimes to the police and on the ability of the police to detect when a crime is hate motivated (as well as on other factors). The issue of victim reporting was discussed earlier; at this point it can be noted that police departments vary considerably in the extent to which they encourage patrol officers to look for hate motivation and the amount of training they provide in the recognition of hate motivation. Many police departments have developed guidelines to tell officers what to look for and how to handle hate crimes when they find them (e.g., see ADL, 1988). In terms of determining whether hate motivation is present, the guidelines typically emphasize overt indications, such as verbal expressions from the offender or the content of graffiti. Other factors mentioned include the occurrence of the crime on a religious or ethnic holiday; whether the victim has been publicly associated with racial, religious, or other issues; whether the victim is a minority who has recently moved into a predominantly nonminority neighborhood; and whether there have been similar occurrences of hate crimes in the same geographic area.

Despite guidelines and training, many situations are ambiguous, and the determination of whether hate motivation exists will be open to a great deal of discretion (see examples in Garofalo & Martin, 1993, pp. 49-51). Thus interpretations of police data on hate crimes should be made with this discretion in mind.

Types of Hate Motivation

The national FBI data for 1993 included 7,587 incidents of hate victimization with complete information. Among the 7,587 incidents, 62% were racially motivated (FBI, 1995, p. 9). This predominance of racially motivated incidents among hate victimizations is consistent with other data sources. For example, 57% and 77% of hate crimes in NYC and Baltimore County, respectively, were found to be racially motivated (Garofalo & Martin, 1993, p. 11), as were 87% of the hate crimes recorded in Minnesota in 1989 (Lane, 1990, p. 35).

There are some indications that the proportional representation of various types of hate victimizations is misleading because of differential willingness among victims to notify the police. For example, Finn and McNeil (1988, p. 3) concluded that gay and lesbian victims were least likely of all hate crime victims to report to the police. Given the special disincentives to reporting that are faced by gay and lesbian victims, it may well be that their victimizations are underrepresented in hate crime data sets (11% in the FBI data, 7% in NYC, and 3% in Minnesota). However, the substantial representation of racially motivated victimizations is not surprising, given the pervasiveness of racial tensions in U.S. society and the fact that race is a characteristic that is relatively easy to identify.

It is interesting to note that despite the claims of some critics that "hate crime" really means "crime against minorities," a sizable number of racially motivated hate victimizations are committed against whites—about a third of the racially motivated incidents in both the FBI and NYC data sets.[3] As pointed out elsewhere (Garofalo, 1991), this reflects the mutual nature of racial antagonisms in the United States as well as the more equal opportunities for racial minorities to become victimizers "on the streets," in contrast to their opportunities in other spheres of life, such as the job and housing markets.

Religious hatred appears to be the second most common motivation for hate crime victimizations. The overwhelming majority of the religion-motivated incidents are directed against Jewish victims. Thus it is not surprising that the proportion of religion-motivated victimizations varies across hate crime data

sets, depending on the proportion of Jews in the underlying population. For example, 27% of the NYC hate crimes were motivated by the religion of the victim, compared to only 5% of the 1989 Minnesota hate crimes (Garofalo & Martin, 1993, p. 11; Lane, 1990, p. 35).

After race and religion, incidents motivated by the sexual orientation and ethnicity of the victims are most common; in the ethnicity-motivated incidents, Hispanic victims predominate. These two types of hate motivation account for similar proportions of the incidents in the FBI data and in the NYC data. The national FBI figures show that 11% and 9% of the hate incidents were motivated by victims' sexual orientation and ethnicity, respectively (FBI, 1995, p. 9); the comparable figures for NYC were 7% and 6% (Garofalo & Martin, 1993, p. 11).

Of course, the proportional representation of various types of hate motivation depends, to some extent, on which types of hate motivation are considered under a particular reporting statute or policy. The Minnesota data set, for example, covers crimes motivated by the victims' sex, age, and disability, although these categories accounted for very few incidents in the 1989 data. On the other hand, the Baltimore County data in the mid- to late 1980s contain no incidents motivated by the victims' sexual orientation because the Maryland definition covered "RRE" (racial, religious, ethnic) incidents but not sexual orientation incidents. (See ADL, 1994, pp. 30-31, for a listing of the provisions of state hate crime statutes.)

Whether a particular characteristic is covered under a hate crime statute or policy is basically a political issue that has raised controversy in some instances. For example, legislative debates about whether sexual orientation should be included as a hate crime category have been especially contentious (see Garofalo & Martin, 1993, pp. 46-48). More recently, the question of whether sex should be included as a category has been a subject of debate. Proponents argue that many crimes committed against women—particularly rapes—are motivated primarily by a general hatred of women. Opponents argue that a generalized hatred of women is difficult to detect in the context of a crime; therefore inclusion of sex as a category in hate crime statutes would place an undue decision-making burden on the criminal justice system. Whatever the outcome of this particular debate, it is almost certain that the exact categories contained in hate crime statutes and policies will vary across jurisdictions and will change from time to time within jurisdictions.

Types of Crime

Hate crime can involve any type of criminal act, from multiple murder to harassment. Although definitions and categories of crime differ from one jurisdiction to another, it is fair to say that less serious forms of face-to-face, confrontational crimes predominate. Intimidation and harassment tend to be the most common, followed by assaults, with simple assaults outnumbering aggravated assaults. The only other type of crime with substantial representation among hate crimes is vandalism or property damage.

There is an interaction between type of hate motivation and type of crime. The overwhelming majority of hate crimes motivated by the race, ethnicity, or sexual orientation of victims consist of face-to-face altercations: assault, harassment, intimidation. In contrast, the majority of hate crimes that target victims because of their religion consist of property crimes, primarily vandalism. This interaction is apparent in both the FBI and NYC data sets (FBI, 1995, pp. 14-15; Garofalo & Martin, 1993, p. 12). Evidently, religious hatred is more likely to be directed at the religion as an institution than at individuals. In addition, religions tend to have a number of easily identifiable physical structures (churches, synagogues, schools, cemeteries) that can be targeted by hate crime offenders. The differential selection of targets is illustrated in the FBI data, in which only half of the hate crimes motivated by the victim's religion were directed against individuals, whereas 87% to 94% of the incidents in the other categories (race, ethnicity, and sexual orientation) were directed against individuals (FBI, 1995, p. 11).

Incident Characteristics

Numbers of Victims and Offenders

The NYC data for 1987-1988 showed that in comparison to a matched sample of victimizations that were not hate motivated, personal hate crime victimizations were more likely to involve multiple offenders and multiple victims, and the victims tended to be fewer than the offenders. For example, in incidents in which a person was victimized directly, the mean number of victims was 1.56 for hate crimes and 1.08 for the comparison, nonhate crimes. Similarly, in cases for which an estimate of the number of offenders was available, the mean number of offenders was 2.93 in the hate crimes and 1.43 in the comparison crimes. In fact, one-victim-one-offender situations were the norm in nonhate crimes (68% of the relevant cases), but this was relatively uncommon (19%) in hate crimes (Garofalo & Martin, 1993, pp. 16, 20-21).

The 1993 FBI data imply a somewhat different pattern of numbers of victims and offenders. Although they do indicate the presence of multiple victims and offenders in hate crimes, they suggest that victims outnumber offenders (FBI, 1995, p. 9). However, the victim count includes individual and nonindividual (e.g., business, religious, government facilities) victims of property crimes, primarily vandalisms, and these are cases in which the number of offenders is usually unknown. The NYC figures referred to above are based only on confrontational crimes in which the victims were able to estimate numbers of offenders.

Although hate crimes often involve multiple offenders, this does not mean that the crimes are committed primarily by organized hate groups. In fact, the view of most observers is that organized hate groups account for a relatively small proportion of all hate victimizations (e.g., Berrill, 1992, pp. 30-31; Finn & McNeil, 1988, p. 2; Levin & McDevitt, 1993, p. 104; Maxwell & Maxwell, 1995, pp. 39-40; Weiss, 1993, p. 176). However, there is concern that organized groups are responsible for some of the most violent hate victimizations and that the groups' ideologies and rhetoric inspire unaffiliated individuals to commit hate crimes (see, e.g., Berrill, 1993, p. 155).

Victim and Offender Characteristics

Victims of hate crimes tend to be young. About half of the hate crime victims in NYC during 1987-1988 and in Minnesota in 1989 were under 21 (Garofalo & Martin, 1993, p. 23; Lane, 1990, p. 38). Furthermore, the NYC data show that the hate crime victims were, on average, younger than the victims in the comparison sample of nonhate crimes. The median age of the hate crime victims was 22, whereas the median age of the victims in the comparison sample was 29 (Garofalo & Martin, 1993, p. 22).

Hate crime offenders tend to be even younger than the victims. In the 1989 Minnesota data, 75% were under 21 (Lane, 1990, p. 37). In the NYC data, among offenders for whom age estimates were available, the median age was 18 for hate crime offenders and 25 for offenders in the sample of comparison crimes (Garofalo & Martin, 1993, p. 17). Similarly, Maxwell and Maxwell (1995, p. 24) reported that the proportion of juveniles among arrestees for hate crimes was more than twice the proportion among arrestees for all offenses in New Jersey from 1988 to 1991.

Victims and offenders in hate crimes are predominantly males, and again, the NYC data

indicate that overrepresentation of male victims and offenders is greater in hate crimes than it is in comparable, nonhate crimes (Garofalo & Martin, 1993, pp. 17, 22).

Hate victimizations are usually committed by offenders who are strangers to their victims. In the 1989 Minnesota data, 61% of the offenders were classified as strangers (Lane, 1990, p. 37). In nearly 90% of the NYC hate crimes, victims reported that the offenders were strangers or that they could not be sure whether the suspects were people they knew; the comparable figure in the comparison sample of nonhate crimes was 65%. In contrast, acquaintances were identified as offenders in 21% of the comparison cases but in only 7% of the hate crime cases in NYC (Garofalo & Martin, 1993, p. 24).[4]

Time and Place of Occurrence

The NYC samples of hate- and non-hate-motivated crimes showed no substantial differences in time of occurrence. When place of occurrence was examined, hate crimes were more likely to have been committed in public places and less likely to have been committed in (or immediately outside of) private homes or apartments (Garofalo & Martin, 1993, pp. 14-15). The FBI and Minnesota data sets also suggest a predominance of public locations for hate victimizations, but both also show a greater proportion of the crimes occurring in homes/residences than does the NYC data set (FBI, 1995, p. 13; Lane, 1990, p. 36). This difference may be at least partially attributable to the fact that both the FBI and Minnesota data sets contain higher proportions of property crimes among their hate victimizations than does the NYC data set.

Weapon Use and Injury

Weapon use by offenders was found about as often among hate-motivated personal crimes as among nonhate personal crimes in the NYC data. However, when weapons were used, hate crimes were *less* likely to involve guns or knives: 22% of the hate versus nearly half of the nonhate crimes in which offenders used weapons. Furthermore, victims in hate-motivated assaults were *less* likely to be injured than were victims in nonhate assaults (Garofalo & Martin, 1993, pp. 19, 25).[5]

Summary

Data from several sources and locations suggest that hate victimizations tend to consist of confrontational crimes committed in public places by small groups of young offenders who are strangers to their victims against lone victims or pairs of victims who are slightly older than the offenders. An exception to these patterns is found among crimes motivated by hatred of the victims' religion, in which property crimes—particularly vandalism—predominate.

Large proportions of hate victimizations involve harassment, intimidation, or simple assault. Likewise, the NYC data showed lower injury rates and use of less lethal weapons in hate crimes as compared to nonhate crimes, suggesting that, in conventional terms, hate victimizations are, on average, not very serious. This observation does not deny the fact that some hate crimes are extremely serious; there are many descriptive accounts of particularly vicious hate crimes. Nor does it deny that the expression of hate itself—independent of the underlying crime—inflicts harms on the victims, as noted in the next section.

Taken together, the findings suggest that (with the exception of crimes motivated by religious hatred) hate victimizations typically involve spontaneous street confrontations initiated by small, unorganized groups of youths. Chance encounters—while passing through a particular neighborhood or during a traffic dispute, for example—can develop into hate victimizations when the encounters are with people who carry real or imagined grudges against groups they consider to be outcasts.

Effects on Victims

As noted earlier, one of the rationales for treating hate crime victimizations separately from other criminal victimizations is the notion that the expression of hatred can have negative effects on victims, aside from any harms derived from the underlying crime itself. Unfortunately, there is very little information available that bears directly on this issue.

Intuitively, we can understand how the fact of hate motivation can create harm independently. For example, a family moves into a new home, encounters a few rude neighbors, and suffers a few acts of vandalism to their property during the first month. Although the family members will be upset, they may not be motivated to give up their new home and move away—unless, for example, it is an African American family, and the rudeness from neighbors consists of racial slurs, and the vandalism consists of crosses burned on the family's lawn.

The NYC study of bias-motivated crimes included a small, pilot, telephone survey of victims of hate-motivated and non-hate-motivated personal crimes. Although only 30 hate crime victims and 28 comparison crime victims were interviewed, some clear patterns of differential effects emerged. Relative to the comparison crime victims, hate crime victims were more likely to rate their crimes as "very serious"; they were more likely to report that being "frightened or scared" was their primary response in the immediate aftermath of the crime and less likely to report being "angry or mad" as their predominant response; they were more likely to report being "very upset" immediately after the crime; they were more likely to say that the crimes had a "great deal" of effect on their lives in both the short term (the week or so after the incident) and the long term (2 or 3 months after the incident); they were more likely to report emotional effects and less likely to report avoidance behaviors as effects (Garofalo & Martin, 1993, pp. 28-29). Similarly, Ehrlich (1992, pp. 110-111) reported preliminary results indicating more numerous traumatic effects being suffered by victims of hate crimes than by other victims.

Thus, although research on the topic is very limited, the findings are consistent with the hypothesis that the expression of hate motivation as part of a crime adds to the negative effects suffered by individual victims of hate crimes. The issue of whether hate crimes have especially negative effects on *communities* remains to be investigated.

Responses to Hate Victimization

An array of civil remedies are available to victims of hate incidents, including hate crimes (see ADL, 1994; Padgett, 1984; Washington, D.C. Lawyers' Committee, 1986). Regulatory agencies and the courts routinely deal with claims of discrimination in housing, employment, and so forth on the basis of race, ethnicity, gender, and other characteristics (but not sexual orientation), even though the U.S. Supreme Court has made such claims more difficult to sustain in recent years. Criminal actions can also be taken under federal civil rights laws (Padgett, 1984; Sandberg, 1993), but most criminal actions are taken under state laws.

In one sense, it is unfortunate that hate *crime* has come to be viewed as a phenomenon separate from hate victimization generally. This perspective puts hate crime squarely in the realm of the criminal justice system, which may not be well prepared to deal with deep-seated intergroup animosities.

Faced with the mandate to "do something" about hate crime, the criminal justice system has tended to respond in typical ways: create new categories—either for reporting crimes or in the substantive criminal law—and increase the penalties associated with hate crimes (see ADL, 1994).

Nearly half of the states have passed hate crime reporting statutes, and, as noted earlier, the 1990 Federal Hate Crime Statistics Act requires the FBI to develop a separate hate crime reporting system within the Uniform Crime Reporting program.

Most states have "institutional vandalism" laws, which encompass a number of hate crimes because they cover defacement, damage, or destruction directed against churches, cemeteries, schools, and other facilities that are often identified with particular groups. Attempts to criminalize forms of hate expression directly have been made, but they face stiff constitutional challenges (e.g., *R.A.V. v. City of St. Paul,* 1992).

Enhancement of available penalties for crimes that are hate motivated has been adopted by more than two thirds of the states. There are two basic approaches. The first is simply to add to the existing penalty for a crime when the court finds that the crime was hate motivated; this is the approach given U.S. Supreme Court approval in *Wisconsin v. Mitchell* (1993). In the second approach, existing crimes are listed as one class or grade higher in the penal code when hate motivation is present.[6]

Separate reporting requirements, creation of new crimes, and enhancement of penalties for hate crimes all have a great deal of support, but there are detractors as well (Gellman, 1992; Jacobs, 1993). In addition, there are disagreements about which forms of hate should be covered by the statutes and policies. Racial, ethnic, and religious hatred are routinely covered, but there is less agreement about hatred directed at victims because of their sexual orientation, gender, age, or disability (see Kelly et al., 1993).

It is difficulty to argue against improved data systems. Creating new crimes and enhancing penalties are more open to criticism. The main purpose of these approaches is to deter hate crimes (and perhaps to incapacitate hate-motivated offenders), but there is precious little evidence to support the deterrent (or incapacitative) effects of criminalization or increased penalties.

Perhaps an even more important criticism of punishment-oriented responses to hate victimization is that they alleviate the demand to engage in other responses that may be more time consuming and expensive but perhaps more effective. Passing a few new laws and then engaging in a few prosecutions under those laws does not require the levels of resources needed to implement extensive, ongoing education, prevention, investigation, and victim services efforts. In Baltimore County, Maryland, a multifaceted approach to dealing with hate victimization is integrated with community policing; in New York City, the police department maintains a separate unit to investigate hate crimes, assist hate crime victims, and coordinate with prosecutors in hate crime cases (see Garofalo & Martin, 1993; Sanderson, 1993). Although some other jurisdictions have also implemented creative responses, penalty enhancements are much more common.

Some Concluding Comments

Hate victimization is an especially disturbing problem in U.S. society, which gives strong vocal support to the ideals of openness, diversity, and tolerance. Hate crimes—a subset of hate-motivated, harm-inflicting behaviors—do involve some heinous, vicious crimes. But the limited data available about hate crimes indicate that more commonly they consist of either (a) relatively less serious forms of spontaneous confrontational crimes committed in public places by young, multiple offenders who are strangers to the victims or (b) vandalisms directed against property identified with particular groups, such as religious or racial groups.

Even more limited data suggest that victims of hate crimes suffer more negative effects than do victims of nonhate crimes. Although

there is no systematic data to support the suspicion that hate crimes can have especially deleterious consequences for communities as well as individuals, a number of anecdotal reports do exist, and it makes intuitive sense that hate crimes can aggravate intergroup tensions. The need for research on the effects of hate crime victimization is particularly important. A systematic understanding of the effects on individual victims and on communities is needed to support the development of individual-level and community-level services and interventions.

Because bias and prejudice are so deeply embedded in the cultural, social, and economic fabric of the nation, effective, long-term responses to hate crime would seem to require efforts that address the sources of friction and ill will. In the short term, the criminal justice system can help by offering services that are geared to the special needs of hate crime victims (or linking the victims to appropriate services provided by others); by applying resources to the detection, investigation, and prosecution of hate crimes; and by treating hate crime as a form of community disorder that falls within the preventive mission of community policing (see Ferry, 1993). Unfortunately, these kinds of "hard work" responses are less common than the presumed "quick fix" of penalty enhancements.

Increasing the penalties for hate crimes is a response that resonates with the public mood of punitiveness, and penalty enhancement has symbolic value in articulating society's condemnation of hate crimes. But the general experience of trying to suppress certain behaviors through increased criminal penalties does not offer much basis for optimism. At the adjudication stage, victim interests might be better served by the development of creative sentencing alternatives, especially for juveniles, who make up a disproportionate share of hate crime offenders (for some examples, see ADL, 1994, pp. 19-21; Maxwell & Maxwell, 1995, p. 52).

Finally, there is a need for conceptual work on hate- and bias-motivated victimization more generally. In one sense, the distinction between hate *crimes* and other forms of bias-motivated harms is artificial. Maintaining the distinction might be useful for limiting the forms of victimization that the criminal justice system (or the law in general, when civil remedies are included) should deal with, but it might also impede insights into how various forms of victimization are linked by common cultural, social, and economic factors. A more comprehensive conceptual understanding of hate victimization is needed to support the development of actions to address such factors.

Notes

1. Many democratic nations prohibit written or verbal expressions of racial, ethnic, and religious hatred. In the United States, judicial interpretations of the First Amendment have been hostile toward efforts to control expression that are based on the content of the expression (see Magnet, 1994; Walker, 1994).

2. The study was funded by the National Institute of Justice (Grant No. 90-IJ-CX-0002). The primary focus here is on the New York City data set because it contains a much larger number of incidents and because hate crimes motivated by the victims' sexual orientation are not included in the Baltimore County data set.

3. Stretesky (1995) has argued that given existing biases in the criminal justice system, there is a danger that hate crime laws will be used disproportionately against minorities rather than to protect them. It is also interesting to note that the leading U.S. Supreme Court case upholding the constitutionality of enhanced penalties for hate crimes involved a white victim and a black offender: *Wisconsin v. Mitchell* (1993).

4. The predominance of strangers in hate crimes occurred even though domestic incidents were purposefully excluded from the comparison sample of nonhate crimes (see Garofalo & Martin, 1993, p. 8).

5. Lower injury rates for hate-motivated assaults were also found in the Baltimore County data set in the same study.

6. See ADL (1994, pp. 8-9) for a more finely differentiated description of statutory approaches to penalty enhancement.

References

Anti-Defamation League. (1988). *Hate crimes: Policies and procedures for law enforcement agencies.* New York: Author.

Anti-Defamation League. (1994). *Hate crimes laws: A comprehensive guide.* New York: Author.

Berrill, K. T. (1992). Anti-gay violence and victimization in the United States: An overview. In G. M. Herek & K. T. Berrill (Eds.), *Hate crimes: Confronting violence against lesbians and gay men* (pp. 19-45). Newbury Park, CA: Sage.

Berrill, K. T. (1993). Anti-gay violence: Causes, consequences, and responses. In R. J. Kelly (Ed.)., *Bias crime: American law enforcement and legal responses* (pp. 151-164). Chicago: University of Illinois at Chicago, Office of International Criminal Justice.

Berrill, K. T., & Herek, G. M. (1992). Primary and secondary victimization in anti-gay hate crimes: Official response and public policy. In G. M. Herek & K. T. Berrill (Eds.), *Hate crimes: Confronting violence against lesbians and gay men* (pp. 289-305). Newbury Park, CA: Sage.

Chalk, F., & Jonassohn, K. (1990). *The history and sociology of genocide: Analyses and case studies.* New Haven, CT: Yale University Press.

Delgado, R. (1993). "Words that wound: A tort action for racial insults, epithets, and name calling." In M. J. Matsuda, C. R. Lawrence III, R. Delgado, & K. W. Crenshaw (Eds.), *Words that wound: Critical race theory, assaultive speech, and the First Amendment* (pp. 89-110). Boulder, CO: Westview.

Ehrlich, H. J. (1992). "The ecology of anti-gay violence." In G. M. Herek & K. T. Berrill (Eds.), *Hate crimes: Confronting violence against lesbians and gay men* (pp. 105-122). Newbury Park, CA: Sage.

Federal Bureau of Investigation. (1995). *Hate crime statistics: 1993.* Washington, DC: Government Printing Office.

Fein, H. (1993). *Genocide: A sociological perspective.* Newbury Park, CA: Sage.

Ferry, T. (1993). Community involvement and interagency cooperation in the prevention of hate crimes. In R. J. Kelly (Ed.)., *Bias crime: American law enforcement and legal responses* (pp. 132-142). Chicago: University of Illinois at Chicago, Office of International Criminal Justice.

Finn, P., & McNeil, T. (1988). *Bias crime and the criminal justice response: A summary report prepared for the National Criminal Justice Association.* Cambridge, MA: Abt.

Garofalo, J. (1991). Racially motivated crimes in New York City. In M. J. Lynch & E. B. Paterson (Eds.), *Race and criminal justice* (pp. 161-173). Albany, NY: Harrow & Heston.

Garofalo, J., & Martin, S. E. (1993). *Bias-motivated crimes: Their characteristics and the law enforcement response* (Final Report to the National Institute of Justice). Carbondale: Southern Illinois University, Center for the Study of Crime, Delinquency, and Corrections.

Gellman, S. (1992). "Brother, you can't go to jail for what you're thinking": Motives, effects, and "hate crime" laws. *Criminal Justice Ethics, 11*(2), 24-28.

Herek, G. M., & Berrill, K. T. (Eds.). (1992). *Hate crimes: Confronting violence against lesbians and gay men.* Newbury Park, CA: Sage.

Jacobs, J. B. (1993). Should hate be a crime? *Public Interest, 113,* 3-14.

Kelly, R. J. (Ed.). (1993). *Bias crime: American law enforcement and legal responses.* Chicago: University of Illinois at Chicago, Office of International Criminal Justice.

Kelly, R. J., Maghan, J., & Tennant, W. (1993). Hate crimes: Victimizing the stigmatized. In R. J. Kelly (Ed.), *Bias crime: American law enforcement and legal responses* (pp. 23-47). Chicago: University of Illinois at Chicago, Office of International Criminal Justice.

Lane, V. (1990). *Bias motivated crimes.* St. Paul: Minnesota Board of Peace Officer Standards and Training.

Levin, J., & McDevitt, J. (1993). *Hate crimes: The rising tide of bigotry and bloodshed.* New York: Plenum.

Magnet, J. (1994). Hate propaganda in Canada. In W. J. Waluchow (Ed.), *Free expression: Essays in law and philosophy* (pp. 223-250). New York: Oxford University Press.

Maxwell, C., & Maxwell, S. R. (1995). *Youth participation in hate-motivated crimes: Research and policy implications.* Boulder, CO: Center for the Study and Prevention of Violence.

Padgett, G. L. (1984). Racially-motivated violence and intimidation: Inadequate state enforcement and federal civil rights remedies. *Journal of Criminal Law and Criminology, 75,* 103-138.

R.A.V. v. City of St. Paul, 112 S.Ct. 2538 (1992).

Rummel, R. J. (1994). *Death by government.* New Brunswick, NJ: Transaction.

Sandberg, M. A. (1993). "Bias crime: The problems and the remedies." In R. J. Kelly (Ed.), *Bias crime: American law enforcement and legal responses* (pp. 193-204). Chicago: University of Illinois at Chicago, Office of International Criminal Justice.

Sanderson, P. M. (1993). Investigation of religious bias-motivated crimes. In R. J. Kelly (Ed.), *Bias crime: American law enforcement and legal responses* (pp. 90-97). Chicago: University of Illinois at Chicago, Office of International Criminal Justice.

Stretesky, P. (1995, March). *The hate crime debate: A utility paradox.* Paper presented at the meeting of the Academy of Criminal Justice Sciences, Boston.

Tafoya, W. (1993). "Rioting in the streets: Déjà vu?" In R. J. Kelly (Ed.), *Bias crime: American law enforcement and legal responses* (pp. 54-63). Chicago: University of Illinois at Chicago, Office of International Criminal Justice.

Walker, S. (1994). *Hate speech: The history of an American controversy.* Lincoln: University of Nebraska Press.

Washington, D.C. Lawyers' Committee for Civil Rights Under Law. (1986). *Striking back at bigotry: Remedies under federal and state law for violence motivated by racial, religious, and ethnic prejudice.* Baltimore: National Institute Against Prejudice and Violence.

Weiss, J. C. (1993). Ethnoviolence: Impact upon and response of victims and the community. In R. J. Kelly (Ed.), *Bias crime: American law enforcement and legal responses* (pp. 174-185). Chicago: University of Illinois at Chicago, Office of International Criminal Justice.

Wisconsin v. Mitchell, 113 S.Ct. 2194 (1993).

8

The Psychological Consequences of Crime

Findings From a Longitudinal Population-Based Study

FRAN H. NORRIS

KRZYSZTOF KANIASTY

MARTIE P. THOMPSON

This chapter summarizes the major findings from a research project entitled "Violence: Psychological Reactions and Consequences." As the title implies, the purpose of the study was to examine the effects of crime and violence on psychological functioning, with a particular focus on identifying various mediators and moderators of those effects. Because the chapter concentrates on our own research, we do not offer detailed descriptions of other studies. Excellent reviews of the psychological impact of crime are available elsewhere (e.g., Frieze, Hymer, & Greenberg, 1987; Koss, 1993; Lurigio & Resick, 1990; Resick, 1993). First, we provide an overview of the project's framework and methodology; then

AUTHORS' NOTE: This research was supported by Grant No. RO1 MH41579 (Fran H. Norris, Principal Investigator) from the National Institute of Mental Health. We thank the staff and interviewers of the Southern Research Corporation (Louisville, Kentucky) and the University of Louisville Urban Research Institute for their efforts in collecting the data. Wes Skogan and Richard McCleary provided valuable consultation and advice during the planning stages of the project.

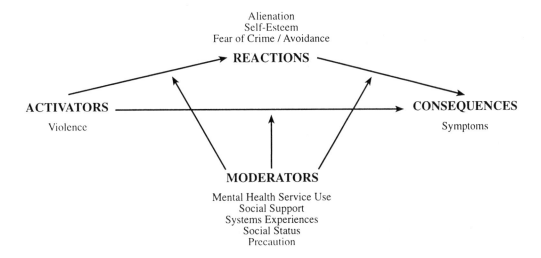

Figure 8.1. Conceptual Framework

we describe our major results. We conclude by identifying the overarching themes that have emerged in our research and others'.

Conceptual Overview

The conceptual framework shown in Figure 8.1 was adapted from the model developed by a panel of stress researchers brought together by the National Academy of Sciences (Eliot & Eisdorfer, 1982). The framework's four key concepts—*activators, consequences, reactions,* and *moderators*—helped to organize our project's constructs. As guided by this framework, our research involved four major questions. The *activator question* was "What elements of the crime 'activate' the individual's reactions and consequences?" We focused primarily on the presence versus absence of violence (force or threat of force) during the commission of the crime. The *consequence question* was "How lasting are the

effects of crime and violence on psychological symptoms (e.g., depression, anxiety)?" We examined the course of recovery over three time points, each 6 months apart. The *reaction question* was "What psychological mechanisms link the occurrence of the event with the occurrence of symptomatology?" Here we focused on victims' beliefs and assumptions about themselves and their worlds. Finally, the *moderator question* was "What social and environmental factors change (i.e., enhance or diminish) the relations between the activators and the consequences, between the activators and the reactions, and between the reactions and the consequences?" We examined numerous potential moderators to identify protective factors for crime victims.

Background and Methodology

When our research team became interested in conducting research on criminal victimization, a decade ago as of this writing, one of the first things we noticed was that there were two very distinct literatures. The psychological literature focused on the experience of victimization. These studies had a lot of heart, were very rich sources of ideas, and often involved excellent and extensive psychological measurement. However, the samples were often quite small, self-selected, or lacking in relevant comparison groups. The criminal justice literature was quite the opposite. Here, the focus was on crime (e.g., its distribution, incidence, and related issues). Samples were large and representative, but psychological aspects were ignored or poorly measured. We sought to build a bridge between these two literatures. We wanted to measure individual experiences accurately and thoroughly using a representative sample of victims and nonvictims.

In recent years, a third type of study has emerged, which was not prevalent when we first began. In this epidemiological literature, studies did capture both population and psychological dynamics but typically used a lifetime perspective for the measurement of crime (e.g., George, Winfield, & Blazer, 1992; Kilpatrick, Saunders, Veronen, Best, & Von, 1987; Resnick, Kilpatrick, Dansky, Saunders, & Best, 1993). For us, the goal to encompass both population and psychological dynamics presented quite a challenge because we desired to interview victims within the first few months after the crime. Whereas crime is all too common from a population perspective, crime victims are rare in a research sense. At that time, the annual violent crime rate was estimated to be about 5%. Hence a sample of 1,000 would provide only about 25 persons who experienced violent crimes in the past 6 months.

Our solution was to use a multistage procedure that provided reasonably large samples of recent victims who had known probabilities of selection. In January 1988, a sample of 12,226 households in Kentucky was generated using random-digit-dialing procedures. A five-item screening instrument was used to classify all contacted households into three groups on the basis of crimes experienced in the past 6 months (violent, property, nonvictim). Because the probability varied that a household would belong to a given category, the probability of selection for an interview also varied according to screener classification. All households reporting violent crime were selected for an interview, whereas only 2 in 5 property crime households and 1 in 28 nonvictim households were selected. Once a household was selected to participate, the potential respondent was chosen according to procedures developed by Kish (1949). For violent and property crime households, one person was selected randomly from all persons experiencing the incident. For nonvictim households, one person was selected randomly from all adults residing in that household. Regardless of screener classification, all respondents were administered an 18-item crime incidence battery that was similar to the one used in the National Crime Survey (Lehnen & Skogan, 1984). Although most persons (88%) were classified correctly by the screener, some persons' categories were switched on the basis of their interview data. Subsequent classification of individuals was based on results from the 18-item battery. Final ns were 171 violent crime victims, 338 property crime victims, and 298 nonvictims.

This sampling plan had three major strengths. First, it provided reasonably large analytical samples that were all approximately representative of their respective populations in Kentucky. Second, the victim samples were heterogeneous. About half of these victims were male, whereas the prototype victim in the literature is female. Also, about half of the victims were rural; stereotypes to the contrary, crime is not simply an urban phenomenon. Third, victims were selected randomly—not because they either reported the crime or sought professional assistance.

The design was longitudinal. Six months after their first interview and again 6 months after that, attempts were made to reinterview all study participants, again by telephone.

Table 8.1 Characteristics of Original and Three-Wave Samples

Time 1 Measure	Original Sample N = 807	Three-Wave Sample N = 522
Mean age	39	39
Mean education	13	13
% female	59	58
% married	57	60
% urban	53	55
% violent crime	21	20
% Property crime	42	44

Table 8.2 Crimes Experienced by the Three-Wave Sample by Time

	Time 1	Time 2	Time 3
Rape	6	3	2
Robbery	19	1	2
Aggravated assault	23	8	8
Simple assault	57	53	17
Any violent crime	105	65	29
Burglary	68	16	25
Larceny	114	55	53
Vandalism	45	21	19
Any Property Crime	227	92	97

NOTE: Table entries are *ns*. The total three-wave sample has an *N* of 522.

Time 2 response rates were reasonably high (80% for nonvictims, 85% for property crime victims, 82% for violent crime victims), as were those for Time 3 (83% for nonvictims, 82% for property crime victims, and 75% for violent crime victims). Altogether, 522 people completed all three interviews and had complete data on all symptom measures. As Table 8.1 shows, the three-wave sample was quite similar to the original Wave 1 sample.

The Activator Question

Our sampling procedures provided sufficient numbers and varieties of crime victims to examine the activator question quite well. Table 8.2 shows the crimes experienced by this sample. Although people were selected on the basis of crimes experienced at Time 1, many people also reported crimes at Times 2 and 3. People who were selected for the study because they were victims at Time 1 were more likely than nonvictims to report crimes at later interviews as well.

In analysis, we focused on the relative impact of violent and property crimes. Figure 8.2 shows the means on the five symptom measures (CONSEQUENCES) for the violent, property, and no-crime groups at Time 1. Depression (DEP), somatization (SOM), hostility (HOS), anxiety (ANX), and phobic anxiety

(PHO) were measured using the Brief Symptom Inventory (BSI; Derogatis & Spencer, 1982). This figure, in addition, shows the means for two more proximal REACTIONS: fear of crime (FR, the extent to which respondents worried about being victimized by crime) and avoidance behavior (AV, the extent to which they actually avoided other people or places because of the threat of crime).

A multivariate analysis of variance (MANOVA) verified the visual impression that the three groups differed in their overall levels of psychological distress. The no-crime group's means were virtually identical to norms provided by Derogatis and Spencer for nonpatient adults (BSI scales only). Although below those established for psychiatric samples, the crime groups' means were well above the nonpatient norms. In the case of violent crime, group means exceeded the norms by no less than one standard deviation. Moreover, about 25% of the violent crime victims reported extreme distress (*T* scores > 70) on BSI Depression, Hostility, and Anxiety scales. An additional 22% to 27% showed moderately severe distress (*T* scores in the 61-70 range) on these same scales.

It can also be observed that crime was associated not with a specific symptom profile but rather with a pervasive elevation of symptoms across domains. For all respondents, fear of

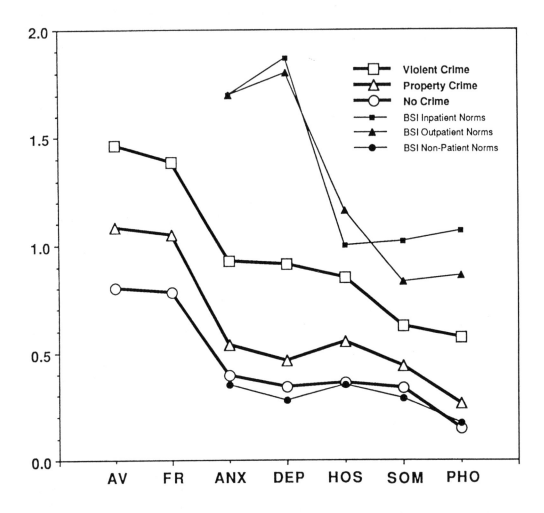

Figure 8.2. Time 1 Symptom Profile and Comparison to Brief Symptom Inventory (BSI) Norms

crime and avoidance were most common; somatization and generalized phobias were least common. Anxiety, depression, and hostility occurred at levels intermediate to these extremes. These findings were described in greater detail by Norris and Kaniasty (1994).

The Consequence Question

However striking, the preceding findings do not in themselves demonstrate that crime is a significant problem from an etiological perspective. The same panel of stress researchers referenced earlier argued that we need to make clearer distinctions between short-term and longer-term consequences. Many reactions to stress are transient and not harmful in themselves. The panel recommended that judgments concerning the ultimate importance of life events be based only on their long-term consequences. Thus our study addressed a basic but important question: How lasting are the psychological consequences of crime and violence?

Total Effects of Crime and Time

Initially, the effects of crime and time on the five symptom measures were tested using MANOVA as the statistical technique. *Crime* (violent, property, no crime, as assessed at Time 1) was the between-subjects factor. *Time* (Time 1, Time 2, Time 3, each 6 months apart) was the within-subjects factor. The effect of crime was highly significant in the multivariate test and in each univariate test. Contrasts revealed that the crime groups showed significantly higher symptoms than the no-crime group and that the violent crime group showed significantly higher symptoms than the property crime group. A multivariate effect of time was observed; for the sample as a whole, symptoms declined over time. This improvement held for all dependent measures.

Of particular interest were the interactions between crime and time. The Crime × Time interaction was significant for depression, anxiety, and phobic anxiety. These interactions indicated that the groups differed in the course of their symptoms over time. The nature of the interaction is easy to see in Figure 8.3. For each dependent measure, this figure shows the means over the three time points for each group. In all cases in which interactions occurred, the symptoms of the crime groups declined while those of the no-crime group did not. Violent crime victims showed a greater change over time than property crime victims. Despite these changes, the groups retained their same rank order throughout the study period.

Unique Effects of Crime Over Time

For longitudinal analyses, mean data have incomparable descriptive appeal. One can easily see both the overall differences between groups and the changes that each group exhibits over time. Here, these data are all the more appealing because each group was approximately representative of its respective population in Kentucky. Thus it seemed particularly worthwhile to observe them as they "naturally" evolved. Nonetheless, we cannot infer causality to the crimes themselves because victims differed from nonvictims in many ways. These differences included not only initial sociodemographic characteristics but also subsequent exposure to crime. Furthermore, the MANOVAs could not establish that the postcrime means differed from precrime symptom levels. (The design, though longitudinal, was not prospective.)

Thus our ability to draw conclusions from these data is limited by three alternative explanations. First, the differences in symptomatology might have been due to (a) differences between victims and nonvictims in background variables such as age, education, and prior victimization; (b) differences between victims and nonvictims in preexisting symptomatology; or (c) the occurrence of subsequent crimes (and the higher likelihood that crime victims would experience them).

To overcome these limitations, we reanalyzed the data using multiple regression as the statistical technique. The outcome measures were again depression, somatization, hostility, anxiety, and phobic anxiety. To provide results parallel to the MANOVAs, two separate series of regressions were performed. The first series was conducted on the total sample ($N = 522$), using dummy-coded (0, 1) variables as measures of Time 1 crime, Time 2 crime, and Time 3 crime. The second series of regressions was conducted using only victim data ($n = 332$) and dummy-coded measures of Time 1 violence, Time 2 violence, and Time 3 violence.

First, let us consider whether crime had effects on symptoms independent of its confounds with background variables. Table 8.3 summarizes the findings by simply noting how many significant effects were observed for crime and violence (the independent variables) across the five dependent variables. Before background variables were controlled for, both crime and violence had significant effects on all five outcome measures. These effects remained when background variables were

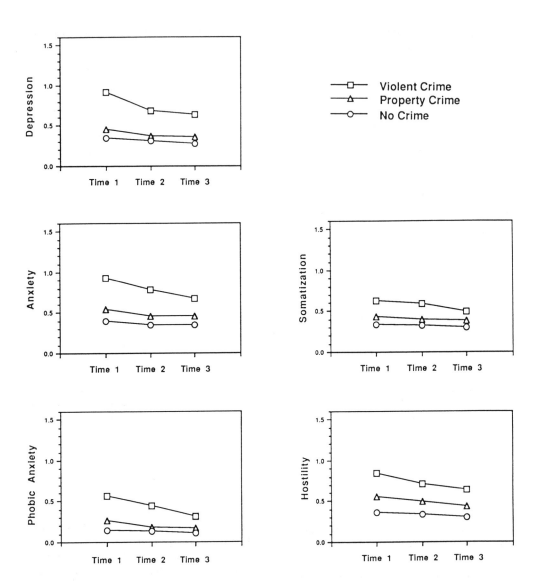

Figure 8.3. Symptoms by Crime and Time

controlled. This finding suggests that the mean differences found at Time 1 cannot be accounted for by status differences between the crime and no-crime groups.

The second alternative explanation was that the findings could be accounted for by preexisting symptom differences. We can never

know for sure that this was not the case at Time 1. However, we can examine the effects of Time 2 and 3 crimes, which occurred after the measures of Time 1 symptoms were taken. At Time 2, the effects of recent crime and violence were significant in all 10 tests (5 for crime, 5 for violence). All of these effects

Table 8.3   Summary of Regression Results: Number of Significant Effects of Crime and Violence on the Five Consequence Measures

	Independent Variable	
	Crime	Violence
Effects of **Time 1** crime and violence **AT TIME 1**		
Before background variables entered	5	5
After background variables entered	5	5
Effects of **Time 2** crime and violence **AT TIME 2**		
Before Time 1 symptoms entered	5	5
After Time 1 symptoms entered	5	5
Effects of **Time 3** crime and violence **AT TIME 3**		
Before Time 1 symptoms entered	2	3
After Time 1 symptoms entered	1	3
Effects of **Time 1** crime and violence **AT TIME 2**		
Before Time 2 crime entered	5	5
After Time 2 crime entered	2	3
Effects of **Time 1** crime and violence **AT TIME 3**		
Before Time 2-3 crime entered	5	4
After Time 2-3 crime entered	0	1

remained when Time 1 symptoms were entered into the equation. The results were not as strong at Time 3, but these measures of crime and violence encompassed crimes of average lesser severity than the earlier measures (see Table 8.2). Four of the five initial effects remained, however, when pre-event symptoms were controlled. Methodologically, this is an important demonstration of the impact of crime on psychological functioning because in this field of inquiry baseline data are very rare.

A third alternative explanation is that long-term effects were exhibited because initial crime victims were disproportionately exposed to subsequent crime. This issue pertains only to the persistence of symptoms rather than to the strength of initial effects. At Time 2, 5 of the 10 effects observed for Time 1 crime and violence dropped out when Time 2 crime or violence was entered into the equation. At Time 3, all five of the crime effects and three of the four violence effects dropped out when subsequent crimes were controlled. This pattern suggests that to a large extent, the

persistence of symptom consequences is mediated by subsequent exposure to crime and violence (see Norris & Kaniasty, 1994).

The Reaction Question

What makes crime such a powerful stressor? Theoretically, the most prominent explanation is that criminal victimization challenges victims' fundamental beliefs about themselves and their worlds. Janoff-Bulman and Frieze (1983), for example, asserted that victimization shatters three basic assumptions: the illusion of invulnerability, the view of oneself in a positive light, and the perception of the world as a meaningful place. Following in their footsteps, McCann, Sakheim, and Abrahamson (1988) derived a model in which cognitive schemas in the areas of safety, esteem, trust, power, and intimacy mediate adaptation to life experiences. In their model, various life experiences, such as victimization, "shape, solidify, or alter" the existing schema.

Empirical verification of these theoretical perspectives lagged far behind the thinking. We therefore developed and tested a causal model, using data from the panel's first wave. We restricted our attention to beliefs about safety, esteem, and trust because victims of crime may be particularly disposed to negative schemas in these domains.

We first tested the hypothesis that beliefs mediated the effects of violent crime. The sample consisted of 154 violent crime victims and 241 nonvictims for a total N of 395. The hypotheses were tested using the Linear Structural Relations (LISREL) program (Jöreskog & Sörbom, 1981). A LISREL model has two parts. The measurement model specifies the relation of the observed measures to underlying constructs or latent variables. (Latent variables are italicized here.) The structural equation model specifies the causal relations among the latent variables.

Three sets of beliefs were examined as mediators of the effects of violent crime on *Distress* (anger, tension, sadness; Derogatis & Spencer, 1982): *Safety* (fear and avoidance; Norris & Johnson, 1988), *Esteem* (low self-worth and inferiority; Rosenberg, 1965), and *Trust* (cynicism and pessimism; Srole, 1956). The indicators of *Victimization* were type and severity. Type was based on the 18-item crime battery and scored on a 4-point ordinal scale (no crime = 0, threat or simple assault = 1, aggravated assault = 2, rape or robbery = 3). Severity was based on the victim's verbatim description of the crime and was also coded on a 4-point scale (no violence = 0, minor = 1, moderately serious = 2, very serious = 3).

Age, education, sex, and urbanicity were included as control variables in all structural equations. Two models were compared. In Model A, all effects of *Victimization* were indirect; *Victimization* was to affect each domain of beliefs (*Safety, Esteem, Trust*), and each domain of beliefs was to affect *Distress*. In Model B, which is illustrated in Figure 8.4, *Victimization* has, in addition, a direct effect

on *Distress*. This model provided a better fit to the data than Model A, though both fit the data adequately. It is instructive to compare path "g" (*Victimization* to *Distress*) in Model B to the coefficient that was obtained without the presumed mediators in the equation. Without the hypothesized mediators, the standardized coefficient (.44) was almost twice as large as the coefficient (.23) obtained with the mediators in the equation. This difference is strong evidence for the mediating role of beliefs.

We next tested the generalizability of the model to property crime. The sample consisted of 295 property crime victims and 241 nonvictims, for a total N of 536. The measurement model was the one previously described except for the indicators of *Victimization*. Here, type related to property crimes (no crime = 0, vandalism = 1, larceny = 2, burglary = 3). Severity was a 4-point scale reflecting the dollar amount of property loss. In this case, Model A fit the data as well as the less parsimonious Model B because *Victimization* had no direct effect on *Distress*. Reactions to property crime were less intense than were those of violent crime. *Victimization* was associated with more negative beliefs in the *Safety* domain but did not lead to more negative beliefs in the *Trust* or *Esteem* domains. It is instructive to compare the nonsignificant coefficient of *Victimization* on *Distress*, obtained in the analysis controlling for the mediators, to the coefficient that was obtained without controlling for beliefs. There, *Victimization* had a small but significant effect on *Distress*. Thus the effects of property crime on distress would appear to be indirect, through the disruption of beliefs in the safety domain. More detail on these analyses can be found in Norris and Kaniasty (1991).

The Moderator Question

Our research project identified a number of factors that moderate the effects of crime and

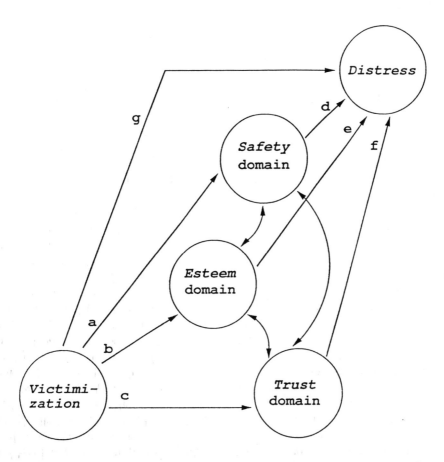

Figure 8.4. LISREL Structural Equation Model (Model B) for Testing Mediating Role of Beliefs in the Victimization-Distress Relation

violence. Moderators, defined as factors that change the strength of the relation between the predictor and outcome variables, may come into play at various points in the sequence (see Figure 8.1). First, they may alter the lasting consequences of crime. Second, they may alter the more proximal reactions (fear, alienation) that mediate crime's effects on symptom outcomes. Finally, they may alter relations between the reactions and consequences. At one point or another in our project, each of these roles has been demonstrated for one or more environmental or psychological constructs.

Moderators of the Activator-Consequence Relation

In our framework, the primary moderators of the more distal or lasting consequences of crime were formal and informal sources of support. Table 8.4 shows the percentage of victims receiving assistance from various sources within the first few months postcrime. Overall, about one in eight victims sought professional mental health services within this interval. Victims of violent crimes were more likely than victims of property crimes to have

Table 8.4   Frequency and Evaluation of Service Use by Crime Victims

	Property Crime		Violent Crime	
	% Using Service	% Stating "Very Helpful"	% Using Service	% Stating "Very Helpful"
Police (% reporting crime)	70	15	61	27
Lawyer or legal aid[a]	12	13	30	33
Medical doctor[a]	2	0	21	46
Clergy[a]	7	31	21	41
Mental health professional[a]	7	56	23	27
Other professional	7	39	11	40

a. Significant difference between property and violent crime victims in use of this service.

contact with professionals. For mental health services, the use rate among property crime victims was comparable to use rates reported for the general population (e.g., Taube, Kessler, & Feuerberg, 1984). Although violent crime victims used services more often, they were less frequently satisfied with them.

We attempted to identify factors that predict use of mental health services among recent victims of crime. A discriminant analysis revealed that by far the two most important predictors of use were depression and the presence of violence in the commission of the crime. The use of services was also more pronounced when the recent incident followed other victimization experiences. This result is consistent with other research showing that a prior crime may exacerbate the symptomatic consequences of a more recent incident. Those whose lives are chronically prone to violence may be an important population for mental health services.

Another interesting finding was that social support correlated positively with service use: The greater the receipt of support from families or friends, the more likely victims of violence were to seek help from professionals. This finding may simply reflect a general tendency of some people to mobilize help from all available sources. However, it could also suggest that responsive social networks facilitate use of services by encouraging or enabling victims to seek the care they need.

Research into the determinants of service use is potentially useful for developing strategies that increase victims' use of or access to mental health services. Ultimately, however, the value of such strategies rests on the assumption that professional support services do, in fact, hasten recovery from the crisis at hand. To test this assumption, we conducted a series of regression analyses in which the Time 2 symptom measures served as the dependent variables. With initial symptoms and crime exposure held constant, professional help was associated with a subsequent reduction in symptoms *if and only if* it was both prompt (reported at Time 1) and continuing (reported at Time 2). This interactive effect is perhaps a disappointing finding in terms of designing intervention strategies. The problems experienced by victims may be too profound, enduring, or variable in onset to be prevented by simple one-shot counseling efforts. For further discussion of these findings, see Norris, Kaniasty, and Scheer (1990).

The contributions of professionals to victims' well-being pale beside the contributions of victims' families and friends (i.e., their "natural" social supports). Indeed, no answer to the "Moderator Question" would be complete without considering social support and all its diverse functions. What types of social support would be most effective in alleviating the psychological consequences of criminal victimization? For guidance, we turned to Cutrona and Russell's (1990) model of optimal stress-support matching. In this model, an event's location on various dimensions, such as controllability, desirability, or life domain, determines the coping needs of people experiencing that event. As these needs differ, so does the importance of different types of social support. Cutrona and Russell classified criminal victimization as an uncontrollable, negative event that may affect psychosocial assets such as material goods or physical health. For uncontrollable events, emotional support is most beneficial because it fosters feelings of acceptance and comfort. When victimization also involves loss, social support capable of replacing the loss (tangible support) is also of help. Although Cutrona and Russell classified victimization as an uncontrollable event—and were no doubt correct in principle—crime may not always be perceived as such. Individuals often believe that their probabilities of victimization are subject to their own control. When victimization is perceived as controllable, informational support would also be of value.

Thus, in our study, we included measures of each type of social support. Moreover, we included measures of both perceived support (i.e., the belief that support would be available if needed; Interpersonal Support Evaluation List [ISEL]; Cohen & Hoberman, 1983) and received support (i.e., the actual receipt of help; Inventory of Socially Supportive Behaviors [ISSB]; Barrera, Sandler, & Ramsay, 1981). Whereas the literature has given more weight to the former, we contended that in this context, believing is not always enough.

We tested the main and interactive effects of these variables in a series of regression analyses. Two consequences, depression and anxiety, were examined. The measures of symptoms were taken 6 months after the measures of social support. Main effects emerged for perceived support (beliefs about support availability) but not for received support (actual assistance). Overall, perceived support was more beneficial, stress levels aside. Significant moderating effects occurred for perceived appraisal support (emotional and informational support) in the regression of anxiety and for perceived tangible support in the regressions of depression and anxiety. However, received support showed no capacity to buffer the direct consequences of crime. For more detail on these results, see Kaniasty and Norris (1992).

Moderators of the Activator-Reaction Relation

Our analysis of the buffering effect of social support also included fear, conceptualized here as a more event-specific reaction to crime. Interestingly, although received support did not interact with crime in predicting symptom consequences, it did in predicting fear. Both informational and tangible aspects of received support showed crime-buffering effects in this case. The limited scope of the effects observed for received support is instructive. In combating more proximal reactions to crime, practical actual support may be especially relevant. Fear of crime is likely to be the first reaction to be noticed by, or acknowledged by victims to, members of their social networks. Fear may also be an outcome that is easier than others to remedy because it is not difficult to assess what kinds of help would alleviate it. Thus, in this case, the event (violence), the reaction (fear), and the needs of the victim (security) may have been easily recognized and understood by people around the victim. These same people, however, may have been less aware of, and thus less capable of alleviating, more diffuse consequences such as depression or general anxiety.

In another paper (Thompson & Norris, 1992), we examined the moderating role of several aspects of social status on fear, avoidance, and alienation. An interesting aspect of this analysis was our inclusion of a measure of community-level crime along with our standard measures of violent and property crime. This community-level measure reflected rates of Part I crimes in the respondent's county of residence in 1987 and was objectively derived. Part I crimes, as defined by the Federal Bureau of Investigation, include murder, rape, robbery, aggravated assault, burglary, lacernytheft, motor vehicle theft, and arson. In this analysis, the most notable finding was the influence of socioeconomic status (SES; i.e., education, occupational status) on reactions to crime. SES moderated both individual-level crime (violence) and community-level crime, but in different directions. Lower-status individuals reacted more strongly to high community crime, but higher-status individuals reacted more strongly when touched by crime on a personal level.

Another question we asked (Norris & Thompson, 1993) was whether victims' experiences in the justice system influenced their reactions to the crime. A criminal act usually lasts only a few minutes, but if the crime is reported, it may require the victim's involvement in the criminal justice system for many months, even years. Despite much speculation, very little is known about how crime victims respond to their experiences in the justice system. Elias (1984) has written that postvictimization experiences can cause considerable disenchantment (i.e., alienation) not only with the offender but also with the justice system and the broader society. This postvictimization period, in which victims come to perceive themselves as rejected by the community, its agencies, and society in general, has been described as the "second injury" to victims (Symonds, 1980).

We again used LISREL to analyze the data (Time 1 only). The sample here was composed of 220 Time 1 victims who had reported their crimes to the police. The model encompassed nine observed variables tapping crime characteristics, system experiences, and victim alienation. Except where noted, latent and observed variables were synonymous in the model. Two crime characteristics were included as exogenous variables: *Crime Severity,* a 5-point scale, and *Acquaintance,* a dichotomous variable, scored 1 if the victim

knew the perpetrator (30%). *Investigation,* the first system variable, had two indicators: whether the police looked for evidence (yes = 1; 42%) and whether they promised to investigate (yes = 1; 54%). *Arrest* was dichotomous, scored 1 if an arrest had been made (12%). *Satisfaction* was the victim's assessment of the overall helpfulness of the police (44% not at all, 34% somewhat, 18% very). Victim *Alienation,* the outcome of interest, had three indicators: pessimism and cynicism from Srole's (1956) anomia scale and the "hopelessness" item from the BSI.

Figure 8.5 shows the model that provided the best fit to the data. As hypothesized, alienation was directly influenced by both the nature of the crime and the nature of the victim's system experience. More severe crimes and acquaintance crimes were associated with greater alienation. Greater satisfaction with police led to lower alienation. The occurrence of an investigation or arrest had only indirect effects on alienation in that both made satisfaction more likely. Relative to each other, actual arrests were less important in reducing alienation than was the simple assurance from police that they would investigate the crime.

Moderators of the Reaction-Consequence Relation

A growing body of evidence suggests that fear of crime may eventuate in impaired mental health (Taylor, Perkins, Shumaker, & Meeks, 1989). It is commonly assumed that precautionary behavior is an effective means of lessening fear of crime. However, prospective research has challenged the long-standing assumption that precaution is inversely related to subsequent fear (see Norris & Johnson, 1988). In our study, we proposed that a more fruitful conceptualization would be to view precaution as a strategy that citizens use to manage their fear rather than as a means to prevent it. This proposition builds on Riger's (1985) characterization of precaution as a form of coping behavior, but in this case, the

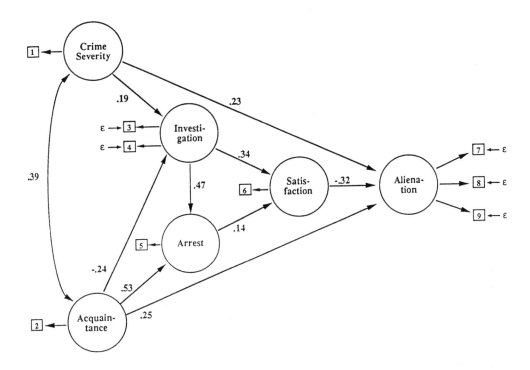

Figure 8.5. LISREL Model for Testing Effects of System Responsiveness on Victim Alienation

function is palliative (emotion focused) rather than instrumental (problem focused). Perhaps precaution provides the individual with a way of "encapsulating" the fear—living with the fear inherent in contemporary life—thereby blunting or buffering its impact on other aspects of mental health. Thus the function is the prevention of more generalized states of distress, rather than the reduction of fear itself.

Before testing this hypothesis, we developed a 16-item scale of precaution that factored into four crime prevention strategies: Vigilance (alertness), Locks (access control), Neighbors (informal cooperation), and Professionals (formal programs). Then LISREL models were specified. *Distress* served as the outcome variable. In each model, one of the four crime prevention strategies, *Fear,* and a latent variable representing the interaction of

the two served as the predictor variables. In their separate analyses, both *Neighbors* and *Locks* significantly interacted with *Fear* to affect *Distress. Fear* was more strongly related to *Distress* when the use of locks or neighbors was low than when the use of these precautions was high. The form of the interaction is illustrated in Figure 8.6 for protective neighboring. A final analysis examined *Neighbors* and *Locks* together in the same model. The effects of *Locks* × Fear dropped out, but the effects of *Locks* × Neighbors remained significant.

Of course, the primary function of precautionary behavior is assumed to be crime prevention. A vigilant and informed citizenry should reduce crime by making it more difficult to commit (Lurigio & Rosenbaum, 1986). Although this hypothesis was not directly pro-

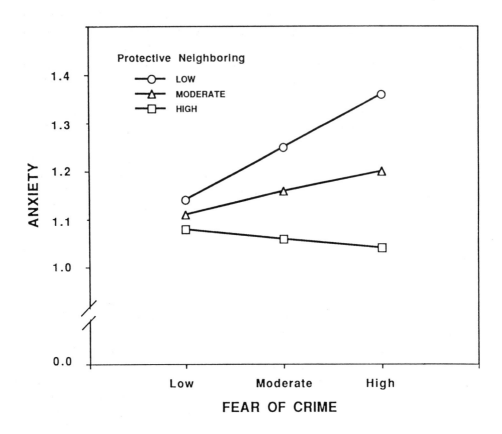

Figure 8.6. Precaution as a Fear-Buffering Strategy

posed within our framework, we thought it was important to investigate such claims. To test the effectiveness of precautionary behavior in preventing crime, we conducted three logistic regressions. Victimization was defined according to crimes occurring over the year-long interval between Waves 1 and 3. Persons with acquaintance crimes were excluded. The same group of nonvictims ($n = 317$) was compared first to victims of larceny ($n = 109$), second to victims of burglary ($n = 72$), and third to victims of violence ($n = 57$).

The predictor variables were various potential risk factors and crime prevention strategies. Because they were all assessed at Wave 1, the predictors could not have been affected by the crimes. Of all the risk factors examined,

prior victimization was the strongest predictor of subsequent experience of crime. Greater levels of fear of crime were also reliably associated with victimization, especially with larceny and violence. As for the predictive power of precaution, all analyses yielded the same conclusion: Not one of the crime prevention strategies discriminated between those who did and did not experience crime over the ensuing year (see Norris and Kaniasty, 1992).

Conclusion

The findings of this study paint a complex picture, but there are recurrent themes amid the isolated facts. The theme of *pervasiveness* is first and foremost. It is important to note that the victims of this study experienced a variety of crimes, ranging in severity from vandalism to rape. Although victims of violence were clearly the most severely distressed, property crime victims also showed considerable distress (see also Cook, Smith, & Harrell, 1987; Davis & Friedman, 1985; Lurigio, 1987; Maguire, 1982; Wirtz & Harrell, 1987a). Property crime, like violent crime, was a sufficiently powerful stressor to evidence effects in prospective analyses that included precrime measures of psychological state. In one analysis or another, we found criminal victimization to be associated with depression, anxiety, hostility, somatic symptoms, fear of crime, avoidance behavior, lower self-esteem, increased alienation, and need for both formal and informal social support. The pervasive nature of these effects is consistent with the literature showing a variety of consequences following criminal victimization (Atkeson, Calhoun, Resick, & Ellis, 1982; Bard & Sangrey, 1986; Davis & Friedman, 1985; Kilpatrick et al., 1985; Kilpatrick & Resnick, 1993; Koss, Woodruff, & Koss, 1990; Resnick et al., 1993; Siegel, Golding, Stein, Burnam, & Sorenson, 1990; Skogan, 1987). Men and women, city dwellers and rural persons, the cautious and careless, were all equally likely to experience these crimes and to experience their adverse effects. Thus these effects were not confined to rare events, specific symptom clusters, high-risk areas, or uniquely vulnerable individuals.

The breadth of crime's effects was especially well evidenced by crime's impact on beliefs and attributions. These results are congruent with current theories that emphasize the mediating role of cognitions in explaining the emotional reactions of crime victims (Janoff-Bulman, 1992; McCann & Pearlman, 1990; Roth & Newman, 1991). Violent crime in particular led to more negative schemas in the domains of safety (Kilpatrick, Veronen, & Resick, 1979; Skogan, 1987; Vitelli & Endler, 1993), self-esteem (Murphy et al., 1988; Shepherd, 1990), and trust (Janoff-Bulman, 1989; Roth & Lebowitz, 1988). And these pessimistic beliefs led to distress (Dutton, Burghardt, Perrin, Chrestman, & Halle, 1994; Ross, 1993). We conceptualized these changes as proximal reactions that shape the more distal consequences of criminal victimization. In addition, the analyses shed light on why property crime victims are less severely distressed than victims of violent crime. Unlike the schemas of violent crime victims, those of property crime victims were relatively unscathed. Property crime did lead to more negative beliefs in the safety domain but otherwise did not alter victims' views of the world and themselves. Their beliefs were affected less, so their distress was less. However, we should not overlook the finding that in a more limited sense, the belief mediational model explained the effects of property crime quite well. The difference between property crime and violent crime, then, was one more of scope than of process.

There is also a theme of *persistence*. Initially, crime victims showed clear signs of recovery, but their improvement leveled off after the first few months. After 15 months, which is where our study ends, violent crime victims were still more distressed than property crime victims, who were still more distressed than nonvictims. Several other studies have also found criminal victimization to have long-lasting effects (Ageton, 1983; Burnam et al., 1988; Calhoun, Atkeson, & Resick, 1982; Cohen & Roth, 1987; Gidycz & Koss, 1991; Kilpatrick et al., 1985; Riggs, Kilpatrick, & Resnick, 1992; Wirtz & Harrell, 1987b).

A troubling analogue to this persistence theme is the theme of *recurrence*. The strongest predictor of recent victimization was prior victimization, a relation that has been documented in a number of other studies (Gidycz, Coble, Latham, & Layman, 1993; Hindelang, Gottfredson, & Garofalo, 1978; Koss & Dinero, 1989; Wyatt, Guthrie, & Notgrass, 1993). Although victims' behavior was not its source, it was nonetheless true that some people were chronically prone to violence and other crimes.

Sadly, crime appears to be a stressor for which prior experience provides no additional coping expertise. Need for professional services was highest when the recent crime followed other victimization experiences. In addition, a meaningful proportion of victims' lasting symptomatology was explained by subsequent exposure to crime and violence. In general, victims of multiple crimes have shown poorer outcomes (Burgess & Holmstrom, 1978; Burnam et al., 1988; Frazier, 1991; Koss & Dinero, 1989; Sorenson & Golding, 1990). Clinically, this finding has vital implications. To treat the victim without "treating" the environment may do little to hasten the course of recovery. Spouse abuse is an obvious and compelling example, but our point is not limited to this case. Clinical assessments should include an assessment of risk for future victimization, based on lifestyle and environmental factors.

In the present study, risk for future victimization had little to do with precautionary behavior as practiced at the individual or household level. In a series of analyses that controlled for 14 separate risk factors, precaution had no preventive effects on the occurrence of larceny, burglary, or violence over the ensuing year. Whereas this is among our most controversial findings, it is actually quite consistent with the results of other investigations of crime prevention (Davis & Smith, 1994; Miethe, Stafford, & Sloane, 1990; Norris & Johnson, 1988; Rosenbaum, Lewis, & Grant, 1986; Van den Bogaard & Wiegman, 1991). The most promising strategy was protective neighboring because it showed no adverse effects and some positive ones, such as the capacity to buffer the effects of fear on generalized distress. However, policy implications are not straightforward. Neighborhood watch programs (included here within the professional subscale) have not been shown to be successful in reducing rates of crime or fear in participating neighborhoods (Bennett &

Lavrakas, 1989; Garofalo & McLeod, 1989). Community organizing may well be of value, but perhaps crime should not be (directly) its theme. Organizers would be well advised to undertake more achievable goals (beautification, traffic reduction, tenant rights) while helping communities to develop protective bonds. Environmental design should likewise be encouraged, as certain features of the physical environment (communal areas, circulation of people) appear "naturally" to facilitate social cohesion and control (Newman, 1972; Perkins, Florin, Rich, Wandersman, & Chavis, 1990).

A more hopeful theme was that of *responsiveness*. Various sources of support were instrumental in diminishing adverse reactions and consequences. Depending on the circumstances, families and friends (Brown & Harris, 1989; Kimerling & Calhoun, 1994; Krause, 1986; Shepherd, 1990), protective neighbors (Perkins et al., 1990; Riger, 1985; Riger, LeBailly, & Gordon, 1981), mental health professionals (Davis & Henley, 1990; Falsetti & Resnick, 1995; Foa, Rothbaum, Riggs, & Murdock, 1991; Golding, Stein, Siegel, Burnam, & Sorenson, 1988; Resick & Schnicke, 1990), and criminal justice officials (Brandl & Horvath, 1991; Kilpatrick et al., 1987; Maguire, 1984; Shapland, 1984; Skogan, 1989; Winkel, 1991; Winkel & Vrij, 1993) are all able to allay victims' fears and distress.

Supporting and assisting crime victims is a complex, involving, and delicate task. Our findings suggest that the most effective support we can provide to crime victims is to restore their tarnished beliefs. As Janoff-Bulman (1985) noted, coping with victimization is in large part the process of "coming to terms with these shattered assumptions and reestablishing a conceptual system that will allow the victim to once again function effectively" (p. 22). Excellent discussions on how this may be accomplished have been presented elsewhere (Frieze et al., 1987; Janoff-Bulman & Schwartzberg, 1991; McCann & Pearlman, 1990; Meichenbaum & Fitzpatrick, 1992;

Taylor, 1983). What is also needed is a more proactive approach of educating the public about the realities of coping with criminal victimization. Being informed about the benefits, difficulties, and risks involved in social support processes may help providers to provide more effectively and victims to believe that supports are available.

What can we say? Crime changes people in fundamental ways that do not lend themselves to quick and easy solutions. We join others (Koss & Harvey, 1991; Rosenberg & Fenley, 1991) who have voiced the position that crime poses a significant threat to our nation's health. This conclusion, which is not made lightly, is justified, even necessitated, by the findings presented here. Crime—common "garden-variety" crime—engenders pervasive and persistent psychological distress. From a policy perspective, this is an important observation because it implies that we must seek solutions to the problem at a population level. Individual psychotherapy, though undeniably of value, is unlikely to meet the needs of a population in which exposure to crime and crime-related distress are shockingly widespread. Our study suggests that crime prevention, improving the responsiveness of the criminal justice system, and the provision of social support to victims are all areas in which further research and program development are sorely needed.

References

Ageton, S. (1983). *Sexual assault among adolescents.* Lexington, MD: D. C. Heath.

Atkeson, B., Calhoun, K., Resick, P., & Ellis, E. (1982). Victims of rape: Repeated assessment of depressive symptoms. *Journal of Consulting and Clinical Psychology, 50,* 96-102.

Bard, M., & Sangrey, D. (1986). *The crime victim's book* (2nd ed.). New York: Brunner/Mazel.

Barrera, M., Sandler, I. N., & Ramsay, T. B. (1981). Preliminary development of a scale of social support: Studies on college students. *American Journal of Community Psychology, 9,* 435-447.

Bennett, S., & Lavrakas, P. (1989). Community-based crime prevention: As assessment of the Eisenhower Foundation's Neighborhood Program. *Crime and Delinquency, 35,* 345-363.

Brandl, S., & Horvath, F. (1991). Crime-victim evaluation of police investigative performance. *Journal Criminal Justice, 19,* 293-305.

Brown, B., & Harris, P. (1989). Residential burglary victimization: Reactions to the invasion of a primary territory. *Journal of Environmental Psychology, 9,* 119-132.

Burgess, A., & Holmstrom, L. (1978). Recovery from rape and prior life stress. *Research in Nursing and Health, 1,* 165-174.

Burnam, M., Stein, J., Golding, J., Siegel, J., Sorenson, S., Forsythe, A., & Telles, C. (1988). Sexual assault and mental disorders in a community population. *Journal of Consulting and Clinical Psychology, 56,* 843-850.

Calhoun, K., Atkeson, B., & Resick, P. (1982). A longitudinal examination of fear reactions in victims of rape. *Journal of Counseling Psychology, 29,* 655-661.

Cohen, L., & Roth, S. (1987). The psychological aftermath of rape: Long-term effects and individual differences in recovery. *Journal of Social and Clinical Psychology, 5,* 525-534.

Cohen, S., & Hoberman, H. M. (1983). Positive events and social supports as buffers of life change stress. *Journal of Applied Social Psychology, 13,* 99-125.

Cook, R., Smith, B., & Harrell, A. (1987). *Helping crime victims: Levels of trauma and effectiveness of service.* Washington, DC: U.S. Dept. of Justice, National Institute of Justice.

Cutrona, C., & Russell, D. (1990). Type of social support and specific stress: Toward a theory of optimal matching. In B. R. Sarason, I. G. Sarason, & G. R. Pierce (Eds.), *Social support: An interactional view* (pp. 319-366). New York: John Wiley.

Davis, R., & Friedman, L.(1985). The emotional aftermath of crime and violence. In C. Figley (Ed.) *Trauma and its wake: The study and treatment of post-traumatic stress disorder* (pp. 90-112). New York: Brunner/Mazel.

Davis, R., & Henley, M. (1990). Victim service programs. In A. Lurigio, W. Skogan, & R. C. Davis (Eds.), *Victims of crime: Problems, policies, and programs* (pp. 157-171). Newbury Park, CA: Sage.

Davis, R., & Smith, B. (1994). Teaching victims crime prevention skills: Can individuals lower their risk of crime? *Criminal Justice Review, 19,* 56-68.

Derogatis, L., & Spencer, P. (1982). *The Brief Symptom Inventory (BSI): Administration, scoring and procedures manual-1.* Baltimore: Author.

Dutton, M., Burghardt, K., Perrin, S., Chrestman, K., & Halle, P. (1994). Battered women's cognitive schemata. *Journal of Traumatic Stress, 7,* 237-255.

Elias, R. (1984). Alienating the victim: Compensation and victim attitudes. *Journal of Social Issues, 40,* 103-116.

Eliot, G., & Eisdorfer, C. (1982). *Stress and human health.* New York: Springer.

Falsetti, S., & Resnick, H. (1995). Helping the victims of violent crime. In J. Freedy & S. Hobfoll (Eds.), *Traumatic stress: Theory and practice* (pp. 263-285). New York: Plenum.

Foa, E., Rothbaum, B., Riggs, D., & Murdock, T. (1991). Treatment of posttraumatic stress disorder in rape victims: A comparison between cognitive procedures and counseling. *Journal of Consulting and Clinical Psychology, 59,* 715-723.

Frazier, P. (1991). Self-blame as a mediator of postrape depressive symptoms. *Journal of Social and Clinical Psychology, 10,* 47-57.

Frieze, I., Hymer S., & Greenberg, M. (1987). Describing the crime victim: Psychological reactions to victimization. *Professional Psychology: Research and Practice, 18,* 299-315.

Garofalo, J., & McLeod, M. (1989). The structure and operations of neighborhood watch programs in the United States. *Crime and Delinquency, 35,* 326-343.

George, L., Winfield, I., & Blazer, D. (1992). Sociocultural factors in sexual assault: Comparison of two representative samples of women. *Journal of Social Issues, 48,* 105-125.

Gidycz, C., Coble, C., Latham, L., & Layman, M. (1993). Relationship of a sexual assault experience in adulthood to prior victimization experiences: A prospective analysis. *Psychology of Women Quarterly, 17,* 151-168.

Gidycz, C., & Koss, M. (1991). Predictors of long-term sexual assault trauma among a national sample of victimized college women. *Violence and Victims, 6,* 175-190.

Golding, J., Stein, J., Siegel, J., Burnam, M., & Sorenson, S. (1988). Sexual assault history and use of health and mental health services. *American Journal of Community Psychology, 16,* 625-644.

Hindelang, M., Gottfredson, M., & Garofalo, J. (1978). *Victims of personal crime: An empirical foundation for a theory of personal victimization.* Cambridge, MA: Ballinger.

Janoff-Bulman, R. (1985). The aftermath of victimization: Rebuilding shattered assumptions. In C. Figley (Ed.), *Trauma and its wake: The study and treatment of posttraumatic stress disorder* (pp. 15-35). New York: Brunner/Mazel.

Janoff-Bulman, R. (1989). Assumptive worlds and the stress of traumatic events: Applications of the schema construct. *Social Cognition, 7,* 113-136.

Janoff-Bulman, R. (1992). *Shattered assumptions.* New York: Free Press.

Janoff-Bulman, R., & Frieze, I. (1983). A theoretical perspective for understanding reactions to victimization. *Journal of Social Issues, 39,* 1-17.

Janoff-Bulman, R., & Schwartzberg, S. (1991). Toward a general model of personal change. In C. R. Snyder &

D. Forsyth (Eds.), *Handbook of social and clinical psychology* (pp. 488-508), Elmsford, NY: Pergamon.

Jöreskog, K., & Sörbom, D. (1981). *LISREL: Analysis of linear structural relations by the method of maximum likelihood (Version VI).* Chicago: National Educational Services.

Kaniasty, K., & Norris, F. (1992). Social support and victims of crime: Matching event, support, and outcome. *American Journal of Community Psychology, 20,* 211-241.

Kilpatrick, D., Best, C., Veronen, L., Amick, A., Villeponteaux, L., & Ruff, G. (1985). Mental health correlates of victimization: A random community survey. *Journal of Consulting and Clinical Psychology, 53,* 866-873.

Kilpatrick, D., & Resnick, H. (1993). PTSD associated with exposure to criminal victimization in clinical and community populations. In J. Davidson & E. Foa (Eds.), *Posttraumatic stress disorder: DSM-IV and beyond* (pp. 113-143). Washington, DC: American Psychiatric Press.

Kilpatrick, D., Saunders, B., Veronen, L., Best, C., & Von, J. (1987). Criminal victimization: Lifetime prevalence, reporting to police, and psychological impact. *Crime and Delinquency, 33,* 479-489.

Kilpatrick, D., Veronen, L., & Resick, P. (1979). Assessment of the aftermath of rape: Changing patterns of fear. *Journal of Behavioral Assessment, 1,* 133-148.

Kimerling, R., & Calhoun, K. (1994). Somatic symptoms, social support, and treatment seeking among sexual assault victims. *Journal of Consulting and Clinical Psychology, 62,* 333-340.

Kish, L. (1949). A procedure for objective respondent selection within the household. *American Statistical Association Journal, 44,* 380-387.

Koss, M. (1993). Rape: Scope, impact, interventions, and public policy responses. *American Psychologist, 48,* 1062-1069.

Koss, M., & Dinero, T. (1989). Discriminant analysis of risk factors for sexual victimization among a national sample of college women. *Journal of Consulting and Clinical Psychology, 57,* 242-250.

Koss, M., & Harvey, M. (1991). *The rape victim: Clinical and community interventions.* Newbury Park, CA: Sage.

Koss, M., Woodruff, W., & Koss, P. (1990). Relation of criminal victimization to health perceptions among women medical patients. *Journal of Consulting and Clinical Psychology, 58,* 147-152.

Krause, N. (1986). Social support, stress, and well-being among older adults. *Journal of Gerontology, 41,* 512-519.

Lehnen, R., & Skogan, W. (1984). *The National Crime Survey: Working papers, volume II: Methodological studies.* Washington, DC: U.S. Dept. of Justice, Bureau of Justice Statistics.

Lurigio, A. (1987). Are all victims alike? The adverse, generalized, and differential impact of crime. *Crime and Delinquency, 33,* 452-467.

Lurigio, A., & Resick, P. (1990). Healing the psychological wounds of criminal victimization: Predicting postcrime distress and recovery. In A. Lurigio, W. Skogan, & R. Davis (Eds.), *Victims of crime: Problems, policies, and programs* (pp. 50-68). Newbury Park, CA: Sage.

Lurigio, A. & Rosenbaum, D. (1986). Evaluation research in community crime prevention: A critical look at the field. In D. Rosenbaum (Ed.), *Community crime prevention: Does it work?* (pp. 19-45). Beverly Hills, CA: Sage.

Maguire, M. (1982). *Burglary in a dwelling.* London: Heinemann.

Maguire, M. (1984). Meeting the needs of burglary victims: Questions for police and the criminal justice system. In R. Clarke & T. Hope (Eds.), *Coping with burglary.* Boston: Kluwer-Nijhoff.

McCann, L., & Pearlman, L. (1990). *Psychological trauma and the adult survivor: Theory, therapy, and transformation.* New York: Brunner/Mazel.

McCann, L., Sakheim, D., & Abrahamson, D. (1988). Trauma and victimization: A model of psychological adaptation. *Counseling Psychologist, 16,* 531-594.

Meichenbaum, D., & Fitzpatrick, D. (1992). A constructivist narrative perspective on stress and coping: Stress inoculation applications. In L. Goldberger & S. Breznitz (Eds.), *Handbook of stress.* New York: Free Press.

Miethe, T., Stafford, M., & Sloane, D. (1990). Lifestyle changes and risks of criminal victimization. *Journal of Quantitative Criminology, 6,* 357-376.

Murphy, S., Amick-McMullan, A., Kilpatrick, D., Haskett, M., Veronen, L., Best, C., & Saunders, B. (1988). Rape victims' self-esteem: A longitudinal analysis. *Journal of Interpersonal Violence, 3,* 355-370.

Newman, O. (1972). *Defensible space: Crime prevention through urban design.* New York: Macmillan.

Norris, F., & Johnson, K. (1988). The effects of "self-help" precautionary measures on criminal victimization and fear. *Journal of Urban Affairs, 10,* 161-181.

Norris, F., & Kaniasty, K. (1991). The psychological experience of crime: A test of the mediating role of beliefs in explaining the distress of victims. *Journal of Social and Clinical Psychology, 10,* 239-261.

Norris, F., & Kaniasty, K. (1992). A longitudinal study of the effects of various crime prevention strategies on criminal victimization, fear of crime, and psychological distress. *American Journal of Community Psychology, 20,* 625-648.

Norris, F., & Kaniasty, K. (1994). Psychological distress following criminal victimization in the general population: Cross-sectional, longitudinal, and prospective analyses. *Journal of Consulting and Clinical Psychology, 62,* 111-123.

Norris, F., Kaniasty, K., & Scheer, D. (1990). Use of mental health services among victims of crime: Frequency, correlates, and subsequent recovery. *Journal of Consulting and Clinical Psychology, 58,* 538-547.

Norris, F., & Thompson, M. (1993). The victim in the system: The influence of police responsiveness on victim alienation. *Journal of Traumatic Stress, 6,* 515-531.

Perkins, D., Florin, P., Rich, R., Wandersman, A., & Chavis, A. (1990). Participation and the social and physical environment of residential blocks: Crime and community context. *American Journal of Community Psychology, 18,* 83-115.

Resick, P. (1993). The psychological impact of rape. *Journal of Interpersonal Violence, 8,* 223-255.

Resick, P., & Schnicke, M. (1990). Treating symptoms in adult victims of sexual assault. *Journal of Interpersonal Violence, 5,* 488-506.

Resnick, H., Kilpatrick, D., Dansky, B., Saunders, B., & Best, C. (1993). Prevalence of civilian trauma and posttraumatic stress disorder in a representative national sample of women. *Journal of Consulting and Clinical Psychology, 61,* 984-991.

Riger, S. (1985). Crime as an environmental stressor. *Journal of Community Psychology, 13,* 270-280.

Riger, S., LeBailly, R., & Gordon, M. (1991). Community ties and urbanites' fear of crime: An ecological investigation. *American Journal of Community Psychology, 9,* 653-665.

Riggs, D., Kilpatrick, D., & Resnick, H. (1992). Long-term psychological distress associated with marital rape and aggravated assault: A comparison to other crime victims. *Journal of Family Violence, 7,* 283-296.

Rosenbaum, D., Lewis, D., & Grant, J. (1986). Neighborhood-based crime prevention: Assessing the efficacy of community organizing in Chicago. In D. Rosenbaum (Ed.), *Community crime prevention: Does it work?* (pp. 109-136). Beverly Hills, CA: Sage.

Rosenberg, M. (1965). *Society and the adolescent self-image.* Princeton, NJ: Princeton University Press.

Rosenberg, M., & Fenley, M. (1991). *Violence in America: A public health approach.* New York: Oxford University Press.

Ross, C. (1993). Fear of victimization and health. *Journal of Quantitative Criminology, 9,* 159-175.

Roth, S., & Lebowitz, L. (1988). The experience of sexual trauma. *Journal of Traumatic Stress, 1,* 79-107.

Roth, S., & Newman, E. (1991). The process of coping with sexual trauma. *Journal of Traumatic Stress, 4,* 279-297.

Shapland, J. (1984). Victims, the criminal justice system and compensation. *British Journal of Criminology, 24,* 131-149.

Shepherd, J. (1990). Victims of personal violence: The relevance of Symonds' model of psychological response and loss-theory. *British Journal of Social Work, 20,* 309-332.

Siegel, J., Golding, J., Stein, J., Burnam, M., & Sorenson, S. (1990). Reactions to sexual assault: A community study. *Journal of Interpersonal Violence, 5,* 229-246.

Skogan, W. (1987). The impact of victimization on fear. *Crime and Delinquency, 33,* 135-154.

Skogan, W. (1989). The impact of police on victims. In E. Viano (Ed.), *Crime and its victims: International research and public policy issues* (pp. 71-77). New York: Hemisphere.

Sorenson, S., & Golding, J. (1990). Depressive sequelae of recent criminal victimization. *Journal of Traumatic Stress, 3,* 337-350.

Srole, L. (1956). Social integration and certain corollaries. *American Sociological Review, 21,* 709-716.

Symonds, M. (1980). The "second injury" to victims. In Kivens, L. (Ed.), *Evaluation and Change: Services for Survivors* (pp. 36-38). Minneapolis: Minneapolis Medical Research Foundation.

Taube, C. A., Kessler, L. G., & Feuerberg, M. (1984). *Utilization and expenditures for ambulatory mental health care during 1980* (DHHS Publication No. 512-A-29). Hyattsville, MD: U.S. Dept. of Health and Human Services, National Center for Health Statistics.

Taylor, R., Perkins, D., Shumaker, S., & Meeks, J. (1989). *Impacts over time of fear of crime and support on mental health.* Unpublished final report to NIMH, Temple University, Department of Criminal Justice.

Taylor, S. (1983). Adjustment to threatening events: A theory of cognitive adaptation. *American Psychologist, 38,* 1161-1171.

Thompson, M., & Norris, F. (1992). Crime, social status, and alienation. *American Journal Community Psychology, 20,* 97-119.

Van den Bogaard, J., & Wiegman, O. (1991). The effectiveness of police services for victims of residential burglary. *Journal of Social Behavior and Personality, 6,* 329-352.

Vitelli, R., & Endler, N. (1993). Psychological determinants of fear of crime: A comparison of general and situational prediction models. *Personality and Individual Differences, 14,* 77-85.

Winkel, F. (1991). Police, victims, and crime prevention: Some research-based recommendations on victim-oriented interventions. *British Journal of Criminology, 31,* 250-265.

Winkel, F., & Vrij, A. (1993). Facilitating problem- and emotion-focused coping in victims of burglary: Evaluating a police crisis intervention program. *Journal of Community Psychology, 21,* 97-112.

Wirtz, P., & Harrell, A.(1987a). Assaultive versus nonassaultive victimization: A profile analysis of psychological response. *Journal of Interpersonal Violence, 2,* 264-277.

Wirtz, P., & Harrell, A. (1987b). Victim and crime characteristics, coping responses, and short-and long-term recovery from victimization. *Journal of Consulting and Clinical Psychology, 55,* 866-871.

Wyatt, G., Guthrie, G., & Notgrass, C. (1993). Differential effects of women's child sexual abuse and subsequent sexual revictimization. *Journal of Consulting and Clinical Psychology, 60,* 167-173.

9

Victims as Agents

Implications for Victim Services and Crime Prevention

ROBERT C. DAVIS

BRUCE G. TAYLOR

RICHARD M. TITUS

The field we have come to refer to as "victimology" has been flourishing for some 20 years. American victimology includes various lines of research, from studies that attempt to count how many people become victims of one kind of crime or another to assessments of the socioemotional and physical consequences of crime to analyses of the role of victims in the court system. Victimologists have examined victims as a group, and various researchers have focused on special needs and problems of subgroups, including sexual as-sault victims, victims of domestic violence, child victims, elderly victims, victims of hate crimes, and so forth.

But with all the diversity of the field, one tenet has been broadly accepted by those who work with and study victims. That is, victims are not responsible for their misfortune. They were simply unlucky enough to be in harm's way. The idea "There, but for the grace of God, go you and I" has held sway since the early days of victimology. For example, one of the early influential works in the field em-

AUTHORS' NOTE: The views expressed are our own and are not meant to represent the official position of Victim Services, the U.S. Department of Justice, or the National Institute of Justice. We would like to thank Camille Wortman, Lucy Friedman, and Daniel Kaizer for comments on earlier drafts of this chapter.

phasized the prominent "role of chance" in determining why a crime is committed against persons who just happen "to be in the wrong place at the wrong time" (Bard & Sangrey, 1979, p. 96).

The notion that crime is capricious has been espoused especially strongly by those victimologists interested in violence against women. Many authors have bristled at the idea that victims are somehow an integral part of the crimes committed against women. For example, Dobash and Dobash (1979) argued that in domestic violence, "The idea of provocation . . . is both naive and insidious. . . . The idea of provocation is a very powerful tool used in justifying the husband's dominance and control" (p. 136).

The principle of asserting the blamelessness of victims is especially strong in sexual assault and domestic violence because there has been a perceived need to counteract years of societal beliefs that these victims, in some way, precipitated the crimes committed against them. Large segments of society in general and of the law enforcement community specifically have believed that sexual assault victims encouraged the attack by wearing seductive clothing or by behaving provocatively. Clark and Lewis (1977) concluded that "the onus has been on the raped woman to prove her innocence from the beginnings of recorded Western history. . . . The assumption has been that, if the victim did not intentionally provoke the rape, she may at least have been reckless or negligent in protecting herself" (p. 156).

Similarly, domestic violence victims have sometimes been seen as behaving in ways that encouraged their spouses to become physically abusive. Dobash and Dobash (1979) deplored social science that espoused the notion of victim precipitation as representing "an acceptance of violence" (p. 135). Walker (1979) asserted that "although some researchers have tried to understand the offender's behavior by studying the possible provocative behavior of the victim, this research leads up blind alleys and simply encourages continuance of such crimes" (p. 15).

The notion of victim precipitation was common in the criminology literature prior to 1970, and not just with respect to sexual or domestic assault. Von Hentig (1948) was looking at victimization in situational terms when he wrote that "in a considerable number of cases, we meet a victim who consents tacitly, cooperates, conspires, or provokes. The victim is one of the causative elements" (p. 436). Wolfgang's (1958) classic study concluded that victim precipitation was a frequent contributor to homicides. One of Wolfgang's students came to a similar conclusion about sexual assault (Amir, 1971).

The belief of modern victimologists in victims as luckless individuals can be seen as a reaction against the earlier conceptions of criminologists. Cressey (1985) made the point that American victimology is dominated by humanists with a social work agenda. The aim of the humanists, according to Cressey, is to obtain justice for those injured by crime. To persuade society and government to prosecute criminals, compensate victims, and afford victims greater protection under the law, it clearly is useful to portray victims as innocent rather than as participants in criminal incidents. Thus the criminologists' view of victims as participants had to be replaced with a view of victims as hapless individuals to proceed with a political agenda. Fattah (1992) lamented that "the search for theory, characteristic of the early days of victimology, gave way to an obsessive preoccupation with policy. Gradually, rhetoric overshadowed research findings and disinterested unbiased scholarship was in danger of becoming eclipsed by political ideology" (p. 19).

The portrayal of victims as innocent was useful as well for conservative politicians interested in promoting tougher crime legislation. McShane and Williams (1992) observed that "the subject matter of the new victimology

lent itself to political and public interest and
. . . was coopted by those interests" (p. 258).
Similar concerns were voiced by Fattah
(1992) and Cressey (1985).

Today, much of the political agenda that
victim activists set in the 1970s has been
achieved. Victims are treated very differently
by the police and the courts today than they
were prior to the 1970s. This is, perhaps, most
true for victims of domestic violence, who, in
most places, now can presume that an arrest
will be made if they so request (see Chapter 4
of this book). In most states, all victims are
entitled to be notified of key events in their
cases, to be present at important hearings, and
to submit statements of crime impact (see
Chapter 13 of this book). Defense attorneys
face greater restrictions in their cross-exami-
nations of sexual assault victims. Most victims
are eligible to apply for state funds for unre-
imbursed losses suffered as a result of crime.
Advocacy groups such as Mothers Against
Drunk Driving have had great success in per-
suading legislators to pass laws consistent
with their agendas.

In the meantime, some researchers and
theoreticians, most notably Ezzat Fattah, have
continued to think about victims in the tradition set by criminologists. That is, they have
continued to develop the concept of victims as
actors in *situational* explanations of crime.
And they have made notable headway in this
endeavor. We now have irrefutable evidence
that victims often are *not* just people who
happen to be at the wrong place at the wrong
time. We will review studies that show that
some individuals, by virtue of demographics
and behavior, are far more prone than others
to become victims. Moreover, persons who
have been victims once are at elevated risk of
becoming victims again.

It is time to ask whether the notion of victims as simply hapless individuals still serves
us well. It is our belief that it is time for victim
researchers, advocates, and service providers
who work with victims to consider giving up

the notion of victims as people who were just
unlucky and consider the alternative view of
victims as agents in criminal incidents. This
"paradigm shift" may be more appropriate today than before because so much of the political agenda of victim advocates has been
achieved. It is time to acknowledge Meier and
Miethe's (1993) observation that "no picture
of predatory crime can ever be complete without information about the victim" (p. 460).

In our view, individuals can be considered
agents in their own victimization in several
respects. First, by virtue of *who* they are. Do
their personal characteristics place them in a
high-risk group for criminal victimization?
Second, by virtue of the choices they make
about places and company they frequent. Are
they with people or in situations that are likely
to lead to a crime? Third, by virtue of how they
respond to the behavior of would-be perpetrators. Do they react in such a way as to defuse
the situation, or do they act in a way that fails
to deter it or even provokes it? Note that none
of these roles implies that people are responsible for their own victimization or that they
should be blamed for it. But who victims are
and what they do represent one set of causes
of victimization.

Surprisingly, rather than leading to denigra-
tion of victims, the view of the victim as an
integral part of criminal incidents is proving
to have significant benefits for victims. By
understanding how their behavior or characteristics make them vulnerable, people can
begin to shift the odds more in their favor.
They cannot, perhaps, change some risk factors, such as socioeconomic status or gender,
but they can change how they travel to and
from work, leisure time activities, and the like.
In fact, the British have developed new and
exciting crime prevention models that build on
the idea that persons once victimized are at
increased risk of future victimization. We will
review this work and propose some extensions
of the British ideas on working with victims to
reduce their risk of crime.

The Victim as an Actor in Situational Models of Crime

Current criminological theories stress the importance of situational explanations of crime. That is, they view criminal incidents as stemming from opportunities and choices made by rational offenders. Rather than looking at criminal behavior as a trait that certain individuals possess, they argue that it is fruitful to study situations that give rise to crime and the interactions that occur between individuals involved in these situations.

There are a number of somewhat different situational models of crime. Various versions have been termed *routine activity theory* (Cohen & Felson, 1979), *lifestyle theory* (Hindelang, Gottfredson, & Garofalo, 1978), and *rational choice perspective* (Cornish & Clarke, 1986). The subtle differences between them need not concern us here. (For a recent comparison, see Clarke & Felson, 1993.) What is important for us are the points of similarity between the different approaches. All assume that criminal activity is opportunistic and rational rather than the result of innate forces within the offender. All emphasize criminal acts as arising from situational variables and from transactions between individuals.

Fattah (1991, 1993) made serious attempts to apply activity theory (the term we will use to refer to current situational models) to the study of victims. He viewed criminal behavior as a "response to environmental stimuli, stimuli that ineluctably include the characteristics, the behavior of the potential victim and the available opportunities for offending" (Fattah, 1993, p. 238). Criminal incidents are reactions or overreactions arising from dynamic processes of interaction among offenders, victims, and others who may be involved in the situation. Particular persons run greater risk of becoming victims because of choices they make (or choices they are forced into by their circumstances) concerning lifestyle, friends, and places frequented—choices that result in their crossing paths with persons with the motivation to engage in criminal behavior.

Once potential victims and offenders have crossed paths, whether a crime will occur hinges on transactions between potential victims and offenders in which victims play a major role. Victim behavior may facilitate crimes, whether through obvious provocation, carelessness, or passive cooperation. The point is that criminal behavior is not a foregone conclusion when potential offenders and victims encounter each other. "Scripts" are played out, and how the victim behaves at each stage affects how the offender will respond at the next.

Fattah also postulated that the roles of victim and offender are not fixed, assigned, or predetermined. Rather, he argued, they are interchangeable. Victims and offenders are seen as coming from the same populations. He claims that the roles of victim and offender are revolving, "with many individuals moving alternatingly between the two roles: yesterday's victims becoming today's offenders and today's offenders becoming tomorrow's victims" (Fattah, 1993, p. 239).

Clearly, the view of the victim-as-agent espoused by Fattah, Cornish (1994), and others is antithetical to the luckless-individual concept that has dominated recent American victimology. But as it turns out, criminologists have amassed an overwhelming amount of data over the past 15 to 20 years to bolster the contention that whether a person becomes a victim can be predicted quite well on the basis of personal history, demography, and behavior patterns.

Evidence Supporting the Activity Theory View of Victims

In the late 1970s, researchers began to examine whether the distribution of victimization in the population could be statistically modeled. These researchers were attempting to test whether the distribution of victimization corresponded to a chance distribution of independent, single-incident victimizations in a population sampled with replacement (also known as a "Poisson model"; Farrell, 1995). If it could be shown that victimization was randomly distributed, it could be argued that those who were victimized were merely "unlucky." However, if it could be demonstrated that victimization was nonrandomly distributed, an argument could be made that victims are a special group of people who possess some qualities that predispose them to victimization.

As pointed out by Gottfredson (1981), common sense would lead us to the conclusion that victimization is not a random event. As far back as the 1960s, Wilkins (1965, as cited in U.S. Dept. of Justice, 1981) made the point very clearly:

> Let any (non-criminal) reader try to imagine himself in the position of being required to commit a crime—say one of the most common crimes like larceny or breaking and entering—within the next twelve hours. Few readers would select the victim completely at random, unskilled at victim-selection though they might be. There will be something approaching rationality in the selection of the victim. (p. 40)

Two major studies in the late 1970s confirmed this commonsense analysis. Hindelang et al. (1978) analyzed victimization data from 26 American cities to establish rates of victimization, using statistical modeling to fit their victimization data to a Poisson distribution. They concluded that this model did not fit the data well and that therefore victimization was not a chance event.

Sparks, Genn, and Dodd (1977) examined victimization data from three London boroughs. They attempted to fit the spread of victimization to both a Poisson model and a "heterogenous" model (basically an attempt to fit a Poisson model to different subgroups of the population). Much like Hindelang et al. (1978), Sparks et al. found evidence of vic-

timization "proneness" clustering around certain subgroups in London. They found that the distribution of the victimization data contained more nonvictims and more multiple victims than would be expected by chance.

The results from the British and American studies definitively answered the question about whether criminals are capricious in their choice of victims. But the question remained, *Who* is likely to be victimized and who is relatively safe? This is the question that drove subsequent research on victimization risk and on repeat victimizations. The factors that have been identified as increasing the risk of victimization can be divided into personal history, demographics, and behavior patterns.

Personal History

One of the earliest and best predictors of victimization that researchers were able to isolate was being a victim on an earlier occasion. In the United States, the issue of repeat victimization was first examined within the early victimization surveys done for the 1967 President's Commission (Ennis, 1967). Repeat victimization has been studied now for over 20 years, and it has been consistently shown that persons once victimized are at elevated risk of victimization in the future (see, e.g., Hindelang et al., 1978; Sorenson, Siegel, Golding, & Stein, 1991). This fact is not surprising for victims of domestic violence: It is common belief that repeat domestic victimization is not only possible but indeed very likely if the victim remains in the situation. Yet research has shown that robbery victims stand a 9 times' greater chance of revictimization than others and sexual assault victims a 35 times' greater chance (Canada Solicitor General, 1988).

Work on repeat victimization has been even more prevalent in Great Britain than in North America (e.g., Anderson, Chenery, & Pease, 1995; Farrell & Pease, 1993; see Farrell, 1995, for a recent summary). Findings from the British studies have been quite consistent with the North American results. For example, a recent research summary by the National Board for Crime Prevention (1994) of British crime rates showed that households once burglarized are reburglarized at four times the rate of unburglarized houses and that 22% of motor vehicle thefts are accounted for by just 8% of the victims.

Findings on repeat victimization prompted Sparks (1981) to wonder whether victimization changes the probability of subsequent victimization (event dependency) or whether it operates as a marker of preexisting risk (risk heterogeneity). In other words, is there some condition created by victimization that makes people more vulnerable to subsequent crime (e.g., offenders revisiting an easy or rewarding target)? Or are certain individuals more vulnerable targets who are more likely to be selected for victimization and for revictimization? Surprisingly, the most recent and strongest study on this issue points to both risk heterogeneity and event dependency as coexplainers of victimization (Ellingworth, Osborn, Trickett, & Pease, 1995).

The risk of revictimization is greatest in the period soon after the previous victimization for crimes as diverse as school crime, residential burglary, bias crime, domestic violence, auto crimes, neighbor disputes, and retail crimes (Farrell & Pease, 1993). In domestic violence cases, for example, the risk of revictimization is highest within the first 11 days and declines thereafter (Lloyd, Farrell, & Pease, 1994). In residential burglary, 40% of repeat burglaries occur within 1 month of the previous burglary (Anderson et al., 1995); after about 6 months the likelihood of repeat burglary returns to the average levels for a given area (Polvi, Looman, Humphries, & Pease, 1991). These studies support the notion of event dependency in repeat victimization: That is, there is something about being victimized a first time that increases the risk of another victimization. For example, burglars visiting a house for the first time may note additional items worth coming back for.

Some studies of sexual assault victims have examined personal history variables other than prior victimization, with equivocal findings. Long and Jackson (1991) found that family dysfunction and initial abuse characteristics were predictors of repeat sexual victimization. Murphy et al. (1988) found that repeat victimization was positively related to higher psychiatric symptoms on the SCL-90. On the other hand, Sorenson et al. (1991) failed to find a difference between single and repeat sexual assault victims on mental disorders or symptoms of general dysfunction. Similarly, Mandoki and Burkhart (1989) found no relationship between repeat victimization and a variety of personality measures, including assertiveness, dependency, self-esteem, and attributional style.

Demographic Factors

Studies have consistently demonstrated that the likelihood of victimization varies dramatically with demographic characteristics. For personal crimes in the United States, victimization rates are substantially higher for the poor, males, blacks, the young, single people, renters, and central city residents (Hindelang et al., 1978; Sparks et al., 1977; U.S. Dept. of Justice, 1981). Over the years, the National Crime Victimization Survey (NCVS) also has shown consistently that these same subgroups of the population are at a greater risk of experiencing not only violent victimization but also *any* victimization (Bastian, 1995; Bureau of Justice Statistics, 1993). For example, 1 in 8 persons aged 12 to 15 becomes a victim of violent crime, compared to just 1 in 279 persons aged 65 or older (Bastian, 1995).

In the United States, some researchers have examined whether demographic factors could be used to identify repeat or "recidivist" (Zeigenhagen, 1976) victims from those victimized a single time. These studies have found that repeat victims tend to be located in poor, predominately black, areas (Hough, 1986; Skogan, 1981; Sparks et al., 1977). In an analysis of the NCVS data by Schwartz (1991), differences were found between repeat and nonrepeat domestic violence victims in terms of marital status, race, and gender (fewer repeat domestic violence victimizations were found for wives, blacks, and males).

Behavior Patterns

Lasley and Rosenbaum (1988), using data from the British Crime Survey, examined the extent to which routine activity predicted repeat victimization. They found that all three of their measures of routine activities were significantly related to repeat victimization, including victims' work schedules, number of weekend evenings spent away from home, and alcohol consumption. Using the same data source, Sampson and Wooldredge (1987) found that victimization risk increased for people who frequently went out at night or left their homes empty. Their final model included both individual-level and community-level variables associated with victimization.

In a similar vein, Smith (1982) found that victims were more likely than nonvictims to engage in unstructured activities that were more likely to bring them into contact with strangers (e.g., going to bars or movies). Hough and Mayhew (1983) found that the chances of victimization increased with alcohol consumption and going out in the evening.

The strongest and the most provocative result to come out of research on behavior patterns is the link between delinquent behavior and victimization. Among adolescents at least, *victims and offenders are not distinct groups:* They come from the same subculture and the same individuals often alternate between victimizing others and being victimized (Fagan, Piper, & Cheng, 1987; Singer, 1981, 1986).

For example, Sampson and Lauritsen (1990) reported that the risk of all types of face-to-face victimizations increased markedly when adolescents engaged in self-reported violent behavior themselves (defined as starting physical fights or inflicting intentional injury on someone outside the family). Moreover, the same principle seems to hold for other types of delinquent behavior. Jensen and Brownfield (1986) found that youths who reported frequenting bars or parties or having been in trouble with the police ran higher rates of both property and violent victimization than other youths. Lauritsen, Laub, and Sampson (1992) found that risk of victimization was increased *two to three times* when adolescents reported using alcohol or marijuana, spending time with friends who were delinquents, or having received traffic citations.

Although few, these studies imply that the risk of victimization increases with exposure to delinquent patterns of behavior. Jensen and Brownfield (1986) have argued that delinquent behavior can be seen as a type of routine activity that increases the odds of victimization because it places adolescents in close proximity to dangerous persons and/or high-risk locations such as bars or social clubs.

Fattah (1991) synthesized other behavioral and situational factors that increase risk of victimization. These factors involve exposure, unwise associations, dangerous times and places, dangerous behaviors, high-risk activities, and lack of care. Here are some examples:

- Employment involving odd hours, handling cash, travel or delivery, or contact with public
- Failure to take reasonable precautions to protect person or property (e.g., locking car, reading contracts carefully, investigating "fabulous bargains," not hitchhiking or picking up hitchhikers)
- Being in unfamiliar territory as a newcomer, visitor, or tourist
- Attendance in settings with large numbers of single males (e.g., sporting events and bars)
- Use of, or association with users of, drugs or alcohol; spending time in places where they are used
- Behavior and places involving thrill seeking, risk taking, or sexual promiscuity
- In a dispute, being the first to throw an insult, make a threat, strike a blow, or show a weapon

- Association with delinquents or criminals; participation in delinquency or crime

Fattah's (1991) classification of victim risk factors can be grouped according to how susceptible these characteristics and behaviors are to change by the victim. First are factors that the victim cannot change—factors having to do with demography and personal characteristics (e.g., age, sex, height, handicap, appearance, social class, race). Next are factors that victims may be able to change, such as income, marital status, choice of domestic partner, neighborhood of residence, place of school or employment, hours of employment, modes of travel, self-confidence and assertiveness, and physical strength. Finally, some factors are unambiguously under victims' control and *can* be changed. These include use of leisure time (hours, places, type of activity); display and securing of property and personal possessions; style of dress; alcohol and drug use; sexual activity; participation in delinquent or criminal activity; thrill-seeking behavior; antagonism and aggressiveness in interpersonal relations; gambling and financial risk taking; negligence and carelessness; and level of cautiousness (investigating persons/places/activities before becoming involved in them).

Victim Responsibility and People's Need to Make Sense Out of Crimes

Ronnie Janoff-Bulman was one of the first modern victimologists to suggest the significance of victims' appraisals of how their own attributes, circumstances, or behavior might have contributed to their misfortune. Her research showed that victims are often very willing to blame themselves (Janoff-Bulman & Frieze, 1983). There is something deeply affecting about this finding; it suggests that victims are desperate for a sense of control, for an assurance that the crime will not happen to them again. Telling themselves that the harm

resulted from behavior that *they* could change allows victims to put themselves back in control—at least in their own minds. Janoff-Bulman (1979) termed this kind of functional blame "behavioral self-blame." She distinguished it from "characterological self-blame"—blaming victimization on perceived defects in one's own character. Whereas Janoff-Bulman saw characterological self-blame as psychologically harmful, she saw behavioral self-blame as facilitating healthy readjustment from the effects of victimization. Several subsequent studies have found support for her hypothesis (e.g., Baum, Fleming, & Singer, 1983; Friedman, Bischoff, Davis, & Person, 1982; Schulz & Decker, 1985), although others have not (e.g., Frazier, 1990; Hill & Zautra, 1989).

Victim Responsibility and Crime Prevention

The view of victim as agent that is inherent in activity theory has significant practical implications. If being victimized once is a good predictor of being victimized in the future, then it makes sense to concentrate crime prevention efforts on persons who report victimization to the authorities. Neatly enough, people are likely to be especially receptive to crime prevention opportunities immediately following victimization. There is a "window of opportunity" during the first weeks after a crime during which victims feel vulnerable and are willing to consider seriously behavioral and lifestyle changes (Anderson et al., 1995; Davis & Smith, 1994).

Davis and Smith (1994) reported the results of a field test of a crime prevention program administered to recent victims. One hundred and ninety-one New York City victims of robbery, burglary, and nonsexual assault were divided into two groups using a quasi-experimental design. One group received traditional crisis counseling; the other received instruction in crime prevention and were offered free upgrades of home security hardware. Relative to the crisis counseling group, victims assigned to the crime prevention training were significantly more likely to believe that the crime could have been avoided, had significantly greater knowledge of crime prevention principles, and were significantly more likely to engage in precautionary behaviors. Victims who had experienced the crime prevention training had a 33% lower rate of revictimization than controls over the next 12 months. However, the sample was small, and the difference attained only marginal statistical significance.

The British have been leaders in working with victims to prevent revictimization. In England, police concentration on those who have already been victimized is seen as a more efficient way to use police resources and identify priorities (Farrell & Pease, 1993; National Board for Crime Prevention, 1994). It is argued that "by pointing to the most probable times and places of future offenses, repeat victimization also helps identify the times and places where offenders may be found and apprehended. There is potential for the development of a symbiotic relationship between crime prevention and offender detection" (National Board for Crime Prevention, 1994, p. 2). Along these lines, it is also clear that any program incorporating the problem-solving approach to policing should pay special attention to repeat victims, who contribute disproportionately to an area's crime statistics, most especially in high-crime areas (Trickett, Osborn, Seymour, & Pease, 1992).

Some applications of this approach in Britain have been reported. In a crime prevention program for victims of residential burglary on a housing estate, the strategies included replacement of coin-operated gas and electricity meters (a frequent target), security upgrades, property marking, victim support and information, and "cocoon" neighborhood watch (involving the victim's six nearest neighbors). The evaluation showed a substantial reduction in burglary for the entire estate over the next 3 years, compared to itself and also compared to the remainder of the police subdivision

(Pease, 1992). Similar programs for burglary victims in three housing estates showed a decrease in repeat victimization; although there was no apparent diffusion of benefits to other residents, neither was there any clear evidence of displacement (Tilley & Webb, 1994).

In a West Yorkshire project, victims of burglary or automobile theft receive an increasing level of police response based on the number of victimizations suffered in the previous year. Strategies include (as appropriate to a particular victim) security upgrades, property/vehicle marking, "cocoon" watch, focused patrol, offender targeting, priority fingerprinting, and the loan of burglar alarms and vehicle location devices. The project is currently in implementation and has not yet yielded evaluation information (Anderson et al., 1995). In a domestic violence reduction project, victims receive wearable alarms linked to the police by cellular phone, responding officers receive en route information on prior calls and on current court orders, victim service workers offer support and develop an action plan with the victim, and lecture and discussion sessions are held with the police to raise victims' awareness of the issue of domestic violence and the police role. Evidence from a limited number of victim interviews indicates that the pendant alarms have greatly increased the recipients' sense of security (Lloyd et al., 1994).

Farrell and Pease (1993) added a word of caution: "The aspirations to model crime prevention strategy on the research reported may be seen as grandiose and premature. The reasons for repeats are diverse, the data on repeat victimization is incomplete, and the range of techniques to combat it are not fully elaborated" (p. 28). Nonetheless, although it is still in an early stage of development, and applications have not been extensively evaluated, this British work appears to have major implications both for crime control and for helping victims. It also raises interesting questions for activity theory: Although prompt and frequent revictimization might be expected in domestic violence and some other nonstranger crimes, the findings on residential and nonresidential burglary, on theft of and from autos, and on crimes against business are less easy to understand. How much is to be explained by victim behavior, target characteristics, situational factors, and offender behavior?

Conclusion

We have argued that activity theory holds much promise as a way to understand more about criminal victimization and about how to help victims and others reduce their vulnerability to crime. We have talked about how knowledge gained from activity-theory-driven research is being put to use in designing effective crime prevention programs.

Clearly, activity theory can contribute much more to understanding why and how victimizations occur. For example, activity theory needs to look more closely at the sequential nature of criminal events that has been noted by some criminologists (e.g., Brantingham & Brantingham, 1993; Cornish, 1994; DeFrances & Titus, 1993). Nonstranger sexual assault often appears to result from a sequence of events that the two parties interpreted differently (Fattah, 1991). Nonsexual assault typically escalates through a distinct series of stages, over either a short (minutes) or long (weeks) time period, often with important roles played by noncombatants (Fattah, 1991; Garofalo, Siegel, & Laub, 1987; Pallone & Hennessy, 1993). The better we understand these sequences in terms of the behavior of victim and offender, the better our chances for disrupting them, preferably in their earlier stages through modifications in the environment or in the behavior of victims. This approach is already being incorporated in school conflict-resolution programs and domestic violence reduction programs.

The ideal vehicle for introducing crime prevention messages to victims is victim assistance programs. These programs deal specifically with victims and intervene in the first days after the crime, when victims are most likely to be amenable to crime prevention education. Anderson et al. (1995) recently argued that "crime prevention and victim support are necessary for the *same* people (recent victims) at the *same* time (promptly after their victimization). *Reaction* to the last offence, if it has a preventive element, is *proaction* to the next" (p. 3). Victim assistance programs should include an immediate response component to meet the victim's needs and to deal with the threat of early revictimization, and a long-term response component of actions that may take more time to implement and that are intended to become permanent (Farrell & Pease, 1993; National Board for Crime Prevention, 1994).

Yet victim programs have not, by and large, taken on the task of educating victims about crime prevention. Skogan, Davis, and Lurigio (1990) found that although crime prevention was the single service most desired by victims, it was the service that they were least likely to receive from victim assistance programs. The strong belief that victims are merely incidental to crimes and not agents has held assistance programs back from any activities that might suggest that victimization is often avoidable. It is time to take a different view of victims, one consistent with the scientific evidence and one that holds out to victims hope that they can do something to improve the quality of their lives.

In the long run, this view of victims may lead to quite practical applications. Titus (in press) has suggested that criminal justice borrow from medicine the concept of self-assessments of risk that have been successful in combating heart disease. Using these assessments, which have been made available in doctor's offices and in the media, individuals calculate an overall heart disease risk score based on factors such as family health history, age, diet, gender, weight, serum cholesterol, physical activity, use of tobacco, life stress, and personality type. The risk factors in these tables and the weights assigned to each are based on research and actuarial data.

Someday we may be able to do something similar for risk of victimization. Creators of a victimization risk assessment instrument would not have access to data of the quality that the cardiologists have. However, weights for various risk factors could be approximated from available research and data on activity theory and victimology. A CDROM version could also incorporate pictures and film clips to clarify assessment questions, to present reenactments of different types of crimes, and to provide some incidental education and crime prevention tips where appropriate. Simply completing the assessment would direct people's attention to what the risk factors are and the importance of taking full advantage of factors over which they have some control. Specially trained counselors could be available to assist people in formulating changes in behavior patterns that would meaningfully reduce their risk levels.

References

Amir, M. (1971). *Patterns in forcible rape.* Chicago: University of Chicago Press.

Anderson, D., Chenery, S., & Pease, K. (1995). *Biting back: Tackling repeat burglary and car crime* (Crime Detection and Prevention Series Paper No. 58). London: Home Office.

Bard, R., & Sangrey, D. (1979). *The crime victim's book.* New York: Basic Books.

Bastian, L. (1995). *Criminal victimization 1993.* Washington, DC: U.S. Dept. of Justice.

Baum, A., Fleming, R., & Singer, J. E. (1983). Coping with victimization by technological disaster. *Journal of Social Issues, 39,* 117-138.

Brantingham, P. L., & Brantingham, P. J. (1993). Environment, routine, and situation: Toward a pattern theory of crime. In R. V. Clarke & M. Felson (Eds.), *Routine activity and rational choice* (pp. 259-294). New Brunswick, NJ: Transaction.

Bureau of Justice Statistics. (1993). *Highlights from 20 years of surveying crime victims* (NCJ-144525). Washington, DC: U.S. Dept. of Justice.

Canada Solicitor General. (1988). *Multiple victimization* (Canadian Urban Victimization Survey Bulletin No. 10). Ottawa: Ministry of the Solicitor General.

Clark, L., & Lewis, D. (1977). *Rape: The price of coercive sexuality.* Toronto: Women's Press.

Clarke, R. V., & Felson, M. (1993). Introduction: criminology, routine activity, and rational choice. In R. V. Clarke & M. Felson (Eds.), *Routine activity and rational choice* (pp. 1-14). New Brunswick, NJ: Transaction.

Cohen, L. E., & Felson, M. (1979). Social change and crime rate trends: A routine activity approach. *American Sociological Review, 44,* 588-608.

Cornish, D. B. (1994). Crimes as scripts. In D. Zahm & P. Cromwell (Eds.), *Proceedings of the International Seminar on Environmental Criminology and Crime Analysis, University of Miami, 1993* (pp. 30-45). Tallahassee: Florida Criminal Justice Executive Institute.

Cornish, D. B., & Clarke, R. V. (Eds.). (1986). *The reasoning criminal: Rational choice perspectives on offending.* New York: Springer-Verlag.

Cressey, R. D. (1985). Research implications in conflicting conceptions of victimology. In Z. P. Separovic (Ed.), *Victimology: International action and study of victims* (pp. 43-54). Zagreb, Croatia: University of Zagreb.

Davis, R. C., & Smith, B. (1994). Teaching victims crime prevention skills: Can individuals lower their risk of crime? *Criminal Justice Review, 19,* 56-68.

DeFrances, C. J., & Titus, R. (1993). Urban planning and residential burglary outcomes. *Landscape and Urban Planning, 26,* 179-191.

Dobash, R. E., & Dobash, R. (1979). *Violence against wives.* New York: Free Press.

Ellingworth, D., Osborn, D. R., Trickett, A., & Pease, K. (1995). *Lifestyle and prior victimization: A logit analysis of crime risk.* Unpublished paper, Quantitative Criminology Group, Manchester University.

Ennis, P. H. (1967). *Criminal victimization in the United States: A report of a national survey* (Field Survey No. 2). Washington, DC: Government Printing Office.

Fagan, J., Piper, E., & Cheng, Y. J. (1987). Contributions of victimization to delinquency in inner cities. *Journal of Criminal Law and Criminology, 78,* 586-609.

Farrell, G. (1995). Preventing repeat victimization. In M. Tonry & D. P. Farrington (Eds.), *Building a safer society: Strategic approaches to crime prevention* (pp. 469-534). Chicago: University of Chicago Press.

Farrell, G., & Pease, K. (1993). *Once bitten, twice bitten: Repeat victimization and its implications for crime prevention* (Crime Prevention Unit Paper No. 46). London: Home Office.

Fattah, E. A. (1991). *Understanding criminal victimization.* Englewood Cliffs, NJ: Prentice Hall.

Fattah, E. A. (1992). Victims and victimology: The facts and the rhetoric. In E. A. Fattah (Ed.), *Towards a critical victimology* (pp. 29-56). New York: Macmillan.

Fattah, E. A. (1993). The rational choice/opportunity perspectives as a vehicle for integrating criminological and victimological theories. In R. V. Clarke & M. Felson (Eds.), *Routine activity and rational choice* (pp. 225-258). New Brunswick, NJ: Transaction.

Frazier, P. A. (1990). Victim attributions and post-rape trauma. *Journal of Personality and Social Psychology, 59,* 298-304.

Friedman, K., Bischoff, H., Davis, R., & Person, A. (1982). *Victims and helpers: Reactions to crime.* Washington, DC: Government Printing Office.

Garofalo, J., Siegel, L., & Laub, J. (1987). School-related victimizations among adolescents: An analysis of National Crime Survey (NCS) narratives. *Journal of Quantitative Criminology, 3,* 321-338.

Gottfredson, M. R. (1981). On the etiology of criminal victimization. In U.S. Dept. of Justice (Ed.), *Victims of crime: A review of research issues and methods* (pp. 37-54). Washington, DC: Government Printing Office.

Hill, J. L., & Zautra, A. J. (1989). Self-blame attributions and unique vulnerability as predictors of post-rape demoralization. *Journal of Social and Clinical Psychology, 8,* 368-375.

Hindelang, M., Gottfredson, M., & Garofalo, J. (1978). *Victims of personal crime: An empirical foundation for a theory of personal victimization.* Cambridge, MA: Ballinger.

Hough, J. M. (1986). Victims of violent crime: Findings from the first British Crime Survey. In E. Fattah (Ed.), *From criminal policy to victim policy* (pp. 117-132). New York: Macmillan.

Hough, M., & Mayhew, P. (1983). *The British Crime Survey: First report.* London: H.M. Stationery Office.

Janoff-Bulman, R. (1979). Characterological versus behavioral self-blame: Inquiries into depression and rape. *Journal of Personality and Social Psychology, 37,* 1798-1809.

Janoff-Bulman, R., & Frieze, I. (1983). A theoretical perspective for understanding reactions to victimization. *Journal of Social Issues, 39*(2), 1-17.

Jensen, G., & Brownfield, D. (1986). Gender, lifestyles, and victimization: Beyond routine activity theory. *Violence and Victims, 1,* 85-99.

Lasley, J. R., & Rosenbaum, J. L. (1988). Routine activities and multiple personal victimization. *Sociology and Social Research, 73*(1), 47-50.

Lauritsen, J. L., Laub, J. H., & Sampson, R. J. (1992). Conventional and delinquent activities: Implications for the prevention of violent victimization among adolescents. *Violence and Victims, 7*(2), 91-105.

Lloyd, S., Farrell, G., & Pease, K. (1994). *Preventing repeated domestic violence: A demonstration project on Merseyside* (Crime Prevention Unit Paper No. 49). London: Home Office.

Long, P. J., & Jackson, J. L. (1991). Children sexually abused by multiple perpetrators. *Journal of Interpersonal Violence, 6,* 147-159.

Mandoki, C. A., & Burkhart, B. R. (1989). Sexual victimization: Is there a vicious cycle? *Violence and Victims, 4,* 179-190.

McShane, M. D., & Williams, F. P. (1992) Radical victimology: A critique of the concept of victim in traditional victimology. *Crime and Delinquency, 38,* 258-271.

Meier, R. F., & Miethe, T. D. (1993). Understanding theories of criminal victimization. *Crime and Justice: An Annual Review of Research, 17,* 459-499.

Murphy, S. M., Kilpatrick, D. G., Amick-McMullan, A., Veronen, L. J., Paduhovich, J., Best, C. L., Villeponteaux, L. A., & Saunders, B. E. (1988). Current psychological functioning of child sexual assault survivors: A community study. *Journal of Interpersonal Violence, 3,* 55-79.

National Board for Crime Prevention. (1994). *Wise after the event: Tackling repeat victimization.* London: Home Office.

Pallone, N. J., & Hennessy, J. J. (1993). Tinder box criminal violence: Neurogenic impulsivity, risk-taking, and the phenomenology of rational choice. In R. V. Clarke & M. Felson (Eds.), *Routine activity and rational choice* (pp. 127-158). New Brunswick, NJ: Transaction.

Pease, K. (1992). Preventing burglary on a British public housing estate. In R. V. Clarke (Ed.), *Situational crime prevention: Successful case studies* (pp. 223-229). New York: Harrow & Heston.

Polvi, N., Looman, T., Humphries, C., & Pease, K. (1991). The time course of repeat burglary victimization. *British Journal of Criminology, 31,* 411-414.

Sampson, R. J., & Lauritsen, J. L. (1990). Deviant lifestyles, proximity to crime, and the offender-victim link in personal violence. *Journal of Research in Crime and Delinquency, 27,* 110-139.

Sampson, R. J., & Wooldredge, J. D. (1987). Linking the micro- and macro-level dimensions of lifestyle-routine activity and opportunity models of predatory victimization. *Journal of Quantitative Criminology, 3,* 371-393.

Schulz, R., & Decker, S. (1985). Long-term adjustment to physical disability: The role of social support, perceived control, and self-blame. *Journal of Personality and Social Psychology, 48,* 1162-1172.

Schwartz, M. D. (1991). Series wife battering victimizations in the National Crime Survey. *International Journal of Sociology of the Family, 19,* 117-136.

Singer, S. (1986). Victims of serious violence and their criminal behavior: Subculture theory and beyond. *Violence and Victims, 1,* 61.

Singer, S. (1981). Homogeneous victim-offender populations: A review and some research implications. *Journal of Criminal Law and Criminology, 72,* 779.

Skogan, W. (1981). *Issues in the measurement of victimization* (U.S. Dept. of Justice, Bureau of Justice Statistics). Washington, DC: Government Printing Office.

Skogan, W. G., Davis, R. C., & Lurigio, A. J. (1990). *Victim needs and victim services: Final report.* Washington, DC: National Institute of Justice.

Smith, S. J. (1982). Victimization in the inner city. *British Journal of Criminology, 22,* 386-402.

Sorenson, S. B., Siegel, J. M., Golding, J. M., & Stein, J. A. (1991). Repeat sexual victimization. *Violence and Victims, 6,* 299-301.

Sparks, R. F. (1981). Multiple victimization: Evidence, theory, and future research. *Journal of Criminal Law and Criminology, 72,* 762-778.

Sparks, R., Genn, H., & Dodd, D. (1977). *Surveying victims.* New York: John Wiley.

Tilley, N., & Webb, J. (1994). *Burglary reduction: Findings from safer cities schemes* (Crime Prevention Unit Paper No. 51). London: Home Office.

Titus, R. M. (in press). Activity theory and the victim. *European Journal on Criminal Policy and Research.*

Titus, R. M., Heinzelmann, F., & Boyle, J. M. (1995). Victimization of persons by fraud. *Crime and Delinquency, 41,* 54-72.

Trickett, A., Osborn, D., Seymour, J., & Pease, K. (1992). What is different about high crime areas? *British Journal of Criminology, 32,* 81-90.

U.S. Dept. of Justice. (Ed.). (1981). *Victims of crime: A review of research issues and methods.* Washington, DC: National Institute of Justice.

von Hentig, H. (1948). *The criminal and his victim.* New Haven, CT: Yale University Press.

Walker, L. E. (1979). *The battered woman.* New York: Harper & Row.

Wolfgang, M. E. (1958). *Patterns in criminal homicide.* Philadelphia: University of Pennsylvania Press.

Zeigenhagen, E. (1976). The recidivist victim of violent crime. *Victimology, 1,* 538-550.

PART II

Providing Assistance to Victims

10 Violence Prevention Through Victim Assistance

Helping People Escape the Web of Violence

LUCY N. FRIEDMAN
SUSAN B. TUCKER

Beyond the social conditions and behaviors traditionally associated with violence, including poverty, racism, gender inequity, substance abuse, and gun ownership, research and practice suggest that violence itself can beget violence. Some crime victims get trapped in a web of violence. They may be subjected to repeated crime and injury or may learn to use violence against others. But by helping people recover from the trauma of violence and lead safer lives, victim assistance programs can reduce the risk of revictimization and make a break in the transmission of abuse from one person to another.

Many violence prevention efforts focus on alleviating broad social conditions and high-risk behaviors—a difficult task, given that these problems are often deeply embedded in the social structure. With violence prevention programs focusing on root causes of crime and early intervention, it might seem that victim assistance after the fact comes too late to make our communities safer. However, victim services can address the socioeconomic context, as well as another, perhaps more malleable, risk factor: victims' personal history of violence. In the wake of crime, people are especially motivated to make changes in their own behavior and surroundings to reduce the risk

AUTHORS' NOTE: We wish to thank Peter Neville and Linda Lausell for their contributions to this chapter.

of future violence. Rather than too little too late, services for victims—including hotlines, support groups, counseling, housing, safety strategies, job training and economic supports, opportunities for activism, and other efforts—suggest a promising strategy for helping people break free from repeated victimization and reducing the incidence of crime.

Caught in the Web of Violence

Research on the causes of violence has identified a broad range of risk factors, from low birth weight and poverty to poor school performance and racism (National Research Council, 1993). But regardless of what causes violence in the first place, people who are victimized often face a greater risk of being hurt again and of becoming violent themselves.

The web of violence is woven in a variety of ways. We suggest three general categories: circular, vertical, and horizontal. A single victim-offender pair, such as a battered woman and her mate, or an abused child and the violating parent, can be locked in a rotating *circle* of repeated abuse. Violence can be transmitted *vertically* through successive generations, as when an abused child becomes an abusing parent, or a child who witnesses domestic violence grows up to become a batterer. The *horizontal* transmission of violence occurs back and forth among family, friends, strangers, and the community: A child abused at home strikes out at classmates, or a teen who has lost friends to street violence becomes resigned to the probability of early death and stops taking normal safety precautions.

The Circular Repetition of Violence

In some relationships, coercion, intimidation, and violence can develop into an ongoing pattern of abuse. Victims may suffer repeated,

and sometimes escalating, violence by a single offender, creating an environment of abuse that is difficult to escape without outside intervention. Child abuse, domestic violence, and elder abuse are often characterized by such repeated episodes of victimization (Langan & Innes, 1986; National Research Council, 1993; Straus, 1990). One national study found that multiple assaults had been reported in 94% of child abuse cases (National Research Council, 1993).

The circular character of domestic violence is illustrative. Battered women are nearly three times more likely than victims of other types of violence to be revictimized within 6 months by their partner (Langan & Innes, 1986). For these women, the web of violence is more intricate than just the repetition of physical violence. According to Stark (1992), "The hallmark of the battering experience [is] 'entrapment' . . . a pattern of control that extends . . . to virtually every aspect of a woman's life, including money, food, sexuality, friendships, transportation, personal appearance, and access to supports including children, extended family members, and helping resources" (p. 282). This type of coercion and control severely restricts battered women's ability to escape abusive situations, especially when there are also other impediments to leaving, such as familial or religious prohibitions, financial dependence, children, or even love. Sometimes the more the woman resists, the tighter these binds become. In some extreme cases, battered women see no way out of the intensifying and suffocating spiral and end up killing themselves or the men who abuse them. Domestic violence is associated with 26% of the suicide attempts by women (Rosenberg, Stark, & Zahn, 1986), and one study of a women's prison in Chicago found that 40% of inmates were incarcerated for killing partners who had repeatedly assaulted them (Lindsey, 1976, cited in Browne, 1987).

Similar patterns of violence can also occur outside the family network, as seen in repeated bullying, violent revenge, feuds, and vigilantism. In our work with students in New York City schools, we have seen taunting and name calling escalate to shoving, beatings, and assaults with weapons, and disputes between groups continue long after the initial incident. In these cases, the close physical or social proximity mirrors family or romantic relationships, trapping the victim in a dangerous pattern of violence.

Vertical Transmission

Given its implications for the future, the vertical transmission of violence to new generations is particularly disturbing. A study by Spatz Widom (1989) found that victims of child abuse and neglect are 38% more likely to be arrested for a violent crime later in life. Children who are sexually assaulted may become aggressive (Kendall-Tackett, Williams, & Finkelhor, 1993; Spatz Widom, 1995) and are more likely than others to be revictimized later in life (Gidycz, Coble, Latham, & Layman, 1993; Wyatt, Guthrie, & Notgrass, 1992).

Even children who are simply exposed to domestic violence are at greater risk for violence. Straus, Gelles, and Steinmetz (1980) found that men who had witnessed physical violence between their parents were three times more likely to beat their own spouses, and Hotaling and Sugarman's (1986) analysis of 52 case comparison studies suggested that witnessing violence in the family is the single most important factor for becoming an aggressor or a victim. In our shelters for battered women, we can see violence taking root in their children, with young boys (and some girls) imitating their fathers' threatening behavior. These are often the children of mothers who themselves grew up in violent homes and gravitated toward partners with a similar family history, increasing the risk that familiar patterns of violence would be reenacted.

Horizontal Transmission

Unlike vertical transmission, which involves successive generations, the horizontal transmission of violence sets up a chain reaction that spreads to other members of a school, neighborhood, or community. A child or adult who is being brutalized at home may carry the violence outside the family network (Hotaling & Straus, 1988), just as violence from outside can infect the home. Young people who live with the direct experience and constant threat of violence often see the world as divided into two camps, victims and victimizers; many opt for the position of apparently greater power, trying to recover their lost sense of control by using force against others. Lashing out at others may be their only outlet for the fear and rage that accompanies victimization.

The Web of Violence in People's Lives

Why some individuals react to trauma by perpetrating violence against others whereas others injure themselves or become more at risk for revictimization is difficult to predict or explain. According to Harvey's (1991) "ecological view of trauma," an individual's response to trauma "emerge[s] from a complex interaction between the person, the event and the environment" (Lebowitz, Harvey, & Herman, 1993, p. 2).

Whether trauma is defined as an "an extraordinarily stressful or disturbing event . . . that is outside the range of usual human experience" (Fullilove et al., 1992, p. 3) or the mark that such an event makes on the body and the psyche of the individual who experiences it, victims of violent crime often suffer from posttraumatic stress disorder (PTSD). Fullilove et al. mentioned nightmares, intrusive thoughts or flashbacks, numbing, avoidance, and feelings of arousal, confusion, and emptiness. The feeling of "disempowerment, meaninglessness and disconnection from oneself and others is central to the experience of inter-personal trauma" (Lebowitz et al., 1993, p. 3).

Children are a special case that painfully illustrates how some people traumatized by violence end up victimizing others:

> Feeling unsafe, helpless, and small runs counter to the developing child's desire and capacity to be in greater control of the self and to achieve increasing mastery of his or her environment. . . . When the child is exposed to the dangers of violence on a regular basis, identification with the exciting and powerful role of perpetrator may become a chronic hedge against feeling helpless and afraid. (Marans, 1993, p. 283)

People who experience violence are also at higher risk for being revictimized. A national survey of crime in Britain showed that across a wide range of crime types, 70% of incidents were reported by the 14% of victim respondents who were repeat victims (Farrell, 1992; see Titus, 1995, for a review of related studies). Other research indicates that a person who has been shot is more likely to be victimized again than someone who has not (Weissbeski Sims et al., 1989), and another study found that college women who had been raped as adolescents were more than three times more likely to be sexually revictimized than those who had not (Gidycz et al., 1993). At Victim Services, we often see battered women with a history of successive violent relationships.

Though the explanation for why victims may be at greater risk is not clear, the literature and our work with crime victims suggest that it may not be a question of choice: High-risk behavior is more likely a symptom of trauma than a willful choice. Some may become so resigned to losing control over their lives or desensitized to dangerous situations that they fail to take normal safety precautions or to resist manipulation by others (Finkelhor & Browne, 1985; Wyatt et al., 1992). Herman (1992) noted that "survivors of prolonged, repeated trauma," such as victims of family vio-lence, often suffer what she calls "complex post-traumatic stress disorder," which can make them "particularly vulnerable to repeated harm" (p. 119). They may explain their victimization by believing they deserved it—that some characterological flaw in themselves triggered the crime (Janoff-Bulman, 1985)—and thus may actually expect to be victimized again. Repeated abuse from parents or mates can make people confused about the meaning of love and so desperate for affection that they become vulnerable to dangerous relationships. Like soldiers in the Vietnam War, some victims adapt to violence by becoming desensitized, resigned, and even attracted to the excitement of escalating levels of risk. They may put themselves in danger as a cry for help or may reenact the traumatic event over and over, unconsciously searching for a more positive outcome (Garbarino, Dubrow, Kostelny, & Pardo, 1992).

The complex and often messy lives of individuals rarely fit neatly into any theoretical paradigm about vertical or horizontal transmission or circles of violence, especially because circumstances beyond individual victimization are major factors. The complex dynamic of poverty and unemployment, shattered families, racism, high-risk behavior patterns (Titus, 1995), and chronic physical and mental health problems makes it impossible to identify which factors led to violence in any given situation. As Fullilove (1994) pointed out, when entire communities suffer these desperate conditions, they become breeding grounds for violence, and those living in them are at an even greater risk. Where whole communities are traumatized by violence, the social ties that normally support and strengthen community members get corroded, leaving them vulnerable and defenseless (Erikson, 1995). In these conditions, violence itself seems to be self-perpetuating.

Two case examples from Victim Services clients help illustrate how victimization can entrap people in a web of violence.

A Battered Woman

Vanessa's[1] earliest memory is of her father hitting her mother. After years of being abused, her mother had a nervous breakdown and was unable to be a supportive and nurturing parent, leaving the teenage Vanessa to search for love and comfort from a series of partners. From then on, Vanessa's life seemed to mirror her mother's and grandmother's—a succession of violent relationships with men and women, drug and alcohol abuse, and occasional welfare dependency. Her first abusive relationship was with a magnetic but controlling older woman who used verbal and physical violence to manipulate Vanessa's life and emotions. She was finally able to escape with the help of her church, but soon thereafter she fell in love with a man who had been abused by the aunt who raised him after he was abandoned by his drug-addicted parents. He was suffering the same pain and insecurities as Vanessa, but he took it out on her. During her second pregnancy, the verbal abuse became physical. Vanessa got an order of protection to expel her husband from the house. She took him back a few months later; once again, he turned on her, throwing her against the wall and threatening, "If I kill you, I'll only get two years. That's how much your life is worth."

A Troubled Youth

When he was 9, Francisco and his family moved to New York City from Jamaica, where his father gave up being an auto mechanic to deal cocaine. Francisco was in the eighth grade when he witnessed his father being shot to death. Devastated by the trauma, his mother returned to her family in Jamaica, leaving Francisco, an only child, behind. Francisco had to be placed with a foster family. Before the death of his father, whom he had loved and idolized, Francisco had been a "B" student with good attendance. Afterward, he became angry and violent: He brought box-cutters and other weapons to school and terrorized his teachers and fellow classmates by shouting, spitting, pushing, and shoving. Big for his age, he was an intimidating figure whom students and teachers alike were afraid to challenge. The single incident of his father's murder had, over the course of a few months, destroyed the stability of Francisco's life and set him on a course of violence and destruction.

The Role of Victim Assistance

As seen in the stories of Vanessa and Francisco and many others like them, violence can subject people to repeated pain and trauma. But this is not inevitable. Our experience working with 100,000 crime victims each year is consistent with the recommendations of experts on repeat victimization (Farrell & Pease, 1993; Trickett, Osborn, Seymour, & Pease, 1992)—that appropriate interventions with victims can create an opening in an otherwise closed system of repeated victimization.

People traumatized by violence often feel locked in, with no way out. As Vanessa described her situation, "To have a choice to stay or leave, women must have a *place* to go." "Place" may mean literally a place to live or work or may mean the conditions of one's life—economic class, employment opportunity, neighborhood safety. It may refer to a person's existential sense of self—his or her culture, beliefs, values, and behavior. To change one's place, in any sense of the word, victims need to believe they have somewhere else to go. To the extent that victims' behavior contributes to the risk of violence, helping victims assess where they are, where they want to go, and how to get there can create opportunities for change. Assistance programs can lead victims to a new place and thereby reduce the risk of future violence.

Working with the victim immediately following the crime is particularly important. At

the point of crisis, people may be more inclined to make changes in their behavior,
their lives, and their surroundings, and this
makes them more receptive to assistance programs (Anderson, Chenery, & Pease, 1995). In
addition, prompt reaction can provide more
effective prevention because the risk of revictimization is greatest immediately after
the incident (Anderson et al., 1995; Polvi,
Looman, Humphries, & Pease, 1991; Titus,
1995).

Though more research is needed, victim
assistance programs seem to offer promising
venues to help extricate victims from the web
of violence because they create opportunities
that range from the individual to the collective.
Addressing the consequences of the crime to
reduce the likelihood of future violence includes teaching victims safety strategies, helping them recover from trauma, and reconnect-
ing them with others. It also means assessing
and addressing the broader socioeconomic
conditions that raise the odds for violence
(poverty, joblessness, lack of housing) on an
individual and community level.

Safety and Shelter

Helping the victim be and feel safer is a
crucial first step in preventing further violence. This may entail providing new locks or
improving the safety of victims' neighborhoods. For battered women and their children,
establishing emergency plans of escape or providing shelter space or medical attention can
mean the difference between safety and injury
or death. Teaching victimization avoidance
and crime prevention skills, including how to
identify and change high-risk behaviors (see
Chapter 9 of this book) or how to resolve
conflicts peacefully, can enable victims to create a safer environment for themselves and
avoid unnecessary risks. Various therapeutic
strategies, including medication, stress management or cognitive techniques, and building
interpersonal and social connections, can enhance the individual's sense of safety by ame-

liorating feelings of danger and isolation (Lebowitz et al., 1993).

Recovering From Trauma

As suggested above, personal history and
environmental factors affect how individuals
react to trauma, influencing how trauma im-
pairs their ability to protect themselves without injuring themselves or others. As a result,
no single approach will work for all people;
rather, "to be effective, interventions must be
tailored to the individual's unique 'ecology';
they must respond to the personal, sociocultural, environmental and interpersonal exigen-
cies of an individual's life" (Lebowitz et al.,
1993, p. 3). A range of education, counseling,
and therapeutic services may be necessary to
help victims recover from trauma.

Therapy and other mental health services
can help people break free from the compulsive reenactment of the traumatic event and
learn to deal with the sense of powerlessness
and loss occasioned by violence. People can
learn nonviolent expressions for the legitimate
fear and anger produced by crime. Given information about the dynamics of violence and
victimization, or the use of power and control
in intimate relationships, victims learn to apportion blame properly, reassess beliefs about
gender roles and acceptable behavior in intimate relationships, and identify danger signs
early on. Drug and alcohol programs tailored
to the needs of victims can help people traumatized by violence regain control over their
lives and surroundings without self-medicat-
ing to numb their pain or fear. Batterers, as
well, many of whom have histories of childhood abuse and violence, need psychological
and educational assistance to address their response to trauma and learn more appropriate attitudes and behaviors in intimate relationships.

Connection to Others

Victims often suffer intense isolation from
friends, family, and community (Herman,

1992). They may feel stigmatized or tainted by
the crime, a feeling reinforced by being
avoided or treated insensitively by others. Iso-
lating the victim is a common strategy for
control by those who abuse women, children,
and older people. Lebowitz et al. (1993) noted
that one of the key steps in recovering from
trauma is breaking down this isolation by re-
connecting with others; hence the benefits of
self-help groups in which people share common experiences and offer mutual support. By
reestablishing ties with family and community
support networks, victims become less vulnerable and, in some cases, more inclined to help
other victims and engage in community efforts
to change the conditions that breed violence.

Economic Viability

Victimization can propel people into dire
economic circumstances: They may lose the
ability to pay their rent or bills. In the case of
domestic violence or elder abuse, financial
control may be one of the abuser's weapons.
Men who batter often exploit and perpetuate
their partner's financial dependence as a
means of maintaining control; in turn, the perceived loss of control that comes with victimization can make improving one's condition
seem an unreachable goal.

Whether through job training, emergency
financial assistance, or other methods, helping
victims to gain an economic toehold is often
an important part of victim assistance that
allows people to lead normal lives again. For
some, economic improvements can also have
a therapeutic effect: Getting a job can rebuild
battered women's eroded self-esteem and reassure them of their strength and resiliency. At
the same time, these services can reduce the
risk of revictimization. In cases of partner or
elder abuse, economic assistance can spring
victims from the trap of economic dependence. For young people, education, job training, and expanded employment opportunities
open up nonviolent paths to achieve a sense of
control, self-worth, and hope for the future.

Economic services can also reduce the risk of
violence associated with poverty (National
Research Council, 1993). Where economic
concerns such as shelter and food take precedence over reducing the risk of injury, assistance programs can help people meet these
more pressing needs and allow them to focus
on avoiding victimization.

Helping Victims Through
Other Social Services

Aside from dedicated victim assistance programs, many other social service institutions
and organizations have the potential to help
victims escape the web of violence. By addressing both the direct results of crime and
the preexisting conditions in people's lives
that put them at risk, health care, business,
criminal justice, education and social service
institutions, and community-based organizations and churches can create opportunities for
safer alternatives, often with only minor
changes in their operations or staff training.
Doctors and other health care providers who
learn to identify the signs of domestic violence
can help battered women develop safety plans
and refer them to domestic violence services.
School-based programs, such as Victim Services' Safe Harbor, create secure places in
schools where students can talk with trained
listeners when they feel threatened or need to
resolve a conflict. Corporations can create employment opportunities and training for battered women and make domestic violence
awareness programs and counseling part of
their employee assistance programs. The frequent co-occurrence of domestic violence and
child abuse (Stark & Flitcraft, 1984) suggests
that child protective services could provide an
opportunity for identifying domestic violence
and linking women with services. Welfare
system reformers could look at how to address
the conditions that cause people to go on welfare in the first place (including victimization)
and work to prevent entry into the system

rather than focusing solely on moving people off public assistance.

Collaborations among victim programs, police departments, mental health providers, and child welfare agencies can provide coordinated attention to crime victims and raise general awareness of these issues. One interesting example is the Child Development/Community Policing Program, a joint project of Yale University's Child Study Center and the New Haven Police Department, which trains police officers to identify and work with children who are victims or witnesses of crime to reduce the risk of trauma and future violence.

Working With Offenders

Victim assistance for offenders is another promising prevention strategy. With youth especially, we see that victims and victimizers are often the same people; many batterers suffered childhood abuse and victimization. Providing victim assistance services to offenders through the juvenile and criminal justice systems may be a particularly effective means of violence prevention. In the current judicial and correctional systems, however, there are few programs to help offenders address their trauma or learn conflict resolution skills to reduce recidivism. As a result, the system is passing up an opportunity to prevent future violence.

Working with individuals in correctional facilities, juvenile boot camps, or community correction programs such as work release centers, victim programs could help people find nonviolent, lawful ways to deal with their own victimization, break away from patterns of violence, and become reintegrated into society. Combined with continuing education that improves economic opportunities on release, which has a proven record in reducing recidivism (Kunen, 1995), these kinds of programs could serve a truly "correctional" role for victim/offenders, giving the opportunities and skills to lead nonviolent lives.

A recent Victim Services intervention program in a residential adolescent youth facility in New York showed promising evidence that young offenders can benefit from victim assistance. Through group discussions on violence and victimization, these long-term wards of the state learned to recognize and avoid abusive behavior in themselves and others. Many were able for the first time to talk about their own histories of victimization, taking the first step in working through their feelings of anger and isolation. With more than half of participating youth revealing some type of past victimization, other facility staff and administrators recognized the value of victim assistance for their own work in helping young people put their lives back together.

Victim Assistance in Action

Victim assistance helped Vanessa and Francisco to break free from the web of violence. For each, help during a crisis created options—a way out of what looked like a closed and violent system. Both have made significant changes in their own lives—moving to a new place, in both senses of the word. By becoming active in community violence prevention, they have become more optimistic about their own futures.

Six years ago, Vanessa called Victim Services' domestic violence hotline—not for herself but for a neighbor who was being beaten. It took her another year before she called the hotline on her own behalf. With the help of a victim assistance counselor, she got an order of protection and moved with her children into a safe house in an emergency shelter program. From there, she moved to a transitional battered women's shelter and finally to permanent housing. These residences gave Vanessa the safety and peace of mind she needed to reassess her situation, explore her options, and address her own and her children's emotional and psychological needs. She began seeing a therapist, who helped her confront the self-blame and aggressive behavior she had used over the years to cope with abuse. She has learned to acknowledge her own self-worth and understand how her mother's lack of support affected her own adult relationships. She also started to attend church regularly, finding strength in religion. A counselor helped get her into job training and life skills programs, which have enhanced her self-confidence and enabled her to support herself so she is not tempted to return to her husband. Working with a social services agency, she has moved up quickly through the ranks. With new confidence in her own abilities, she is finding satisfaction helping others find employment and economic self-sufficiency. Most significantly to Vanessa, her children are leading peaceful lives; her daughter is an honor student at a high school for gifted students, and her son is making progress with a therapist. Vanessa credits victim assistance and her religious faith with helping her escape from violence.

When Francisco's threatening behavior got out of hand, he was referred to a counselor in his school's victim assistance program. For the first time, Francisco talked about the death of his father and all the difficult changes he had been through. Over the course of the year, he was able to step back and understand how his father's murder had affected him and why he was reacting so violently. He learned to verbalize his feelings instead of acting out—to say, "I need to be left alone," instead of pushing a classmate down the stairs and to say, "I'm sorry," instead of striking out. The counselor worked with the foster care system to get Francisco placed with his aunt until his mother returned. She was referred to trauma counseling as well, and eventually she and Francisco were able to live together again and move to a safer neighborhood. In the beginning, Francisco had felt hopeless and betrayed, trapped by his emotions and scared at how quickly his life had decayed. Gradually, he began to recapture his enthusiasm for life. Having learned nonviolent ways to express his emotions and

his needs, Francisco decided to take on violence prevention as his personal mission. With training, he became a peer counselor in an alternatives-to-violence program and helped launch a student safety campaign at his school.

Victims in Violence Prevention

Francisco's decision to help other young people and Vanessa's commitment to assisting others in need show that victim assistance programs have another powerful yet overlooked preventive benefit for society as a whole. At Victim Services, we first noticed the desire of some crime victims to help their communities in our Families of Homicide Victims Program. Through this support group for surviving family members, participants found that they were not alone in their suffering and that they could give each other valuable understanding and support. Members who wanted to influence legislation created a spin-off advocacy group for victims' rights and violence prevention. Some members wanted to reach out to others in need and were trained to cofacilitate support groups with Victim Services staff. One member who lost three sons to violence started an after-school program for at-risk youth.

The participation of these individuals in addressing the broader social context of violence prevention is not unique. Mothers Against Drunk Driving, the Stephanie Roper Committee and Foundation, and Parents of Murdered Children are three examples of violence prevention and advocacy organizations established in response to a particular violent crime and supported in large part by the efforts of crime victims and their families.

Victim activism is often beneficial for those who choose to become involved. Herman (1992) noted that victims who take on a "survivor mission" to improve society may be able to "transform the meaning of their personal tragedy by making it the basis for social action" (p. 207). They are often able to "transcend [their] personal grievance against the perpetrator" (p. 209) and focus on the needs of other victims and the social conditions that contribute to crime. Others may find an outlet for their energy and emotions in other social movements such as civil rights, the environment, or AIDS, which, though not directly related to crime, do reflect other "victimizing" conditions. Regardless of the forum, feelings of anger and rage are translated into constructive social action, at the same time that victims come to feel less isolated and more strongly connected to their communities. As a result, activism can reduce many of the effects of victimization that contribute to future violence.

In addition, victims who become involved in their communities can be a powerful force for reform and prevention. As peer counselors and advocates, victim activists have helped others recover from violence and escape repeated crime. Working in groups, they can reduce the causes of violence on a much broader scale than as individuals. They have launched antiviolence campaigns, such as MADD's Designated Driver program, to change social behavior and reduce the risk of violence on a community-wide basis. They have lobbied for legislation and services that are more supportive of victims' needs and that address the broader social conditions that can lead to violence, such as discrimination, poverty, and unemployment. They have spoken out about their own experiences to change the public's behavior and beliefs, showing potential victims and offenders what can result from crime.

Having reduced the chances of their own victimization through assistance programs, a number of victims are turning their attention to helping others avoid the web of violence. However, victim activism is not yet broadly recognized or sufficiently supported, even among victim assistance professionals. Expanded opportunities for involvement would create new avenues for victims away from violence and mobilize a dedicated force for violence prevention.

Conclusion

As a society increasingly alarmed about violence even as solutions to the problem continue to elude us, we need to step back and think about the most effective means of violence prevention. Though more research is needed on the transmission of violence through victimization and the most effective programs for breaking the web of violence, victim assistance in the aftermath of crime offers a prime opportunity for intervention. Those who work with victims need to recognize that our task is not merely to bind the wounds after the fact—it is also to reduce the risk of future injury. In a time of limited service resources, this dual goal becomes particularly important. And when victims build on their recovery by becoming involved in violence prevention efforts, they further extend the preventive value of victim assistance, creating a powerful new force for strengthening the safety of our communities.

Note

1. Names in case studies have been changed.

References

Anderson, D., Chenery, S., & Pease, K. (1995). *Biting back: Tackling repeat burglary and car crime* (Crime Detection and Prevention Series Paper No. 58). London: Home Office.

Browne, A. (1987). *When battered women kill*. New York: Macmillan.

Erikson, K. (1995). Notes on trauma and community. In C. Caruth (Ed.), *Trauma: Explorations in memory* (pp. 183-199). Baltimore: Johns Hopkins University Press.

Farrell, G. (1992). Multiple victimization: Its extent and significance. *International Review of Victimology, 2,* 85-102.

Farrell, G., & Pease, K. (1993). *Once bitten, twice bitten: Repeat victimization and its implications for crime prevention* (Crime Prevention Unit Paper No. 46). London: Home Office.

Finkelhor, D., & Browne, A. (1985). The traumatic impact of child sexual abuse: A conceptualization. *American Journal of Orthopsychiatry, 55,* 530-541.

Fullilove, M., Fullilove, R., Smith, M., Winkler, K., Michael, C., Panzer, P., & Wallace, R. (1992). *Violence, trauma and posttraumatic stress disorder among women drug users.* New York: New York State Psychiatric Institute.

Fullilove, M. (1994, July). *Poverty: The unmentionable, unavoidable fact.* Paper presented at the Human Resource Association of the Northeast, Arlington, VA.

Garbarino, J., Dubrow, N., Kostelny, K., & Pardo, C. (1992). *Children in danger: Coping with the consequences of community violence.* San Francisco: Jossey-Bass.

Gidycz, C. A., Coble, C. N., Latham, L., & Layman, M. J. (1993). Sexual assault experience in adulthood and prior victimization experiences: A prospective analysis. *Psychology of Women Quarterly, 17,* 151-168.

Harvey, M. (1991). *An ecological view of trauma.* Unpublished manuscript.

Herman, J. L. (1992). *Trauma and recovery.* New York: Basic Books.

Hotaling, G. T., & Straus, M. (1988). Violence in the family and violence and other crime outside the family. *Crime and Justice: An Annual Review of Research, 11,* 315-375.

Hotaling, G. T., & Sugarman, D. B. (1986). An analysis of risk markers in husband to wife violence: The current state of knowledge. *Violence and Victims, 1,* 101-124.

Janoff-Bulman, R. (1985). The aftermath of victimization: Rebuilding shattered assumptions. In C. R. Figley (Ed.), *Trauma and its wake* (pp. 15-33). New York: Brunner/Mazel.

Kendall-Tackett, K. A., Williams, L. M., & Finkelhor, D. (1993). Impact of sexual abuse on children: A review and synthesis of recent empirical studies. *Psychological Bulletin, 113,* 164-180.

Kunen, J. S. (1995, July 10). Teaching prisoners a lesson. *New Yorker,* pp. 34-39.

Langan, P. A., & Innes, C. A. (1986). *Preventing domestic violence against women* (Bureau of Justice Statistics Special Rep. No. NCJ-102937). Washington, DC: U.S. Dept. of Justice.

Lebowitz, L., Harvey, M. R., & Herman, J. L. (1993). A stage-by-dimension model of recovery from sexual trauma. *Journal of Interpersonal Violence, 8,* 378-391.

Marans, S. (1993). Children and inner-city violence: Strategies for intervention. In L. Leavitt & N. Fox (Eds.), *The psychological effects of war and violence on children* (pp. 281-301). Hillsdale, NJ: Lawrence Erlbaum.

National Research Council. (1993). *Understanding and preventing violence.* Washington, DC: National Academy Press.

Polvi, N., Looman, T., Humphries, C., & Pease, K. (1991). Time course of repeat burglary victimization. *British Journal of Criminology, 31,* 411-414.

Rosenberg, M. L., Stark, E., & Zahn, M. A. (1986). Interpersonal violence: Homicide and spouse abuse. In J. M. Last (Ed.), *Public health and preventive medicine* (12th ed., pp. 1399-1425). Norwalk, CT: Appleton-Century-Croft.

Spatz Widom, C. (1995, March). *Victims of childhood sexual abuse: Later criminal consequences* (National Institute of Justice Research in Brief). Washington, DC: U.S. Dept. of Justice, Office of Justice Programs, National Institute of Justice.

Spatz Widom, C. (1989). The cycle of violence. *Science, 244,* 160-166.

Stark, E. (1992). Framing and reframing battered women. In E. Buzawa (Ed.), *Domestic violence: The criminal justice response* (pp. 271-289). New York: Auburn House.

Stark, E., & Flitcraft, A. (1984). Women-battering, child abuse and social heredity: What is the relationship? In N. Johnson (Ed.), *Marital violence* (pp. 147-172). London: Routledge & Kegan Paul.

Straus, M. A. (1990). Injury and frequency of assault and the "representative sample fallacy" in measuring wife beating and child abuse. In M. A. Straus & R. A. Gelles (Eds.), *Physical violence in American families: Risk factors and adaptations to violence in 8,145 families* (pp. 75-91). New Brunswick, NJ: Transaction.

Straus, M. A., Gelles, R. J., & Steinmetz, S. K. (1980). *Behind closed doors: Violence in the American family.* Garden City, NY: Doubleday.

Titus, R. M. (1995, August). *Criminology, crime prevention, and the victim.* Paper presented at the 1995 annual meeting of the National Organization for Victim Assistance, Maui.

Trickett, A., Osborn, D., Seymour, J., & Pease, K. (1992). What is different about high crime areas? *British Journal of Criminology, 32*(1), 81-89.

Weissbeski Sims, D., Bivins, B., Obeid, F., Horst, H., Sorensen, V., & Fath, J. (1989). Urban terrorism: A chronic recurrent disease. *Journal of Trauma, 29,* 940-947.

Wyatt, G., Guthrie, D., & Notgrass, C. (1992). Differential effects of women's child sexual abuse and subsequent sexual revictimization. *Journal of Consulting and Clinical Psychology, 60,* 167-173.

11 Victim Rights and Services

A Modern Saga

MARLENE A. YOUNG

At 9:01 a.m. on April 19, 1995, people in downtown Oklahoma City, Oklahoma, were stunned by an explosion at the Alfred P. Murrah federal building. That shock was soon felt across the country and around the world; the worst terrorist attack on civilians in recent U.S. history had killed 169 people and shattered the lives of the survivors. The physical and human devastation caused by the crime was palpable to the millions who spent much of the next few weeks watching television. But what was not seen on television—the response to the victims—was also extraordinary.

The U.S. Departments of Justice and Education supported teams of crisis responders who flew to Oklahoma within hours of the event to provide crisis intervention and counseling to rescue workers, community members, and survivors of the bombing. Suzanne Breedlove, the director of the state's crime victim compensation program, quickly began mobilizing to donate financial aid to injured victims and the families of those who were killed. The local U.S. Attorney's Office began preparing to assist the hundreds of victims and survivors as they faced the possibility of a lengthy criminal investigation and trial. One might say that concern for victims was the central focus of most people involved in the aftermath of the crime, from the victim assistance coordinators on the scene to the Attorney General of the United States.

The response in Oklahoma City was indicative of the impact that the victims' movement has exerted on American society over the last 30 years. The movement has transformed the status of "crime victim" from one of lonely insignificance to one commanding legal status, an expanding array of social services, and public concern. Because the movement has been so powerful, it is useful to review its origins, what it has accomplished, and where it may lead in the future.

The Past: The Infancy of the Victims' Movement

The emergence of the victims' movement was triggered by the confluence of five virtually independent activities: (a) the introduction of state victim compensation programs, (b) the development of a field of study known as victimology, (c) the women's movement, (d) a crime wave and a parallel growth in public dissatisfaction with the criminal justice system, and (e) the growth of victim activism.

Victim Compensation

The idea that the state should provide financial reimbursement to victims of violent crime for their losses was propounded initially by English penal reformer Margery Fry in the early 1960s. Spurred by the impulse to grant a new kind of welfare to people in need, New Zealand's was the first legislature, in 1963, to adopt a victim compensation program, with Great Britain passing a similar law shortly thereafter. In 1965, California became the first state in North America to establish a compensation program in 1965, soon followed by New York.

The idea spread methodically in the United States, with 32 states administering compensation programs by 1979. Most evolved from a welfare to a justice orientation, in which victims were seen as deserving compensation whether they were in need or not. Compensation programs also sought to promote involvement by victims in the criminal justice system because they required victims to report to the police and, in many cases, to cooperate with the prosecution.

In the early years, administrators of victim compensation programs were not always passionate advocates of victims' broader concerns, but from the start, their programs were of both practical and symbolic value—they represent the first public recognition of society's responsibility to victims and have been the cornerstone of all the victim service schemes that have followed.

Victimology

The study of victimology arose in Europe after World War II primarily to understand the criminal-victim relationship. In retrospect, it is ironic that early victimology at times suggested that victims themselves might be one of the causes of criminal behavior. Benjamin Mendelssohn (1956) first coined the term *victimology* to propose a separate discipline from criminology, one that focused on the victim's role in criminal behavior. His initial typology classified victims in accordance with the degree of their guilt in contributing to the crime. Similarly, Hans von Hentig (1948) argued that the reciprocal relationship between criminals and victims called for not only greater victim participation in the criminal justice system but also a greater share in criminal responsibility.

The importation of victimology to the United States correlated with increasing concern about crime in the late 1960s. That concern spawned the President's Commission on Law Enforcement and the Administration of Justice in 1966, which, in turn, prompted national crime victimization surveys showing that criminal victimization was far higher than law enforcement reports indicated and that victims often did not report crime due to lack of faith in the criminal justice system. This captured the attention of researchers, who began to examine more closely the impact of crime on victims as well as victim disillusionment with the system.

Studies done during the 1970s on rising crime rates, rape trauma, crime's impact on the elderly, and the battered women's syndrome had a profound influence on program strategies for helping victims to cope. Research on victim and witness participation in the criminal justice system was the catalyst for experimental programs in prosecutors' offices that provided better notification, support, and aid to victims and witnesses. Victimology began to embrace a more compassionate view of victims.

The Women's Movement

There is little doubt that the women's movement was central to the development of the victims' movement. Leaders of the women's movement saw sexual assault and domestic violence —and the poor response of the criminal justice system to these crimes—as potent illustrations of women's lack of status, power, and influence. Consciousness-raising groups soon acknowledged the need to focus special attention on victims of rape or spouse abuse. It is significant that of the three first victim programs in the United States, two were rape crisis centers in Washington, D.C., and the San Francisco Bay Area. One of the interesting contributions of these programs was their emphasis on crisis intervention and counseling for victims. Recognition that the criminal justice system could not (because no one was arrested) or would not give rape victims much satisfaction made it all the more important to concentrate on helping women cope with the trauma of rape and empowering them to begin a new life.

Crime and Dissatisfaction

The growth of victimology helped to generate data that confirmed what the public already sensed during the 1970s: Crime and fear of crime were at unacceptably high levels, and victims received little attention or assistance in the aftermath of crime. The application of this knowledge led to initiatives by the Law Enforcement Assistance Administration (LEAA) that awarded funding to criminal justice agencies to improve services to victims. In 1974, the first victim/witness programs were created through LEAA in the District Attorney's Offices in Brooklyn, New York, and Milwaukee, Wisconsin. The National District Attorneys Association also received a grant to create model victim assistance programs in seven other prosecutors' offices.

These programs were fertile ground for the development and implementation of new ideas for victim services. The leadership from program directors helped to mold the new movement, and many directors remain actively involved today. In addition, LEAA supported crime victim programs in law enforcement agencies. In 1974, Indianapolis, Indiana, and Ft. Lauderdale, Florida, became the first communities to establish law-enforcement-based crisis intervention programs responding to all victims of crime with counseling and other assistance.

Victim Activism

Finally, the victims' movement was given its energy and determination from victims themselves. The women's movement raised the consciousness of women concerning the oppression of criminal violence, but it was rape survivors and battered women who most often founded programs and shelters for other victims. Families and Friends of Missing Persons and Violent Crime Victims was organized in 1974 in Washington State as a result of the efforts of survivors of homicide victims. Parents of Murdered Children was founded by Charlotte and Robert Hullinger in 1978 in the aftermath of their daughter's murder. Mothers Against Drunk Driving was organized in 1980 by Candy Lightner when her daughter was killed. Protect the Innocent in Indiana was strengthened by Betty Jane Spencer after she was attacked in her home and her four boys were killed.

The five forces of victim compensation, victimology, women's movement, rising crime, and victim activism worked together at first in a loose coalition, but the formation of the National Organization for Victim Assistance (NOVA) in 1975 helped to consolidate the purposes and the goals of the victims' movement. The organization grew out of ideas developed at the first national conference on victim assistance in Ft. Lauderdale in 1973. NOVA's initial contributions to the field were to sponsor annual national conferences to promote victim issues and to make available early training opportunities to those working with victims.

In the late 1970s, LEAA funding gave communities the support they needed to replicate pioneering programs and to translate knowledge and practice into educational materials. The National District Attorneys Association developed a Committee on Victims to assist in disseminating information. And the American Bar Association established a Victims Committee as a part of its Criminal Justice Section to increase awareness of victim issues among lawyers.

By the end of the 1970s, many states had at least a few victim assistance programs, networks of programs had been established in 10 states, and there was a common understanding of the basic elements of service: crisis intervention, counseling, support during criminal justice proceedings, compensation, and restitution. LEAA sought to consolidate this information by commissioning a Victim Assistance Prescriptive Package and by holding regional training seminars to assist in the development of new programs. LEAA continued to promote victim assistance through its state block grant program as well as through the first National Victim Resource Center, which it established in 1978. In 1979, NOVA incorporated the growing demand for victims to have legiti-mate access to the criminal justice system into a new policy platform on victim rights. Furthermore, NOVA initiated a National Campaign for Victim Rights, which had as its core a National Victim Rights Week, endorsed in 1981 by President Ronald Reagan.

The 1970s were marked by rapid progress in improving responses to victims, but they were also marked by turbulence, caused in part by the waxing and waning of federal financial support. As national priorities shifted, stable funding became elusive, and programs often entered into internecine warfare over limited resources. Controversy also arose between programs that were driven by grassroots energy and those that were based in traditional criminal justice institutions. Many felt that there was an inherent conflict between the goals of prosecutors or law enforcement officials and the interests of victims. Some sought legal changes in the system, whereas others felt that change should take place through the formulation and revision of policies and procedures. Tensions within the movement led to new national organizations: The National Coalition Against Sexual Assault was formed at a NOVA meeting in 1978 to serve as a leader for rape crisis programs; the National Coalition Against Domestic Violence was founded at the end of 1978 to provide an advocacy network for shelters.

Adolescence: Growth and Acceptance

The loss of significant federal funding for local programs in 1980 due to the abolition of LEAA by Congress served as a powerful reminder of how tenuous the movement's gains were in the 1970s. The impact of the new organizations, victim activist groups, and public awareness of the plight of crime victims came at a critical time. Their influence helped the victims' movement make progress on three fronts: public policy, program implementation, and public awareness.

Public Policy

Public policy leaders at the state level realized that state action was necessary to ensure the permanency of victim assistance. California was a leader again as it became the first state to establish funding for victim assistance in 1980. At the same time, Wisconsin became the first state to pass a victim's bill of rights, and the concern for victims at the national level was enhanced by the receptivity of the new administration in Washington, D.C. President Reagan followed up his endorsement of National Victim Rights Week with an Attorney General's Task Force on Violent Crime in 1981, which recommended the establishment of a Presidential Task Force on Victims of Crime. The President acted on that recommendation in 1982. His task force held six hearings and produced a final report with 68 recommendations for improving assistance to crime victims.

In anticipation of that report, NOVA undertook two major projects to consolidate knowledge on victim services. The first, with the support of the Office of Justice Assistance, Research, and Statistics (LEAA's successor), was a field study of 50 victim assistance programs in which narrative accounts of program directors and their staff were collected to document the kinds of services provided. In addition, policies, protocols, and practices were gathered as reference materials and resources for other programs. The second project was a strategic planning process to examine the threats and opportunities facing victim service programs and to identify the main steps that should be taken to ensure program viability and stability. That process helped to establish a long-range plan for developing comprehensive training for victim advocates and their allied professionals in criminal justice, medicine, mental health, the clergy, and education.

The President's Task Force Report was instrumental in launching four critical initiatives in the 1980s. First, it recommended the development of federal legislation that would establish a federal Office for Victims of Crime (OVC) in the U.S. Department of Justice and federal funding to support state victim compensation programs and local victim assistance programs. That recommendation was a precipitating force in the enactment of the Victims of Crime Act (VOCA) of 1984. The act established a Crime Victims Fund, based on the collection of fines from federal criminals, that is used to support state compensation and local victim assistance programs.

Second, it recommended to professionals in the criminal justice system and associated professions ways in which they could improve the treatment of crime victims. These recommendations were crucial to the development of training programs for law enforcement, prosecutors, judges, corrections personnel, health and mental health professionals, and the clergy. The 1983 National Conference on the Judiciary and Victim Rights was a direct spin-off of the task force's recommendations on the judiciary and served as a major force to change judicial policies and attitudes.

Third, it recommended an additional task force on violence within families, which resulted in the establishment of the Attorney General's Task Force on Family Violence in 1983. Its 1984 report stimulated federal action requiring state compensation programs to cover victims of family violence who receive federal funds.

Fourth, it recommended an amendment to the U.S. Constitution according victims the right to be present and heard at all critical stages of judicial proceedings. That recommendation sparked the interest of victims and their advocates, and by 1986, a national Victims Constitutional Amendment Network had been formed to seek state constitutional amendments on victim rights.

Program Implementation

In the 4 years that followed the President's Task Force Report, the Office for Justice

Programs and the OVC worked closely with NOVA to implement the recommendations. States began receiving funds under VOCA in 1985, training programs for criminal justice professionals were designed and implemented widely, standards for victim program services were developed, and regional training programs for victim service providers were presented throughout the nation.

In 1985, victim-oriented justice gained international recognition with the adoption by the United Nations of the Declaration of Basic Principles of Justice for Victims of Crime and Abuse of Power. This document encouraged other nations to institute or expand victim rights and services. The United Kingdom had established victim support schemes in the early 1970s; their orientation was primarily toward counseling and crisis intervention. The 1980s brought new proposals for victims' involvement in the criminal justice system. Germany, which had a long tradition of allowing victims a voice in the criminal justice process, began to consider victim assistance as a way of garnering support for that voice. France had the opportunity for victim participation through the *partie civile* system, in which civil claims of victims are merged with criminal proceedings. The impetus of the U.N. declaration encouraged France to develop a nationwide network of victim assistance programs. These and other international steps toward broader victim participation served as examples for victim programs in the United States.

The development of a new Model Victim Assistance Program Brief in 1986-1988 by NOVA, with the support of OVC, served as a planning, management, and evaluation tool. It articulated eight basic services that programs should provide: (a) crisis intervention, (b) counseling and advocacy, (c) support during criminal investigation, (d) support during prosecution, (e) support after case disposition, (f) crime prevention, (g) public education, and (h) the training of allied professions. It became a standard reference for many states. States were also moving rapidly to institutionalize victim assistance through legislation and the formation of statewide networks of service programs. Victim's bills of rights were adopted in every state by 1990. Six states had passed constitutional amendments, and more than twice that many would follow suit within half a decade. Funding for victim services and compensation programs was given increasing priority so that by the end of the decade, over 8,000 programs could be identified as serving victims through crisis intervention, criminal justice support, and advocacy.

Public Awareness

The 1980s brought new contributors to the victims' movement and expanded its reach to new constituencies. The National Victim Center was founded in 1985 to commemorate Sunny von Bulow. The Victim Assistance Legal Organization (VALOR) became prominent as its founder, Frank Carrington, helped to develop and promote civil litigation on behalf of crime victims. The National Center for Missing and Exploited Children was established. The International Association of Chiefs of Police formed a Victims Committee and announced a law enforcement bill of rights for victims. The American Correctional Association issued 16 recommendations for better treatment of victims. The American Probation and Parole Association developed program goals relating to crime victims. The Spiritual Dimension became a source of education and training for clergy on victim issues. Neighbors Who Care was initiated by Justice Fellowship to develop victim assistance within religious congregations. The International Society of Traumatic Stress Studies and the International Association of Trauma Counselors were established to serve as research and education resources for individuals working in the field of trauma.

The growth in understanding the trauma of victimization was particularly important during the 1980s. In 1980, the third edition of the American Psychiatric Association's *Diagnos-*

tic and Statistical Manual (*DSM-III;* 1980) included a description of posttraumatic stress disorder (PTSD) that became a fundamental component in the training of victim and trauma counselors. Revisions in the *DSM-III* and continuing studies of trauma and its impact increased our understanding of crisis interventions and of long-term therapy and counseling. Greater emphasis was placed on early intervention and the need for supportive follow-up services. As survivors of trauma began to tell their stories in more detail, service providers began to realize that not only were direct victims of crime affected by criminal attack but so were many of their friends and family members—indeed, whole communities could experience crisis.

NOVA drew on the experience of seasoned crisis intervenors, trauma research, and psychological intervention strategies developed for emergency responders after critical incidents to initiate a practical model for community crisis intervention in the aftermath of tragedy. Its first national Crisis Response Team was dispatched in 1986 following the mass murders committed by Patrick Sherrill in the Edmond, Oklahoma, Post Office. The success of that effort engendered the birth of a National Crisis Response Team Project that made trained volunteer crisis interveners available to communities in crisis to address the emotional impact of crime and other disasters. It also influenced the growth of new local and state networks of crisis response teams in many jurisdictions, all designed to plan for and coordinate crisis response efforts should a catastrophe occur.

Victim rights and the need for more compassionate treatment of victims became ingrained in the consciousness of common citizens toward the end of the 1980s. It was not unusual to see television programs and made-for-television docudramas on victim-related issues. Yet the media seemed to have a contradictory relationship with victims. Some reporters and writers took victim issues to heart as reflected in articles and documentaries on the trauma of victimization, yet victims and their advocates continued to see the media sensationalize sensitive topics and exploit victims in crisis.

The double-edged sword of public acceptance of victim concerns was apparent in other ways. Citizens began to expect victim rights to be honored and victim services to be available. At the same time, it became obvious that unless legal action was taken, bills of rights for victims or constitutional amendments on victim rights were not enforced. Funding of victim assistance programs remained unstable. As states faced budget cuts, victim services were often the least recognized programs. Even when victims were allowed to participate in the system, the outcomes of cases were uncertain or ambiguous. And, most important, crime and violence remained at unacceptably high levels. In short, the victims' movement had matured, but there remained much work to do before victims could be guaranteed fair and compassionate responses to their plight.

The Present: Maturity and Transition

The history of the victims' movement has been marked by many diverse influences that have shaped the emerging multidisciplinary profession of victim services and have radically reformed the legal system. In 1995, the victim assistance field can be divided into three key areas: theory and research, program and professional development, and public policy.

Theory and Research

The victim assistance field has benefited greatly from the progress made in trauma research. The *Diagnostic and Statistical Manual*'s fourth edition (*DSM-IV;* American Psychiatric Association, 1994) altered the description of PTSD to include a subjective perception of trauma that confirmed victim service providers' observations that not all victims of crime or other crises suffer long-term trauma. It included a description of acute stress disorder that is useful in helping to define further what many victims experience as the crisis reaction.

In their studies leading up to the publication of the *DSM-IV,* mental health professionals also began to examine another dimension in long-term stress relating to victimization, termed the *diagnosis of extreme stress not otherwise specified* (DESNOS). The symptoms characterizing this proposed diagnosis may occur in persons who have survived complex, prolonged, or repeated trauma in which they have been subjected to coercive control. Such control may be imposed through violence or threat of violence, control of bodily functions, capricious enforcement of petty rules, intermittent rewards, isolation, degradation, and forced participation in violence. Although not yet included in the *DSM,* this description may be useful in designing interventions for chronically abused persons such as battered women, sexually abused children, torture victims, and victims of hostage taking or kidnapping. The value of these advances in trauma research is twofold. First, victim service providers have found that describing the symptoms of trauma to victims helps them to validate their experience and to understand their own reactions better. Second, the descriptions help service providers in determining when a mental health referral may be useful.

A consensus on the nature of traumatic stress reactions has spurred research into how such reactions might be manifested differently in children, adults, the elderly, and various ethnic groups. Of equal interest are the reactions of communities as a whole to traumatic events and how such reactions affect individuals. Similarly, increasing attention is being paid to what has been termed "vicarious victimization" or "compassion fatigue" suffered by caregivers working with victims.

Although studies of the effects of trauma have made great strides in our understanding of victims' reactions, less progress has been made on the issue of what constitutes effective intervention or counseling. Victims often complain (although less often now than in the early years of the victims' movement) that therapists do not know how to respond appropriately to their needs. And although most victims say that immediate crisis response is useful, there remains little research on whether various crisis intervention techniques have long-term effects or on which models are best. There have also been few studies on the impact of victim participation in the criminal justice system. Victimization surveys continue to demonstrate a significant lack of reporting of crime (although reporting rates have crept up slightly over the years). Few data support the hypothesis of the early 1970s that attention to victims and witnesses results in better cooperation, increases convictions, or affects sentencing. However, criminal justice professionals seem to view such participation as useful if it only increases citizens' understanding of the criminal justice system. It also appears that participating increases victims' satisfaction with the criminal justice system.

Program and Professional Development

Federal funding, standards for victim services, and legislated victim rights in the 1980s have resulted in expansion of victim services. All U.S. Attorneys' Offices now have victim and witness coordinators. Most prosecutors' offices, at least in urban and suburban jurisdictions, have victim assistance units. A study of law enforcement agencies with over 100 sworn officers in 1990 indicated that over 37% housed victim services. NOVA's Program Directory, which captures most of the universe of victim service programs (including chapters of Parents of Murdered Children and some but not all chapters of Mothers Against Drunk Driving), contains listings for nearly 10,000 programs.

Despite the growth of programs, coverage of all eight elements of service in any given community is still spotty. A number provide crisis intervention services and supportive counseling to particular kinds of victims (usually victims of sexual assault or domestic violence). Law enforcement agencies and prosecutors often provide support in the criminal justice system from investigations through prosecution. Many correctional agencies have victim notification units, and some have victim education programs, victim impact panels, or victim-offender dialogue programs for inmates. Comprehensive programs provide services from the time of criminal victimization through sentencing, but there are still only a few of these.

What is notable, however, is the expansion of specialized services. There are now Child Advocacy Centers throughout the United States, all using an interdisciplinary model first developed in Huntsville, Alabama. More programs are addressing the needs of victims who are ethnic or racial minorities. Programs currently provide services to burglary victims. Some also provide specialized services to victims of gang-related crimes. And efforts have been made to develop services for elder abuse victims and victims of bias crimes.

Telephone-based victim services are increasing. Statewide hotlines or information and referral services are common. NOVA has maintained a national hotline for nearly a decade. With the enactment of the 1994 Violence Against Women Act, a federal appropriation was approved for a national domestic violence hotline that will be in service during 1996. In addition, many victim compensation programs offer toll-free assistance to crime victims.

Professional education and development opportunities have expanded considerably during the first half of the 1990s. Through increased funding from OVC, new training programs have been offered on the following topics: law enforcement and domestic violence, bias crimes, civil litigation on behalf of victims, victim services and the clergy, federal victim service, the impact of HIV and AIDS on the victim assistance field, working with survivors of homicide, prosecution and sexual assault, elder abuse, victim services in corrections, community policing and victim assistance, working with grieving children, the media and victim services, victim assistance in the military, victim assistance in public housing, victim assistance and drug-related crime, and victim assistance in Indian country.

Statewide training conferences are now being held in most states. Several have started statewide training academies or institutes, and several more are integrating victim assistance training into state law enforcement academy curricula. And institutions of higher education have developed courses and curricula on victim assistance or victimology. New initiatives from OVC will address the integration of victim assistance curricula into education requirements for criminal justice, medicine, psychology, theology, and social work. Other OVC initiatives will promote additional specialized training for law enforcement, prosecutors, judges, correctional personnel, victim service providers in rural areas, emergency room workers, community crisis responders, practitioners in the juvenile justice system, and victim service providers working with white-collar crime victims. The expansion of program services and education has been accompanied by a recognition that victim assistance is a multidisciplinary profession. That recognition is reflected in the development of a new National Code of Ethics for victim assistance professionals.

Public Policy

Public policy changes in 1995 on behalf of victims of crime have affected all levels of government. The Victims of Crime Act of 1984 has become permanent federal legislation and in 1994 brought in more than $220 million of federal criminal fines to support victim assistance and compensation. A federal Bill of Rights for Victims of Crime resulted in new federal programs for victims that involve an estimated 1,000 victim and witness coordinators government-wide (although most also have other duties in their job descriptions). It also resulted in a Department of Defense directive that ensures victim and witness protections and participation in the military system of justice.

The 1994 Violence Against Women Act attracted bipartisan support to increase shelters and domestic violence and sexual assault programs as well as to provide a federal cause of action for gender-based crimes. The state bills of rights and the growing number of state constitutional amendments—20 through the 1994 election cycle—have spawned a new national coalition working toward a federal constitutional amendment in support of crime victims.

Such legislative change has, by necessity, been accompanied by the need for interpretation of policy initiatives. Victim rights issues are being litigated in the courts. The first such issue, concerning the rights of victims to provide input at sentencing, reached the Supreme Court in 1987 in *Booth v. Maryland*. The Supreme Court ruled that victim impact statements at sentencing in death penalty cases heard by a jury are unconstitutional. However, in 1991, the Court reversed that decision in *Payne v. Tennessee*, which may prove a harbinger for future cases. By 1995, a whole field of case law existed on victim rights at the state level regarding issues of protection; intimidation; notification; victim input at bail proceedings, plea bargain negotiations, sentencing, and parole hearings; the use of victim trauma as evidence; and due-process rights for victims. Despite the pervasiveness of such litigation, what remains unaccomplished is any comprehensive cataloging or interpretation of these cases. As a result, it is unclear whether there are trends in the jurisprudence of crime victims' rights.

The Future

It is clear that in the next decade, the field of victim assistance will continue to build on

its successes. It is probable that victim services will be fully integrated into the criminal justice system, crisis services will be available in most communities, victim rights will be incorporated into the constitutions of most states (if not in the federal government), victimology (by whatever term it is called) will be a part of most educational curricula from elementary school through graduate-degree programs, and victim assistance will become a recognized and respected profession.

Change is occurring faster than ever before in human history. The process of change itself has become so rapid, so complex, so turbulent, and so unpredictable that some have called it "whitewater change." Change in the criminal justice system that has been engendered by the victims' movement over the last 20 years has been seen by most as positive. But change now both threatens and offers opportunities that will transform the movement itself. That change will involve, at a minimum, the following issues.

Demographics

The new population emerging in the United States will be characterized by three critical attributes. First, the United States has the fastest-growing population in the industrialized world. It adds nearly 3 million people a year to its total population. A large number of these are immigrants (800,000 in 1992), and the United States now absorbs through immigration about 1% of the people added to the world population each year. Trends suggest that this country will reach a total population of 383 million by the year 2050 (Nelan, 1993). The impact of such population acceleration has the potential for devastation. Unless a substantial redistribution of resources occurs, it is likely that the population boom will result in increased poverty, illiteracy, homelessness, and violence.

Second, the population will be driven by a demographic tilt away from children and toward the elderly. Even now, for the first time in history, the average American has more parents living than children. At the beginning of the 20th century, fewer than 1 in 10 Americans was age 55+, and only 1 in 25 was age 65+. By 1989, 1 in 5 Americans was at least 55 years old and 1 in 8 was at least 65. Between 1989 and 2030, the 65+ population is expected to double. There will be over 100,000 people over the age of 100 by the year 2000 (U.S. Bureau of the Census, 1996). Medical advances and disease prevention strategies have contributed to a continuing rise in longevity.

Social attitudes and information on the aging process have not kept stride with the promise of that longevity. Future elderly will be challenged by growing concerns with health care, housing, poverty, loneliness, and a technological estrangement from younger groups. If the future is characterized by violence, it is likely that the elderly will be one of the most vulnerable population groups.

Minority population groups, such as those defined by race or ethnicity, sexual orientation, or disabilities, will become more prominent. Their increase will affect both the delivery of victim services and the political process by which decisions about victim services and victim rights are made. The racial and ethnic makeup of the country will change due both to higher birth rates among minority populations and to the impact of immigration and migration from around the globe. The ability of the United States to respond equitably and expeditiously to new and competing demands for access to opportunity, justice, power, and freedom may be seriously threatened. Optimists suggest that increased population diversity will provide the impetus for developing deeper understandings of different human perspectives and resolutions of old conflicts based on ignorance. Pessimists worry that diversities based on ever-smaller units of differences may create even greater conflicts, as evidenced by the conflict in the former Yugoslavia.

Victim assistance providers must become more adept at reaching out to different population groups. They must increase their knowledge of the aging process and appropriate services for the elderly. They should make diversity training a mandatory part of their professional development and, even more important, they should become better connected with their colleagues around the world. International networking will be a necessity in the future. They should also explore new methods of ensuring victim rights in alternative justice systems. An understanding of the concepts of justice and equity and the mechanisms for achieving fairness in other cultural systems will be needed to provide assistance to a broader range of victims as well as to propose modifications in our own system.

Economics

Today, the federal Crime Victims Fund has collected more contributions than ever before. Should collections continue to rise, funds to establish and sustain victim assistance and compensation programs could reach a point at which the movement's dreams can be realized. All crime victims could have access to comprehensive services from the time of criminal attack through case disposition.

But this possibility raises real concerns. Is the victims' movement ready to use such resources effectively and efficiently? Are personnel available who could be quickly trained to fill needed victim service positions? Are there adequate training opportunities if the demand for service expansion suddenly increases? Are program managers trained in service expansion? Have program managers planned for service expansion so that it can be effected in an orderly manner? Do programs have adequate facilities and equipment to handle service expansion? The answer to most of these questions today is "no." If the victims' movement is to benefit from new economic largesse, it must be prepared to answer these questions or confront the likelihood that political forces will divert the monies to other social needs.

A dramatic increase in the Crime Victims Fund will be accompanied by political demands that its purpose be expanded to address additional needs such as homelessness or illiteracy or that, once again, the fund be capped and excess monies be used for balancing the budget or funding alternative governmental programs. As states have faced budgetary crises, some have chosen to "raid" victim funding or abolish funding altogether to meet other governmental mandates. Such a possibility could result in a severe loss of funding for victim services and would force the victims' movement to consider how to defend its political and economic well-being as well as how to survive in an age of economic austerity.

Technology

The tremendous advances in technology over the last 10 years have been hailed as the predecessors to an era that will revolutionize life as we know it. The information superhighway and telecommunication technologies promise instant exposure to new knowledge and to a worldwide community of resources. Interactive computers and augmented or virtual reality systems offer unique training and service opportunities and improved health and mental health interventions for injured victims. These possibilities are encouraging, but other effects of new technologies hold difficult challenges. Technology is, even now, changing concepts of criminal behavior and the instruments by which criminal acts take place. Child pornography on the Internet, stalking and harassment through computer networks, and fraudulent conversion of funds through computer authorizations are only a present-day sample of what might occur in the future.

Technology will change how justice itself is processed. The new world holds the potential for "paperless" courts, computer-assisted law enforcement, on-scene crime adjudication, and computer monitoring of offenders. Max Winkler, a Colorado parole officer, predicted that custom-programmed microprocessor chips implanted under the skin will be available to monitor and respond to offenders' physiological patterns and reactions sometime after 2001. These technological changes may require new interpretations of constitutional concepts such as rights to confrontation, to not incriminate oneself, and to keep and bear arms, and even freedoms of speech, press, and assembly.

In this new world, the victim assistance providers of today will be obsolete. Most are technologically illiterate. Many have no experience or knowledge in working with basic computers. A world in which technology is a dominant force of communication and an arbiter of life and death is difficult to contemplate and understand, but we must be prepared to do so.

Communication

The technological basis for communication may also change the nature of communication itself. Today, the world remains separated by language barriers. Many see such barriers eradicated in the future because of the ability of computers to achieve instant translations and perhaps even because of the evolution of a universal language. To accommodate language-translation technologies, crisis interveners and counselors need to find ways of communicating critical concepts that can be cross-linguistically meaningful in trauma situations. Language will also be enhanced more than ever before by visual stimuli. Color, form, and the impact of various mediums on communication must be explored.

Health and Health Care

National health care has been a hotly debated issue in the last few years. The majority of people in the United States seem to favor some type of national health care system, but political leaders are largely divided on how such a system should be designed and implemented. The possibility of a national health care system should raise immediate issues for victim services. To what extent will victim compensation programs need to be reevaluated and reorganized if national health care becomes available to all victims? To what extent will a national health care program address crisis and long-term trauma care for victims? Should national health care include crisis and trauma programs, and will they effectively replace currently established victim assistance programs? Will the elevation of crisis and long-term trauma care to the status of health care mean that all providers must be health professionals?

Issues of national health care may be the most immediate health issue affecting the victims' movement, but technological advances in health care will raise additional issues. Medical advances are giving doctors more power to make decisions of life or death and to determine the impact of physical injury on victims. The result may make irrelevant certain traditional measures of the seriousness of crime. It is arguable, for example, that someone who intends to commit murder and would have succeeded if not for the intervention of new medical technologies should then be tried for murder. Similarly, sentences that are based on the level of victim injury may become different if doctors can completely repair the injury. An eye for an eye becomes another issue if a doctor can replace a blind eye.

Organ transplantation is now routine enough in some cases that theft of vital organs is legally prohibited. In addition, doctors now make decisions concerning priority patients for transplants. When a patient dies who needed a transplant as a result of a crime but was given less priority than another patient who also needed a transplant, is the resulting death a homicide? Many believe that we will soon be able to create a healthy child sustainable outside the uterus as a result of test-tube fertilization. Will such births result in laws that regulate birth under these conditions, reduce the need for abortions, or require parental licensing?

Mental health issues may also be seen from a different perspective. Experiments are being conducted to transplant memory from adult bees to bee larvae with surprising success. Some scientists view this research as a precursor to more advanced experiments that might eventually result in the ability to transplant memory from one human being to another. If memories can be eradicated, replaced, or reinvented either physiologically or psychologically, is this a meaningful way to reduce trauma to crime victims?

Environment

Population trends in the United States are echoed even more devastatingly in the growth of worldwide population. Estimates suggest that the population will double by the year 2050 to nearly 11 billion people. In an article in a *Time* magazine special edition entitled "Beyond the Year 2000," Eugene Linden (1996) described a worst-case scenario in which millions of people might become environmental refugees, overwhelming nations that tried to conserve their soil, water, and forests. These people would share a planet on which rats, cockroaches, weeds, and microbes were the dominant species. The world would consist primarily of deserts, patches of tropical forests, eroded mountains, dead coral reefs and barren oceans, all buffeted by extremes of weather.

Competition for dwindling environmental resources among a rapidly expanding population could well lead to increased conflict both within and between nations, producing not only countless victims but an enormous need for victim services.

The threat to our environment today suggests that we may have to impose new laws and regulations to achieve needed responses to population increases. At a futures conference for the courts held by the State Justice Institute a few years ago, judges envisioned a justice system that would address cases in which flora, fauna, and other features of the environment would be treated as victims and need representation in court. Would this call for a new kind of victim services that considered the financial and physical impact of crime on those "new victims" as well as providing social and psychological support to communities damaged by environmental crimes?

Ethics

Many of the future possibilities I discuss in this chapter are interlaced with a reconsideration of values and their ethical consequences. The United States has operated as a society with general principles that all individuals have a "right to life, liberty and the pursuit of happiness" and are due "liberty and justice" and that "all men are created equal." Its Bill of Rights also enshrines the rights of the accused, implies rights to privacy, and articulates freedoms of speech, press, and assembly. In the 220 years since the Declaration of Independence was written, these values have often been called into question. Futurists predict that our social hierarchy of values and our individual ethical interpretations of such values will be tested as never before. The following is a sample of ethical questions that we face as we go into the next millennium:

- In a society that is densely populated and interdependent for goods and services, should individual needs take priority over the needs of a community?
- If individuals have a right to life, do they also have a right to die?
- Does the right to life mean that society cannot prioritize whose death takes place and when, where, or how that death occurs?
- Does an individual's right to happiness interfere with another's right to freedom? If so, how are such contradictions resolved?
- Because rights of the accused are identified in our constitution, is there justification for including rights of the accuser—whether the accuser be society, an individual victim, or both?

- Do rights to privacy conflict with the public's right to know and the freedom of the press? If so, how are such conflicts resolved?
- Does equality mean being equal in the eyes of God or being treated equitably by government and the system of justice?
- Do rights to assemble or free speech imply the rights to network through telecommunication and to broadcast any message at any time?

Religion

John Naisbett (1982) considered the next decade and the next century a time of spiritual revolution, partly because the turn of a calendar year, a decade, or a century tends to spark reflection and concern for the future and partly because of the historical and religious prophecies of an Armageddon that will accompany the new millennium. Further, in a time of rapid change and uncertainty, individuals may turn to God or religion to explain the unknown.

Recent psychological studies suggest that people who have faith survive disaster better than people who do not. Perhaps that is why nearly 60% of the American public expect religion to play a greater role in the lives of people in this country after the year 2000. Some futurists expect that Catholicism and Eastern Orthodoxy will survive and that Mormonism will have a global impact. Hinduism and Buddhism may become more acceptable, with sizable followings in the United States. And Judaism and Islam will maintain their influence. Ancient religions or spiritual beliefs are expected to reemerge. In the midst of this spiritual revival, science and spirituality will accommodate themselves in a new "Age of Faith." What implications does such a merger have for working with victims? Many would project a need for victim assistance providers to be better equipped to help victims deal with spiritual issues. Perhaps more important is the need for people who deal with victimization concerns, death and dying, and the random nature of crime to explore how they themselves resolve the eternal questions of existence and its consequences.

Crime and Violence

Crime in the United States has been on the decline. However, the most recent data from the redesigned National Crime Victimization Survey reported by the Bureau of Justice Statistics (1995) indicated that levels of certain completed, violent crimes have been declining or holding steady, whereas levels of attempted victimizations have generally been increasing. In addition, victimization levels and rates between 1992 and 1993 showed little change. There were 43.6 million criminal victimizations in 1993, of which 10.9 million were rapes, robberies, or assaults. There were 32 million property crimes among the almost 100 million households in the United States.

These facts do not contain much hope for a nonviolent society in the near future. Furthermore, many would argue that brutality and mass violence is on the increase. In the last 20 years, there have been between 10 and 30 mass murders each year (incidents in which more than four people were killed at one time). Bystander injuries and deaths have increased 400% in the last decade. Carjackings occur 30,000 times each year. Workplace violence has risen by about 20%. The rise in juvenile crime is significant. Arrests for violent crime by youths under 18 have risen over 90% in the last 20 years. From 1982 to 1992, the number of 13-, 14-, and 15-year-olds who were arrested for murder doubled. The impact of such crimes goes far beyond the offenders and their immediate victims. A 1992 study of South Side Chicago high school students between the ages of 13 and 18 reported that 47% had seen a stabbing, 61% had witnessed a shooting, 45% had seen someone killed, and 25% had experienced all three. By the year 2005, the number of 15- to 19-year-olds will have increased by 25%. Hence the potential for violent chaos throughout our nation is imminent (Bureau of Justice Statistics, 1995).

"Ordinary" crime is only one aspect in the threat of future violence. Many futurists believe the world is on the edge of war. Ramsey (1993) identified four challenges to world peace: regional, ethnic conflict (the sovereignty of nearly 200 nation-states will be challenged by some 4,000 ethnic minorities); trafficking in arms and engineers; regional pariah regimes (such as Iraq's Saddam Hussein and Serbia's Slobodan Milosevic); and the focused economic grievance syndrome. Chief among the potential global conflicts are a sixth Arab-Israeli war; a fourth India-Pakistan war; a civil war in Russia; a second war for Africa; the third Gulf war; the second Korean war; the Sandinista war; the war for Transylvania; a war involving Egypt, Libya, and the Sudan; and a Sino-Russian war (Dupuy, 1993).

These grave predictions on both domestic and international fronts suggest that violence prevention must become an integral part of all victim assistance programs. Research should continue on how to eradicate violent behavior, and increased education about violence is also necessary. Community-wide partnerships between public and private organizations and among individuals must be cultivated at the local level to address poverty, racism, and illiteracy. Those partnerships should work together to provide immediate assistance to victims as well as assistance, wherever possible, to restore offenders to healthy social functioning.

The potential for world war has caused some people to call for an international crisis response capability, similar to the national and state crisis teams in the United States, to assist a permanent world peacekeeping force. Such teams should include trained crisis interveners and individuals experienced in facilitating victim-offender dialogue and community restoration.

Trauma

With so many profound changes facing us over the next decade, it should not be surprising that our understandings of crisis, trauma, and appropriate responses will also change.

Over the last decade, we have broadened our understanding of the concept of trauma in several important ways. Although this understanding will continue as a foundation for victim assistance providers, the future is likely to address additional questions, such as:

- To what extent is the impact of crisis and trauma transmitted intergenerationally?
- Does repeated exposure to chronic crime and violence establish trauma as a "normal state" from which victims may find it difficult to disengage?
- Is the state of crisis or trauma contagious?
- To what extent are crisis reactions manifested differently among cultures?
- Can crisis and supportive counseling techniques be successfully adapted to new technologies that allow for remote interventions through telecommunication?
- Can crisis reactions be ameliorated through interactive computer interventions?

Transnationalism

Many different governing schemes have been projected for our future world: a gradual breakdown of the nation-state into smaller and smaller fragments so that peoples in specific geographic areas govern themselves on the basis of their own specific needs; a realignment of nation-states; a One World Government in which the world is united under one order, one law, and one set of values; or a network of nations that allows each nation to be integrated into the global whole and yet remain an independent entity and substantially self-reliant. But no matter what form governance takes in the next century, there is one sure projection: Responses to crime and violence will be driven by international forces that transcend national barriers. It is likely that victim service programs will become a part of international networks of assistance. Victim assistance will become a foundation for transnational responses to crime and other severe crises in the world. Crime not only will be

redefined in terms of future technologies but will need to sort out reciprocal agreements and a mutuality of process such that victims in one country may be treated similarly to victims in another country. More international tribunals may take precedence in areas addressing global corporate crime, environmental crime, drug trafficking, and miniwars. The United Nations may serve as a leadership body in this effort, but international cooperation and understanding will be essential.

Justice

Finally, it can be expected that the U.S. justice system will be radically changed. The victims' rights movement has already pushed the system in the direction of greater participation by victims and witnesses, and some people predict that a completely new paradigm of justice will emerge, with victims as a third party. This possibility becomes more likely as states continue to pass constitutional amendments and as victim advocates push harder for federal constitutional amendments on behalf of victims' rights.

The goals of justice will also be reexamined. The debate over "restorative community justice" versus "retributive justice" (or restitutive justice) will continue until the public feels that justice is indeed being served. More thought is being given to whether the system should focus on individual justice or social justice. Many of the ethical questions I raised earlier are also questions that affect the distribution of justice. Similarly, the mechanisms that search for truth and justice may be reinvented. The call for community involvement in the justice process may create direct citizen involvement in law enforcement activities, case prosecutions, judicial functions, and the sanctioning and monitoring of those who violate the social order. New responses to such violations include not only those invested in new technologies but a return to historical sanctions such as shaming, exile, or isolation. The role of victims and victim advocates in this redefinition of justice and the justice system will be critical if the new system is to continue to improve responses to victims.

Conclusion

The aftermath of the Oklahoma City bombing of April 19, 1995, revealed what the victims' movement has accomplished for victims of crime in the United States. The event was also a vivid example of the movement's limits. Although crisis responders were quickly dispatched to the scene, there was clearly a need for more knowledge of how to cope with the immediate and long-term effects of the crime. Although the survivors will have opportunities for participation in the criminal justice process, victim service coordinators will be challenged to accommodate families of the 169 who died and the hundreds of others who were injured or who witnessed the destruction. Although state victim compensation was offered in Oklahoma, the funds available at the time could not possibly meet the needs of all the victims of that one crime. And perhaps, most important, the tragedy was testimony to our inability to control and prevent violence in our midst. These issues and how we address them will determine the fate of the victims' movement.

References

American Psychiatric Association. (1980). *Diagnostic and statistical manual of mental disorders* (3rd ed.). Washington, DC: Author.

American Psychiatric Association. (1994). *Diagnostic and statistical manual of mental disorders* (4th ed.). Washington, DC: Author.

Attorney General's Task Force on Family Violence. (1984, September). *Final report.* Washington, DC: Government Printing Office.

Attorney General's Task Force on Violent Crime. (1981). *Final report.* Washington, DC: U.S. Dept. of Justice.

Bard, M. (1970). *Training police as specialists in family crisis intervention.* Washington, DC: Government Printing Office.

Bard, M., & Sangrey, D. (1979). *Crime victims handbook.* New York: Basic Books.

Booth v. Maryland, 482 U.S. 497 (1987).

Bureau of Justice Statistics. (1995). *Criminal victimization in the United States.* Washington, DC: U.S. Department of Justice, Bureau of Justice Statistics.

Burgess, A., & Holmstrom, L. (1974). Rape trauma syndrome. *American Journal of Psychiatry, 131,* 981-986.

Burgess, A., & Holmstrom, L. (1978). *The victim of rape.* New York: John Wiley.

Dupuy, T. N. (1993). *Future wars: The world's most dangerous flashpoints.* New York: Warner.

Fry, M. (1957, July 7). Justice for victims. *Observer.*

Linden, Eugene. (1996, July 8). Global fever. *Time Magazine,* Vol. 148, No. 2, pp. 56-57.

Mendelsohn, B. (1956, July-September). The victimology. *Etudes Internationales de Psycho-Sociologie Criminelle,* 239-244.

Mendelsohn, B. (1963, May-June). The origins of doctrine of victimology. *Excerpta Criminologica, 3*(3).

Naisbett, J. *Megatrends: Ten new directions transforming our lives.* New York: Warner.

Nelan, B. (1993). Not quite so welcome any more. *Time Magazine,* Special Issue, Vol 142, No. 21.

Payne v. Tennessee, 501 U.S. 808 (1991).

President's Task Force on Victims of Crime. (1982, December). *Final report.* Washington, DC: Government Printing Office.

Ramsey, R. (1993, April). World systems, challenges: 1993-2025. *Officer.*

U.S. Bureau of the Census. (1996). *Current population report, special studies: 65 plus in the United States.* Washington, DC: Government Printing Office.

Victims of Crime Act, 42 U.S.C. § 10601 et seq. (1984).

von Hentig, H. (1948). *The criminal and his victim: Studies in the sociology of crime.* New Haven, CT: Yale University Press.

Walker, L. (1978). *The battered woman.* Harper & Row.

Young, M. (1988). The crime victims' movement. In F. Ochberg (Ed.), *Post-traumatic therapy and victims of violence.* New York: Brunner-Mazel.

Young, M. (1990). Victim assistance in the United States: The end of the beginning. *International Review of Victimology, 1,* 181-199.

12   Provision for Victims in an International Context

MIKE MAGUIRE

JOANNA SHAPLAND

The main purpose of this chapter is to provide an international perspective on issues that are discussed elsewhere in the book primarily in the context of the United States. The central focus will be on Europe, although countries in other continents will be referred to in passing. Even with this limitation, it is difficult in a short chapter to cover the huge range of developments in rights and services for crime victims that have taken place in recent years. A few general statements may be made with a fair degree of confidence. For example, it would not be a gross exaggeration to speak of a sea change in attitudes toward victims in most European countries, whereby the rhetoric, at least, of the major relevant agencies—police, prosecutors, courts, social services, and policy makers in the criminal justice field—now regularly includes concern for the interests of victims. Yet at the same time there are major differences between countries and between agencies in the levels of resources

committed, in the relative priority attached to particular aspects of victimization, and in the extent to which genuine changes in practice have been effected. All we can do here is to convey a broad outline of what has been occurring and to pick out for special attention a few particularly significant or interesting developments.

The shape of the chapter is as follows. After a few general remarks about the varying social and legal contexts in which concern about victims has grown, we move to a discussion of specific developments. We begin with a brief overview of the progress made by voluntary organizations, particularly in the area of victim support, in countries where these have played a leading role. We then consider developments in compensation to victims by the state and by offenders, moving to more general comments on victims' services and victims' rights within the criminal justice system. We end with an assessment of the role and importance of research in encouraging change and with some predictions about the future.

Similarities and Differences

Internationally, the "victims' movement" has been in serious motion for less than 20 years, although there were isolated earlier developments (such as the introduction of state compensation for victims of violent crime in Britain and in New Zealand in the 1960s). Indeed, in most Western countries, the real thrust has occurred only over the past 10 years. In Europe, victims received a considerable boost from a number of important initiatives in the mid-1980s, including a Convention and two important Recommendations by the Council of Europe in 1983, 1985, and 1987 (on, respectively, state compensation, the position of the victim in the criminal justice system, and assistance to victims). Before this, in only three countries—the United Kingdom, Germany, and the Netherlands—had victims' issues achieved any prominence. More recently, many former Eastern bloc and Third World countries have begun to give serious attention to victims, a key impetus deriving from the United Nations Declaration on Basic Principles of Justice for Victims of Crime and Abuse of Power (Shapland, 1989). The reasons for the recent, unprecedented growth of interest in crime victims across the world are not totally clear, but its primary causes are related to public reactions against increasing crime rates, combined with increasingly impersonal, uncaring, and ineffective criminal justice systems and growing awareness of the serious impact of crime on individuals.

Yet despite wide agreement about the basic nature of the problem, responses to it have varied considerably. At a very broad level, it is possible to draw some fundamental distinctions between the victims' movement in Europe and in the United States. For example, from the early 1970s onwards, many provic-

tim groups in the United States have adopted an aggressive, overtly political and campaigning approach, with an emphasis on the *rights* of victims—if necessary, at the expense of offenders' rights—and a commitment to promoting new legislation to secure them; some, indeed, have campaigned for tougher sentences, including capital punishment (Davis, Kumeuther, & Connick, 1984; Fattah, 1986; Hudson, 1984; Lamborn, 1986; National Organization for Victim Assistance [NOVA], 1985). In Europe, by contrast, few major groups have taken an analogous approach. There tends to be greater consensus within each country, with the rhetoric of government departments, police forces, and the most influential voluntary organizations alike referring much more often to desirable improvements in *services* for victims than to victims' rights or radical legislation on their behalf (as has, e.g., been the position of the main English and Welsh victim support agency, Victim Support; see Maguire, 1991; Maguire & Corbett, 1987; Mawby & Gill, 1987; van Dijk, 1988). There are also fewer "self-help" groups formed by victims of particular types of crime; the typical victim organization in the major European countries is a generalist service provider, staffed largely by volunteers with some trained, professional guidance and assistance.

Of course, there are exceptions to this pattern: Many American groups are totally service oriented, and some in Europe (e.g., Justice for Victims in England and to a lesser extent the Weisser Ring in Germany) project a strong, campaigning, "antioffender" profile. Nevertheless, it is a fair generalization. The reasons behind the contrast are complex but clearly include differences in legal and political tradition and in the overall volume and seriousness of crime (see also Joutsen, 1991). Another major difference—the much greater focus on the criminal justice system in North America, typified by the prominence of victim-witness assistance schemes—can likewise be explained by American victims' lack of cooperation with their court system and progressive disillusionment with its well-publicized defects (Elias, 1983). Hitherto, this problem has been perceived as less serious in Europe, though there are signs of change, including the emergence of small campaigning groups and increasing debate about such issues within Victim Support (see, e.g., Brew, 1993).

Yet although it may be useful to draw broad comparisons of this kind between America and Europe, it is also evident that, as we shall illustrate, differences between individual European countries in their social and legal traditions have helped to produce some very different perceptions of and responses to victims' issues. In Germany, for instance, it has long been the practice in certain categories of criminal trials to allow the presence of an extra lawyer (the *Nebenklager*) to argue the case for the victim, whereas in Britain, the victim has traditionally been treated simply as another witness with no right to an audience. Again, each country has its own traditions of social and medical services, ranging from the highly developed welfare state in Sweden and the Netherlands to the much lower level of public provision for social or medical needs that obtains in most Mediterranean countries. Although the flow of information and discussion between European countries about victims' issues has increased enormously, although international initiatives are under way, and although some standardization of practice is already occurring, basic differences of the above kind will continue to work against the development of anything resembling a homogeneous victims' movement across Europe.

In the last 10 years in Europe, there are signs that the initial enthusiasm and political will to create change in provisions for victims has subsided, perhaps because of the growing institutionalization and acceptance as "mainstream" of certain services, such as victim support and assistance, or information about the progress of cases in court. In general, however, the services being institutionalized are not those perceived as threatening to the accepted model of criminal justice services: They are support, information, and assistance, rather than victims' rights in court, compensation, or alternative forms of dispute resolution.

This general picture of absorption of some victim requirements coupled with resistance to more far-reaching reforms we consider to be true of provisions for victims in general. For certain specific groups of victims, however, major changes have come about, particularly in relation to prosecution and court procedures. So, for example, it is now possible for child victims (especially child victims of sexual or physical abuse) in England and Wales to give videotaped evidence and for victims in sensitive cases (child victims, some adult victims of sexual assaults, terrorist cases) to give evidence behind a screen erected in the courtroom (Davies, 1991; Morgan & Zedner, 1992). Legislative provisions to limit the questioning of sexual assault victims in court have been enacted in England and Wales and in Germany (Joutsen, 1991). Outside the courtroom, concern about victims of racial attacks in England and Wales and in Germany has led to the development of policing tactics designed to show a high police profile in areas where any such attacks have occurred and to reassure ethnic minority communities. It is noteworthy that many of these more recent initiatives for change in both criminal justice and support policies have been influenced by groups representing specific kinds of victims, rather than stemming from the generic victim associations.

Another very recent development in Europe has been a growing awareness of the extent and cost of commercial victimization. Spurred by the initial commercial crime surveys carried out in the Netherlands[1] and by an increasing emphasis on cost reduction in the face of recession, as well as by concern about the safety of staff, business has begun to devote much higher priority to evaluating its risks, costs, and security measures. This has brought a different emphasis in relation to victim issues: a risk management philosophy, a public health model in relation to health and safety issues facing employees (with associated duties on employers and guidance for managers and staff), and, above all, an emphasis on prevention rather than the detection and prosecution of offenders (Shapland, 1995). It has combined with the increased stress on crime prevention in crime policy generally to bring to the fore the need for the provision of crime prevention advice to victims. Here again, however, the developments fit well with the tradition of victim support and assistance rather than of victims' rights—and again, much reliance is being placed on essentially voluntary agencies to help employers develop appropriate models for victim care.

The Voluntary Movement and Victim Support

Voluntary groups set up expressly to assist victims of crime are now in existence in virtually every European country. "Generalist" support services provided by volunteers have reached a particularly high level of organization in two countries, Great Britain and Germany, where pioneering groups formed in the early 1970s paved the way for the growth of Victim Support (formerly called the National Association of Victims Support Schemes) and the Weisser Ring, respectively. Both are already major organizations with continuing influence on government policy toward victims, and Victim Support in particular has promoted a model for the support of victims that has influenced the development of schemes in several other countries—notably, in the Netherlands, Ireland, France, and Sweden.

More specialized services are provided by other voluntary groups in many countries—notably, the counseling and assistance from rape crisis centers to victims of sexual assault and the shelter offered to battered women by women's refuges. Another important development, of which there are examples in France,

Spain, and Italy, is the voluntary provision, by suitably qualified groups, of legal advice and assistance to victims, principally in the area of claims or actions for compensation.

In this section, we explore some ramifications of one of the major issues currently affecting and preoccupying voluntary groups. The main voluntary organizations in the European countries that pioneered generalist services to victims—the UK, the Netherlands, and Germany—have all experienced such massive increases in demand for their services that they have been forced into major expansion and reorganization. This has created practical necessities for much greater financial resources and for more efficient management that have had important consequences for the whole character and ethos of the victim support movement. Moreover, countries that have come late to the provision of victim services by volunteers (notably, France and Switzerland) have tended to begin operations at a much more sophisticated and more centralized level of organization and with more secure funding—conditions that, again, have greatly influenced their basic philosophy and approach. The results have varied between countries, but there is no doubting the general trend.

One of the most significant consequences has been what van Dijk (1988) has called the "institutionalization of victim support." This term can be applied both literally and metaphorically. In more and more European countries, funding for the management and administration of voluntary schemes has come from central government. Although direct government interference in the way they operate is unusual, there is clearly a degree of informal control: organizations dependent on the renewal of short-term grants not only are accountable for how they have spent public money but tend to listen carefully to their funders' general policy wishes. Moreover, the need to "keep their own house in order" tends to hasten any trend toward centralization and bureaucratization.

Perhaps the most interesting situation is that in Great Britain, where the National Association of Victims Support Schemes, which had struggled financially for several years, was suddenly in 1986 presented with a government grant of £9 million for the next 3 years. Those sums have increased in subsequent years, to be over £10 million in 1995. The advent of significant government financial support is, however, double-edged. It has enabled the organization to transform its organizational character at the local level, with paid coordinators and an increasing emphasis on a "professional service," but it has also made the provision of victim support and the very survival of Victim Support increasingly dependent on securing agreement to annual renewals of this funding (Corbett & Maguire, 1988; National Association of Victims Support Schemes, 1988; Russell, 1990). It does not encourage overt criticism of government policy or easy adoption of experimental models of service delivery.

Victim support in Britain began very definitely as a community-based, grassroots movement. Between 1974 and 1979, it consisted of no more than 30 independent voluntary groups, mostly funded on a shoestring by charitable donations and often administered virtually single-handed from a coordinator's own home. The names and addresses of victims, mainly of burglary or other crimes of low to medium seriousness, were passed to the coordinator by the police a day or so after the event, and volunteers were dispatched to visit them with offers of emotional or practical support. Any problems the volunteers were unable to deal with were, in theory, referred on to agencies better equipped to handle them, although in practice it was often difficult to arrange this (Maguire & Corbett, 1987). Although most of the early schemes operated according to this basic model, there were wide variations in, for example, their commitment to training, the kinds of victim they took on, and their concepts of service delivery. Moreover, they were fiercely independent and proud of their own mode of operation.

Even after 1979, when the National Association (later called Victim Support) was formed by a group of these schemes, many remained reluctant to allow any common standards or conditions to be imposed on them: The central office could suggest basic policies and minimum standards in matters such as training, referral policy, record-keeping, or management structure but had few effective sanctions against those who ignored them. Yet over the years, Victim Support gradually achieved a stronger influence over local schemes through giving standard advice and information to new groups as they were formed, through conferences and newsletters, and through its own higher profile in the media. This influence was enhanced above all by the new government funding. Schemes receive grants (mainly to pay coordinators, whose tasks now border on the Herculean in high-crime areas) only if they meet certain centrally agreed standards and requirements (Russell, 1990).

At the same time, Victim Support itself was drawn closer to government, and there are fairly frequent meetings and discussions between senior Victim Support staff and both Home Office officials and government ministers. Although Victim Support has taken few public stances on controversial issues involving victims, there is no doubt that it is both increasingly influenced by, and influential on, policy making behind the scenes.

What effect has this institutionalization been having on schemes at a local level? First of all, committees have been pushed to improve their systems of management and record keeping, and volunteer visitors are being asked to undergo more training and to meet higher standards generally. Second, schemes are being asked to handle much more serious crime than has been the general practice in the past. Whereas the bread-and-butter work of volunteers has traditionally been single visits to burglary victims, most schemes are now assisting victims of rape and other very serious assaults, as well as the families of murder victims. This work often involves long-term support, which requires a much more professional approach, some training in counseling techniques, and expert backup for the volunteers—a much more costly endeavor that is difficult to fund. In addition, the organization has now made a major commitment to the operation of Crown Court Witness Services, providing support services to victims and witnesses at the higher courts, throughout England and Wales (Raine & Smith, 1991; Wright, 1995). Although these developments are obviously beneficial to victims, there is some worry among local schemes that they are gradually becoming professionalized to the extent that they could lose the very aspect of their character that contributed most to their rapid growth in earlier years—their voluntary spirit or community base.

These issues are most acute in Britain, partly because of the relatively early and independent development of victim services and partly because of its distinctive voluntary tradition: Britain has aptly been described as a nation of volunteers. A similar debate has been taking place in the Netherlands, although the effects have been less dramatic because several schemes there have employed professionals for many years. In Germany, the Weisser Ring, which maintains over 200 offices, has remained nominally independent of government funding, but the fact that it has for many years been allocated large amounts of money from fines paid by offenders in lieu of imprisonment, and that a large proportion of its membership is made up of ex-police officers and other criminal justice professionals, makes its status as a grassroots organization questionable. Although it, too, has expanded significantly, it has always had a firm organizational base (Eppenstein, 1991). Moreover, because a much smaller proportion of its work is concerned with the emotional support of victims (unlike in Britain, where personal visits to homes and the provision of a "listening ear" form the keystones of victim support work) and because its main services lie in the fields of legal advice and compensation, "pro-

fessionalization" has not been experienced as traumatic to anything like the same extent.

Perhaps the most fortunate country in the above respect is France, which has achieved a good balance of professional and voluntary input without any major dissension, largely because in coming late to the field, it learned from others' experiences. France had little tradition of victim support before 1983, when a central organization was set up under generous funding from the Ministry of Justice with the express purpose of developing (and hence directing) victim support across the country. By the end of the 1980s, there were over 150 local schemes in existence, with a 10-to-1 ratio of volunteers to professionals.

Finally, on the subject of generalist victim assistance, it should be mentioned that although one may speak of Britain, the Netherlands, and Germany as the pioneers in victim services in Europe, and France and some Scandinavian countries as the "second wave" benefiting from lessons learned by the pioneers, there are still several countries—notably, those around the Mediterranean—in which there are few, or no, groups in existence with the specific objective of assisting crime victims. On the other hand, as we discuss below, some of these countries are more geared in other ways toward victims' interests: for example, in legal provisions facilitating the recovery of damages from offenders.

We end this section with a few comments about organizations that have seen less of the limelight recently but have been very influential in bringing the needs of particular categories of victims to public attention. Rape crisis centers and battered women's refuges, which have in most countries been run mainly by feminist groups, provide an important alternative model of victim assistance to that of the increasingly institutionalized, generalist organizations. They are usually fully independent of, and sometimes antagonistic toward, the police, encouraging victims to telephone them directly, even if they have not officially reported an offense. (By contrast, victim support schemes in Britain, for example, rely almost exclusively on the police for the names and addresses of victims, whom they then contact with an offer of assistance.) Further, rape crisis centers often attempt to "radicalize" victims (or "survivors," as they prefer to call sexually assaulted women in Britain) at the same time as assisting them. They do not normally form national associations, and few receive government funding of any consequence, so their voice is heard less often now than that of their wealthier counterparts. Nevertheless, they have achieved a great deal in changing attitudes among police officers, sentencers, and the general public—for instance, in reducing the amount of victim blaming by judges in rape cases and in securing better treatment for women who report sexual assaults to the police. On the other hand, it seems that in European countries, they have been less in the vanguard of the victims' movement as a whole than has been the case in the United States (where some would argue that they began the whole thing).

State Compensation for Violent Crime

As the messages of the victims' movement have influenced public consciousness and hence the political arena, ministers have looked around for measures that they can introduce to show their government's willingness to support victims. One of the most obvious measures is state compensation for victims of violent crime. It is attractive because it is normally nationally introduced, administered, and controlled and because it seems to give clear benefit to some of the most stereotypically deserving victims—victims of violent crime. In most countries, it has required legislation for its introduction. This is also an attractive option for states; legislation is something they can themselves control (as opposed to the amorphous diffusing of support networks throughout the voluntary sector), and legislation, once passed, can thereafter be cited as a positive action by government. Given the striking popularity of victim issues throughout the political spectrum (Phipps, 1988; van Dijk, 1984b), passing the legislation rarely poses many problems. The main disadvantages of state compensation schemes, as far as governments are concerned, are their high initial cost and the relative inability of government to control cost and take-up thereafter. The first has deterred some countries from starting and has led to restrictions in others. The second is becoming increasingly apparent in the older schemes.

The first state compensation scheme in Europe was the Criminal Injuries Compensation Scheme and Board (CICB) set up in England, Wales, and Scotland in 1964. This was created, in a peculiarly British way, not by legislation but by administrative fiat, and was run by a board of senior advocates under the supervision of the Home Office and Scottish Office. It was originally created as a very wide-ranging scheme, providing compensation to any victim of violent crime (or person assaulted in the course of preventing crime) of any nationality who was victimized or injured in Britain. It remains one of the most generous in Europe, paying out well over £100 million annually (CICB, 1994). Even so, it has come in for intense criticism from victims' organizations and opposition from political parties, particularly over the fact that although legislation was enacted to place the scheme on a statutory footing, this has not been implemented. The potential cost to the state of an open-ended commitment alarmed the government, which has further stirred up hostility by, in 1995, trying to introduce a tariff based on types of injury rather than consideration of the damages in individual cases. The political debates on this issue should not be seen as peculiar to the victims issue; they mirror the attempts in many Western countries to pull back the boundaries of the state and decrease state costs. However, it must be recognized that the costs of provision for victims remain minuscule in relation to other criminal justice costs.[2]

State compensation schemes are now operative in Austria, Belgium, Canada, Denmark, Great Britain, Germany, Finland, France, Ireland, Luxembourg, the Netherlands, Northern Ireland, Norway, Poland, Sweden, and the United States (Joutsen, 1991). The Convention of the Council of Europe on state compensation for victims of violent crime (Council of Europe, 1983) set out minimum provisions that it recommended member states to provide. It seeks to ensure that victims resident in or working in a state will be compensated by that state (thereby getting over the problem of migrant workers). It has currently been ratified by four member states (Denmark, Luxembourg, the Netherlands, and Sweden) and signed by many more. The convention was agreed on with little dispute, after having been produced by a committee in record time (Tsitsoura, 1989), and delays in ratification seem largely to be for budgetary reasons.

A comprehensive scheme is costly, as is shown by the example of the CICB. In addition to its advocacy of a tariff scheme, the British government has further limited the costs of the scheme by setting a minimum limit for claims to succeed, by restricting payment for clothing, spectacles, and so forth damaged in the course of violent crime, and by ensuring that any payments of compensation by offenders are deducted from the scheme's award. However, the relatively small numbers of offenders who are prosecuted and convicted, combined with their impecunious state, sets an intrinsic limit to the amount that can be raised from offenders to offset costs (probably less than 10% overall).

Miers (1983, 1990) argued that state compensation is essentially a symbolic act by governments to show their concern for victims, but with little real intention of following it through with hard cash. Though this seems to be true in some parts of the world, it demands qualification in Europe. The Convention may be said to fall into this category (rapid passage, little implementation), but the fact remains that where European countries have set up schemes, they have attracted applications and made awards.

What is clearly pertinent, however, is Miers's other assessment of the implications of the symbolic nature of state compensation—that awards define the kinds of victims seen as deserving by states. Most states—and the Convention—allow for awards to be reduced or refused if victims are not truly "innocent" victims: that is, if they have a criminal record (even if this is not directly linked to the victimization), have contributed to the crime through provocation, or have not helped the police quickly and without protest. Several studies have cast doubt on the number of victims who are enabled to apply to state compensation schemes, stating that many victims are not aware of the schemes' existence (the schemes may not publicize themselves very well because of fears about cost) and that the schemes exclude victims who do not fit the political stereotype of the "innocent victim" (Eppenstein, 1991; Shapland, Willmore, & Duff, 1985; Villmow, 1991). These illustrate the difference between governmental and victim perceptions of such compensation. Victims see it (quite correctly) as a judgment by the state on the worth of their claim and their status as victim. But the state and the law's view of incidents and violence as black and white with a clear offender and a clear victim does not match up with real life or with victims' perceptions of situations. Real incidents are often muddy shades of grey, with no "ideal victim" (Christie, 1986) to be found. Disillusionment is to be found in the mismatch.

Though there are good commentaries on the setting up and procedures of the different state compensation schemes (see HEUNI, 1989; Joutsen, 1987; Miers, 1978, 1990), research into the operation of the schemes and the reactions of victims is rarer. Results of studies in Britain (Shapland et al., 1985) and the Netherlands (Cozijn, 1984) parallel those of Elias (1983) on the New York and New Jersey Boards. In Britain, in the early 1980s, awards were given to most victims who applied, and delays were running at less than 1 year. Victims were in general satisfied with the operation of the board, but their experiences did not affect their attitudes toward other parts of the criminal justice system (Shapland et al., 1985). More recently, delays have increased, and there are signs of increasing dissatisfaction with the paper-based, centralized system. In the Netherlands, the procedures are very bureaucratic, require the participation of lawyers, and ensure delays of over 2 years before awards are made. There is great dissatisfaction with the operation of the scheme, such that victim support associations are not recommending it to victims (van Dijk, 1989). Victims who have been through the scheme have been found to be more dissatisfied with the criminal justice system than those who never applied (Cozijn, 1984). Most important of all, in both countries, it seems that victims would prefer compensation from offenders to state compensation, even if this meant that they did not receive full compensation (due to the limited means of offenders; Maher & Docherty, 1988; Newburn & De Peyrecave, 1988; Shapland et al., 1985; van Dijk, 1984a).

Compensation From Offenders

Compensation from offenders can occur by means of three different models in Europe: the *partie civile* procedure, the award of a compensation order as part of a sentence against the offender, and restitution made informally or as part of a diversion arrangement by the prosecution. The first two models have tended to be seen as mutually exclusive in jurisprudential terms, so that one country has favored one and one another, though the Netherlands is currently considering introducing compensation orders while retaining the possibility of using *partie civile*.

The *Partie Civile* Model

In the *partie civile* model, the victim pursues a civil claim against the offender at the same time and in the same proceedings as the criminal trial. It is active in countries with continental law jurisprudence, in particular, France, Austria, and Germany and also, to a lesser extent, the Netherlands. The advantages for the victim include the fact that he or she is an officially recognized participant in the trial so that information regarding charges, court dates and so forth must be sent to the victim. In most countries, questioning by the victim or the victim's advocate is restricted to matters affecting damages, though the German *Nebenklage* procedure, available over a range of relatively minor offenses, allows for the victim to become, in effect, an ancillary prosecutor with wide-ranging powers of questioning and commentary on the trial and sentence.

There are several disadvantages. In some countries, there are very low limits on the amounts of damages that can be awarded under this procedure (though there have been moves in several countries to raise these). Typically, no mechanism is provided for enforcement, so the victim is forced to fall back on civil distraint procedures, which are slow and relatively ineffective. In some countries, to be a *partie civile,* the victim must attend all the relevant sessions, which imposes an impossible burden for victims who are working or have small children. And finally, in common with all compensation mechanisms, there is a problem of victims knowing about the procedures, so that they have low take-up rates. In France, leaflets explaining all the procedures are available at police stations, and victim support associations will give aid and advice. The first victim support scheme in Spain (at Valencia) has also adopted this as its chief role. Nonetheless, use of the *partie civile* is low in all countries in which research has been undertaken (France, Germany, the Netherlands; HEUNI, 1989). In the Netherlands, for example, compensation was awarded to the victim in only 7% of cases in which there was a civil trial (Wemmers & Zeilstra, 1991). Similarly, an evaluation of the *partie civile* procedure in Austria has shown that only a minority of victims (primarily property crime victims) take advantage of their rights under this procedure (such as looking at the file or presenting information to the court), primarily because judges fail to give proper instructions to the lawyers involved or information to victims (Kraintz, 1991). It is now thought unlikely that the mechanism can be reformed to provide an adequate avenue for compensation from offenders (due to the intrinsic problems of using civil procedures, which are most suitable for wealthy or institutional victims, for victims of crime, who are relatively poor and legally ill informed). Countries are increasingly looking with interest at the compensation order model or at mediation or compensation paid at an earlier prosecutorial stage.

Compensation Orders

Compensation orders were first introduced in England and Wales under the 1972 Criminal Justice Act. They permitted the sentencer to award compensation for any loss, damage, or injury suffered by any identifiable victim of crime as part of the sentence, though such compensation, like all financial penalties, had to take into account the means of the offender. They were extended in the 1982 Criminal Justice Act such that in the case of impoverished offenders, they could form the sole sentence and such that if both a fine and compensation were to be ordered, the compensation would take priority. Similar provisions were enacted in Scotland in 1980. Since the 1988 Criminal Justice Act in England and Wales, sentencers have to give reasons if they do not order compensation in a case with an identifiable victim (though there have not been any appeals when this has not happened). Compensation may be ordered for immaterial damages (pain and suffering, solatium, etc.) as well as for material loss.

The idea of compensation found immediate favor with magistrates in England and Wales, and the latest figures show awards in 57% of criminal damage cases.[3] Initially, there were problems with injury cases, because sen-

tencers were unclear how to quantify awards (Newburn, 1987, 1988; Shapland et al., 1985) and did not always think to award compensation. In fact, both research studies found that one of the principal reasons differentiating cases in which an award was made from those in which no order occurred was whether the prosecution mentioned the word *compensation* in any context. There remains the problem that sentencers are not being provided with sufficient information to enable them to quantify compensation. The amount of information on losses, injuries, and so forth that is necessary to prove the elements of the offense for conviction is much less than that needed for sentence. The move toward codification of the law, which makes convictions technically easier to obtain, has put a greater burden on sentencers (Thomas, 1978), and the information mechanisms have not responded (Shapland, 1987). This is one reason for recent government proposals to introduce forms of victim impact statements in England and Wales (following their relatively successful introduction in the United States), though this remains very controversial among lawyers, many of whom see it as significantly affecting the rights of the offender (Ashworth, 1993).

In the Crown Court in England and Wales and in the sheriffs' courts in Scotland, judges originally clearly felt greater unease about mixing what they saw as an essentially civil matter with criminal sentencing. Orders have been correspondingly less frequent (Maher & Docherty, 1988; Shapland et al., 1985). This essential ambiguity about the role of compensation in sentencing has dogged both practice and academic debate. Should it be seen as civil? Has it then a place in a procedure that is designed solely to match the punishment demanded by the state with the resources of the offender? Or should a criminal trial also address the wrong done to the victim? If so, should these needs be subordinated to the state's overall right to decide on sentence according to its perceptions of what is important? How can they be? Or is there no problem because, in fact, punishment should include compensation and because compensation, no less than the fine, should be regarded as punishment? Is then the real difficulty that we have not yet sorted out a criminal scale for compensation and that merely translating across a civil scale produced in personal accident cases is insufficient? In different countries, the extent of the jurisprudential and practical divide between civil and criminal law varies. Accordingly, so do their answers to the above questions. These are questions currently under active consideration in Germany (Hertle, 1991; Jung, 1988) and in the Netherlands.

Victims have fewer doubts about these questions. In England and Wales and in Scotland, most victims clearly approve of compensation orders made by offenders, even if the orders do not cover all their losses—even, indeed, if the payments come in the halting and uneven dribs and drabs of installments (Maher & Docherty, 1988; Newburn & De Peyrecave, 1988; Shapland et al., 1985). The national victimization survey conducted in 1984 reflected these feelings (Hough & Mayhew, 1985). Dissatisfaction arises largely if awards are derisory (for the reasons cited above) and if courts do not inform victims about the amount of the award or about the reasons for nonpayment and the means being taken for enforcement.

Restitution and Diversion

Payment of money from offender to victim—restitution or compensation—can also occur earlier in the criminal justice process. There have now been many attempts in numerous countries at setting up mediation schemes (HEUNI, 1989; Wright, 1995). Restitution may be arranged informally and may prevent any referral of the crime to the police at all. Or the police, alone or in combination with other social agencies, may supervise payment in return for dropping proceedings. Similar processes can occur with prosecutors. In all countries, it is likely that informal arrangements of

this kind operate at least in a small minority of cases, even where a strict principle of legality applies. Their disadvantage is their relative invisibility and the lack of effective remedies if they go wrong—for enforcement of payment by offenders or, indeed, for uncovering corruption among criminal justice personnel.

We now have the results of evaluation of a number of local schemes in several countries (e.g., Dignan, 1992; Kerner, Marks, & Schreckling, 1991; Nergard, 1993; Schoch & Bannenberg, 1991; Wright, 1995). The conclusions seem universal. Financial restitution figures in only a small proportion of the cases sent for mediation (the majority ending with an apology or in some contract concerning the offender's behavior). Mediation cases themselves remain very much a minority disposal in terms of the flow of criminal justice cases overall. The dominant model is still prosecution, or some form of discontinuance (such as a formal caution in England and Wales), sometimes accompanied by work with the offender—but rarely involving the victim.

More formal arrangements have tended to start with juveniles. In Britain, juvenile liaison bureaus' diversion strategies can include the payment of restitution to a victim, but this is rarely achieved. In the Netherlands, prosecutors can take into account compensation paid by the offender and require fines for certain offenses. Compulsory compensation may be introduced by this method, as opposed to at the time of sentence. In Germany, prosecutors can drop cases if compensation is paid, fines are paid to the state, or donations are made to certain charities. However, the form of the question posed to defendants and the attitudes of prosecutors have resulted in the situation that over 90% of this money is paid to the state or charity and only 10% to individual victims (HEUNI, 1989).

In general, there are three sets of issues to be addressed. First, mediation has tended to be offender oriented, with the dominant model that of changing offending behavior, not securing redress for the victim or meeting any symbolic or emotional needs of victims. Second, mediation is a discretionary way of disposing of cases within the criminal justice system. Any new discretionary option runs into the difficulty of changing prosecutors' attitudes and ensuring uniformity in practice throughout the country. Training, guidelines, and pronouncements by senior functionaries are all helpful (and are being increasingly tried, e.g., in the Netherlands). But disparities will still remain. The third issue is the inevitable lack of openness of such a system and related problems of enforcement and potential corruption—as well as the need to consult and inform victims properly. Very few schemes have devoted much attention to these kinds of due-process "rights" for victims (see Dignan, 1992). The only way around this is the establishment of formal mechanisms of rules, review, and appeal. However, in doing this, we may be in danger of reinventing all the mechanisms already set up for sentence—of recreating a sentencing system lower down the process, with police or prosecutor as judge. Would it not be better to sort out compensation at the sentencing stage?

Helping Victims to Participate in the Criminal Justice Process

There are three main ways in which victims' participation in the criminal justice system can be increased from its current very low level (where, for instance, in many countries, there are no routine mechanisms even for informing victims of the results of cases) and their satisfaction with the system improved. One is to reform criminal procedures by *instructing* professionals (police, prosecutors, court staff, etc.), through guidelines and orders, to be more sympathetic to the needs of victims. A second is to *create a climate for changes of attitudes* among those who operate the system. Here, research, victim support agencies, media publicity, and official pronouncements can all play a part. The final way is to *change procedures through legislation or administra-*

tive ordinances so that victims themselves have usable rights in the process or so that enforceable duties are placed on agencies. All three of these means have been used in Europe, but the balance to date has lain with the first two. Victims' rights have only occasionally been changed or been important in effecting change. Indeed, the whole idea of bestowing greater justiciable rights on victims has been regarded with some suspicion and occasionally horror.

The pattern of change has varied in different countries more strongly in this respect than with compensation or victim support. Partly, this reflects different legal systems. In the common-law tradition, which reaches its apogee in England and Wales, the accusatorial mode of discovering evidence has placed victims more firmly under the command of the prosecution and has made it more difficult to change procedures without affecting the experiences and rights of defendants and others. In inquisitorial jurisdictions, the use of examining magistrates to take evidence and prepare a case for trial has enabled victims to tell their story as a matter of course (France, Spain, Germany, Finland, Poland, etc.), though the Dutch Ministry of Justice has considered changing the practice whereby the police read out their statements first, to allow the victim instead to have the first word (HEUNI, 1989).

There are also cultural differences concerning victims' wish to participate. In the Netherlands, research has shown that few victims wish to attend the main trial (they will already have given their story to the prosecutor). In Germany, on the other hand, more victims express a desire to appear at the trial and to have the opportunity to challenge the defense. This is congruent with the fact that the greatest opportunity for victims to have rights to appear and speak is also to be found in Germany, under the *Nebenklage* procedure. In Finland, Aromaa (1991) has found that victims vary considerably in their desire to participate. A few want to participate in every way. A few want definitely not to take part. Most would like to avoid court procedures but do attend to make sure that their cases are dealt with properly (because of their distrust of criminal justice personnel). In France, the victim assistance movement helps victims to go through the court process. They have found that victims are now more ready and more eager to play an active role, so that more now wish to speak out in court about their experiences. This may reflect the greater support they receive, greater acceptance of victim issues by the system, or media publicity (HEUNI, 1989).

Schadler (cited in HEUNI, 1989) has queried whether it is possible to determine what victims might like if professionals' attitudes and practices were sympathetic to their needs, or whether victims' views merely reflect the cultural position of legal and court thinking in a country. However, it seems that countries are beginning to move toward an acceptance of the diversity of victim views on participation (as set out in the Recommendation of the Council of Europe, 1985) and to set up ways in which these views can be taken into account.

In all countries, it seems easier to influence police and prosecution thinking and procedures than those of court staff (see Shapland & Cohen, 1987, for the results of an English national survey and HEUNI, 1989, for the views of researchers in several European countries). Governments have agreed that police and prosecutors have duties toward victims. Acceptance of the idea that courts have duties toward victims and that judges and court administrative personnel should ensure that victim requirements are met has not yet ensued. As a result, though different methods have been adopted in different countries, all have been biased toward police and prosecution practices. It is rare to find provision of separate waiting rooms at court (HEUNI, 1989; Shapland & Cohen, 1987). Changing court procedures produces considerable controversy. But guidelines have been issued for prosecutors in the Netherlands and backed up both by training and by the institution of an ombudsperson to whom victims may appeal and who has indeed awarded damages against the Ministry of Justice if procedures have not been correctly followed. Guidance for police in the form of several Home Office circulars has been set out in England and Wales (Shapland, 1989), with corresponding advice in Scotland. Sweden and the Netherlands have training for prosecutors (Joutsen, 1991). Similar measures are being considered or introduced in most European countries.

A variation of this approach is the adoption of a Victims' Charter (England and Wales). This sets out the kinds of services victims can expect, such as to be informed of the result of the case. It is not, however, enforceable, and the levels of service are not precisely formulated.

Up to the mid-1980s, the idea of forcing change through the claiming and establishment of victims' rights was considered impractical, unlikely, and even unthinkable in most European countries, a considerable difference from the United States. There are several reasons for the difference. One is the lack of reliance on written constitutions. Another is the difficulty for individuals in bringing cases that are designed to test new rights without, in most states, provision for legal aid (though this is changing in several continental jurisdictions) or a contingency fee basis for actions. Yet another is the relative lack of vocal pressure groups for victims in Europe.

Perhaps most important is the seemingly greater paternalism in the operation of the criminal justice systems in Europe and in the ways legislation relating to them is introduced. The tradition is, once a need for change has been accepted by a profession or by an influential group reflecting professional interests within the legislature, for that group to consider how best to bring the change about itself within the administrative or legislative structures of the professions. A successful test case by an individual would be seen as a failure to anticipate the change. The difficulty is, of course, that this method of creating change is rather conservative (see Rock, 1988). Changes that fit the profession's self-image have a high chance of happening eventually. Changes that are inimical to professional self-images or that require fundamental, structural alterations can be stalled (Shapland, 1988). Yet change produced through evolution of service delivery, as opposed to individual rights, does at least mean change that may be delivered effectively and relatively evenly across the country. Change based on individual cases in which rights have been exercised can lead to patchy, limited effects.

In the late 1980s and early 1990s, the attitude toward rights for victims and enforceable duties on agencies started to change. Germany has introduced the Victim Protection Act 1986 (which came into effect in 1987). It provides, among other things, victim rights to inspect court files, to have the assistance of counsel, to improve the "adhesion" (*partie civile* type) procedure, and to protect the victim by removing the accused from the courtroom when the victim's life or physical health is in danger. Kury and Kaiser (1991), however, found that knowledge of these rights among both victims and court personnel (including judges and prosecutors) was very limited and hence that they were not being appropriately implemented. They commented—and we would agree—that "passing a law is merely the first step. If this law is not put into practice it becomes something which is idling and at most feigns progressive victim politics" (p. 610).

This is the major difficulty with rights that individuals, such as victims or witnesses, have to claim for themselves. Those individuals have a position of little power within the legal and criminal justice structures and are highly unlikely to be able to undertake test cases unless there is support from a victims' group. Unless victims' groups see themselves as in this rights-enforcing mold (and they have typically not taken this line in Europe), action will not occur. Increasing dissatisfaction with the operation of both the services and the rights model and the failure of the agencies within

the criminal justice system to provide even a base level of services for victims is, however, beginning to create some momentum for a different means of enforcing change on criminal justice. This is the idea of legally enforceable duties on agencies, which would combine the legislative/executive order input to the agency with the justiciable rights for individuals to claim damages or compel action if the service is not provided. Clearly, such duties will be resisted by government agencies because they will compel a higher standard of service. Only if political will to support victims increases (the inclusion of victims' powers to use the ombudsperson scheme in the Netherlands occurred at a time at which victim issues were politically important) are such effective means to spur change likely to emerge.

Patterns of Change for Victims

What of the future? It is very difficult to produce predictions when the history of concern over victim issues is so recent in many countries. Nonetheless, there are a few pointers.

One is the increasing institutionalization of victim issues. In Britain and France, for example, the idea of considering victim needs has now become embedded in the political way of life. Victims are not just the latest fashion— they are here to stay. In Britain, for example, ministers' speeches on most criminal justice problems are likely to contain a reference to victims—a fact that would have been unheard of only 5 years ago. In France, changes in government have not led to the abolition of the previous government's initiatives on victim assistance and support but, if anything, to their strengthening.

With permanence have come consolidation and broadening of the issues tackled. This is most clearly seen in victim assistance. As we discussed earlier, the largely volunteer-motivated and -run schemes of a few years ago in Britain are taking on a more professional ethos as their sources of funding become slightly more secure and the number of paid coordinators rises. Professionalization tends to imply a more conscious questioning of standards and philosophy, as well as a cementing of links with other agencies. As yet, however, we are not seeing the incorporation of victim support into the mainstream criminal justice response, with the victim support scheme taking its place alongside the probation service, forensic psychiatry, and police. Nor are we seeing agencies within criminal justice taking responsibility for providing victim services within their own domain (for example, separate waiting areas in courts—although Germany and England and Wales are beginning to move toward this).

Victim services have always been dogged by the question of whether they are operating for the benefit of victims (as defined by victims) or for the benefit of other groups (such as promoting the rehabilitation of offenders or making court officials' lives easier). In Europe, victims themselves have no organized voice. Unless there continues to be research on victims' own beliefs and needs, there is the danger that agencies set up for their benefit will come to serve only organizational goals. Moreover, the move back toward rehabilitation of offenders, both in Europe and in Australia and New Zealand, is leading to an increasing emphasis on diversion of offenders or changes in criminal justice procedures to allow more effective work with offenders. Are we to see victim needs in criminal justice recognized in principle, only to be frustrated by the perceived greater needs of offenders? Will this, in time, lead to a more antioffender profile on the part of victim groups, increasingly blocked in their pursuit for services already agreed in principle?

We need to bring in, at this point, the continuing development of alternative paths for offenders within criminal justice and consider the implications of this for victims. One of the most interesting developments has been the introduction of "family group conferences" in New Zealand and Australia (Braithwaite & Mugford, 1994; Morris, Maxwell, & Robertson, 1993). These involve victims, as well as families of the defendant and other community leaders, in deciding on the action to be taken as the result of an offense. Here victims are major participants. Similar kinds of schemes are starting to be developed in England and Wales. However, these are new developments. We also need to recognize that in most European countries, the traditional criminal justice system pattern of prosecution, trial, and sentence has already been supplemented by parallel paths for dealing with crimes. A substantial proportion of cases, even a majority, are being dealt with by discontinuance by police or prosecutor when the offenders are juveniles. In this instance, however, the victim may not be involved at all or may merely be informed or "consulted" by the police and prosecutor. As such parallel paths develop, we would argue that it is vital that procedures consider the implications for victims and the need for "informed consent" to be obtained, not just from offenders, but also from victims. It is important that such developments be monitored and their effects and procedures evaluated—particularly because, by their nature, they need to be locally based and often locally diverse.

In general, in fact, we would argue that research results have been crucial in the spread of consideration of victim issues and of possible remedies in Europe. Research to date has been concentrated in a few countries, notably Britain and the Netherlands, with recent surges in Germany and France. But those studies, though they may be ignored on occasion in their own land because they are seen as inappropriate to present political views, have informed debate in other countries, both directly through publications and conferences and more indirectly through their influence on the debates of the Council of Europe and the United Nations. It is now characteristic of countries thinking of expanding their repertoire of victim services to find out about research and practice in other countries with such a provision. Conferences may be held, individual academics or policy makers may make visits to other countries, and supranational documents will be consulted. The effect has been a greater catholicism of provision. Countries within Europe are now prepared to consider provisions, such as compensation orders that stem from an alien legal system. The influence of particular legal systems is waning, though services will still reflect national cultural and social differences.

This greater willingness to share and to learn from others is also sparking greater interest in forming pan-European links. There is a European Association of Victim Support Organisations. There are more links among European criminologists and legal researchers. This is not to deny the continuing relevance and influence of North American thought and practice. But there now seems to be an intermediate step between importation of an idea and its implementation: examination of its effects in another European country. Similar regional debates are going on in America, Australasia, and Africa.

Perhaps paralleling wider political developments, however, there seems in the 1990s to be less interest in worldwide discussions about how to move forward on issues affecting victims. This may well be because victim issues have moved beyond the phase of increasing awareness and the first, tentative steps at implementation of policies to support victims and address their needs, and toward a more significant implementation and routinization that has begun to touch on criminal justice. The shape of criminal justice depends on and is crucially bound up with national and legal cultures—and tends to be more resistant to homogenization than assistance and support measures. Yet in the introduction of new ideas, it is still possible for an initiative in one country (such as mediation or family conferencing) to spark experimentation in another across the globe. What is becoming very clear, however,

is that the needs of victims for respect, support, information, and consultation seem very similar everywhere. What seems far more difficult for states, communities, or criminal justice is to work out how to address those needs in practice for all victims.

Notes

1. The Netherlands undertook a survey of companies in nine business sectors in 1989 (van Dijk & van Soomeron, 1990). Calculations stemming from this indicated that half the cost of crime in the Netherlands was falling on the business sector. A similar victimization survey was carried out for a bigger sample of retail establishments in 1991 (van Dijk & van Soomeron, 1992). An International Commercial Crime Survey has been conducted in Australia, the Netherlands, England and Wales, Germany, and some other European countries in 1993-1994, and results are currently available for Australia (Walker, 1994).

2. In the Criminal Justice Audit of the British town Milton Keynes, about 1% of criminal justice system costs were devoted to victim services by the total of criminal justice agencies (state compensation payments excluded). This covered victim support and assistance, as well as policing services (Shapland, Hibbert, I'Anson, Sorsby, & Wild, 1995).

3. The high point of awarding compensation orders produced levels of over 70% awards in criminal damage cases, but the ability to award compensation, which must be proportional to the offenders' means in England and Wales, has declined with increasing unemployment among offenders, as has the rate of awarding financial penalties in sentencing generally. However, increasing confidence among sentencers in calculating amounts of compensation in assault cases has led to a significant increase in compensation orders, such that in 1993, compensation was awarded against 64% of offenders convicted of offenses against the person at the magistrates' court (Home Office, 1993).

References

Aromaa, K. (1991). Notes on the victimization experience: Interviews with victims of violence. In H. Kury & M. Kaiser (Eds.), *Victims and criminal justice*. Freiburg, Germany: Max Planck Institute.

Ashworth, A. (1993). Victim impact statements and sentencing. *Criminal Law Review*, pp. 498-509.

Braithwaite, J., & Mugford, S. (1994). Conditions of successful reintegration ceremonies: Dealing with juvenile offenders. *British Journal of Criminology, 34,* 139-171.

Brew, H. (1993). Angry victims. *Victim Support, 52,* 3-4.

Christie, N. (1986). The ideal victim. In E. A. Fattah (Ed.), *From crime policy to victim policy.* New York: Macmillan.

Corbett, C., & Maguire, M. (1988). The value and limitations of Victims Support Schemes. In M. Maguire & J. Pointing (Eds.), *Victims of crime: A new deal?* Milton Keynes, UK: Open University Press.

Council of Europe. (1983). *European Convention on the Compensation of Victims of Violent Crime.* Strasbourg, France: Author.

Council of Europe. (1985). *Recommendation No. R(85)11 of the Committee of Ministers to member states on the position of the victim in the framework of criminal law and procedure.* Strasbourg, France: Author.

Cozijn, C. (1984). *Schadefonds geweldsmisdrijven* [Criminal injuries compensation]. The Hague: Ministerie van Justitie.

Criminal Injuries Compensation Board. (1994). *Annual Report 1993-4.* London: H.M. Stationery Office.

Davies, G. (1991). Children on trial? Psychology, videotechnology and the law. *Howard Journal, 30,* 177-191.

Davis, R. C., Kumeuther, F., & Connick, E. (1984). Expanding the victim's role in the criminal court dispositional process. *Journal of Criminal Law and Criminology, 2.*

Dignan, J. (1992). Repairing the damage: Can reparation be made to work in the service of diversion? *British Journal of Criminology, 32,* 453-472.

Elias, R. (1983). *Victims of the system.* New Brunswick, NJ: Transaction.

Eppenstein, D. (1991). Weisser Ring: Lobby for victims of crime. In G. Kaiser, H. Kury, & H.-J. Albrecht (Eds.), *Victims and criminal justice.* Freiburg, Germany: Max Planck Institute.

Fattah, E. A. (1986). Prologue: On some visible and hidden dangers of victims movements. In E. A. Fattah (Ed.), *From crime policy to victim policy.* New York: Macmillan.

Hertle, D. (1991). Compensation in the context of sanctioning and victim's interest: Result of court practices and victim survey. In G. Kaiser, H. Kury, & H.-J. Albrecht (Eds.), *Victims and criminal justice.* Freiburg, Germany: Max Planck Institute.

HEUNI. (1989). *Changing victim policy: The United Nations Victim Declaration and recent developments in Europe* (HEUNI Pub. No. 16). Helsinki: Author.

Home Office. (1993). *Criminal statistics England and Wales 1992.* London: H.M. Stationery Office.

Hough, M., & Mayhew, P. (1985). *Taking account of crime: Key findings from the Second British Crime Survey* (Home Office Research Study No. 85). London: H.M. Stationery Office.

Hudson, P. S. (1984). The crime victim and the criminal justice system. *Pepperdine Law Review, 11.*

Joutsen, M. (1987). *The role of the victim of crime in European criminal justice systems* (HEUNI Pub. No. 11). Helsinki: HEUNI.

Joutsen, M. (1991). Changing victim policy: International dimensions. In G. Kaiser, H. Kury, & H.-J. Albrecht (Eds.), *Victims and criminal justice.* Freiburg, Germany: Max Planck Institute.

Jung, H. (1988). Compensation order: Ein Modell der Schadenswiedergutmachung? *Zeitschrift fur die gesamte Strafrechtswissenschaft, 99*(3).

Kerner, H.-J., Marks, E., & Schreckling, J. (1991). Implementation and acceptance of victim/offender mediation programs in the Federal Republic of Germany. In G. Kaiser, H. Kury, & H.-J. Albrecht (Eds.), *Victims and criminal justice.* Freiburg, Germany: Max Planck Institute.

Kraintz, K. (1991). The position of injured parties in the Austrian criminal procedure. In G. Kaiser, H. Kury, & H.-J. Albrecht (Eds.), *Victims and criminal justice.* Freiburg, Germany: Max Planck Institute.

Kury, H., & Kaiser, M. (1991). The victim's position within the criminal proceedings: An empirical study. In G. Kaiser, H. Kury, & H.-J. Albrecht (Eds.), *Victims and criminal justice.* Freiburg, Germany: Max Planck Institute.

Lamborn, L. (1986). The impact of victimology on the criminal law in the United States. *Canadian Community Law Journal, 8,* 23-44.

Maguire, M. (1991). The needs and rights of victims of crime. *Crime and Justice: An Annual Review of Research, 14,* 363-433.

Maguire, M., & Corbett, C. (1987). *The effects of crime and the work of Victims Support Schemes.* Aldershot, UK: Gower.

Maguire, M., & Pointing, J. (1988). *Victims of crime: A new deal?* Milton Keynes, UK: Open University Press.

Maher, G., & Docherty, C. (1988). *Compensation orders in the Scottish criminal courts* (Scottish Office Central Research Unit Papers). Edinburgh: Scottish Office.

Mawby, R. I., & Gill, M. L. (1987). *Crime victims: Needs, services and the voluntary sector.* London: Tavistock.

Miers, D. (1978). *Responses to victimisation.* Abingdon, UK: Professional Books.

Miers, D. (1983). Compensation to victims of crime. *Victimology, 8,* 204-212.

Miers, D. (1990). *Compensation for criminal injuries.* London: Butterworths.

Morgan, J., & Zedner, L. (1992). The Victims' Charter: A new deal for child victims? *Howard Journal, 31,* 294-307.

Morris, A., Maxwell, G., & Robertson, J. (1993). Giving victims a voice: A New Zealand experiment. *Howard Journal, 32,* 304-321.

National Association of Victims Support Schemes. (1988). *Victim support, annual report 1987-88.* London: Author.

Nergard, T. (1993). Solving conflicts outside the court system: Experiences with the Conflict Resolution Boards in Norway. *British Journal of Criminology, 33,* 81-94.

Newburn, T. (1987). Compensation for injury in the magistrates' courts. *Home Office Research Bulletin, 23,* 24-27.

Newburn, T. (1988). *The use and enforcement of compensation orders in magistrates' courts* (Home Office Research Study No. 102). London: H.M. Stationery Office.

Newburn, T., & De Peyrecave, H. (1988). Victims' attitudes to courts and compensation. *Home Office Research Bulletin, 25,* 18-21.

National Organization for Victim Assistance. (1985). *Victim rights and services: A legislative directory.* Washington, DC: U.S. Department of Justice.

Phipps, A. (1988). Ideologies, political parties, and victims of crime. In M. Maguire & J. Pointing (Eds.), *Victims of crime: A new deal?* (pp. 177-186). Milton Keynes, UK: Open University Press.

Raine, J., & Smith, R. (1991). *The Victim/Witness in Court Project: Report of the research programme.* London: Victim Support.

Rock, P. (1988). Governments, victims and policies in two countries. *British Journal of Criminology, 28,* 44-66.

Russell, J. (1990). *Home Office funding of Victims Support Schemes: Money well spent?* (Research and Planning Unit Paper No. 58). London: Home Office.

Schoch, H., & Bannenberg, B. (1991). Victim-offender-reconciliation in Germany: Stocktaking and criminal-political consequences. In G. Kaiser, H. Kury, & H.-J. Albrecht (Eds.), *Victims and criminal justice.* Freiburg, Germany: Max Planck Institute.

Shapland, J. (1987). Who controls sentencing? Influences on the sentencer. In D. Pennington & S. Lloyd-Bostock (Eds.), *The psychology of sentencing: Approaches to consistency and disparity.* Oxford, UK: Centre for Socio-Legal Studies.

Shapland, J. (1988). Fiefs and peasants: Accomplishing change for victims in the criminal justice system. In M. Maguire & J. Pointing (Eds.), *Victims of crime: A new deal?* Milton Keynes, UK: Open University Press.

Shapland, J. (1989). Producing change for victims in the criminal justice system: The U.K. experience. In *Changing victim policy: The United Nations Victim Declaration and recent developments in Europe* (HEUNI Publ No. 16). Helsinki: HEUNI.

Shapland, J. (1995). Preventing retail sector crimes. *Crime and Justice: An Annual Review of Research, 19.*

Shapland, J., & Cohen, D. (1987). Facilities for victims: The role of the police and the courts. *Criminal Law Review,* pp. 28-38.

Shapland, J., Hibbert, J., I'Anson, J., Sorsby, A., & Wild, R. (1995). *Milton Keynes criminal justice audit: Summary and implications.* Sheffield, UK: University of Sheffield, Institute for the Study of the Legal Profession, Faculty of Law.

Shapland, J., Willmore, J., & Duff, P. (1985). *Victims in the criminal justice system.* Aldershot, UK: Gower.

Thomas, D. (1978). Form and function in criminal law. In P. R. Glazebrook (Ed.), *Reshaping the criminal law.* London: Stevens.

Tsitsoura, A. (1989). Victims of crime: Council of Europe and United Nations instruments. In *Changing victim policy: The United Nations Victim Declaration and recent developments in Europe* (HEUNI Pub. No. 16). Helsinki: HEUNI.

van Dijk, B., & van Soomeron, P. (1990). *Bedrijfsleven en criminaliteit* [Crime in the business world]. The Hague: Directie Criminaliteitspreventie.

van Dijk, B., & van Soomeron, P. (1992). *Criminaliteit en de detailhandel* [Crime in the retail trade]. The Hague: Ministry of Justice, Directie Criminaliteitspreventie.

van Dijk, J. J. M. (1984a, October). *Public perceptions and concerns: On the pragmatic and ideological aspects of public attitudes towards crime control.* Paper presented at the British Society of Criminology Day Conference, London.

van Dijk, J. J. M. (1984b). *Compensation by the state or by the offender: The victim's perspective.* The Hague: Ministry of Justice.

van Dijk, J. J. M. (1988). Ideological trends within the victim movement: An international perspective. In M. Maguire & J. Pointing (Eds.), *Victims of crime: A new deal?* Milton Keynes, UK: Open University Press.

van Dijk, J. J. M. (1989). Recent developments in the criminal policies concerning victims in The Netherlands. In *Changing victim policy: The United Nations Victim Declaration and recent developments in Europe* (HEUNI Pub. No. 16). Helsinki: HEUNI.

Villmow, B. (1991). Victim compensation in some Western countries. In G. Kaiser, H. Kury, & H.-J. Albrecht (Eds.), *Victims and criminal justice.* Freiburg, Germany: Max Planck Institute.

Walker, J. (1994). *The first Australian national survey of crimes against businesses.* Canberra: Australian Institute of Criminology.

Wemmers, J., & Zeilstra, M. (1991). Victim policy and restitution in the Netherlands. In G. Kaiser, H. Kury, & H.-J. Albrecht (Eds.), *Victims and criminal justice.* Freiburg, Germany: Max Planck Institute.

Wright, M. (1995). Victims, mediation and criminal justice. *Criminal Law Review,* pp. 187-199.

PART III

The Criminal Justice Response

13 Victim Participation in the Criminal Justice System

DEBORAH P. KELLY

EDNA EREZ

It was not long ago that if crime victims were mentioned at all, it was usually in passing to discuss what people were really interested in: the latest grisly crime, who did it, why, and what would happen to (usually) him. The offenders were well known: the more infamous, the more indelible the names—Charles Manson, Jeffrey Dahmer, Ted Bundy. With few exceptions, the names of the victims were forgotten—if they were ever remembered. Although today, public interest in offenders is big business and dwarfs public interest in victims,[1] such inattention is no longer true of the courts and legislatures.

The federal government and virtually all states now have some form of legislation that grants procedural rights to crime victims, ranging from information about the status of their offenders' cases, through compensation and restitution, to rights to participate in the judicial process (Hall, 1991, pp. 234-235).

The National Victim Center estimates that victim-related statutes now number in the thousands.[2] Debates about crime victims have even captured the attention of the Supreme Court, prompting six much-discussed decisions in only 4 years.[3]

Although victims' rights to information about compensation, restitution, and the status of their cases generally were accepted, victims' rights to participate in the judicial process provoked heated debate. This chapter focuses on the reforms that were adopted to increase victims' participation in the criminal justice system and why, more than a decade after such reforms were adopted, passions about them still run high. First, we summarize the background from which victim participation emerged. Second, we summarize a number of the reforms that have been adopted and the varying degrees of participation allowed by each. Third, we discuss some of the legal

AUTHORS' NOTE: Both authors contributed equally to this chapter.

attacks on these participatory reforms. Fourth, we consider some arguments for and against victim participation and then discuss which side of the debate is supported by research. Finally, we offer preliminary conclusions as to the wisdom and future of victim participation in the criminal justice system.

The Evolution of Crime Victims' Role in the Judicial System

The role of victims in criminal prosecution has changed drastically—from an eye-for-an-eye system in which victims were expected to deal with their offenders directly, through a system in which the king assumed the job of punishment and kept whatever fines were imposed, to the present system, in which the state is the surrogate victim and the real victims are relegated to a role of (at best) lead witness (Zeigenhagen, 1977).

For most victims, even their role as lead witness never comes. With a system based on attrition, most cases do not result in arrest, much less prosecution (Brosi, 1979). Victims' principal role is as backup—a threat waiting in the wings if plea bargaining breaks down. Unlike their counterparts in continental legal systems (Joutsen, 1994), victims have no formal standing in the prosecution of their offenders, and until recently, victims had no say in what, if anything, would happen to their offenders. Indeed, for the most part, crime victims have no rights at all, only courtesies to be extended or withheld at the whim of the police or prosecutor. The result is a curious blend of independence and dependence such that victims have no clout as to if or how the state chooses to proceed against their assailants but the state depends completely on their cooperation, without which any chance for a conviction is dashed.

In the early 1970s, victims' roles in the criminal justice system began to improve, largely thanks to an unlikely alliance of feminists (lobbying to ease the plight of rape vic-

tims) and law-and-order groups (lobbying to "get tough" on crime). As a result of their combined efforts, criminal justice procedures were adopted to make the system more sensitive to victims' concerns. Initially, efforts focused on solutions to the economic and psychological problems that victims experienced. Victim compensation programs, the grand-daddy of victims' reforms, were adopted in all states, as well as the District of Columbia and the Virgin Islands.[4] Approximately 26 states provide for restitution. Under the Victim Witness Protection Act of 1982, in the federal system, restitution is presumed and treated like a judgment in a civil case. In *Kelly v. Robinson* (1986), the Supreme Court held that court-ordered restitution could not be evaded by declaring bankruptcy. Victim assistance programs were established to assist victims in dealing with the psychological consequences of the crime (Erez, 1989). Police departments began to train their officers about the special needs of rape victims in particular and to minimize victim-blaming behavior in general. Rape shield laws were enacted in the federal system as well as most states to limit the permissible scope of defense efforts to bring up a victim's past sexual history.

Such reforms were not motivated primarily by a newfound compassion for victims. Studies suggested that the criminal justice system would benefit by "being nicer to victims." The National Crime Survey revealed that, at best, 50% of crimes were reported to the police (Bureau of Justice Statistics [BJS], 1983). One major reason that victims did not report was that they were apprehensive about how they would be treated and whether they would be believed (Kidd & Cajet, 1984; Kilpatrick & Otto, 1987). Others studies showed that although prosecutors blamed high dismissal rates on victim and witness noncooperation, most often victims and witnesses were not uncooperative—they were just intimidated by the criminal justice system and uninformed as to what they were expected to do (Cannavele, 1975). Accordingly, victim-witness units were designed to address the victims' needs for better treatment and more information, as well as the state's need for cooperative witnesses. Victims began to be notified when hearings were scheduled so that they would not be kept waiting unnecessarily. In many courthouses, separate waiting rooms were established for defense and state witnesses.

Although these changes were certainly welcome, crime victims wanted more than pity and politeness; they wanted to participate in the criminal justice system. Studies corroborated the importance of victim participation (e.g., Kelly, 1984; Shapland, Villmore, & Duff, 1985), as did committees that were established to study victims in the criminal justice process (e.g., in the United States, the President's Task Force on Victims of Crime, 1982; in Canada, the Federal-Provincial Task Force on Justice for Victims of Crime, 1983; in New Zealand, the Victim's Task Force in 1987). The international community also recognized the need to integrate victims into the criminal justice process. In 1985, the United Nations Seventh Congress on the Prevention of Crime and Treatment of the Offender, meeting in Milan, adopted a declaration that required that victims be allowed to present their views and concerns at appropriate stages of the criminal justice process.

As advocates pushed to increase victims' rights to participation, however, their demands were met with resistance. Victim participation threatened to disturb established patterns within the courthouse. Studies showed that within the judicial branch, prosecutors, defense attorneys, and judges operated as a "work group," sharing the mutual goal of disposing of cases as fast as time and justice would allow (Eisenstein & Jacob, 1977). Critics feared that if victims were allowed to intrude in this process, it would upset the efficiency of this "work group" and slow down an already overloaded docket. As researchers concluded after studying a project promoting victim involvement in Brooklyn Criminal Court:

Prosecutors are particularly likely to resist consideration of the victims' point of view because it is prosecutors' control that would be most eroded if the victims were given a greater voice. . . . Courthouse professionals have a substantial interest in processing cases in summary fashion and . . . may tend to become insensitive to human suffering involved in the "normal crimes " they process. (Davis, Kunreuther, & Connick, 1984, pp. 504-505)

Widespread Adoption of Participatory Reforms

In the midst of this debate, a new generation of participatory reforms was adopted. Many such reforms were prompted by the recommendation of the President's Task Force on Victims of Crime (1982) that the Sixth Amendment be amended to guarantee victims a right to be present and to be heard at all critical stages of judicial proceedings. Alabama was the first state to act on this recommendation when in 1983 it exempted victims from sequestration requirements. Victims were allowed to sit at the prosecutor's table during the trial and to be included in all bench conferences or hearings, except for those circumstances when the defendant could also be excluded (Ala. Code § 15-14-50 et seq.). About 24 other states passed statutes that allow victims to attend most criminal justice proceedings, subject to judicial discretion.

The 1991 Omnibus Crime Bill (Pub. L. No. 101-647) adopted a watered-down version of the task force report and stated that victims have a right to "be present at all public court proceedings related to the offense." Title V, the Victims' Rights and Restitution Act of 1990, provides that victims in federal courts have rights to restitution; to be present "at all public court proceedings related to the offense" (unless the court determines that the victim's testimony would be affected by the testimony of others at trial); to confer with the U.S. attorney; and to be informed of the arrest, conviction, sentencing, imprisonment, parole, release, or death of the offender. The statute also instructs government officials to inform victims about available medical and social services and who can help them secure those services.

Forty-five states have enacted victim bills of rights. The scope of these statutes varies from mandating politeness toward victims (Rhode Island), to establishing a victim's right to be present and heard (Florida), to allowing victims to sit at the prosecutor's table during trial (Alabama). In most states, victims' rights legislation is by statute. However, some 20 states adopted constitutional amendments to give victims' rights greater permanence and visibility.

Forty states now allow for victim participation in parole hearings, and at least half the states provide for victim participation in plea bargaining. The extent to which victims are allowed to participate in plea bargaining varies widely. In Nebraska, for example, prosecutors must make a good faith effort to consult with victims about negotiations (Neb. Rev. Stat. §§ 29-2261, 29-120, 23-1201). In Arizona, participation extends only to surviving families of homicide victims. Minnesota requires prosecutors to notify victims about the planned disposition and allows victims to file an objection (Minn. Stat. Ann. § 611A *et seq.*). No state gives victims a veto over plea bargains.

Recognizing that adversary rules are premised on confrontation with an adult, not a child (Whitcomb, 1983), 44 states adopted special procedures for when children testify. Legislation ranges from extending the statute of limitations for offenses against children (29 states) to requiring speedy trials for offenses against children (21 states). The National Association of Attorneys General developed model statutes that eliminated competency requirements for child victims of sex offenses. Approximately 31 states passed such legislation. Roughly a dozen states have enacted child victim and witness bills of rights. The use of closed-circuit cameras and videotaped statements or depositions of children's testimony is a common element of these reforms.

In the last 10 years, the way the criminal justice system characterizes domestic violence also has changed, from that of a problem suitable for family counseling to that of an assault suitable for criminal prosecution. The Victims of Crime Act of 1984 targeted domestic violence as a priority. In its final report that same year, the Attorney General's Task Force on Family Violence (1984) instructed law enforcement that "an assault is a crime regardless of the relationship of the parties" and that domestic violence victims should be treated as seriously as any other crime victims.

Landmark decisions such as *Thurman v. City of Torrington* (1984) laid the groundwork for state attention to the significance of domestic violence. In *Thurman,* city police officers were found liable for $2.3 million in compensatory damages because, over a period of 8 months, they did not adequately respond to the plaintiff's requests for protection from her estranged husband's repeated assaults and death threats. The court found that the police department's inaction denied equal protection as it provided less protection for victims who were abused by intimates than for victims who were abused by nonintimates.

Eleven states (Connecticut, Iowa, Louisiana, Massachusetts, Minnesota, Nevada, Oregon, Rhode Island, Washington, West Virginia, and Wisconsin) passed legislation mandating that if probable cause exists, police must make arrests in domestic violence cases, regardless whether the victim signs the complaint. Iowa's statute goes so far as to prohibit a prosecutor from dropping charges without judicial review (Iowa Code chaps. 236.6, 236.12[2]). These mandatory prosecution laws recognize that victims of domestic violence are uniquely vulnerable to retaliation for pressing charges and therefore take that decision away from the victims. Notably, this aspect of domestic violence reforms conflicts with what otherwise is a principal goal of victims' advocates: to give victims a say in decisions that affect their lives. In 1994, the landmark Violence Against Women Act was enacted. Among other provisions, this statute makes it a federal crime to cross interstate lines for the purpose of committing a crime based on gender and creates a federal civil cause of action in the event such an offense occurs.

Of all these participatory reforms, victim impact statements (VIS) are the most common generic reform (as opposed to a reform limited to one type of crime victim), and the research on their effects is the most common type of research on reforms. VIS allow victims to describe the medical, financial, and emotional injuries that resulted from the crime. VIS differ in content and form, ranging from simple checklists in some states to lengthy descriptive statements in others (McLeod, 1988). This information is usually provided to a probation officer, who then writes up a summary that is included in the defendant's presentencing packet. The report then goes to the judge, who may give it as little or as much weight as he or she likes. Although few states provide guidelines on what information may be included in such statements or how this information may be used by parole authorities (Bernat, Parsonage, & Helfgott, 1994), VIS are now permitted in virtually every state, and in the federal system they are required by the Victim Witness Protection Act of 1982.[5]

Compared to victim impact statements, victim statements of opinion (VSO) are considered more subjective. VSO allow victims to tell the court, in writing or in person, their opinion on what sentence the defendant should receive. Currently, about 35 states permit victims' opinion at sentencing to be introduced.

Legal Challenges to Victims' Participation

Not surprisingly, the adoption of reforms to increase victims' rights prompted legal challenges from defendants. In *The Florida Star v. B.J.F.* (1989), the Supreme Court reversed a damages award to a rape victim whose name was published by the *Star* in violation of state law. The Court balanced the state's interest in protecting the privacy of rape victims (thereby encouraging them to report and cooperate with the police) against the First Amendment rights of the press. The Court found that circumstances could exist in which a state's interest in protecting the privacy and safety of rape victims overwhelmed the First Amendment rights of the press, but it held that these circumstances must be narrowly drawn and did not exist in this case (p. 541). In *Maryland v. Craig* (1990), the Court upheld the use of one-way closed-circuit television to protect child abuse victims from the trauma of seeing their assailant while they testified. The Court rejected the argument that the confrontation clause required a face-to-face meeting between accused and accuser. In doing so, the Court affirmed that a state's interest in "the protection of minor victims of sex offenses from further trauma and embarrassment" is "compelling." Not all reforms to protect child witnesses have survived judicial scrutiny. In *Coy v. Iowa* (1988), the Supreme Court held that a screen placed between the defendant and his two 13-year-old sexual assault victims to block their view of him while they testified violated the confrontation clause of the Sixth Amendment because there had not been a case-specific finding that this screen was necessary (p. 1025).

Issues concerning victims' rights were especially prominent in the 1991 term. In *Michigan v. Lucas* (1991), the Court considered the aspect of Michigan's rape shield statute that required defendants to provide 10 days' notice if they intended to raise issues concerning the victims' sexual past. In her decision, Justice O'Connor noted that the statute represented a valid legislative determination that rape victims deserve heightened protection against surprise, harassment, and unnecessary invasion of privacy. In a dramatic turnabout, in *Payne v. Tennessee* (1991), the Court upheld the use of victim impact testimony at the sentencing stage of a capital case, thereby reversing its two prior decisions, *Booth v. Maryland*

(1987) and *South Carolina v. Gathers* (1989), in which VIS had been barred in capital cases as violating the Eighth Amendment.

The Debate Over Victim Participation

Arguments in Favor of Victim Participation

Advocates of victims' rights to participate in the criminal justice process present a host of arguments in its favor, ranging from the moral to the penological. Some argue that sentencing will be more accurate if victims convey their feelings (Erez, 1990) and that the criminal justice process will be more democratic and better reflect the community's response to crime (Rubel, 1986). Victim participation also acknowledges victim's wishes to be treated as a party and with dignity (Henderson, 1985). In addition, it reminds judges, juries, and prosecutors that behind the "state" is a real person with an interest in how the case is resolved (Kelly, 1987). Victim participation may also lead to increased victim satisfaction (Australian Law Reform Commission, 1988; Kelly, 1984) and cooperation with the criminal justice system, thereby enhancing the system's efficiency (McLeod, 1986). Moreover, when the court hears from offenders' family and friends, fairness dictates that the people who actually were injured should be allowed to speak (Sumner, 1987).

Some researchers suggest that victims' participation promotes psychological healing (Erez, 1990) by allowing them to recover faster from the emotional difficulties associated with their victimization and court experiences (Erez, 1990; Ranish & Shichor, 1985). In contrast, a criminal justice system that provides no opportunity for victims to participate may exacerbate the feelings of helplessness and lack of control that arise as a result of the crime (Kilpatrick & Otto, 1987, p. 19). Victim participation may also promote rehabilitation as the offender confronts the reality of the

harm that he or she caused to the victim (Talbert, 1988).

Arguments Against Victim Participation

Objections to victims' participating in any capacity other than as a witness run the gamut from assumptions that retribution will result to predictions that the system will grind to a halt (Erez, 1990). Some argue that allowing victims to participate will expose the court to precisely the public pressure from which it should be insulated (Rubel, 1986) or will result in substituting the victim's "subjective" approach for the allegedly "objective" one practiced by the court (Victorian Sentencing Committee, 1988). Critics argue that similar cases could be disposed of differently depending on whether a VIS is available and how persuasive the victim is (Grabosky, 1987, p. 147).[6] For all these reasons, critics argue that a victim's view of sentencing is "irrelevant to any legitimate sentencing factor, lacks probative value in a system of public prosecution, and is likely to be highly prejudicial" (Hellerstein, 1989, p. 429).

Prosecutors often object to victims' input in sentencing because they fear that their control over cases will be eroded, the predictability of outcomes will be reduced (Davis et al., 1984), and the system will be overburdened (Australian Law Reform Commission, 1988). Others argue that victim input adds very little information that is not already available to the court given that the criminal law already takes into account the harm done to the victim through its definitions of crime and charging decisions (Hellerstein, 1989). Moreover, as the law typically punishes foreseeable consequences, critics argue that only effects on the "normal" victim should be considered (Victorian Sentencing Committee, 1988) and that unforeseen consequences or effects on particularly vulnerable victims should be excluded (Ashworth, 1993). Indeed, this was a basis for the Supreme Court's decision in *South Carolina v. Gathers* (1989).

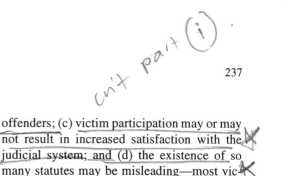

'Some argue that VIS are bad for victims because they create expectations that are not or cannot be met (Fattah, 1986). For example, if a judge is precluded from considering a victim's request, the victim whose opinion is ignored may become embittered and resentful (Henderson, 1985). Although victims are not compelled to fill out VIS, some may feel compelled, and the process may be traumatic for victims who do not want offenders to know the harm they caused (Australian Law Reform Commission, 1988). Victims also may not want to feel responsible for the sentencing outcome and may prefer the criminal justice system to mandate their involvement.

Other objections to victim input are based on ideological grounds. Opponents allege that a gain for victims is a loss for defendants. Because victims are presumed to be vindictive and unforgiving, it is assumed that their participation will result in harsher sentences (Hall, 1991, pp. 245-246). They argue that to bring victims back into the criminal process is to revert to the eye-for-an-eye system (Sebba, 1989) that inappropriately breaks down the distinction between civil and criminal law (Abrahamson, 1985). Others argue that victims have been exploited by "law-and-order" advocates whose real goal is to get tough on offenders, not to help victims (Henderson, 1985).

Assessing the Effects of Victim Participation on the Criminal Justice System

Clearly, many statutes have been passed in the name of crime victims. Victim advocates suggest that both victims and the judicial system will benefit as a result. Critics assert that both defendants and the judicial process will suffer. Who is right? A decade after many reforms were adopted, research provides some answers. It suggests that (a) victim participation does not bog down the criminal justice system; (b) victim participation does not necessarily result in more harsh punishment of offenders; (c) victim participation may or may not result in increased satisfaction with the judicial system; and (d) the existence of so many statutes may be misleading—most victims are unaware of and never benefit from these reforms.

The Effect of Victim Participation on Criminal Justice Administration

Research in jurisdictions that allow or mandate victim participation indicates that including victims in the criminal justice process does not cause delays or additional expense (Davis & Smith, 1994a; Erez, Roeger, & Morgan, 1994; Heinz & Kerstetter, 1979) and that very few court officials believe that victims' input creates or exacerbates problems or slows down the proceedings (Erez et al., 1994; Hillenbrand & Smith, 1989). Even officials (prosecutors as well as judges) in the Bronx, one of the nation's busiest jurisdictions, generally view victim input positively (Henley, Davis, & Smith, 1994). Further, court officials in this country and Australia report that challenges to VIS are rarely raised by the defense, particularly as concerns mental harm (Erez et al., 1994; see also Talbert, 1988). Defense attorneys as well as judges and prosecutors fear that calling victims to testify about the impact of the crime and cross-examining victims on their VIS statement may have devastating effects for the defense and avoid it for that reason (Erez et al., 1994).

Although defense lawyers express concern that victim statements are inaccurate, research indicates that in fact VIS rarely include inflammatory, prejudicial, or other objectionable statements (Erez et al., 1994; Henley et al., 1994). Similarly, exaggerations in VIS are not commonplace. If they do occur, judges and prosecutors in one study report that they involve financial matters, not emotional or mental suffering (Erez et al., 1994). Surveys of judges, however, suggest that they prefer to consider "objective" VIS information (e.g., the physical and financial impact of the crime)

rather than "subjective" types of information, such as social or psychological effects and the VSO (Erez et al., 1994; Hillenbrand & Smith, 1989).

Some studies reveal that VIS have positive effects on the criminal justice process. There is conflicting research as to whether VIS improve the quality of justice by influencing restitution awards (Erez et al., 1994; Hillenbrand & Smith, 1989). Some studies report that most judges and prosecutors believe it does. These findings accord with research in England suggesting that compensation is more likely to be ordered if it was mentioned in court proceedings (Shapland et al., 1985). Because prosecutors may be unaware of victims' preferences, or for various reasons may fail to convey them to the court, allowing victims to express their wishes through VIS may be the only way to guarantee that the sentencing authority learns of their requests. Research in one jurisdiction in Australia, however, did not find any increase in the rate of restitution or compensation orders since VIS legislation was passed because, unless offenders have the means to pay, judges are precluded from imposing restitution or compensation orders (Erez et al., 1994, chap. 3).

The Effect of Victim Participation on Sentencing Outcomes

Research largely refutes assumptions that victim participation results in harsher sentences for defendants. Studies suggest that sentences are usually determined on the basis of legal considerations and the offender's prior record (Davis & Smith, 1994a; Erez & Tontodonato, 1990; Erez & Roeger, 1995). Victims' participation either has no effect on sentences or cuts both ways. As a practical matter, VIS will have limited relevance in the federal system or in jurisdictions that employ a determinate sentencing scheme (Hellerstein, 1989). Judges and prosecutors in one study (Erez et al., 1994) reported that VIS result in increased sentences in some cases (e.g., when

the intended harm was particularly serious or the crime was especially heinous) and in lesser sentences in other cases (e.g., when no harm occurred or it was much less than would be expected). This may explain why aggregate studies (e.g., Erez & Tontodonato, 1990) do not find any effect of victims' participation on sentencing (Erez & Roeger, 1995).

With regard to victims' views on sentencing, a study of victims' sentencing requests in sexual assault cases found that the court was most likely to recognize the desires of the victim when they were consistent with the court's own view of an appropriate sentence. Most interestingly, this study refutes the stereotype that all victims thirst for vengeance. It revealed that the court was *more* punitive than victims and was likely to ignore victims' desire for probation sentences over imprisonment (Walsh, 1986). Moreover, once a prison sentence was imposed, victims' views on sentencing did not significantly affect its length (Erez & Tontodonato, 1990).

Other studies reaffirm that victim participation does not result in increased sentences. One study that used an experimental design to examine the effect of VIS on sentences found that the use of VIS did not result in harsher sentences for offenders or increase the likelihood of incarceration as opposed to probation. Instead, the researchers concluded that the severity of the charge, rather than the harm described in the VIS, most affected the sentence imposed (Davis & Smith, 1994a).

In contrast to victims' rights to file a written statement, one study of victims' right to speak, or allocute, in court found that it was victims' presence rather than their allocution that had an effect on the length of sentence. Typically, victims who attend court during sentencing tend to be involved in many phases of the trial process, thus providing a constant reminder to the judge that the real person, not the state, is the injured party (Erez & Tontodonato, 1990).

When a case goes to sentencing, the decision has already been made, so allocution is unlikely to affect the outcome. In this sense, the right to allocution is more symbolic than effective. By the time the victim comes to the court, a well-prepared judge has already received the probation report and leaves little reason for modification of an intended decision. A victim's emotional appeal to the court cannot carry more weight than facts and sentencing criteria (Villmoare & Neto, 1987, p. 37). In contrast, because the written VIS is submitted *prior* to sentencing, it has a greater chance to influence sentencing, if at all (Erez & Tontodonato, 1990).

The conclusion that emerges from these combined findings is not surprising. Judges use their discretion and judgment when considering victims' views. Although much of the information in VIS should already be reflected in the charge, at times VIS may provide additional information useful to the judge when determining a sentence. To include this additional information does not mean that the court will adopt the victim's opinion. Studies of judges in the United States and in Australia suggest that judges find VIS helpful for learning how victims are affected by crime (Davis & Smith, 1994a; Erez et al., 1994). Judges in one study also indicated that without VIS they would not know the impact of the crime on the victim (Davis & Smith, 1994a). Furthermore, judges in Australia reported that VIS not only educated them about the effects of crimes on victims but sometimes benefited the defendant—for example, when the information disclosed that the injury was not as severe as one might expect from the charge (Erez et al., 1994). Prosecutors in these studies, however, expressed skepticism about judges' interest in the impact of the crime on the victims and whether they actually considered the VIS when sentencing (Davis & Smith, 1994a; Erez et al., 1994).

These inconsistent findings and conflicting perceptions of key players as to the effect of VIS on sentencing suggest that the effect of victim participation on sentencing is ambiguous. VIS may be as likely to mitigate a sentence as to increase it. Alternatively, although they may make the victim feel better, they may have no effect at all on sentencing.

The Effect of VIS on Victims' Welfare and Satisfaction With Justice

Do opportunities for victim participation increase victims' satisfaction with the criminal justice system? Research results are divided and suggest at best modest effects. One study found that filing VIS usually results in increased satisfaction with the outcome (Erez & Tontodonato, 1992). Another found that victim participation generally increases victims' satisfaction (Kelly, 1984). Sometimes merely filing a VIS heightens victims' expectations that they will influence the outcome. When that does not happen, victims' satisfaction may actually be reduced (Erez et al., 1994).

Another study that randomly assigned victims' cases to various treatments found that VIS had no effect on victims' feelings of involvement or satisfaction with the criminal justice process or its outcome (Davis & Smith, 1994a). These results are consistent with an earlier quasi-experimental study by Davis (1985) that also did not find any effect of VIS on satisfaction with justice. Similarly, studies of the VIS program in Canada (Department of Justice Canada, 1990) and in Australia (Erez et al., 1994) revealed that victims who provide information for VIS are not necessarily more satisfied with the outcome or with the criminal justice system.

In contrast, a comparative study of victims in the continental criminal justice systems (which allow victims a party status and significant input into the proceedings) suggests that victims who participated as subsidiary prosecutors or acted as private prosecutors were more satisfied than victims who did not participate (Erez & Bienkowska, 1993). These differences suggest that the more participation a jurisdiction affords crime victims, the greater victims' levels of satisfaction.

Research on victims' involvement in parole proceedings indicates that participation at this stage may salvage victims' views toward the criminal justice system. One study found that many victims who testified in parole hearings were dissatisfied with the criminal justice system's handling of their cases because they had been excluded from earlier proceedings. These victims especially appreciated the opportunity to be heard by parole authorities (Parsonage, Bernat, & Helfgott, 1992). Victim satisfaction also tends to increase when victims are informed about what judges consider in determining sentences and know that their views are one of these considerations. Simply put, studies show that the more victims understand the sentencing process, the more satisfied they are with it (Department of Justice Canada, 1990; Erez et al., 1994; Gardner, 1990; Hagen, 1982).

The effect of victim participation on victims' distress levels has not been systematically studied. Those few studies conducted were limited to rape victims, and their results are inconclusive (Lurigio & Resick, 1990, pp. 60-61). The only study that has examined the effect of VIS on victims' distress levels (Tontodonato & Erez, 1994) suggests that although victims' distress is not directly influenced by VIS, opportunities for such participation nonetheless may be important because it may influence the type of sentence (Erez & Tontodonato, 1990) and whether a request for restitution is awarded. Restitution in turn influences victims' perception of equity and their satisfaction with justice (Erez & Tontodonato, 1992; see also Boers & Sessar, 1991).

Indirect evidence also suggests that victims may be interested in participating for the purpose of "justice," even though it means reliving the crime. A study in Australia found that victims of serious crimes in particular were interested in receiving information concerning the case at all stages of the process (Gardner, 1990). Most victims also expressed the belief that for the purpose of sentencing, the court should have information not only on the medical and financial consequences of the crime but also on the impact of the crime on their emotional state, their family and lifestyle, and their concern for safety (Erez et al., 1994; Gardner, 1990, p. 48).

The Delivery of the Victims' Statutory Rights to Participate in the Criminal Justice System

In practice, most reforms never reach victims. Preliminary studies show that victims either are unaware of their rights to participate or do not exercise them. For example, some studies estimate that no more than a quarter of victims fill out a VIS and that only 6% to 9% exercise their right to allocute (Erez & Tontodonato, 1990; Hillenbrand & Smith, 1989; Villmoore & Neto, 1987). A national survey of probation administrators (McLeod, 1987) found that in felony cases only 50% or less were VIS prepared. This study also found that about 18% of victims were in attendance when their offenders were sentenced but that oral statements were made by fewer than 10% of crime victims (McLeod, 1987, pp. 164-165). Higher estimates for sentencing recommendations were documented in a study of victims of sexual assault (Walsh, 1986). Almost 60% of the victims made sentencing recommendations regarding their assailants, and many of the recommended sentences were less punitive than the ones actually imposed by the court.

Studies also reflect confusion about VIS. Victims often do not know what VIS are or claim that they did not fill out such statements when in fact they did (Erez & Tontodonato, 1992; Erez et al., 1994). This may be because victims are questioned by a seemingly endless array of people and may become confused about the purpose of particular interviews. South Australia's solution to this problem is to have victims prepare their own VIS rather than merely provide the information to the investigating officer (the counterpart of probation or victim assistance officers in other countries).

Why do comparatively few victims invoke their right to participate through VIS? Research offers many possible explanations. To the extent that victims learn of their right to VIS only if court officials tell them, victims' involvement depends on the court officials' level of enthusiasm toward such reform. Court officials sometimes believe that VIS are redundant and contain no new information (Department of Justice Canada, 1990). Prosecutors may be reluctant to have the judge know the full impact of the crime for fear that it would jeopardize a negotiated plea (Corns, 1988) and may be skeptical about the extent to which judges consider victims' views (Davis & Smith, 1994b; Erez et al., 1994). In addition, there may be practical problems in obtaining a VIS or an ideological resistance to giving victims a voice in criminal justice decisions, despite legislative authority to do so (e.g., Department of Justice Canada, 1990; Hellerstein, 1989; Victorian Sentencing Commission, 1988). The low percentage of victims who actually allocute, as opposed to submitting a written VIS, may also reflect that victims are more comfortable talking with a sympathetic criminal justice official than speaking in open court (Villmoare & Neto, 1987). If victims' rights to participate are triggered by court officials' first telling them about this right, rates of participation are likely to remain low. The tendency to ignore or even "lose" victim impact information is well established (Corns, 1988; Douglas, Laster, & Inglis, 1994).

Perhaps most important, usually there is no legal sanction for criminal justice officials who fail to inform victims of options for their participation. Most laws explicitly provide that a sentence cannot be challenged due to noncompliance with VIS. Exceptions exist. South Carolina and Minnesota have ombudspersons who investigate complaints of noncompliance with reforms. Colorado allows for a suit to be filed by the attorney general against the officials who failed to extend to victims their rights. Maryland permits victims to ask for leave to file an appeal to the State Court of Special Appeals for any final order that denies victims their statutory rights. Arizona allows

victims to sue the government for damages if there is "intentional knowing or grossly negligent violation of the victims' rights." As a rule, however, most victims' rights are neither known nor delivered. At base, victims' rights often remain privileges to be granted or denied depending on the whim of the police, the prosecutor, or the judge (Kelly, 1990). Some have warned that

> promising victims rights that are not delivered may involve a certain danger: providing rights without remedies would result in the worst of consequences, such as feelings of helplessness, lack of control and further victimization. . . . Ultimately, with the victims' best interests in mind, it is better to confer no rights than "rights" without remedies. (Kilpatrick & Otto, 1987, p. 27)

Conclusion

As the foregoing has demonstrated, when the legislative reforms adopted on behalf of crime victims are counted, it looks as if victims have hit a proverbial home run. Yet the criminal justice system is still standing. Reports from the field indicate that no administrative problems, serious defense challenges, longer trials, or increased sentences result from victim participation. Yet legal scholars and professionals persist in believing the contrary. Similarly, there is no evidence that the high rates of incarceration in the United States have spiked due to victims' participation in the criminal justice system. In fact, there is no definitive evidence at all on the effects of victim participation on the criminal justice system. Perhaps this is explained by the increased use of sentencing guidelines, which limit judges' discretion. Perhaps it is explained by the fact that victims are just people with as different opinions about sentencing as they would have on any other subject; the act of being victimized does not make them the same and erase natural differences caused by values, social background, or varying relationships to their offenders. Perhaps it is explained by the woeful underuse by victims of the very rights for which victim advocates long campaigned.

Because victim participation in sentencing decisions challenges traditions and established patterns within the criminal courts, these rights often amount to lip service (Davis & Smith, 1994a; Erez & Tontodonato, 1990, 1992; Erez et al., 1994; Kelly, 1991; Kury, Kaiser, & Teske, 1994). Legislative reforms typically lack remedies for noncompliance. Victims' rights, such as VIS, become well-kept secrets that only a few victims know about or use (Kelly, 1990). Victims' participation depends on the luck of the draw. If a victim encounters criminal justice personnel who support victims' rights and inform him or her what they are, there is a greater likelihood that the victim will actually participate (see Douglas et al., 1994; Kury et al., 1994).

Although legislatures were probably most motivated to adopt victims' reforms by a desire for victim cooperation with its resulting judicial efficiency, ultimately the decision of whether to allow or require victim participation largely rests on subjective moral judgments (Erez, 1994). Clearly, victims' participation is viewed skeptically by many in the legal community (e.g., Hall, 1991; Hellerstein, 1989) and the social science community (e.g., Davis & Smith, 1994a, 1994b) precisely because of its low participation rates and attendant fears that if only the elite victims avail themselves of these rights, the disparate treatment of defendants in the criminal justice system will be increased. Clearly, there is a need for further research on the effect of victims' reforms.

Even if such research confirmed that victims' rights pose no great danger to the system or to its defendants and resulted in recommendations to put "the teeth" in such statutes (presumably by creating causes of actions against those who fail to notify victims of their rights), such recommendations would probably never be adopted. Creating rights with remedies would cause the fragile alliance of victims' advocates, legislators, and prosecutors to shatter. As a result, victims are likely to remain where they are, hoping to work with sympathetic criminal justice personnel who will inform them of their rights and help to exercise them, but more likely to remain ignorant of their rights to participate in the criminal justice process.

Notes

1. Profits made by criminals prompted the passage of "Son-of-Sam laws" (so named after serial criminal David Berkowitz). These statutes mandate that any proceeds derived by convicted criminals from selling works that recount their crimes must be escrowed to satisfy any civil judgments obtained by their victims. In *Simon & Schuster v. New York State Crime Victim's Board* (1991), the Supreme Court struck down New York's Son-of-Sam statute as violating the First Amendment. Subsequently, New York revised its law to comport with the Court's mandate.

2. The National Victims Center in Rosslyn, Virginia, maintains a Legislative Database Project that analyzes state and federal statutes dealing with victims according to 931 categories.

3. In addition to the *Simon & Schuster* case, the Supreme Court ruled in *Michigan v. Lucas* (1991), *Payne v. Tennessee* (1991), *Maryland v. Craig* (1990), *South Carolina v. Gathers* (1989), and *Booth v. Maryland* (1987). For commentary on the implications of the Court's ruling in *Booth* on sentencing, see Sebba (1994).

4. Eligible programs are funded with federal grants (up to 40% of the state payouts) authorized under the Victims of Crime Act of 1984 (VOCA) and financed by penalties assessed against federal offenders. To be eligible for VOCA funding, a state program must agree to compensate for mental health counseling and to provide coverage for nonresidents and victims of all federal crimes that occur within state borders. VOCA forbids states to exclude victims of nonstranger violence from consideration, a requirement that has induced many states to do away with their previous policy of "household exclusions," which effectively denied compensation to victims of domestic violence. As a result of this financial incentive, many states expanded the scope of their victim compensation programs.

5. VIS are not limited to the United States. Canada, as well as New Zealand and Australia, permits VIS prepared by the police to be introduced at the time of sentencing. In 1988, South Australia became the first state in Australia to

permit victim impact material to be included in sentencing hearings, followed by the state of Victoria in 1994. South Australia and New Zealand, however, allow victims only to submit written VIS, not to allocute or provide their opinions concerning sentencing.

6. Of course, although sentencing guidelines reduce this effect, it has always been true that defendants may receive varying sentences depending on how sympathetic, articulate, or persuasive they are.

References

Abrahamson, S. S. (1985). Redefining roles: The victims' rights movement. *Utah Law Review*, pp. 517-567.

Ashworth, A. (1993). Victim impact statements and sentencing. *Criminal Law Review*, pp. 498-509.

Attorney General's Task Force on Family Violence. (1984). *Final report*. Washington, DC: Government Printing Office.

Australian Law Reform Commission. (1988). *Sentencing* (Rep. No. 44). Canberra: Attorney General's Publication Service.

Bernat, F. P., Parsonage, W. H., & Helfgott, J. (1994). Victim impact laws and the parole process in the United States: Balancing victim and inmates rights and interests. *International Review of Victimology, 3*, 121-140.

Boers, K., & Sessar, K. (1991). Do people really want punishment? On the relationship between acceptance of restitution, needs for punishment and fear of crime. In K. Sessar & H.-J. Kerner (Eds.), *Developments in crime and crime control research: German studies on victims, offenders and the public*. New York: Springer-Verlag.

Booth v. Maryland, 482 U.S. 497 (1987).

Brosi, K. B. (1979). *A cross-city comparison of felony case processing*. Washington, DC: Institute for Law and Social Research.

Bureau of Justice Statistics. (1983). *Reports to the nation on crime and justice*. Washington, DC: U.S. Dept. of Justice.

Cannavele, F. (1975). *Witness cooperation*. New York: Lexington.

Corns, C. (1988). Offender and victims. In D. Biles (Ed.), *Current Australian trends in corrections* (pp. 204-216). Sydney, Australia: Federation.

Coy v. Iowa, 487 U.S. 1012 (1988).

Davis, R. C., Kunreuther, F., & Connick, E. (1984). Expanding the victim's role in the criminal court dispositional process: The results of an experiment. *Journal of Criminal Law and Criminology, 75*, 491, 504-505.

Davis, R. C. (1985). *First year evaluation of the victim impact demonstration project*. Unpublished report, Victim Services Agency, New York, NY.

Davis, R. C., & Smith, B. (1994a). The effects of victim impact statements on sentencing decisions: A test in an urban setting. *Justice Quarterly, 11*, 453-469.

Davis, R. C., & Smith, B. (1994b). Victim impact statements and victim satisfaction with justice: An unfulfilled promise? *Journal of Criminal Justice, 22*(1): 1-12.

Department of Justice Canada, Research Section, Research and Development Directorate. (1990). *Victim impact statements in Canada: Vol. 7. A summary of the findings*. Ottawa, Canada: Author.

Douglas, R., Laster, K., & Inglis, N. (1994). Victim of efficiency: Criminal justice reform in Australia. *International Review of Victimology, 3*, 95-110.

Eisenstein, J., & Jacob, H. (1977). *Felonious justice: An organizational analysis of criminal courts*. Lanham, MD: University Press of America.

Erez, E. (1989). The impact of victimology on criminal justice policy. *Criminal Justice Policy Review, 3*, 236-256.

Erez, E. (1990). Victim participation in sentencing: Rhetoric and reality. *Journal of Criminal Justice, 18*, 19-31.

Erez, E. (1994). Victim participation in sentencing: And the debate goes on. *International Review of Victimology, 3*, 17-32.

Erez, E., & Bienkowska, E. (1993). Victim participation in proceedings and satisfaction with justice in the Continental systems: The case of Poland. *Journal of Criminal Justice, 21*, 47-60.

Erez, E., & Tontodonato, P. (1990). The effect of victim participation in sentencing on sentence outcome. *Criminology, 28*, 451-474.

Erez, E., & Tontodonato, P. (1992). Victim participation in sentencing and satisfaction with justice. *Justice Quarterly, 9*, 393-415.

Erez, E., Roeger, L., & Morgan, F. (1994). *Victim impact statements in South Australia: An evaluation* (Series C, No. 6). Adelaide, South Australia: Office of Crime Statistics, Attorney General's Department.

Erez, E., & Roeger, L. (1995). The effect of victim impact statements on sentencing patterns and outcomes: The Australian experience. *Journal of Criminal Justice, 23*(4), 363-375.

Fattah, E. A. (Ed.). (1986). *From crime policy to victim policy*. New York: Macmillan.

The Florida Star v. B.J.F., 491 U.S. 524 (1989).

Gardner, J. (1990). *Victims and criminal justice* (Research Report). Adelaide, South Australia: Office of Crime Statistics, Attorney-General's Department.

Grabosky, P. N. (1987). Victims. In J. Bastan, M. Richardson, C. Reynolds, & G. Zdenkowski (Eds.), *The criminal injustice system* (Vol. 2). Sydney, Australia: Pluto.

Hagan, J. (1982). Victims before the law: A study of victims' involvement in the criminal justice process. *Journal of Criminal Law and Criminology, 73*, 317-329.

Hall, D. J. (1991). Victim voices in criminal court: The need for restraint. *American Criminal Law Review, 28*, 233-266.

Heinz, A. M., & Kerstetter, W. G. (1979). Pre-trial settlement conference: Evaluation of reform plea bargaining. *Law and Society Review, 13,* 349-366.

Hellerstein, D. R. (1989). Victim impact statement: Reform or reprisal? *American Criminal Law Review, 27,* 391-430.

Henderson, L. N. (1985). The wrongs of victims' rights. *Stanford Law Review, 37,* 937-1021.

Henley, M., Davis, R. C., & Smith, B. E. (1994). The reactions of prosecutors and judges to victim impact statements. *International Review of Victimology, 3,* 83-93.

Hillenbrand, S. W., & Smith, B. E. (1989). *Victim rights legislation: An assessment of its impact on criminal justice practitioners and victims.* Washington, DC: American Bar Association.

Joutsen, M. (1994). Victim participation in proceedings and sentencing in Europe. *International Review of Victimology, 3,* 57-67.

Kelly, D. P. (1984). Victims' perceptions of criminal justice. *Pepperdine Law Review, 11,* 15-22.

Kelly, D. P. (1987). Victims. *Wayne Law Review, 34,* 69-86.

Kelly, D. P. (1990). Victim participation in the criminal justice systems. In A. J. Lurigio, W. A. Skogan, & R. C. Davis (Eds.), *Victims of crime: Problems, policies, and programs* (pp. 172-187). Newbury Park, CA: Sage.

Kelly, D. P. (1991, Fall). Have victims reforms gone too far or not far enough? *American Bar Association Criminal Justice Magazine,* Vol. 6, pp. 22-28, 38. Chicago, IL: American Bar Association.

Kelly v. Robinson, 479 U.S. 36 (1986).

Kidd & Cajet. (1984). Why victims fail to report: The psychology of criminal victimization. *Journal of Social Issues, 40,* 34-50.

Kilpatrick, D. G., & Otto, R. K. (1987). Constitutionally guaranteed participation in criminal justice proceedings for victims: Potential effects of psychological functioning. *Wayne Law Review, 34,* 7-28.

Kury, H., Kaiser, M., & Teske, R. (1994). The position of the victim in criminal procedure: Results of a German study. *International Review of Victimology, 3,* 69-81.

Lurigio, A. J., & Resick, P. A. (1990). Healing the psychological wounds of criminal victimization: Predicting postcrime distress and recovery. In A. J. Lurigio, W. A. Skogan, & R. C. Davis (Eds.), *Victims of crime: Problems, policies, and programs* (pp. 50-68). Newbury Park, CA: Sage.

Maryland v. Craig, 497 U.S. 836 (1990).

McLeod, M. (1986). Victim participation at sentencing. *Criminal Law Bulletin, 22,* 501-517.

McLeod, M. (1987). An examination of the victim's role at sentencing: Results of a survey of probation administrators. *Judicature, 71,* 162-168.

McLeod, M. (1988). *The authorization and implementation of victim impact statements.* Washington, DC: National Institute of Justice.

Michigan v. Lucas, 500 U.S. 145 (1991).

Parsonage, W. F., Bernat, F., & Helfgott, J. (1992). Victim impact testimony and Pennsylvania's parole decision making process: A pilot study. *Criminal Justice Policing Review, 6,* 187-206.

Payne v. Tennessee, 501 U.S. 808 (1991).

President's Task Force on Victims of Crime. (1982). *Final report.* Washington, DC: Government Printing Office.

Ranish, D. R., & Shichor, D. (1985). The victim's role in the penal process: Recent developments in California. *Federal Probation, 49,* 50-57.

Rubel, H. C. (1986). Victim participation in sentencing proceedings. *Criminal Law Quarterly, 28,* 226-250.

Sebba, L. (1989). Victims and parameters of justice. In Z. P. Separovic (Ed.), *Victimology: International action and study of victims* (pp. 13-24). Zagreb, Croatia: University of Zagreb.

Sebba, L. (1994). Sentencing and the victims: The aftermath of *Payne. International Review of Victimology, 3,* 141-165.

Shapland, J., Villmore, J., & Duff, P. (1985). *Victims in the criminal justice system.* Aldershot, UK: Gower.

Simon & Schuster v. New York State Crime Victim's Board, 501 U.S. 808 (1991).

South Carolina v. Gathers, 490 U.S. 805 (1989).

Sumner, C. J. (1987). Victim participation in the criminal justice system. *Australian and New Zealand Journal of Criminology, 20,* 195-217.

Talbert, P. A. (1988). The relevance of victim impact statements to the criminal sentencing decision. *U.C.L.A. Law Review, 36,* 199-232.

Thurman v. City of Torrington, 595 F.Supp. 1521 (D. Conn. 1984).

Tontodonato, P., & Erez, E. (1994). Crime, punishment and victim distress. *International Review of Victimology, 3,* 33-55.

Victims of Crime Act, 42 U.S.C. §§ 10601 *et seq.* (1984).

Victim Witness Protection Act, 18 U.S.C. § 1801 *et seq.* (1990).

Victims' Rights and Restitution Act, 18 U.S.C. § 1501 *et seq.* (1984).

Victorian Sentencing Committee. (1988). *Sentencing: Report of the Committee.* Melbourne, Australia: Attorney-General's Department.

Villmoare, E., & Neto, V. V. (1987). *Victim appearances at sentencing hearings under the California Victims' Bill of Rights* (NIJ Executive Summary). Washington, DC: U.S. Dept. of Justice.

Walsh, A. (1986). Placebo justice: Victim recommendations and offender sentences in sexual assault cases. *Journal of Criminal Law and Criminology, 77,* 1126-1171.

Whitcomb, D. (1983). *When the victim is a child.* Washington, DC: U.S. Dept. of Justice.

Zeigenhagen, E. (1977). *Victims, crime, and social control.* New York: Praeger.

14 Making Victims Whole Again

Restitution, Victim-Offender
Reconciliation Programs, and Compensation

BARBARA E. SMITH
SUSAN W. HILLENBRAND

There are a number of ways crime victims can obtain reimbursement for financial losses associated with their victimization. They can sue their offender. They can sue a third party, such as a landlord whose carelessness about building security indirectly led to their victimization. They can file an insurance claim or apply to the state crime victim compensation fund. They can request that the court order their offender to pay restitution. Or they can enter into an agreement with their offender whereby the offender voluntarily agrees to repay them.

Individual victims have fared well from each of these tactics. Unfortunately, however, for the typical victim, all are wanting. Civil remedies are often expensive and time consuming; their outcome is uncertain; and they require the victim, who may already have un-

dergone the rigors of the criminal justice system, to initiate and endure what is likely to be a further ordeal in the civil justice system. Moreover, it is the relatively rare case that features an identifiable third party to sue or a perpetrator who can satisfy a judgment even to the extent of covering the victim's expenses of bringing suit. Private insurance for medical bills and property loss, of course, benefits only those victims who had the foresight and means to purchase it in advance of the crime; even for insured victims, high deductibles may preclude substantial reimbursement.

Most victims who receive financial recompense do so through state compensation programs, court-ordered restitution, or restitution obtained through victim/offender reconciliation programs. Each of these has certain (though different) advantages over civil suits and private insurance, but each also has drawbacks. State-funded compensation programs are relatively dependable; however, many are limited to victims of violent crimes and reimburse only for losses above a certain minimum and below a certain maximum. Moreover, victims must know about the programs, make application, and adhere to certain requirements, such as reporting the crime and cooperating with law enforcement officials. Restitution also requires victim cooperation, and although the victim need not initiate the process, he or she has relatively little control over whether the imposed "minimums" or "maximums" to restitution orders (except, of course, the amount of the loss), the victim's ability to collect depends on the offender's ability—and willingness—to pay. Offenders who enter into agreements with victims in victim offender reconciliation programs may be more willing to pay, but here, too, the offender's limited means are a major impediment to meaningful reimbursement for the victim. In fact, victims who meet face to face with their offenders may recognize the futility of even requesting that restitution be an element in the reconciliation agreement.

The rationale for compensation programs is quite different from the rationale for restitution and victim offender programs. The latter are based on early theories that crime is primarily a conflict between individuals, with the victim having a right to bring the perpetrator to justice and to benefit directly from restitution that the perpetrator has a responsibility to pay. Compensation came about at a time when crime was viewed primarily as a wrong against the state, with the state not only assuming responsibility for law enforcement but also reserving to itself the right to impose and benefit from sanctions against the perpetrator. Because victims were no longer able to pursue restitution themselves, it was argued that the state should assume some responsibility for reimbursing the victim (Carrow, 1980).

In this chapter, we discuss restitution, victim-offender reconciliation programs, and compensation as means of making victims "whole" following their victimization. The discussion includes their origin and evolution, their development in recent years, and their effectiveness in terms of both financial reimbursement for victims and victim satisfaction.

Restitution

From the crime victim's perspective, little is more axiomatic than the criminal justice system's ordering the offender to pay restitution. Not only can offender restitution help make the victim "whole," but it does so by placing the onus on the offender who caused the loss. Moreover, restitution has certain advantages over other means of victim recompense: It can apply to property as well as personal crimes, has at least in theory no minimum or maximum limitations, can be included as part of the criminal process, and requires no anticipatory action by the victim. It is not surprising, therefore, that restitution as a matter of justice to crime victims has been a persistent, if relatively low-key, theme of the victims' rights movement.

History

In a sense, restitution to crime victims has come full circle. In Colonial times, victims, rather than the state, investigated and prosecuted crimes; their success, particularly in theft and property crimes, resulted in awards of multiple damages from the offender (Gittler, 1984; McDonald, 1976). The impact on offenders was rarely considered; in fact, victims were sometimes authorized to sell indigent offenders into service for a period corresponding to the amount of the multiple damages (McDonald, 1976, p. 653).

Once the state, rather than the individual victim, began to be viewed as the injured party and public prosecutors became responsible for criminal prosecutions, restitution to the individual victim became a less obvious sanction. Although many offenders still were literally required to "pay for their crimes," the "victim" they were required to pay was the public through fines rather than the individual through restitution. The advent of the penitentiary further diminished the use of restitution as a criminal sanction. Accordingly, victims who wished offenders to make good the losses they caused were steered to the civil justice system.

Though the original rationale for victim restitution (making good victims' losses by those responsible for them) diminished over the years, restitution as a sanction made somewhat of a comeback in the late 19th and early 20th centuries, when it was viewed as a means to achieve what was then a major criminal justice goal — offender rehabilitation (Gittler, 1984, p. 137).

Today, there is little public confidence in rehabilitation as a sentencing goal. Now retributive justice is in vogue, as evidenced by the considerable outcry for more and lengthier prison sentences. Nonetheless, in the light of unprecedented prison populations, even those who prefer more "punitive" sanctions are recognizing the practical need for alternative sanctions for less serious offenses (American Bar Association [ABA], 1994; Hillsman & Greene, 1988). It is not surprising that restitution is viewed favorably, as it costs relatively little in terms of public funds and requires at least some sacrifice on the part of the offender. It is also responsive to the renewed belief that the criminal justice system should recognize and address the needs of crime victims.

In 1982, President Reagan's Task Force on Victims of Crime released its final report, which contained 68 recommendations for improving the plight of crime victims (President's Task Force on Victims of Crime, 1982), two of which related to restitution. The report urged that "legislation should be proposed and enacted to . . . require restitution in all cases,

unless the court provides specific reasons for failing to require it" (p. 18). It also recommended that "judges should order restitution to the victim in all cases in which the victim has suffered financial loss, unless they state compelling reasons for a contrary ruling on the record" (p. 72).

The rationale for the restitution recommendations was reflected in the accompanying commentary:

> It is simply unfair that victims should have to liquidate their assets, mortgage their homes, or sacrifice their health or education or that of their children while the offender escapes responsibility for the financial hardship he has imposed. It is unjust that a victim should have to sell his car to pay bills while the offender drives to his probation appointments. The victim may be placed in a financial crisis that will last a lifetime. If one of the two must go into debt, the offender should do so. (President's Task Force, p. 79)

Though at first somewhat more cautious, the legal community also began to endorse restitution as a matter of justice to crime victims. A Statement of Recommended Judicial Practices adopted by the first National Conference of the Judiciary on the Rights of Victims of Crime in early 1983 included a recommendation that "judges should order restitution in all cases unless there is an articulated reason for not doing so, whether the offender is incarcerated or placed on probation" (National Institute of Justice, 1983).

In August 1983, the ABA adopted a set of Guidelines for Fair Treatment of Crime Victims and Witnesses, with a recommendation that "victims of a crime involving economic loss, loss of earning, or earning capacity should be able to expect the sentencing body to give priority consideration to restitution as a condition of probation" (ABA, 1983, p. 22). A comprehensive set of Guidelines Governing Restitution to Victims of Criminal Conduct approved by that same body 5 years later were considerable more expansive, providing that if the sentencing court finds that a victim or victims have suffered damages as a result of the criminal conduct of the defendant, and finds that the amount of such damages has been established by reliable and probative evidence, the court should make a finding as to the amount of those damages in addition to or in lieu of any other sentence or as a condition of probation. (ABA, 1988, Guideline 1.5, p. 3)

Restitution also was included among the community-based sanctions of the ABA Model Community Corrections Act approved in 1992 (ABA, 1992). Finally, the third edition of the *ABA Sentencing Standards* approved in 1993 assigned restitution priority over other economic sanctions, such as fines, forfeitures, or other payments to governmental bodies (ABA, 1994). Like the previously adopted guidelines, they recognize that the actual amount of restitution paid will, of necessity, depend on the offender's ability to pay. Unlike the guidelines, however, the standards recommend that the restitution sanction itself be fixed by the benefit to the offender or the actual loss to the victim, whichever is greater, and that the offender's ability to pay be reflected only in the schedule of payments.

Legislation

Judicial authority to order defendants to make restitution to their victims is long-standing in the common law and has been codified in the federal system and in many, if not most, states for some time. However, since the 1970s there has been a spate of legislation on the subject. Much of this is novel in that it recognizes restitution as a matter of justice to crime victims, rather than solely as a punitive or rehabilitative measure for offenders.

In 1982, Congress enacted the Victim Witness Protection Act (VWPA; Pub. L. No. 97-291), which included a provision authorizing restitution "in addition to or in lieu of" other authorized penalties in the federal courts. (The provision was amended in 1986 to authorize restitution as an additional penalty for felonies and either an additional or sole penalty for misdemeanors.) This significant advancement beyond the previous authorization of restitution only as a condition of probation was incorporated into the U.S. Sentencing Guidelines through the Sentencing Reform Act of 1984 (Pub. L. No. 98-473). Restitution was further strengthened in several ways by the 1990 Crime Control Act (Pub. L. No. 101-647). Responding to the Supreme Court's decision that restitution was dischargeable in bankruptcy if not explicitly exempted,[1] Congress adopted a provision that placed "restitution included in a sentence on the debtor's conviction of a crime" among the nondischargeable debts.[2] It also added a provision allowing federal courts to accept plea agreements requiring restitution for acts beyond the "offense of conviction."[3]

On the other hand, Congress has not indiscriminately adopted restitution "reforms." In 1986, it deleted an original VWPA requirement that the court state on the record the reasons for declining to order restitution. It refused to accept a provision in the 1990 crime legislation to extend restitution in cases not involving pleas beyond the "offense of conviction."[4] Moreover, in that same bill, Congress refused to approve a provision to require, rather than merely authorize, restitution in all cases.

State legislatures were also extremely active amending and enacting restitution statutes in the years following the President's Task Force report. By 1988, restitution was authorized or required in virtually every state as a condition of probation. In addition, over half the states provided for restitution in addition to, or in lieu of, other sentences. Some authorized restitution as a condition of parole, a condition of suspended sentence, and a condition of work release.[5]

In addition to successfully promoting legislation authorizing court-ordered restitution, the civil rights movement has successfully promoted legislation to *facilitate* restitution orders. The federal VWPA includes a requirement that the presentence report contain "information concerning any harm, including financial, social, psychological, and physical harm, done to or loss suffered by any victim of the offense" and "any other information that may aid the court in sentencing, including the restitution needs of any victim of the offense." Every state now allows some form of victim impact statement at sentencing (National Victim Center, 1994, p. 42). Thirty-nine explicitly allow for the inclusion of financial impact as an element of the victim impact statement, and 16 allow for the inclusion of a statement of the need for restitution (p. 42). In addition, some states passed laws to allow victims to provide information to officials before important decisions are made—for example, through consulting with prosecutors before cases are dismissed or before plea or sentencing negotiations are finalized, or through addressing the court before plea agreements are accepted.

The Courts

Several judicial surveys conducted in the 1970s before the victim movement gained momentum found judges strongly supportive of monetary restitution and confident about its rehabilitative effectiveness (Chesny, Hudson, & McLargen, 1978). By the late 1980s, judges seemed similarly supportive of restitution as a matter of justice to crime victims. In a 1987 nationwide survey of 77 state trial judges for a study on implementation of victim rights legislation, a considerable majority reported that victim impact information substantially affected both the number and size of restitution orders. Moreover, *all* said that they ordered restitution whenever the victim had suffered financial loss and the defendant seemed able to pay (Hillenbrand & Smith, 1989).

Although there are no national figures showing trends in restitution orders, there is little doubt that both the number and size of restitution orders have increased in recent years. For instance, in the federal courts (where many crimes such as drug-related ones are not subject to restitution), the percentage of total criminal sentences involving restitution rose from 9% to 16% between 1988 and 1991, and the median payment ordered rose from $525 to $2,500 (Tobolowsky, 1993, p. 94, citing annual reports from the U.S. Sentencing Commission). The increase in state courts is undoubtedly even greater. According to unpublished data from the Brooklyn, New York, Criminal Court, between 1978 and 1987 the restitution cases that the Victim Services Agency was asked to enforce increased from 480 cases totaling $97,000 to 4,447 cases totaling over $1 million—a 1,000% increase (Davis, Smith, & Hillenbrand, 1991).

In recent years, both federal and state appellate courts have addressed a number of restitution issues. Victims have often fared well, despite considerable reluctance of these courts to acknowledge legislatures' increasingly compensatory rationale for restitution statutes.[6] Somewhat ironically, it might be to victims' advantage not to force the issue. Courts clearly rely on an offender-based rationale to justify restitution in the criminal justice system. Acknowledgment that compensation is its primary purpose might result in relegating restitution to the civil justice system—where, as a practical matter, few victims would receive any compensation from their offenders.[7]

Improving Compliance and Victim Satisfaction

Victims, understandably, are most satisfied with restitution when the restitution order is for the entire amount of loss and is complied with in full by the offender (Davis, Smith, & Hillenbrand, 1992). Unfortunately, it appears that these two goals are often mutually exclusive because high compliance rates generally occur when the offender's means have been a factor in fashioning economic sanctions (Davis et al., 1992; McDonald, Greene, & Worzella, 1992). In fact, it is possible that if the increased emphasis of courts and legislatures on victims' rights results in larger restitution orders, compliance rates—and accordingly, victim satisfaction—will decrease. And compliance is already notoriously low. One study of four restitution programs with supposedly high compliance rates found that fewer than half the dollars awarded were collected (Smith, Davis, & Hillenbrand, 1989), and another found that only about a third of the dollars ordered in Chicago were collected (Lurigio, 1984, as cited in Lurigio & Davis, 1990).

Despite the impact of offenders' limited means on the amount of restitution they pay, most offenders probably could make more restitution than they typically do.[8] Studies have identified a number of ways—other than reducing the amount of the order itself—that compliance rates can be increased. Allen and Treger (1994) have shown that offenders' perceptions of the seriousness of the sanction as conveyed by the judge and the probation officer influence restitution payments. For example, compliance increases when full payment is articulated in the court order and decreases when the court order contains no payment plan, reflects only that the offender should make a "best effort" to comply, or leaves payment requirements to the probation officer's discretion. Moreover, in light of their finding that repeated contacts with courts and probation officers diminish probationers' initial fear that failure to pay the ordered restitution will result in their incarceration, these researchers were not surprised to find that the probability of compliance increases when the first payment is made within 30 days of the order. Lurigio and Davis (1990) have found that sending warning letters to delinquent offenders increases compliance, especially of employed offenders and offenders with few prior arrests and probations. Still other research has shown that compliance can be increased by monitoring payments and consistently taking actions when delinquencies occur, recommending extensions of time for delinquent offenders to pay restitution, and monitoring offenders with criminal records particularly closely (Smith et al., 1989).

To the extent that these strategies result in improving the collection of restitution dollars, they presumably will also increase victim satisfaction. Moreover, aside from compliance, it has also been shown that victim satisfaction can be increased if victims are informed about the award, told when to expect payments, and given the name of a person to contact about the award (Davis et al., 1992).

Victim-Offender Reconciliation Programs

Victim-offender reconciliation programs (VORPs) and victim-offender mediation programs are grounded in restorative justice theory. That theory rejects the premise that the state is the primary victim of the crime. Rather, restorative justice theory returns to a way of thinking about crime commonplace prior to the Norman invasion of Britain, in which crime is seen primarily as a conflict between individuals (Umbreit, 1994). Under this theory, the individual is the primary victim, and the state is the secondary victim. This contradicts the assumptions of our current system of justice and places the emphasis on holding the offender accountable for the crime and responsible to repay the victim for his actions (Zehr, 1990). As a result, restitution and apologizing to the victim become more important than punishment. Zehr (1990, as cited in Umbreit, 1994) best summarized the difference between the paradigm in which the state is viewed as the primary victim and the restorative justice paradigm in which the individual is viewed as the primary victim (see Table 14.1).

VORPs are intended to make offenders personally accountable for their behavior, instill in the offenders a sense of the human impact of crime, present offenders with the chance to face their victim and repay the damage done to the victim, enhance victim participation in the justice system, and improve the quality of justice rendered to both victims and offenders (Umbreit, 1994). VORPs typically involve a juvenile offender accused of a property crime,

Table 14.1 Zehr's Paradigms of Justice

Old Paradigm (State as Victim)	New Paradigm (Restorative Justice)
1. Crime defined as violation of state.	1. Crime defined as violation of one person by another.
2. Focus on establishing blame based on guilt, on past (did he/she do it?).	2. Focus on problem solving, on liabilities/obligations, on future (what should be done?).
3. Adversarial relationship and process are normative.	3. Dialogue and negotiation are normative.
4. Imposition of pain to punish and deter/prevent future crime.	4. Restitution as means of restoring both parties; goal of reconciliation/restoration.
5. Justice defined by intent and process: right rules.	5. Justice defined as right relationships; judged as outcome.
6. Interpersonal, conflictual nature of crime obscured, repressed; conflict seen as individual versus the state.	6. Crime recognized as interpersonal conflict; value of conflict is recognized.
7. One social injury replaced by another.	7. Focus on repair of social injury.
8. Community on sidelines, represented abstractly by state.	8. Community as facilitator in restorative process.
9. Encouragement of competitive, individualistic values.	9. Encouragement of mutuality.
10. Action directed from state of offender—victims ignored; offender passive.	10. Victim and offenders recognized in problem/solution: victim rights/needs recognized; offender encouraged to take responsibility.
11. Offender accountability defined as taking punishment.	11. Offender accountability defined as understanding impact of action and helping to decide how to make things right.
12. Offense defined in purely legal terms, devoid of moral, social, economic, or political dimensions.	12. Offense understood in whole context—moral, social, economic, political.
13. "Debt" owed to state and society in the abstract.	13. Debt/liability to victim recognized.
14. Response focused on offender's past behavior.	14. Response focused on harmful consequences of offender's behavior.
15. Stigma of crime unremovable.	15. Stigma of crime removable through restorative action.
16. No encouragement for repentance and forgiveness.	16. Possibilities for repentance and forgiveness.
17. Dependence on proxy by professions.	17. Direct involvement by participants.

usually a misdemeanor; less common are cases involving violent acts or felonies.

The first VORP began in 1974 in Canada. The idea spread to the United States in 1978, and as of 1994, there were more than 120 victim-offender mediation programs in the United States, most of which handled misdemeanor property cases involving strangers (Umbreit, 1991a).

Coates and Gehm (1989) first evaluated VORPs in four cities in Indiana. They found that 83% of the offenders and 59% of the victims were satisfied with the VORP process. Further, 97% of the victims expressed interest in using the VORP system in the future. Vic-

tims who were satisfied noted the following reasons: They had the chance to meet with the offender personally and gain an understanding of why the offender committed the crime, they received restitution for their losses, they realized that the offender was sorry for the harm inflicted on them, and they were pleased with the concern expressed by the mediator. Victims who expressed dissatisfaction listed the following reasons: Offenders did not pay the restitution they promised, an unreasonable amount of time elapsed between the crime and the VORP session, and the VORP process consumed too much of the victim's time. Offenders named the following aspects as most satisfying: The victim was willing to listen to their story, the process saved them from serving jail time, and they were able to arrange a practical restitution schedule. Ironically, offenders who were least satisfied with the VORP process most often named the reason other offenders found most satisfying: meeting the victim face to face (Coates & Gehm, 1989).

Umbreit (1989, 1990, 1994) has conducted much of the seminal work on VORP programs. He examined the "fairness" of VORPs from the victim's perspective. On the basis of 50 in-person interviews with victims of burglary committed by juveniles in Hennepin County, Minnesota, he concluded that of the victims referred to the VORP program, 62% chose actually to participate in the process. He measured three aspects of fairness: punishment of the offender, compensation of the victim, and rehabilitation of the offender. Victims were most concerned about the offender receiving rehabilitation, next most concerned about receiving restitution, and least concerned about punishing the offender through the imposition of jail time (Umbreit, 1994). Victims expressed high levels of satisfaction with the VORP process, with 97% stating that they were treated fairly in the session, 94% stating that the mediator was fair, 93% stating that the restitution agreement reached was fair, and 86% stating that it was helpful to meet the offender and talk with him or her about the offense (Umbreit, 1994).

A later study by Umbreit (1991b) analyzed data from 379 cases referred to the Center for Victim Offender Mediation in Minneapolis. This program, like many VORP programs, deals with juvenile offenders exclusively, offenders whose victims might be most open to giving the offender another chance through rehabilitation rather than jail time. Half of the referred cases resulted in a mediation session; the most common reasons for a VORP's not occurring were that the victim (35%) or the offender (25%) was not willing to mediate the case. In interviews with 51 victims and 66 juvenile offenders, Umbreit again found high rates of satisfaction, with three general areas named by victims as most satisfying. First, victims liked communicating to the offender the emotional and financial toll the crime inflicted on them. Second, they found satisfaction in directly confronting the offenders. Third, they wanted to help the offender receive the rehabilitation services they thought were indicated. Victims were also very satisfied with the process, with 90% stating that they liked the mediation program (Umbreit, 1994). In addition, 90% of the juvenile offenders were satisfied with the process, with four reasons cited most frequently. They liked (a) having the opportunity to explain why they had committed the offense, (b) agreeing to a mutually agreeable restitution plan, (c) paying the victim back, and (d) apologizing to the victim (Umbreit, 1994).

Building on his previous work, Umbreit (1994) conducted a large-scale quasi-experimental evaluation of four victim-offender mediation programs in Albuquerque, New Mexico; Minneapolis, Minnesota; Oakland, California; and Austin, Texas. A total of 1,153 interviews with victims and offenders were conducted among three groups: an experimental group of victims and offenders who participated in the mediation, a comparison group of victims and offenders who were referred to the programs but did not participate, and a second comparison group of victims who were not referred to the programs but matched those who were on key variables. Premediation interviews were conducted within a week of the mediation, and postmediation interviews were conducted about 2 months after the mediation (except in Austin, which was added to the study design later in the process, a feature that limited the study to one comparison group and a postmediation interview only).

Umbreit's (1994) large-scale study mirrors the high levels of satisfaction found in other studies. He found that 79% of the victims and

87% of the offenders were satisfied with the mediation and that 83% of the victims and 89% of the offenders were satisfied with the fairness of the mediation. The fear of being victimized again by the same offender lessened after the mediation, with 25% of the victims stating that they were afraid of such recidivism before the session and 10% after the session. Offenders who participated in the program were much more likely to pay the agreed-on restitution than those who did not participate but were court ordered to pay restitution (81% compared to 58%).

On the basis of previous studies, VORPs hold considerable promise for helping victims to understand the crime and the offender, helping victims to receive restitution and an apology, and securing high rates of satisfaction with the process and the outcome. The ABA passed a resolution in April 1994 urging their use in appropriate cases (as specified in 13 different qualifications about how and when the process should be used) that protect the rights of both victims and offenders. But VORPs are not without their critics in the victim advocacy community. The coordinator of a Victim/Witness Service program in Milwaukee, Wisconsin, for the last 20 years disputed Umbreit's findings and succinctly summarized the concerns of some members of the advocacy community:

> Most victims find face-to-face contact with offenders, even in the relative safety of a courtroom, frightening and anxiety arousing. The *very small* numbers of victims with whom we have had contact who wanted a face-to-face meeting with a defendant were typically sexual assault victims who wanted such a meeting in the extremely secure, post conviction setting of a maximum security prison. They do not seek "reconciliation," nor forgiveness; they seek only to know "why me?" . . . Victims' interests are only secondary concerns, at best in VORP programs, and at worst, VORP programs exert pressure on victims to participate, even though the programs vehemently proclaimed that participation was

"voluntary." (Kolandra, personal communication, July 16, 1993)

Victim Compensation Programs

Two major arguments have been advanced for public compensation to crime victims. One is an "obligation of the state" argument that the state has monopolized law enforcement and prosecution, reducing victims' access to redress, and that therefore the state creates a contract to protect the victim and should help compensate for its failure to do so. The other is a "social welfare" argument that the state has a moral obligation to help innocent victims (Galaway & Rutman, 1974).

The first crime victim compensation program began in California in 1965 and quickly spread to other states. The federal government's role and responsibility to help crime victims began with the passage of the Victims of Crime Act in 1984 and has been strengthened every year since. In 1990, the National Institute of Justice asked Abt Associates to update their earlier 1983 national overview of victim compensation programs. The update revealed the proliferation of programs and growth of such programs, as well as an increase in the types of victims of crimes eligible for compensation. According to the update (Parent, Auerback, & Carlson, 1992), 32 states and the Virgin Islands had crime victim compensation programs in 1983. By 1990, every state except Maine and South Dakota had such programs, and these states were planning to introduce such legislation in 1991.

In 1984, the federal government enacted the Victims of Crime Act (VOCA) to use federal dollars to supplement state funding of victim compensation programs and to provide more uniformity in eligibility requirements across states. VOCA established a Crime Victims Fund with revenues from fines, penalty assessments, and forfeited appearance bonds from federal offenders. The federal monies available to the states have steadily increased since VOCA began. Initially, Congress authorized a $100 million ceiling on the fund, but in 1986 it was raised to $110 million, in 1988 to $125 million, and in 1994 to $150 million (Parent et al., 1992).

In 1983, the Office for Victims of Crime (OVC) under the U.S. Department of Justice was created, and in 1986 OVC began VOCA funding to the states. If states meet the VOCA requirements, as much as 40% of their compensation awards can be reimbursed through federal grants (Parent et al., 1992). VOCA requirements dictate that the crime victim compensation program be available statewide. Further, amendments were made to VOCA in 1988 specifying four additional requirements: A state program must allow compensation (a) in domestic violence cases, (b) to victims who sustained injuries/death at the hands of drunk drivers, and (c) to residents who are victims in another state that does not have a victim compensation program, and (d) states that have an "unjust enrichment" provision to deny claims must establish rules delineating what constitutes "unjust enrichments" (Parent et al., 1992).

According to the 1994 Abt study, state programs awarded 50,200 claims in 1986, 56,200 in 1987, and 65,799 in 1988. This represents a total dollar award of $93.6 million in 1986, $110.5 million in 1987, and $125 million in 1987 (Parent et al., 1992). There is some variation across states in who is eligible for compensation. All states require that the victim report the crime to the police and cooperate in the prosecution of the offender. In addition, all states allow surviving family members to be compensated for funeral expenses and loss of support, but compensation for rehabilitation services is allowed in 37 states, for replacement services in 35 states, and for property losses in 8 states (Parent et al., 1992).

One of the primary criticisms of victim compensation programs is that they promise much but deliver little to victims. A number of studies of state violent crime compensation boards have documented that few victims of

violent crime apply for benefits, primarily because few victims know of their existence (Elias, 1986; Friedman, Bischoff, Davis, & Person, 1982; Gattuso-Holman, 1976; Karmen, 1984; McCormack, 1988). According to Elias (1986), compensation programs are chronically underfunded and represent only a symbolic commitment to make the public think their elected leaders are concerned about them. As he stated, "The public lauds its politicians for their concern, hoping it will never need the assistance, yet, if it ever should, it will effectively find little or no hope forthcoming" (p. 239).

Using the U.S. Department of Justice's *National Crime Survey* (NCS) and the Federal Bureau of Investigation's *Uniform Crime Report* (UCR), McCormack (1991) explored the use of victim compensation programs across states. He found that the proportion of violent crime victims requesting compensation ranged greatly from state to state, from a high of 31% in Colorado and Montana to 23% in Hawaii, 21% in Washington, and a low of 1.2% in Illinois and Louisiana. Interestingly, he also found that the states with the most requests were those that granted the most claims and that the states with the least requests also granted the least number of claims (McCormack, 1991). Unlike Elias (1986) and Karmen (1984), who had reported that most claims are rejected, McCormack (1988) found fairly high rates of claims awarded, but again with substantial variation across states. Nationally, the awards-to-claims ratio was 66%, with a high in Washington State of 100% and a low in New Jersey of 31%.

Thus evidence from previous studies is mixed. Some paint a picture of an underfunded burdensome system that few victims are made aware of, whereas others document large dollar payments to a good percentage of victims who apply for the funds. A further problem is that much of the compensation research is fairly dated; thus it is difficult to know whether studies from many years ago are applicable to today's programs.

Conclusion

In this chapter, we have discussed three ways that victims may be repaid for the financial harm inflicted on them. Restitution and VORPs are designed for the offender to reimburse the victim. Compensation programs allow for reimbursement by the state, often supplemented with federal dollars. All hold promise for "making victims whole," but it is important to recognize that only a small minority of victims benefit from these programs, for such reasons as lack of awareness about the programs, inability or unwillingness of defendants to pay restitution, insufficiency of state funds to compensate victims, and limits on which victims are eligible for compensation. Much has been accomplished to help victims with the financial burdens suffered as the result of crimes inflicted on them, but many victims remain uncompensated.

Notes

1. In *Kelly v. Robinson* (1986), the Supreme Court had ruled that state restitution obligations were not dischargeable under Chapter 7 of the Federal Bankruptcy Act because they were criminal penalties explicitly exempted from discharge under that chapter. In *Pennsylvania Department of Public Welfare v. Davenport*, (1990), the Court found that restitution obligations were dischargeable under Chapter 13 of the Bankruptcy Act because Congress had not explicitly exempted debts arising from a "fine, penalty, or forfeiture" in this chapter as it had in Chapter 7.

2. 11 USC 1328; 11 USC 523 (a) (13). The legislative history makes clear that Congress' action to ensure that restitution orders were not dischargeable was based on a concern for victims rather than for the rehabilitative interests of the state.

3. 18 USC 3663 (a) (3).

4. *Hughey v. U.S.* (1990), holding that a Victim Witness Protection Act restitution award is authorized only for the loss caused by the specific conduct that is the basis of the offense of conviction.

5. Compiled from information in National Organization for Victims Assistance (1987) and primary sources.

6. For example, the U.S. Supreme Court's ruling in *Kelly v. Robinson* (1986) that restitution obligations were not dischargeable under Chapter 7 of the Federal

Bankruptcy Act was heralded as a victory for victims. However, its basis was hardly victim oriented. "Because criminal proceedings focus on the State's interests in rehabilitation and punishment, rather than the victim's desire for compensation, we conclude that restitution orders . . . operate for the benefit of the State" (pp. 362-363). Several circuit courts have based their conclusion that the VWPA's failure to include Seventh Amendment jury requirements does not render the act unconstitutional on the finding that restitution is a criminal, rather than a civil, penalty. See *U.S. v. Palma* (1985), *U.S. v. Brown* (1984), *U.S. v. Satterfield* (1984/1985), *U.S. v. Keith* (1985). For an exception, see *U.S. v. Dudley* (1984), in which the court observed "an order of restitution, even if in some respects penal, also has the predominantly compensatory purpose of reducing the adverse impact on the victim" (p. 177).

7. Courts do not always agree about the purpose of restitution statutes. For example, one federal court found that "in drafting the restitution provisions of the VWPA, Congress made clear in both the language of the statute and its accompanying legislative history that victim restitution would be imposed as a criminal, rather than civil, penalty" (*U.S. v. Satterfield*, 1984, p. 836). Another federal court proclaimed that under the VWPA, "An order of restitution, even if in some respects penal, also has the predominantly compensatory purpose of reducing the adverse impact on the victim" (*U.S. v. Dudley,* 1984, p. 177).

8. National income figures are not available for probationers, the class of offender most likely to be ordered to make restitution. However, figures for prison inmates indicate that in 1991, 70% had earned less than $15,000 the year before their incarceration, and only 15% had earned more than $25,000. On the other hand, two thirds were employed at least part-time (Bureau of Justice Statistics, 1993, p. 3).

References

Allen, G., & Treger, H. (1994). Fines and restitution orders: Probationers' perceptions. *Federal Probation, 58,* 34-40.

American Bar Association. (1983). *Guidelines for fair treatment of crime victims and witnesses.* Washington, DC: Author.

American Bar Association. (1988). *Guidelines governing restitution to victims of criminal conduct.* Washington, DC: Author.

American Bar Association. (1992). *Model adult community corrections act.* Washington, DC: Author.

American Bar Association. (1994). *ABA criminal justice standards: Sentencing* (3rd ed.). Washington, DC: Author.

Bureau of Justice Statistics. (1993). *Survey of state prison inmates, 1991*. Washington, DC: U.S. Dept. of Justice.

Carrow, D. M. (1980). *Crime victim compensation: Program model*. Washington, DC: National Institute of Justice.

Chesny, S., Hudson, J., & McLargen, J. (1978). A new look at restitution: Recent legislation, programs and research. *Judicature, 61,* 348-357.

Coates, R., & Gehm, J. (1989). An empirical assessment. In M. Wright & B. Galaway (Eds.), *Mediation and criminal justice.* Newbury Park, CA: Sage.

Crime Control Act of 1990, 18 U.S.C. 1328 (1993).

Davis, R. C., Smith, B., & Hillenbrand, S. (1991). Increasing offender compliance with restitution orders. *Judicature, 74,* 245-248.

Davis, R., Smith, B., & Hillenbrand, S. (1992). Restitution: The victim's viewpoint. *Justice System Journal, 15,* 746-758.

Elias, R. (1986). *The politics of victimization: Victims, victimology and human rights.* New York: Oxford University Press.

Friedman, K., Bischoff, H., Davis, R., & Person, A. (1982). *Victims and helpers: Reactions to crime.* Washington, DC: Naitional Institute of Justice.

Galaway, B., & Rutman, L. (1974). An analysis of substantive issues. *Social Service Review, 28.*

Gattuso-Holman, N. (1976). Criminal sentencing and victim compensation legislation: Where is the victim? In E. Viano (Ed.), *Victims and society* (pp. 363-367). Washington, DC: Visage.

Gittler, J. (1984). Expanding the role of the victim in a criminal action: An overview of issues and problems. *Pepperdine Law Review, 11,* 117-182.

Hillenbrand, S., & Smith, B. (1989). *Victims rights legislation: An assessment of its impact on criminal justice practitioners and victims.* Unpublished report.

Hillsman, S., & Greene, J. (1988). Tailoring criminal fines to the financial means of the offender, *Judicature, 72,* 38-45.

Hughey v. U.S., 495 U.S. 411 (1990).

Karmen, A. (1984). *Crime victims: An introduction to victimology.* Monterey, CA: Brooks/Cole.

Kelly v. Robinson, 107 S.Ct. 353 (1986).

Lurigio, A., & Davis, R. (1990). Does a threatening letter increase compliance with restitution orders? A field experiment. *Crime and Delinquency, 36,* 537-548.

McCormack, R. (1988). *United States victim assistance programs.* Trenton, NJ: Trenton State College.

McCormack, R. (1991). Compensating victims of violent crime. *Justice Quarterly, 8,* 329-346.

McDonald, D., Greene, J., & Worzella, C. (1992). *Day fines in American courts: The Staten Island and Milwaukee experiments.* Washington, DC: National Institute of Justice.

McDonald, W. (1976). Toward a bicentennial revolution in criminal justice: The return of the victim. *American Criminal Law Review, 13,* 649-673.

National Institute of Justice. (1983). *Statement of recommended judicial practices.* Washington, DC: National Institute of Justice.

National Victim Center. (1994). *Impact statements: A victim's right to speak . . . a nation's responsibility to listen.* Arlington, VA: Author.

Parent, D., Auerback, B., & Carlson, K. (1992). *Compensating crime victims: A summary of policies and practices.* Washington, DC: National Institute of Justice.

Pennsylvania Department of Public Welfare v. Davenport, 110 S.Ct. 2126 (1990).

President's Task Force on Victims of Crime. (1982). *Report of the President's Task Force on Victims of Crime.* Washington, DC: Government Printing Office.

Sentencing Reform Act of 1984, 18 U.S.C. 3556 (1985).

Smith, B., Davis, R., & Hillenbrand, S. (1989). *Improving enforcement of court-ordered restitution to victims: Executive summary.* Washington, DC: American Bar Association.

Tobolowsky, P. M. (1993). Restitution in the federal criminal justice system. *Judicature, 77,* 90-95.

Umbreit, M. S. (1989). Victims seeking fairness, not revenge: Toward restorative justice. *Federal Probation, 53*(3), 52-57.

Umbreit, M. S. (1990). The meaning of fairness to burglary victims. In B. Galaway & J. Hudson (Eds.), *Criminal justice, restitution and reconciliation.* Monsey, NY: Criminal Justice Press.

Umbreit, M. S. (1991a, July). Having offenders meet with their victims offers benefits for both parties. *Corrections Today,* pp. 164-166.

Umbreit, M. S. (1991b, August). Minnesota mediation center gets positive results. *Corrections Today,* pp. 194-197.

Umbreit, M. (1994). *Victim meets offender: The impact of restorative justice and mediation.* Monsey, NY: Criminal Justice Press.

U.S. v. Brown, 744 F.2d 905 (2d Cir.), cert. denied, 469 U.S. 1089 (1984).

U.S. v. Dudley, 739 F.2d 175 (4th Cir. 1984).

U.S. v. Keith, 754 F.2d 1388 (9th Cir. 1985), cert. denied, 106 S.Ct. 93.

U.S. v. Palma, 760 F.2d 475 (3d Cir. 1985).

U.S. v. Satterfield, 743 F.2d 827 (11th Cir. 1984), cert. denied, 471 U.S. 1117 (1985).

Victim Witness Protection Act, 18 U.S.C. § 1801 *et seq.* (1982).

Victims of Crime Act, 42 U.S.C. § 10601 *et seq.* (1984).

Zehr, H. (1990). *Changing lenses: A new focus for crime and justice.* Scottsdale, PA: Herald.

15   Toward a Victim Policy Aimed at Healing, Not Suffering

EZZAT A. FATTAH

On Victims and Victimization

The Social Construction and Deconstruction of Victims

Although the word *victim* is one of the staples of the criminological language, and although it was used to coin the term *victimology*, its real criminological meaning remains unclear, and its utility remains in doubt. Just what does the term, as used in criminology and victimology, mean? Is it a label, a stereotype? Is it a state, a condition? Is it meant to assign a status, a role, to the one so described? Is it a self-perception, a social construction, an expression of sympathy, a legal qualification, a juridical designation? (Fattah, 1994b, p. 83).

Quinney (1972) suggested that the "victim" is nothing but a social construction. He pointed out that we all deal in a conventional wisdom that influences our perception of the world around us and that this wisdom defines for us just who the victim is in any situation,
which also means that alternative victims can be constructed.

In every society, there is a continuous process of constructing and deconstructing victims. The same witches who were burnt at the stake for being criminal and dangerous are now defined as victims of witch hunts. Fifty years ago, women beaten by their husbands, as well as children subjected to acts of violence in the process of upbringing, were neither defined as victims nor assigned victim status. As social attitudes changed, both groups were seen as legitimate candidates to the status of victim. When the age of consent to sexual practices was set at 21 or 18 years, those underage were defined and treated as victims. When the age was lowered to 14, teenagers between 14 and 18 or 21 were deconstructed as victims.

In recent years, the general tendency among victimologists has been to broaden the notion of victimization, to define it too widely and too loosely, and to apply the victim label to a wide variety of individuals and groups. In the process, victims have been constructed and created and have included persons who neither define nor perceive themselves as victims. The discrepancy between the self-perception and the external label is well illustrated in Boutellier's (1993) study of prostitutes in Holland. External observers tend to view the relationship of a prostitute to her pimp as one of exploitation and victimization. No one cares to see whether this diagnostic label, imposed from without, is shared by the prostitute herself, whether *she* defines and perceives herself as victim. Boutellier contrasted the "structuralist" and "subjectivist" views of prostitution. The structuralist (one may say the ideological) view argues that prostitution, by definition, is sexual violence, one of the ways in which men oppress women. The "subjectivist" position, on the other hand, takes as its point of departure the experiences of the women involved. In this perspective, prostitution is seen as a legitimate form of labor freely chosen by thousands of women. Boutellier pointed out that in the Netherlands women are no longer seen as just victims of sexuality. Prostitutes are viewed as being able to decide their own lives, as having freely chosen their occupation. This does not necessarily mean that there are no situations where women are forced into prostitution. But, generally speaking, prostitutes are no longer viewed or defined as victims.

Victimization is, therefore, a personal, subjective, and relative experience. Victimization defined according to the normative standards, a specific ideology, or the law may not be defined as such by those who are involved. Inversely, people may define and perceive themselves as victims although what they suffered does not fit the legal definition of victimization. The discrepancy is well described by Bilsky and Wetzels (1992):

> Obviously, individual thresholds come into play that reflect the ability and readiness to tolerate distressing or harmful events without feeling vic-

timized. The harmfulness of an event, the probability of its occurrence, and the personal vulnerability as perceived by the afflicted person may differ significantly from a bystander's point of view. Consequently, categorization of an incidence may fall apart and people may consider themselves victims of crime although this judgement neither fits the perception of others nor bears legal examination. (pp. 5-6)

Furthermore, "There are cases in which people have definitely been victimized according to normative (legal) standards although they do not understand their situation this way. The discrepancy in judgement can be attributed to different reasons, depending on the respective situation" (p. 6).

So what exactly are victimization surveys trying to measure? Despite the proliferation of these surveys in recent years, both nationally and internationally, it is far from clear whether their target is to measure those criminal victimizations that meet the criteria set by the criminal code or to measure the subjective victimizations experienced by the respondents. These, needless to say, are two different realities. Or to put it bluntly, are the surveys designed to measure crime or victimization? The terms *crime survey* and *victimization survey* continue to be used interchangeably.

Rape is a good case in point because of the enormous gap that may exist between the legal definition and the subjective experience of the female and because the sexual act can be experienced in very different ways by different women. Katie Roiphe (1993), for example, insisted that one person's rape may be another's bad night. She referred to current definitions of rape according to which "verbal coercion" or "manipulation" constitute rape.

One problem with current victim policies is that they are limited, almost by definition, to those to whom the legal label of "victim" has been attached. They are not inclusive policies but ones that exclude many, perhaps most, victims.

On Victims' Policy

The Eclipse and Reemergence of Crime Victims

Crime victims have long been a disenfranchised and disentitled group, exploited and mistreated by the criminal justice system and forgotten or ignored by the larger society. In the distant past, when all harmful actions were civil torts, when there was no differentiation between private wrongs and public crimes, victims enjoyed an unchallenged legal status. They were the principal protagonists when prosecutions were private, handled not by the Crown but by the person who suffered or his or her representative. The reduction of the victim to an inconsequential figure coincided with the emergence of the public prosecutor (Galaway & Hudson, 1981). But the real decline started with the emergence of a criminal law that viewed the criminal act not as an offense against the victim but as an offense against the sovereign and later the state. Gradually, the victim, who used to be the central figure, in whose name and on whose behalf the proceedings were conducted, was reduced to the status of a witness who was used to buttress the Crown's case and abused if he or she refused to cooperate or to testify. Once the state monopolized the right to criminal prosecution and converted the "wergeld" or the compensation, that used to be paid to the victim, into a fine destined to the king's coffers, the victim became the "forgotten figure," a legal nonentity.

As professionals and third parties (judges, prosecutors, lawyers, experts) assumed an increasingly important role in the criminal justice system, the victim's role became more and more peripheral, and victims were increasingly treated as irrelevant (see Galaway & Hudson, 1981, p. 229). According to Christie (1977), the root problem is that conflicts have become the property of professionals rather than people.

Victims' current plight stems from the fact that crime is no longer regarded as a conflict between two individuals, two human beings, but as a conflict between the offender and society. Viewed as such, crime generates not an obligation to the victim but a debt to society, and once the criminal is punished, the debt is paid. In this scenario, there is no place for the victims, no part for them to play. Even in an era of raised consciousness of victims' plight, the report of the Canadian Sentencing Commission (1987) leads to the painful realization that despite all the talk about victims, their rights, and their plight, this basic outlook has not changed. Instead of stating that the primary goal of sentencing is to repair the harm done to the victim by the offense and to prevent future harm, the commission regrettably declared that "the fundamental purpose of sentencing is to preserve the authority of, and promote respect for, the law through the imposition of just sanctions" (p. 151).

Such abstract goals are responsible for the depersonalization and dehumanization of the justice system. In an era meant to become the golden age of the victim, there seems to be a growing obsession with punishment, euphemistically called "just deserts." Yet having punishment as the central focus of the criminal justice system is neither morally legitimate nor practically effective. It can only act to the detriment of the victim. The constructive practices of dispute settlement, conflict resolution, mediation, reconciliation, and reparation are foreign to a system centered on punishment, a system that regards the crime not as a human action but as a legal infraction. Such a system acts to intensify the conflict rather than solve it. And instead of bringing the feuding parties closer to one another, it widens the gap that separates them.

Having been forgotten or ignored for several centuries, victims of crime are being rediscovered. Recent years have witnessed a revival of interest in those who suffer as a consequence of a criminal offence. In the 1960s, Margery Fry and others called for state compensation to crime victims, and their pleas led to the creation of government indemnification programs in New Zealand, the United Kingdom, North America, and Europe. In the 1970s, under the mounting influence of the women's movement, the plight of the victims, particularly victims of domestic violence and of sexual predations, became the object of a great deal of research and social action (Fattah, 1979, p. 199). The following decade witnessed the politicization of the cause of crime victims and the proliferation of groups claiming to speak on their behalf. Although in many cases the action of these groups is neither orchestrated nor coordinated, the term *victims' movement* is being widely used in both the popular and criminological literature (Fattah, 1986, p. 2). Surprisingly, there has been very little scrutiny of the actions of the victims' movement and very few critical assessments of its achievements. In fact, the quasi-unanimous response to the rhetorical cry of "justice for victims" has been favorable. The reaction to what has been described as "redressing the balances of justice" has been overwhelmingly (and rather surprisingly) noncontroversial and uncritical. One can say that the issue of victims' rights has not generated much negative concern, any serious criticism, or any meaningful confrontation. Victims' rights legislation and programs to help victims of crime have been greeted with enthusiasm and have encountered very little or no opposition (Fattah, 1992b, p. xi). The lack of any meaningful challenge or critique is all the more surprising because some of the implemented or proposed "reforms" do have far-reaching implications and the potential for fundamentally changing the system of criminal justice as we know it today (Fattah, 1992b, p. xi). Be this as it may, the enthusiastic approval of victim legislation and of the initiatives touted as essential to help and assist crime victims, despite their negative potential, is not difficult to understand. After all, no one wants to oppose or to speak against such a seemingly humanitarian endeavor. As Henderson (1992, p. 106) pointed out, the symbolic strength of the term *victims' rights*

overrides careful scrutiny: Who could be antivictim? The same view was expressed by Geis (1990):

> The movement to aid crime victims made both logical and emotional sense. Their case is compelling, and they traditionally have been ignored. Strong overt opposition to programs providing assistance to crime victims is not likely to surface. Who, after all, is willing to go on record as opposed to so preeminently worthy a cause? (p. 260)

The Victims' Movement: Achievements and Dangers

Few would disagree with the statement that the victims' movement has been very successful. Its achievements are many. First, it has focused attention on the plight of crime victims in modern, industrialized society and has sensitized the general public, the politicians, and the functionaries of the criminal justice system to the traumatic and long-lasting effects of certain types of criminal victimization. Victim groups have managed to raise public consciousness about certain harmful and traumatizing behaviors, such as sexual victimization, child abuse, family violence, and drunken driving, to mention but a few. The movement has been influential in changing social attitudes to victims of rape and domestic violence, among others, and in changing the practices of the criminal justice system regarding those victims and in general all crime victims.

On the applied side, the achievements of the victims' movement have been both emphatic and dramatic. The growth of service programs for victims of crime in the United States, Canada, the United Kingdom, and many other countries has been nothing short of phenomenal. During the 1980s legislation was passed, services were created, and programs were set up, all aimed at helping crime victims and improving their often unhappy lot.

At the First National Conference of Victim of Crime in Canada (Toronto, 1985), the victims' movement was called the growth industry of the decade ("Justice for All," 1985). In the United Kingdom, it is considered the fastest developing voluntary movement (see National Association of Victims Support Schemes, 1984). In 1990, Davis and Henley estimated the number of victim service programs in the United States to be in excess of 5,000, whereas 20 years earlier there had been none (p. 157).

One of the most significant achievements of the victim lobby was the formal approval by the General Assembly of the United Nations, on November 11, 1985, of the *United Nations Declaration of Basic Principles of Justice for Victims of Crime and Abuse of Power*. In adopting it, the General Assembly stated that it was "*cognizant* that millions of people throughout the world suffer harm as a result of crime and abuse of power and that the rights of these victims have not been adequately recognized" (p. 2).

In view of these spectacular achievements, could anything negative be said about the victims' movement, or is the balance sheet exclusively positive? Certain critics (Elias, 1992, 1994; Fattah, 1986, 1992a, 1992b; Henderson, 1992) have wondered whether there are ulterior motives behind the cry of "justice for victims" and the rhetoric of victims' rights. They have wondered whether there is a hidden agenda behind the sympathy exhibited toward crime victims.

It is, of course, an indisputable fact that victims of crime have long been a forgotten group, a group that suffered for centuries not only from society's neglect (see Fattah, 1989) but also from the expropriation of their rightful dues (fines) by the state. It is also true that they had their personal conflicts stolen by professionals and by the criminal justice system (Christie, 1977). However, the exceptional speed with which they were rediscovered and their cause adopted by politicians,

let alone the political climate that prevailed at the time of their rediscovery, is bound to raise questions about the real interests and motives behind what has been portrayed as a genuinely humanitarian and disinterested cause (Fattah, 1992b, p. 4).

Now that the legislative changes and the applied measures designed to help crime victims have been in place for over a decade, certain questions seem to be in order. Did the new initiatives achieve their goals? Did they tangibly improve the lot of crime victims? Are there negative side effects to the implemented and proposed changes? Have they redressed the balance of justice, or have they tipped the scale to one side? All these and many, many others are legitimate questions in search of answers.

The Danger of Using Crime Victims as Pawns in Law-and-Order Policies

Elias (1994) claimed that victims and the movement have been largely co-opted and politically manipulated for official purposes. He criticized victimologists for wanting to maintain the current course of action and to continue victim policy and research that largely reflect a conservative, law-and-order ideology (p. 6).

Conservative politicians, in particular, have been quick to adopt the cause of crime victims as their own and to advocate all kinds of punitive measures as necessary to do justice to the victims. The real intentions behind this rhetoric are not difficult to detect. As Phipps (1988) pointed out, when right-wing politicians speak of the crime problem and when they invoke outrage and sympathy on behalf of crime victims generally, citing instances of injuries, sufferings, and degradation of actual victims, their main purpose is to excite hostility against the offender or to discredit the laxity of the criminal justice system. Phipps added that the cause of crime victims "is also used to promote support for deterrence and retribution rather than for environmental measures to prevent crime. In this sense, the victim in conservative thinking is maintained in a role similar to that which he or she occupies in the prosecution process—a means to an end" (p. 180).

This view is quite similar to that of Henderson (1992). According to her, conservatives realized that victims can be an effective political symbol and thus began rhetorically to paint "the victim" as a sympathetic figure whose rights and interests could be used to counterbalance the defendant's rights. Henderson explained how the conservatives reinforced the image of the "victim" as a blameless, pure stereotype with whom all could identify. She related how the word *victim* was used almost exclusively to describe someone who is preyed on by strangers, a nonprovoking individual hit with violence of "street crime." The heart-rending (and rather atypical) cases selected by President Reagan's Task Force on Victims of Crime (1982) for inclusion in their final report leave no doubt as to the validity of Henderson's claim.

Elias, Henderson, Walker, and others believe that the victims' rights movement (which might originally have been viewed as a populist movement) has become increasingly co-opted by the concerns of advocates of the "crime control" model of criminal justice. Walker (1985) insisted that conservatives have seized the victims' rights issue and made it their own. He reminded us, for example, that in California the advocates of Proposition 8 (the Victims' Bill of Rights) were the traditional prosecution-oriented law-and-order leaders, whereas civil libertarians were the primary opponents. Another example he gave in support of his view was that of President Reagan's Task Force on Victims of Crime, which was dominated by traditional conservative spokespersons.

Crime victims are not the first group to have their cause exploited by unpopular governments seeking a higher rating in opinion polls, opportunist politicians seeking electoral votes, or incompetent public officials trying to

detract attention from their failure to control crime or to reduce its incidence. Showing concern for crime victims acts as a cover-up for the inefficiency of the system and its inability to prevent victimization. Demanding that something be done to help and to alleviate the plight of victims masks society's unwillingness to deal squarely with the problem of crime. In times of growing concern about crime, showing sympathy for the victim and committing a handful of dollars to victim programs and services relieves the pressure on politicians to confront social injustices, ethnic conflict, inequalities in wealth and power, and the frustrations of seeing too much and having too little (Fattah, 1992b, p. 45).

The Danger of Turning Sympathy for Crime Victims Into a Cry for Vengeance

Pity, sympathy, and empathy are among the most noble and worthy human sentiments. Socially, these altruistic emotions are indispensable for group solidarity, for caring for and sharing with those members of the group who suffer as a result of some misfortune or mishap. Unfortunately, these noble and altruistic human sentiments can be and sometimes are exploited to achieve utilitarian goals or political ends. Sympathy for crime victims has been increasingly (and successfully) used in recent years to generate a backlash against criminal offenders. The declared objectives of victim groups in North America bear this out (Fattah, 1992b, p. 8).

In Canada, victims' groups have been vociferous in their attempts to bring back the death penalty, to tighten eligibility for parole, to abolish early release (resulting from statutory remission), and so forth. They have also been relentless in their demands for tougher sentences and longer prison terms. Sex offenders, most of whom are in desperate need of treatment because of sexual, social, or mental inadequacies, are usually singled out for particularly tough penalties. In a brief presented at Toronto City Hall (November 23, 1982) on behalf of Victims of Violence, an advocacy group, the group president, Don Sullivan, made the following statement:

> We firmly believe that the sentences that are being handed down in Ontario are far too lenient for sexual offences. The incarceration of such offenders is far too short. They are getting out far too soon, either on parole or "by law" on automatic release after only two thirds of their sentences. This has become the norm rather than the exception. (Amernic, 1984, p. 190)

The brief then went on to demand mandatory minimum sentences for all first-time sex offenders. It stated, "We firmly believe that mandatory sentences must be prescribed by law for all rapists and sex offenders. A sentence of at least five years, and preferably seven years, must be given for all first offenders" (p. 191).

What Canadian victims' groups were doing was merely to echo what their counterparts south of the border had been saying for many years. The increasing militancy of the so-called victim advocates in the United States has had many consequences, including a resurgence of vigilante justice (Karmen, 1990) and the formation of vigilante groups such as the Guardian Angels in New York, a group that served as a model for similar groups in several American and Canadian cities. The group received a great deal of publicity through the case of Bernhard Goetz, who shot four unarmed young men who accosted him on a subway train but was found guilty only of possessing an illegal weapon (Dershowitz, 1988; Fletcher, 1988; Karmen, 1990).

In addition to street vigilance, there is also what may be called "court vigilance." Mawby and Gill (1987) reported that a California group called Citizens for Law and Order operated a "court watcher" program and published attacks on judges considered lenient. They also cited other groups' attempts to influence court decisions through direct intervention, such as having a victim advocate representing the victim in court and demanding harsher penalties than those asked for by the prosecutors.

The "horror story syndrome" (Walker, 1985), which has been the trademark of the victim movement in Canada and the United States, gained a stamp of approval in the final report of the President's Task Force on Victims of Crime (1982). A brief excerpt from the report will illustrate the tone and the tactics used by task force members who, for all practical purposes, served as the spokespersons for the American victim lobby. After claiming that murder, kidnap, and rape are commonplace, the task force went to great lengths to show that offenders are not being punished enough but are being "pampered" by the criminal justice system:

> The judge sentences your attacker to three years in prison, less than one year for every hour he kept you in pain and terror. That seems very lenient to you. Only later do you discover that he will probably serve less than half of his actual sentence in prison because of good-time and work-time credits that are given to him immediately. The man who broke into your home, threatened to slit your throat with a knife, and raped, beat, and robbed you will be out of custody in less than 18 months. . . .
>
> The defendant's every right has been protected, and now he serves his time in a public facility, receiving education at public expense. In a few months his sentence will have run. Victims receive sentences too; their sentences may be life long. (p. 11)

Helping Crime Victims: What Needs to Be Done?

A close look at the so-called victims' initiatives and at the measures supposedly designed to help crime victims and alleviate their plight reveals that the rhetorical cry of "justice for victims" has been nothing more than an empty slogan. Measures introduced to assist crime victims such as victim compensation, victim impact statements, and victims' right of allo-

cution have been described as political pallia-
tives (Burns, 1980), political placebos (Chappell, 1972), and Band-Aid measures.

Negative assessments come from both sides
of the Atlantic. In the United States, Elias
(1992) painted a rather gloomy picture of victims' initiatives:

> Yet for all the new initiatives, victims have gotten
> far less than promised. Rights have often been
> unenforced or unenforceable, participation spo-
> radic or ill-advised, services precarious and un-
> derfunded, victim needs unsatisfied if not further
> jeopardized, and victimization increased, if not in
> court, then certainly in the streets. Given the
> outpouring of victim attention in recent years,
> how could this happen, and who benefits instead?
> (p. 91)

In Britain, Paul Rock (1990) argued that victims' interests were never the motivating or
mobilizing force behind the new initiatives:

> Criminal injuries compensation was supposed to
> mollify the reactionary victim-vigilante, and
> reparation was a device to divert offenders from
> custody. In both instances, victims were the crea-
> tures of penal imperatives, invested with the char-
> acters needed to get on with the business of
> reforming prisons. Compensation and reparation
> did not have much of a foundation in the declared
> or observed requirements of victims themselves:
> they were bestowed on victims in order to achieve
> particular ends. (p. 408)

As suggested earlier, victims' current plight
stems from the fact that crime is no longer
regarded as a conflict between two individuals, two human beings, but as a conflict between the offender and society. It is difficult
to understand how an act that hurts, injures, or
harms a human being, an act that might thoroughly affect the person's life and disrupt his
or her existence, can be considered an offense
not against that individual but against society.
How is it that such a personal offense does not
create an obligation to the victim but rather a
debt to society? And how is it that when the

wrongdoer is sentenced to a fine, the money
goes not to the victim but to the state? Approximately 90% of the cases that come before
the criminal courts end up in a sentence to a
fine of varying amounts. It does not seem fair
that if the source of injury, harm, or loss happens to be an act defined as a criminal offense,
the money paid by the person who caused it
goes to the state, whereas if the source happens
to be a civil matter, such as negligence, accident, or medical malpractice, the damages are
paid to the person who suffered. Why is it that
plaintiffs in civil disputes are entitled to all the
damages ordered by the courts, whereas victims of acts arbitrarily defined as crimes get
very little or nothing (Fattah, 1995)? All this
points to the need for a new justice paradigm.
The mounting concern for crime victims suggests that the punishment system, as detrimen-
tal as it is to the interests of the victim, will
have to give way to another system in which
victim needs are met and victim wishes are
respected. Replacing the retributive model of
criminal justice by a restorative model will
signal the dawning of a new era for crime
victims. As the Friends World Committee for
Consultation (n.d.) stated in its brief to the
United Nations:

> Restorative justice respects the basic human
> needs of the victim, the offender and the commu-
> nity. The administration of justice, according to
> the restorative model, includes the active partici-
> pation of people directly involved and affected
> by the criminal activity. Settlements provide re-
> dress to the victim and make it possible for the
> offender to fulfil agreed obligations. (p. 1)

What Do Crime Victims Really Want?

But is the restorative justice model truly
superior to the punitive model from the victims' point of view? To answer this question,
let us examine two related ones: (a) What do
victims get from the present punitive, retributive justice system? and (b) What do the victims want: vengeance or redress?

A punitive, retributive system of justice offers nothing to the victim of crime, except maybe for the very few whose vindictive sentiments are satisfied by nothing other than seeing the offender suffer. Whatever satisfaction vengeance may provide is usually ephemeral and short-lived. More important still is that the criminal law not be used to promote revenge and retaliation or to offer blood to those who are bloodthirsty. This is the main rationale behind abolishing the death penalty in so many countries. The primary aims of the criminal law should be to restore peace, heal the injury, and redress the harm. Its main function should be to achieve conciliation, not retaliation; to settle human conflicts, not perpetuate them; and to bring the two feuding parties closer together instead of setting them apart. One has to keep in mind that a high percentage of violent crime is committed between people who are related to each other by some family or other personal relationship. This fact alone shows how essential it is to have a conflict-resolving mechanism that settles the dispute and prevents further violence while maintaining those vital relationships intact. The system of punishment does exactly the opposite. It breaks the ties, disrupts the harmony, and generates a great deal of hostility and antagonism. This hostility and antagonism render any future reconciliation either very difficult or virtually impossible.

The answer to the second question—do victims want vengeance or redress from the justice system?—is an easy one. Studies by Boers Sessar (1992), by Umbreit (1989) in the United States, Pfeiffer (1993) in Germany, Waller and Okihiro (1978) in Canada, and many others show unequivocally that victims are not as vindictive or as bloodthirsty as the advocates of the punishment model would want us to believe. Their primary concern is to have redress: to have the stolen goods returned, the broken window fixed, the vandalized car repaired, the destroyed bike replaced. Their expectations and their demands are realistic, not moralistic.

The television documentary *From Fury to Forgiveness,* shown on the Canadian Broadcasting Corporations's program *The Passionate Eye,* demonstrates in a vivid and deeply moving manner that even victims who lose their young children or close relatives to homicidal killers can show genuine forgiveness and can plead with the justice system for the lives of their victimizers.

They have down-to-earth goals, quite different ones from the divine and metaphysical goals, such as expiation, atonement, or retribution, that are pursued by a theocratic criminal justice system. Victims see the offence committed against them as creating a direct obligation for redress, not as creating a debt to society or to divinity that can be settled only by an expiatory punishment.

In its attempt to achieve divine, metaphysical, and abstract goals, the criminal justice system ignores the basic needs of the victims; it leaves their wishes unfulfilled and their desires unmet. This is particularly true of the primary need for compensation.

Because the vast majority of victims of property crime cannot afford and have no insurance, because three quarters of crimes are property crimes, and because state compensation programs are strictly limited to violent crime, the majority of victims do not get any compensation for whatever loss they have suffered. In punitive systems, there are two losers: Victims lose their property, and offenders lose their liberty.

Policies of Inclusion and Policies of Exclusion

Victims of crime, long ignored, neglected, and at times abused, have finally been rediscovered. Their plight and their rights have been universally recognized. At present, there seems to be a consensus that they are entitled to the help, support, and redress that other victims get. There is less unanimity, however, regarding the philosophy of reform, the means by which victims' needs could best be met, and the nature of the policies needed to improve their lot and alleviate their plight. Although many firmly believe that crime victims are better served by policies of inclusion that promote healing, reconciliation, and redress (Fattah, 1995; Wright, 1991; Zehr, 1990), many of the policies introduced in the last decade in North America have been policies of intrusion and exclusion. Such policies, warned Scheingold, Olson, and Pershing (1994), enhance the power of the State and pose obvious threats to freedom. Scheingold et al. stated that the new policy process is being driven by extreme and atypical events, and they reiterated Reiss's (1981, p. 225) warning that victim advocacy tends to build idiosyncratically on the public's reaction to extreme crimes. One good example of the contentious policies is that of offender registration and community notification when someone is released from prison or placed in a halfway house. But there are many, many others.

The policies of exclusion are based on an erroneous premise, the assumption that victim and offender populations are not only distinct but mutually exclusive. This false dichotomy between offenders and victims is in flagrant contradiction to a sizable and growing body of evidence pointing to a strong link between victimization and offending and to a substantial overlap between offenders and victims (see Fattah, 1991, 1994a; Johnson, Kerper, Hayes, & Killinger, 1973; Mayhew & Elliott, 1990; Sampson & Lauritzen, 1990; Singer, 1981, 1986; Thornberry & Figlio, 1972). Criminological studies in Europe, the United States, Canada, and Australia show that offenders and victims involved in the types of crimes covered by victimization surveys share many characteristics and that the demographic profiles of crime victims and of convicted criminals are strikingly similar (Gottfredson, 1984). These findings led Reiss (1981) to state:

Not only does considerable overlap exist between populations of victims and offenders as demonstrated by the substantial proportion of violators having also been victims, but considerable evidence exists that the experience of being victimized increases the propensity for offending and that populations of victims and offenders have homogeneous characteristics. . . . Clearly any theory that assumes no overlap exists between populations of victims and offenders or that they are distinct types of persons distorts the empirical research. (pp. 710-711)

Criminological and victimological research is increasingly showing that the roles of victim and offender are neither fixed nor antagonistic, but rather revolving and interchangeable. Studies of abused children who grow up to become abusive parents, sexually molested children who become sexual offenders, and battered wives who kill their batterers are only a few examples of how the victims of yesterday are the offenders of today and how the offenders of today may become the victims of tomorrow. The fact that retaliation is a major ingredient in expressive violence (Black, 1983; Fattah, 1994a; Felson & Steadman, 1983) explains well the frequent transformation of victims into victimizers and aggressors.

Policies of exclusion are an attempt to deny, minimize, or deemphasize the affinities, similarities, and substantial overlap between victim and offender populations. They imply, to use David Miers's (1989) words, "that there is a qualitative disjunction between victims and offenders" (p. 9), an implication that is contrary to the empirical evidence.

Policies of exclusion perpetrate the distorted stereotypes of offenders and victims and reinforce the predator-prey model of criminal victimization as well as the normative distinction between the active aggressor and the passive sufferer.

Respecting the Rights of Victims and the Rights of Offenders

The politicization of the cause of crime victims has not been without its negative side effects. In the last decade, victim advocates targeted many of the traditional legal safeguards for abolition and created a false contest between the rights of offenders and the rights of victims (Elias, 1992; Fattah, 1992b; Henderson, 1992; Karmen, 1990). They claimed that much concern has been shown for the "rights of criminals" and not enough for the plight of the innocent people they harm, and they demanded that the rights of victims be restored at the expense of offenders' rights (Karmen, 1990). Summarizing the demands of victims' advocates, Karmen wrote:

> To restore some semblance of balance to the scales of justice, which have been tipped in favor of criminals, some of the "anti-victim" opportunities and privileges offenders have accumulated must be stripped away. According to this analysis, victims need rights to counterbalance, match, or even "trump" the rights of criminals. In this context, reform means reversing previous court decisions and legal trends, shifting the balance of power away from wrongdoers and toward injured parties. (p. 331)

The report of the President's Task Force on Victims of Crime in the United States (1982) and its recommendations can be read as a damning indictment of many of the legal safeguards that the American justice system has established over the years to protect against the conviction of the innocent and to uphold the rights and freedoms so deeply cherished in a democracy (Fattah, 1992b). One of the main recommendations of the report is the abolition of the exclusionary rule, something that President Reagan had advocated as a major step in the fight against crime. The exclusionary rule, which stipulates that illegally obtained evidence cannot be used in court to obtain a conviction of an accused in a criminal case, is used predominantly in drug cases. One has to wonder about the benefits that victims would gain by having it abolished! In fact, its abolition in California following the "yes" vote on Proposition 8 (the Victims' Bill of Rights) has worked not for but against victims, particularly victims of rape, by making it possible for defense lawyers to have the victims examined by psychiatrists or to question the victim about sexual activity she had engaged in shortly prior to the alleged rape (Paltrov, 1982). Another recommendation of the U.S. Task Force on Victims of Crime was to impose severe restrictions on the right to be released on bail, a right that is derived directly from the presumption of innocence.

The fight to have some of the traditional legal safeguards abolished has been successful. For instance, rules of evidence used to require that the testimony of alleged rape victims be corroborated to protect against false accusations. Almost all American states have by now relieved the prosecution of the burden of providing corroboration of the rape accusation (Feher, 1992).

In some cases, such as cases of child sexual abuse, the burden of proof has almost been reversed. Noting that child sexual abuse is a crime that will often leave no physical evidence even when it actually has occurred, Feher (1992) drew attention to the inherent danger:

> In the context of an *actual* occurrence of abuse, the repeal of this rule [corroboration] would appear beneficial. But in the context of a man on trial for accusations which are the product of the interviewing process, the result is that one more procedural safeguard to incorrect convictions has been removed. (p. 22)

In addition to eliminating the corroboration requirement, some jurisdictions have introduced new rules that severely inhibit the defendant's ability to cross-examine the child witness. Other changes include permitting a videotaped statement or live testimony through closed-circuit television instead of the normal under-oath deposition followed by cross-examination (see Fattah, 1992b, p. 22).

Another important change has been the introduction of the so-called rape-shield laws, which prohibit the use of either reputation or opinion evidence of an alleged rape victim's past sexual behavior, thus restricting the circumstances in which and the extent to which the defendant in a rape case may present this type of evidence to the jury ("Texas Rape-Shield Law," 1988). In 1991, the Supreme Court of Canada, in a 7-2 ruling, declared the rape-shield provision of the criminal code to be unconstitutional because it could lead to the conviction of innocent defendants (see Fattah, 1992b, p. 23).

The right of allocution, victim impact statements, and victim involvement in parole hearings can only lead to harsher sentences, longer terms of imprisonment, and delayed release from penal institutions. They are incompatible with less punitive measures, such as diversion and decarceration. It is difficult to see what victims in general can gain from such punitive measures. Despite the rhetorical justifications, it seems clear that their primary objective is not to ensure justice for crime victims or to alleviate their suffering, but simply to reverse the humanitarian trend of the 1950s and the 1960s (Fattah, 1992b). Even the terminology used, such as the popular statement that "the scales of justice have been tipped in favor of the offender and need to be rebalanced to ensure justice for the victim," betrays the punitive intentions and retributive motives of the new ideology. It is undeniable that the demands for retribution symbolized in the rhetorical cry "justice for victims" have contributed to a general punitive climate and have played in the hands of conservative politicians who were anxious to use the victims as pawns in their law-and-order policy.

What is overlooked by the new initiatives and the new policies is that a fair, humane, and efficient justice system serves the interests of both victims and offenders. Inhumane treatment of the offender is not and need not be an outcome or a corollary of humanitarian consideration for the victim. And it is not necessary to sacrifice the basic or the constitutional rights of the offender to affirm or safeguard the rights of the victim (Fattah, 1986, p. 12). Surely the suffering of the victim is not diminished by increasing the suffering of the offender. Inflicting undue pain on the perpetrator of the crime does not alleviate the victim's distress, and the humiliation suffered by the victim is not erased by the degradation of the offender. Humaneness is indivisible. The concern for the victim should not obliterate the fact that those who are labeled as criminals are more often than not victims themselves.

Helping Crime Victims: What Works?

Although victim services have been in existence for several years, there are still many unknowns and several unanswered questions. Maguire and Shapland (1990) have warned that unless research continues to be done on victims' own beliefs and needs, there will always be a danger that agencies set up for their benefit will come to serve only organizational goals. The crucial question of what works to help victims recover from postvictimization trauma remains without answer. Davis and Henley (1990) reviewed research findings and found little indication that counseling of any sort is effective in reducing postcrime trauma. They insisted that the effects of counseling are not easy to measure and that the methodological problems involved in trying to measure those effects are substantial. Despite this, much money is being spent on crisis intervention services for victims in the absence of knowledge as to which forms of treatment work and which do not. This is surprising because it is well known that certain forms of intervention can do more harm than good and can aggravate or perpetuate the psychological wounds rather than healing them. Some interventions can be effective in some cases and totally ineffective in others or beneficial to some recipients and deleterious to others. A decade ago, I warned that victim services might have a side effect of delaying the natural healing process and prolonging the trauma of victimization (Fattah, 1986). I suggested that there might be a relationship between the new interventionist techniques with crime victims and the manifestly growing pains of victimization. I asked, "Could the heightened fear of victimization reported in recent years be related in any way to the increasing attention, the outpour of sympathy and the wide publicity being given to the victims of crime? Do policies of intervention prolong rather than shorten the traumatic effects of victimization?" (1986, p. 11).

Lurigio and Resick (1990) insisted that because reactions to crime and other deleterious experiences are often quite varied, it is important to study individual differences in response to criminal victimization. They stated that variability in victim recovery can be a function of victim characteristics and predispositions, the nature of the incident, victims' perceptions and interpretations of the occurrence, and events that occur in the aftermath of the crime. It is clear that the emphasis here is on the individual correlates of postcrime distress and recovery. But sociocultural factors and attitudes can be of great importance as well and do play a significant role in speeding up or delaying the recovery process. In our society, there is a tendency to stress, even overblow, the negative effects of victimization, whereas in others only the positive effects are emphasized. Even physical injuries resulting from victimization do not carry the same weight everywhere, and their impact, therefore, is bound to be greater or lesser according to a host of variables. It is undeniable that psychological wounds heal faster and better in some cultures than in others. Research is necessary to find out the characteristics of the cultures that facilitate and accelerate the healing process and those of the cultures that hinder or delay the victim's recovery. Why are the coping mechanisms and coping strategies better developed in certain cultures than in others? What role does the social network have? It is well known that the network is stronger and more cohesive in certain cultures than in others.

Although cross-cultural research of the type described above is lacking and urgently needed, certain things appear rather obvious. Healing and recovery are bound to be faster and more complete in cultures in which victimization, particularly minor forms of victimization, is not taken too seriously and its effects are minimized. If this is true, could recent efforts in Western societies to provide professional help to crime victims backfire? Might emphasizing the seriousness of victimization and magnifying its effects delay the healing process and make it more difficult for the victims to recover from the trauma they might have suffered? Is it possible that stressing over and over again how traumatic and long-lasting the effects of victimization are acts as a constant reminder to the victim that the process of recovery is difficult, complicated, and lengthy and that becoming whole again is not easily achieved? Could it become a self-fulfilling prophecy? After all, this seems to be the opposite strategy to what physicians and psychiatrists generally employ when dealing with physical and mental illness. In these cases, they assume a comforting and reassuring stance and try to convey to the patient a positive and optimistic outlook. Could the provision of professional help to victims, which is usually done with the best intentions, have the opposite effect by giving victims the impression that there is no way they can cope on their own, that to recover they will have to receive professional and continuing help?

Yet another area provides excellent opportunities for comparative research of the cross-cultural variety, namely the impact of the social response to victimization on the recovery of the victims. Do victims recover better or worse in retributive justice systems as compared to those in restorative justice systems? Do mediation, reconciliation, restitution, and compensation have a more positive impact on the victim's recovery than retaliatory sanctions, or is recovery conditional on the satisfaction of the victim's vindictive instincts by a punishment that inflicts pain and suffering on the victimizer?

Conclusion

Attempts to exploit the cause of crime victims for political ends and to sell the policies of law and order under the pretext of doing justice to victims have often required the portrayal of victims as vengeful, vindictive, retributive, and even bloodthirsty. Those claiming to represent and speak on behalf of victims have given the impression that concern for crime victims invariably requires harsh, punitive justice policy. Although the distress of some victims may be so overwhelming that they will demand the harshest possible penalty for their victimizer, this can hardly be said of the majority of victims. Healing, recovery, redress, and prevention of future victimization are the primary objectives of most crime victims.

If the primary purpose of social intervention is to restore the peace, redress the harm, heal the injury, and stop the repetition of the offence, it is easy to understand how and why the restorative system (based on mediation, reconciliation, restitution, and compensation) succeeds where the punishment system fails.

Mediation and reconciliation bring the two parties face to face, and ensure that they see each other as human beings in a state of distress. When faced with the victim, it becomes impossible for the victimizer to deny the victim's existence or the injury or harm he or she has caused. The victimizer can no longer depersonalize or objectify the victim. He or she can no longer avoid postvictimization cognitive dissonance. The confrontation between the offender and the victim in a mediation situation is the surest and most effective means of sensitizing him or her to the victim's plight, of countering and reversing the mental process of desensitization that he or she has gone through to avoid guilt feelings or bad conscience (Fattah, 1991).

The mediation process, when done properly, can be very effective in awakening and activating any positive emotions the offender might have lying beneath his or her cruel and indifferent facade. Emotions such as sympathy, empathy, and compassion can be brought to the surface and reinforced.

On the side of the victim, the mediation situation can also have salutary effects. The feared, strong, cruel, and unemotional victimizer is bared to his or her weak and often helpless being, a being that evokes more pity than fear, more compassion than anger. Distorted but long-held stereotypes disappear when checked against the real offender. Both parties end up by gaining a realistic view of one another, and reconciliation becomes possible (Fattah, 1995, p. 312).

Thus, in the long run, the interests of crime victims and of society at large are best served by humanity, empathy, compassion, tolerance, and forgiveness, by the development of conciliatory and forgiving communities rather than hostile and vengeful ones (Fattah, 1986, p. 13). Constructive healing, not destructive punishment, should be the primary and foremost goal of both victim policy and victim services.

References

Amernic, J. (1984). *Victims: The orphans of justice.* Toronto: McClelland & Stewart-Bantam.

Bilsky, W., & Wetzels, P. (1992). Victimization and crime: Normative and individual standards of evaluation. *International Annals of Criminology, 32,* 135-152.

Black, D. (1983). Crime as social control. *American Sociological Review, 48*(1), 34-45.

Boers, K., & Sessar, K. (1991). Do people really want punishment? On the relationship between acceptance of restitution, needs for punishment, and fear of crime. In K. Sessar & H. J. Kerner (Eds.), *Developments in crime and crime control research* (pp. 126-149). New York: Springer.

Boutellier, J. C. J. (1993). *Solidariteit en slachtofferschap: De morele betekenis van criminaliteit in een postmoderne cultur.* Nijmegen, The Netherlands: SUN.

Boutellier, J. C. J. (1993). *Solidarity and victimization.* English summary of a Dutch Ph.D. dissertation. Nijmegen, The Netherlands: SUN.

Burns, P, (1980). *Criminal injuries compensation.* Toronto: Butterworths.

Canadian Sentencing Commission. (1987). *Final report.* Ottawa: Ministry of Supply and Services.

Chappell, D. (1972). Providing for the victims of crime: Political placebos or progressive programmes? *Adelaide Law Review, 4,* 294-306.

Christie, N. (1977). Conflicts as property. *British Journal of Criminology, 17,* 1-15.

Claster, D. S. (1992). *Bad guys and good guys: Moral polarization and crime.* Westport, CT: Greenwood.

Davis, R. C., & Henley, M. (1990). Victim service programs. In A. J. Lurigio, W. G. Skogan, & R. C. Davis (Eds.), *Victims of crime: Problems, policies, and programs* (pp. 157-171). Newbury Park, CA: Sage.

Dershowitz, A. (1988). *Taking liberties: A decade of hard cases, bad laws, and bum raps.* Chicago: Contemporary Books.

Elias, R. (1992). Which victim movement? The politics of victim policy. In E. A. Fattah (Ed.), *Towards a critical victimology* (pp. 74-99). London: Macmillan.

Elias, R. (1994, Autumn). Has victimology outlived its usefulness. *Journal of Human Justice, 6,* 4-25.

Fattah, E. A. (1979). Some recent theoretical developments in victimology. *Victimology: An International Journal, 4,* 198-213.

Fattah, E. A. (1986). On some visible and hidden dangers of the victim movement. In E. A. Fattah (Ed.), *From crime policy to victim policy: Reorienting the justice system* (pp. 1-14). London: Macmillan.

Fattah, E. A. (1989). Victims and victimology: The facts and the rhetoric. *International Review of Victimology, 1,* 43-66.

Fattah, E. A. (1991). *Understanding criminal victimization.* Englewood Cliffs, NJ: Prentice Hall.

Fattah, E. A. (1992a, June). *The positives and negatives of the victim movement: A critical assessment.* Paper presented at the 4th Symposium on Violence and Aggression, Saskatoon, Canada.

Fattah, E. A. (1992b). *Towards a critical victimology.* London: Macmillan.

Fattah, E. A. (1994a). *The interchangeable roles of victim and victimizer.* Helsinki: European Institute for Crime Prevention and Control.

Fattah, E. A. (1994b). Victimology: Some problematic concepts, unjustified criticism and popular misconceptions. In G. F. Kirchoff, E. Kosovski, & H. J. Schneider (Eds.), *International debates of victimology* (pp. 82-103). Mönchengladbach: WSV.

Fattah, E. A. (1995). Restorative and retributive justice models: A comparison. In H. Heiner-Kühne (Ed.), *Festschrift in Honour of Professor Koichi Miyazawa* (pp. 305-315). Baden-Baden: Nomos Verlagsgesellschaft.

Feher, T. L. (1992). The alleged molestation victim, the rules of evidence and the Constitution: Should children really be seen and not heard? In E. A. Fattah (Ed.), *Towards a critical victimology* (pp. 260-291). London: Macmillan.

Felson, R., & Steadman, H. (1983). Situational factors in disputes leading to criminal violence. *Criminology, 21,* 59-74.

Fletcher, G. (1988). *Bernhard Goetz and the law on trial.* New York: Free Press.

Friends World Committee for Consultation. (n.d.). *A statement on restorative justice.* London: Author.

Galaway, B., & Hudson, J. (1981). *Perspectives on crime victims.* St. Louis: C. V. Mosby.

Geis, G. (1990). Crime victims: Practices and prospects. In A. J. Lurigio, W. G. Skogan, & R. C. Davis (Eds.), *Victims of crime: Problems, policies and programs* (pp. 251-268). Newbury Park, CA: Sage.

Gottfredson, M. (1984). *Victims of crime: The dimensions of risk* (Home Office Research Study No. 81). London: H.M. Stationary Office.

Henderson, L. N. (1992). The wrongs of victim's rights. In E. A. Fattah (Ed.), *Towards a critical victimology* (pp. 100-192). London: Macmillan.

Johnson, J. H., Kerper, H. B., Hayes, D. D., & Killinger, G. G. (1973). The recidivist victim: A descriptive study. *Criminal Justice Monographs, 4*(1).

Justice for all. (1985). *Liaison Magazine, 11*(4), 12.

Karmen, A. (1990). *Crime victims: An introduction to victimology* (2nd ed.). Monterey, CA: Brooks/Cole.

Lurigio, A. J., & Resick, P. A. (1990). Healing the psychological wounds of criminal victimization: Predicting postcrime distress and recovery. In A. J. Lurigio, W. G. Skogan, & R. C. Davis (Eds.), *Victims of crime: Problems, policies and programs* (pp. 50-68). Newbury Park, CA: Sage.

Maguire, M., & Shapland, J. (1990). The "victims movement" in Europe. In A. J. Lurigio, W. G. Skogan, & R. C. Davis (Eds.), *Victims of crime: Problems, policies and programs* (pp. 205-225). Newbury Park, CA: Sage.

Mayhew, P., & Elliott, D. (1990). Self-reported offending, victimization, and the British Crime Survey. *Violence and Victims, 5,* 83-96.

Mawby, R. I., & Gill, M. L. (1987). *Crime victims: Needs, services and the voluntary sector.* London: Tavistock.

Miers, D. (1989). Positivist victimology: A critique. *International Review of Victimology, 1,* 3-22.

National Association of Victims Support Schemes. (1984). *Fourth annual report 1983/84.* London: Author.

Paltrov, S. J. (1982, November 26). Opposite effects: New anticrime law in California is helping some accused felons. *Wall Street Journal.*

Pfeiffer, C. (1993). *Opferperspektiven: Wiedergutmachung und Strafe aus der Sicht der Bevölkerung* [Victim perspectives: Public views of restitution and punishment]. Unpublished manuscript.

Phipps, A. (1988). Ideologies, political parties, and victims of crime. In M. Maguire & J. Pointing (Eds.), *Victims of crime: A new deal* (pp. 177-186). Milton Keynes, UK: Open University Press.

President's Task Force on Victims of Crime. (1982). *Final report.* Washington, DC: Government Printing Office.

Quinney, R. (1972). Who is the victim? *Criminology, 10,* 314-323.

Reiss, A., Jr. (1981). Foreword: Towards a revitalization of theory and research on victimization by crime. *Journal of Criminal Law and Criminology, 72,* 704-710.

Roiphe, K. (1993, August 21). No means no. But what does rape mean? *Independent,* p. 27.

Rock, P. (1990). *Helping crime victims: The Home Office and the rise of victim support in England and Wales.* Oxford, UK: Clarendon.

Sampson, R. J., & Lauritzen, J. L. (1990). Deviant lifestyles, proximity to crime, and the offender-victim link in personal violence. *Journal of Research in Crime and Delinquency, 27,* 110-139.

Scheingold, S. A., Olson, T., & Pershing, J. (1994). Republican criminology and victim advocacy. *Law and Society Review, 28*(4).

Sessar, K. (1992). Wiedergutmachungen oder Strafen: Einstellungen in der Bevölkerung und der Justiz. Pfaffenweiler: Centaurus: Verlagesgesellschaft.

Singer, S. (1981). Homogeneous victim-offender populations: A review and some research implications. *Journal of Criminal Law and Criminology, 72,* 779-788.

Singer, S. (1986). Victims of serious violence and their criminal behavior: Subcultural theory and beyond. *Victims and Violence, 1*(1), 61-69.

The Texas rape-shield law: Texas Rule of Criminal Evidence 412. (1988). *American Journal of Criminal Law, 14,* 281-306.

Thornberry, T. P., & Figlio, R. M. (1972). *Victimization and criminal behavior in a birth cohort.* Paper presented at the meetings of the American Society of Criminology, Caracas, Venezuela.

United Nations. (1985). *Declaration of basic principles of justice for victims of crime and abuse of power.* New York: U.N. Dept. of Public Information.

Walker, S. (1985). *Sense and nonsense about crime: A policy guide.* Monterey, CA: Brooks/Cole.

Waller, I., & Okihiro, N. (1978). *Burglary: The victim and the public.* Toronto: University of Toronto Press.

Wright, M. (1991). *Justice for victims and offenders.* Milton Keynes, UK: Open University Press.

Zehr, H. (1990). *Changing lenses.* Scottsdale, PA: Herald.

Index

About the Editors

Robert C. Davis is Senior Research Associate at New York's Victim Services and a consultant to the American Bar Association. He is the author of numerous journal articles, book chapters, and books. His recent publications have been on domestic violence, sexual assault, elder abuse, crime prevention, drug enforcement, and specialized courts. He is currently conducting two large field tests of treatment interventions for domestic violence.

Arthur J. Lurigio is Professor of Criminal Justice at Loyola University of Chicago. His extensive research experience includes publication of 70 articles, more than 20 book chapters, and 15 books. He has also been very active in professional conferences, presenting more than 60 papers. His research interests are in the areas of crime victim recovery and services, community policing, community crime prevention, probation and intermediate sanctions, community antidrug strategies, and organized crime.

Wesley G. Skogan holds a joint appointment in the Department of Political Science and the Center for Urban Affairs and Policy Research at Northwestern University. His research focuses on the interface between the public and the criminal justice system. In addition to research on criminal victimization, his 1990 book, *Disorder and Decline,* examined public involvement in crime prevention and community policing. He is the author of two Home Office Research Series monographs examining citizen contact and satisfaction with policing in Britain. He also conducts research on neighborhood and community responses to crime. He is currently evaluating a new community policing program in Chicago.

About the Contributors

Esther S. Battle is a licensed psychologist who currently maintains a private practice in Yellow Springs, Ohio. In addition to 25 years in clinical practice treating children, adults, and families, she has had extensive experience with Children's Services Boards evaluating custody and abuse cases and providing court testimony. She also conducts psychological evaluations of individuals and families whose loved ones have suffered a wrongful death in her capacity as consultant for Wortman & Associates, Inc., in New York.

Edna Erez is Professor of Criminal Justice Studies at Kent State University and is currently at the Sociology Department of the University of Haifa. She has a law degree from the Hebrew University of Jerusalem and a Ph.D. in sociology/criminology from the University of Pennsylvania. She has published extensively in the areas of victims and women in the criminal justice system and the sociology of law. She is the outgoing editor of *Justice Quarterly* and has recently served as the Chair of the Task Force on Violence Against Women established by the American Society of Criminology.

Jeffrey Fagan is Director of the Center for Violence Research and Prevention at the Columbia University School of Public Health. His research focuses on the causes, contexts, and control of violence. He recently served on the Committee for the Assessment of Family Violence Interventions for the National Research Council.

Ezzat A. Fattah is the founder of the School of Criminology at Simon Fraser University in Vancouver, Canada. He is one of the pioneers in victimology, having published in the discipline as early as 1966. He is the author, coauthor, or editor of 12 books and has written over 100 papers published in scholarly journals. Among his recent books are *Towards a Critical Victimology; Understanding Criminal Victimization; The Plight of Crime Victims in Modern Society;* and *From Crime Policy to Victim Policy*. He is a Fellow of the Royal Society of Canada and an elected member of the Board of Directors of the International Society of Criminology.

David Finkelhor is Research Professor of Sociology at the University of New Hampshire and Codirector of the Family Research Laboratory. He has done extensive research on topics within the field of child victimization and family violence. He is the author of several books on sexual abuse, including *Sourcebook on Child Sexual Abuse* (1986) and *Nursery Crimes: Sexual Abuse in Daycare* (1988, coauthored with Linda Williams). He was the Principal Investigator of the National Incidence Study of Missing, Abducted, Runaway and Thrownaway Children. He is currently working on a book on child victimization called *Growing Up Scared: Abuse and Victimization in the Lives of Children and Youth.*

Lucy N. Friedman is Executive and Founding Director of Victim Services, the largest victim assistance organization in the nation. A longtime advocate for victim rights, she has written extensively on various aspects of crime, its impact on victims and their families, and the treatment of victims in the criminal justice system. She served as Executive Director of Mayor Dinkins's Study Group on Drug Abuse and as Associate Director at the Vera Institute of Justice and participated on a National Research Council Panel on the Understanding and Control of Violent Behavior.

Joel Garner is Research Director of the Joint Centers for Justice Studies, Inc., a nonprofit research corporation based in Shepherdstown, West Virginia. He formerly was a research program manager at the National Institute of Justice, where he was responsible for the Minneapolis Domestic Violence Experiment and the experiments that replicated that landmark study. His other research interests include the use of force by and against the police and the deterrent effectiveness of criminal sanctions.

James Garofalo is Professor of Criminal Justice and Director of the Center for the Study of Crime, Delinquency, and Corrections at Southern Illinois University in Carbondale. He has conducted research on a variety of topics, including victimization, policing, and community crime prevention, and his publications appear in a number of books and journals. He directed a study of law enforcement responses to hate crimes that was funded by the National Institute of Justice.

Susan W. Hillenbrand is Director of Special Projects for the American Bar Association Section of Criminal Justice and Staff Liaison to the section's Victims Committee. She holds

a degree in political science from Marymount College, Tarrytown, New York, and a paralegal certificate from the New York Paralegal Institute.

Krzysztof Kaniasty is Associate Professor in the Department of Psychology at Indiana University of Pennsylvania. His research concentrates on social support exchanges in the context of stressful life events at both individual and community levels.

Deborah P. Kelly has been active in research and advocacy on behalf of crime victims for almost 20 years. She is a principal with the Washington, D.C., law firm of Dickstein Shapiro and Morin & Oshinsky LLP. She served as Chair of the American Bar Association's Victims Committee from 1991 to 1994 and as its Vice Chair from 1988 to 1991. She has been a frequent commentator and author on legal issues concerning crime victims.

John H. Laub is Professor in the College of Criminal Justice at Northeastern University and Visiting Scholar at the Henry A. Murray Research Center of Radcliffe College. He is also currently serving as Vice President of the American Society of Criminology and is the former editor of the *Journal of Quantitative Criminology.* His areas of research include crime and deviance over the life course, the correlates of victimization, juvenile justice, and the history of criminology. Recent publications include *Crime in the Making: Pathways and Turning Points Through Life,* with Robert J. Sampson (1993).

Jeanne Parr Lemkau is Professor at Wright State University School of Medicine and Director of Behavioral Science at the Yellow Springs Family Health Center. She maintains a part-time clinical practice and works as a consultant for Wortman & Associates, Inc., providing psychological evaluations and referral services for individuals and families dealing with catastrophic loss and related litigation. She has also served as a visiting clinical fellow at the Harvard Geriatric Education Center.

Mike Maguire is Reader in Criminology and Criminal Justice at the University of Wales, Cardiff. He has published widely in the fields of policing, prisons, crime patterns, and victim issues. His victim-related publications include *The Effects of Crime and the Work of Victim Support Schemes* (1987, with Claire Corbett), *Victims of Crime: A New Deal?* (1988, with John Pointing), and "The Needs and Rights of Victims of Crime" (in *Crime and Justice,* 1991, Vol. 14).

Pallavi Nishith is Assistant Research Professor in the Department of Psychology at the University of Missouri-St. Louis. Her research interests are in the areas of posttraumatic stress disorder, substance use disorder, and related symptomatology. She is currently working at the Institute for Trauma Recovery as Co-Project Director on a grant from the National Institute of Mental Health studying treatment outcome in sexual assault survivors.

Fran H. Norris is Associate Professor and Director of Graduate Studies in the Department of Psychology at Georgia State University. Her research focuses on the effects of serious stressors such as crime and natural disasters on individuals and communities.

Patricia A. Resick is Professor of Psychology and Director of the Institute for Trauma Recovery at the University of Missouri-St. Louis. She is the Principal Investigator on two National Institute of Mental Health grants concerned with natural recovery from and treatment of rape-induced symptoms. She has published one book and 60 scientific articles and book chapters. She works actively with community agencies in St. Louis that assist victims of crime. In 1988, she was the recipient of an award by the National Association of Victim Assistance for outstanding research

contributions to the victims' assistance field. In 1995, she was the recipient of the Chancellor's Award for Excellence in Research from the University of Missouri.

Joanna Shapland is Professor of Criminal Justice and Director of the Institute for the Study of the Legal Profession at the University of Sheffield, U.K. She has published widely on victim issues, recently on commercial victimization, and has acted as a consultant to the Council of Europe and the United Nations. She is currently chairing a Committee of Justice on the role of victims in criminal justice and is also coeditor of the *International Review of Victimology.*

Barbara E. Smith is a sociologist with a specialty in criminal justice. Over the last two decades, she has researched a variety of criminal justice issues, including the areas of victimization, restitution, domestic violence, child abuse and neglect, specialized courts, crime prevention, prosecutorial decision making, and drug abatement. In her capacity as a consultant to the American Bar Association, she has served as the principal investigator or project director on numerous grants from the National Institute of Justice, the Office of Juvenile Justice and Prevention, the Bureau of Justice Assistance, the State Justice Institute, the National Center for Child Abuse and Neglect, and the Children's Bureau.

Bruce G. Taylor is Research Associate at New York's Victim Services. He is currently working on projects examining the effects of joint police and social service responses to domestic violence and elder abuse.

Martie P. Thompson was a doctoral student at Georgia State University at the time this research was conducted and is now a Postdoctoral Fellow at Emory University Department of Psychiatry and Behavioral Science in Atlanta, Georgia. She is currently conducting research on the effects of homicide and other forms of traumatic bereavement on adults and children.

Richard M. Titus is a Program Manager at the National Institute of Justice. His areas of interest include victimization, environmental crime prevention, and computer crime mapping. His recent research has examined victimization by burglary and fraud.

Susan B. Tucker is Senior Policy Analyst at Victim Services. Previously she was Director of the Office of Alumni Activities at Cardozo Law School and taught law at the New York University (NYU) School of Law and other New York area law schools. She has practiced criminal defense and matrimonial law and has written documentary and feature film screenplays. A graduate of Barnard College and the NYU School of Law, she is a candidate at the National Psychological Association for Psychoanalysis.

Camille B. Wortman is Professor of Psychology and Director of the Social/Health Psychology Graduate Training Program at the State University of New York at Stony Brook. A social psychologist, her major research interests include how people cope with the traumatic loss of a spouse or child. In addition to her work in academia, for the past 10 years she has operated a consulting service which pro-

vides evaluations and expert witness testimony in wrongful death cases. She helps to educate the jury about what happens to families who are faced with a sudden, traumatic death.

Marlene A. Young is Executive Director of the National Organization for Victim Assistance, Washington, D.C. In her capacity as NOVA's Executive Director, she developed the first 40-hour victim-oriented training curricula published for law enforcement patrol officers, law enforcement managers, prosecutors, and mental health providers. She has also designed training courses for victim advocates, victim counselors, and victim service program managers.

Her 1993 trip to Croatia and Bosnia, at the request of the government of Bosnia-Herzegovina, led to the establishment of a volunteer crisis intervention service to victims of displacement and war crimes in refugee camps of the former Yugoslavia. In 1995, she led a similar crisis team to earthquake-ravished Kobe, Japan, and organized a series of Crisis Response Teams to aid the victims of the bombing of the Murrah Federal Building in Oklahoma City. In recent years, she has helped develop new methods to assist Hispanic/Latino crime victims and to bring specialized services to victims of drug-related crime in American inner cities.

UNIVERSITY OF WOLVERHAMPTON
LEARNING RESOURCES